The Coming of the
American Civil War

D0027096

PROBLEMS IN AMERICAN CIVILIZATION

The Coming of the American Civil War

Third Edition

Edited and with an introduction by

Michael Perman
University of Illinois at Chicago

D. C. HEATH AND COMPANY
Lexington, Massachusetts   Toronto

Address editorial correspondence to:
D. C. Heath
125 Spring Street
Lexington, MA 02173

Acquisitions Editor: James Miller
Developmental Editors: Sylvia Mallory and Karen Myer
Production Editor: Carolyn Ingalls
Designer: David Libby
Photo Researcher: Martha Shethar
Production Coordinator: Michael O'Dea
Permissions Editor: Margaret Roll

Cover: Deck of the gunboat *Hunchback* on the James River. Mathew Brady Collection, The National Archives.

To my father, Jack, and the memory of my mother, Sybil

The Editor

Michael Perman was born in London, England, and grew up there. He received his B.A. from Oxford University, his M.A. from the University of Illinois at Urbana, and his Ph.D. from the University of Chicago, where his dissertation adviser was John Hope Franklin. Since then, he has taught at Ohio State University, Manchester University in England, and the University of Illinois at Chicago, where he is currently Professor of History and Research Professor in the Humanities.

His main publications have been *Reunion Without Compromise: The South and Reconstruction, 1865–1868* (1973); *The Road to Redemption: Southern Politics, 1869–1879* (1984); and *Emancipation and Reconstruction, 1862–1879* (1987). He has also edited two volumes of readings in American history, entitled *Perspectives on the American Past* (1989), and an anthology on *Major Problems in the Civil War and Reconstruction* (1991).

He won three book awards for *The Road to Redemption*—the Avery O. Craven Award of the Organization of American Historians, the Fred W. Morrison Prize of the Board of Governors of the University of North Carolina Press, and the V. O. Key Prize of the Southern Political Science Association (cowinner). His research has been supported by the National Endowment for the Humanities, and he has been awarded fellowships by the Charles Warren Center at Harvard University and the John Simon Guggenheim Foundation.

Preface

This anthology first appeared in 1961 under the title *The Causes of the American Civil War*. It proved to be one of the most widely used volumes in the Problems in American Civilization series, known popularly as the Heath books or the Amherst series. The author was Edwin C. Rozwenc of Amherst College, who was also general editor of the series and the editor of seven of its volumes. In 1972 Professor Rozwenc published a second edition. Now, twenty years later, a thoroughly revised and updated version appears, and I am pleased and honored to be the new author.

Retitled *The Coming of the American Civil War*, the new edition follows the format of the original Rozwenc versions. That is, it arranges the readings chronologically so as to show how the interpretation of the origins of the Civil War has changed over the intervening century and a half. Unlike its predecessors, however, this edition gives far less attention to the writings of the first hundred years. These earlier explanations occupy only about a fourth of the book, and they comprise just seven selections—all of them quite brief. The first three pieces were written by contemporaries who themselves played prominent roles in the sectional conflict. The next four essays come from professional historians writing between 1910 and 1960, all of whom were participating in a scholarly debate over whether the contest between North and South involved deep-seated and fundamental issues or whether their differences were less basic and therefore capable of resolution.

The rest of the anthology features selections by historians of the past generation or so. Thus far, their work has not been classified as a school, unlike the writings of proponents of the "irrepressible conflict," who have been identified as the traditional school, and their rivals, the revisionists, who espoused the "repressible conflict" approach. An argument can be made—and I shall make it in the Introduction—that these recent interpretations do actually have a sufficient amount in common that they can be categorized as a distinct group. To give them coherence in this anthology, I have divided them according to the particular approach each author has taken, namely, political and institutional, social and economic, or cultural and ideological. I have also created a fourth category, topical in nature, exploring the secession crisis of 1860–1861 that brought the sectional conflict to a climax. Because the secession crisis precipitated the outbreak of war, this short-term, proximate cause of the Civil War needs to be separated from the long-term origins of the sectional dispute itself.

One additional comment on the selections is that, because of this collection's emphasis on the causes of the Civil War, I have limited myself to essays that shed light on the conflict's origins. I considered writings on other aspects of the history of the United States before the war to be inappropriate and irrelevant, even though many interesting topics could have been included if I had contemplated a reader of such broad scope and coverage. Had this book strayed beyond the focus on causes, however, it would almost certainly have become so wide-ranging and diverse as to be of little use. Moreover, it would no longer have been the third edition of Edwin C. Rozwenc's original anthology.

Finally, I want to thank those historians who evaluated the outline of this new edition. Some of them endured a second round of this process and are therefore doubly in my debt. These reviews were very helpful indeed, because the reactions and suggestions they generated gave me a good sense of what other scholars and teachers see as the most important and useful writings on this subject. I am most grateful for the help offered by Richard H. Abbott, Eastern Michigan University; O. Vernon Burton, University of Illinois at Urbana–Champaign; Mary A. DeCredico, United States Naval Academy; Paul D. Escott, Wake Forest University; John M. McCardell, Middlebury College; Robert E. May, Purdue University; Lawrence N. Powell, Tulane University; and Harry L. Watson, University of North Carolina at Chapel Hill. I should add that this advice was given anonymously; the names are revealed only so that those who participated could be thanked publicly. One of my colleagues at the University of Illinois at Chicago, Richard John, also offered good suggestions, and I want to thank him for his interest in the project.

Others whom I would like to thank for their help with this book are Olivia Mahoney and Eileen Flanagan of the Chicago Historical Society and the editorial staff at D. C. Heath: Carolyn Ingalls, Karen Myer, Margaret Roll, and especially Sylvia Mallory, who was wonderfully supportive and thorough as always. And to my wife, Karen, thanks for everything.

M. P.

Contents

II. Recent Explanations

Introduction

The Civil War was an event of enormous scope and significance in the history of the United States. Mobilizing troops and resources on a scale that justified its characterization as "the first modern war," the military conflict also shattered Americans' notions about their country's immunity to the travails and problems that afflicted other societies, particularly those of Europe. Not surprisingly, the need arose immediately after the war to explain how such a terrible thing could have happened; and this concern has not diminished in the century and a half since then.

Within a decade or so after the war ended, several of the leading public figures who had been involved in the sectional dispute published accounts of how and why the conflict had occurred. Among them were Alexander H. Stephens and Jefferson Davis, the highest officials in the Confederacy, as well as Senators Henry Wilson and John A. Logan and the editor of the *New York Tribune*, Horace Greeley, all of whom wrote from the Union side. Each of their histories was a multivolume treatise intended to justify the course of the author's own section and to blame the opposition for actively fomenting the dispute and precipitating armed conflict.

These partisan apologies were followed after the turn of the century by the first wave of books written by professional historians with positions in universities. Although these authors felt less compulsion to accuse their sectional opponents of bringing on the war, they were, for the most part, identified with one side or the other. What distinguished these historians' explanations was their focus on impersonal forces—usually material but sometimes cultural—as the impetus behind the struggle. Whereas the participants had assumed that human will and agency controlled events, these later scholars, claiming to be more scientific and objective, concluded that economic interests, cultural systems, and social institutions had shaped the developments that led to war. In their view, the contest took on the features of "an irrepressible conflict between opposing and enduring forces," as Senator William H. Seward had depicted it in his celebrated speech of 1858. Proponents of this approach included such historians as Charles A. Beard, Frederick Jackson Turner, Ulrich B. Phillips, and, a little later, Frank L. Owsley.

In the 1930s and 1940s, new views directly challenged the claim that the sectional conflict had stemmed from fundamental differences and therefore had been irrepressible. The revisionists, as the proponents of this position were called, contended that the differences between the sections had *not* been insuperable and thus could have been resolved. Regrettably, however, either extremism on both sides or the incompetence of the nation's political leadership at the time forestalled this more favorable outcome. In effect, the revisionists reintroduced human agency as a crucial ingredient in history, but unfortunately, in this particular instance, it proved inadequate. The specific circumstances of the 1850s precluded the settlement of a "repressible conflict" that American political and intellectual leadership normally could have produced.

The issues stressed by the revisionists went to the heart of the problem of causation in history because, in a direct, almost confrontational, manner, they raised the question of whether the event was inevitable or whether an alternative course or outcome had been possible. Moreover, either explicitly or subtly, most scholarship on the coming of the Civil War until the late 1960s would focus on the issue of inevitability. Since then, a shift in tone and in emphasis has occurred that, I believe, amounts to a departure from the central preoccupations of past historians. Although the break has not been clean—as is ever the case, because there is always continuity as well as change in history—it nonetheless has considerable significance.

Three features of previous discussion of Civil War causation have now declined in salience and relevance. They are as follows:

• *The Question of War Guilt*

Because the war was so devastating, and because everyone who wrote about it came from one or other of the two opposing regions, an instinctive loyalty to either the North or the South, as well as a compulsion to blame the other side, remained strong, especially in the first fifty years after the war's end. Even the revisionists, who felt that the war had not been worth the cost and should have been prevented, assigned blame. They usually pointed the finger at extremists—in particular, the northern abolitionists—or at national politicians who first provoked the South and then could not put out the fire once it had started. Indeed, among revisionists, sectional sympathies and moralizing about who was guilty of starting, or at least not stopping, the war assumed a greater intensity than ever before.

In recent years, however, historians have paid a good deal less attention to this matter of war guilt. Explaining the coming of the war no longer seems to require that the writer affirm a sectional loyalty and deliver a judgment about culpability. The reasons for this shift are not altogether clear. Perhaps the passage of time has made such identifications less necessary. Perhaps the increasing similarity between the regions since the 1960s on a whole set of attitudes and experiences has made sectional partisanship less warranted or reasonable. Certainly, the change has not occurred because historians in general have become more objective and dispassionate, despite the premium often placed on scholarly detachment and objectivity.

• *The Role of Slavery*

Probably the most surprising feature of the first hundred years or so of historical debate about the causes of the Civil War has been the deemphasis of slavery as the primary factor. Of course, the "peculiar institution" has never been absent from discussion. At the same time, however, historians have frequently downplayed or qualified its centrality.

Beginning with Alexander H. Stephens's forceful assertion that slavery was not the war's cause but merely the question on which the contest turned, historians have regarded other aspects of the conflict as more basic or essential. Stephens himself believed that the dispute really revolved around constitutional interpretation and the nature of the federal system. Others have viewed slavery as merely incidental in a struggle that substantially was waged between competing economic interests in the North and South or between two distinct and incompatible societies. Some have even claimed that North and South differed so much from each other that they constituted separate civilizations with their own value systems and institutions. The revisionists, who by contrast felt that the two contestants' differences were reconcilable short of war, nevertheless concurred in reducing the role of slavery in the conflict. Because slavery had flourished for a long time before the crisis of the 1850s, the revisionists argued that logically problems arising later on must have precipitated the war. Besides, their assumption that the war

was avoidable compelled the revisionists to focus attention on proximate and short-term causes, as well as on the question of why the
nation's leaders did not settle a solvable problem. As a result, the
institution of slavery, which was an underlying element and a cause
that could be considered only long-term, fell outside their explana-
tory framework.

Today, historians accept slavery's centrality in bringing on the
Civil War. Scholars widely acknowledge the proposition that, if
slavery had not existed or had not been confined to one location
within the country, then a civil war would not have occurred, or at
least not in the way it did. Moreover, historians now understand
that southern slavery was not just a system of labor and property
but an institution that affected every aspect of the region's existence,
even the lives of nonslaveholders. Accordingly, the issue that concerns historians is no longer whether slavery caused the Civil War,
but how and why it did. In other words, what configuration of
events and forces was brought about by slavery's continuing existence in the southeastern United States? Also, how did this institution, and the resistance to it outside the South, shape the dispute
and the events arising from it?

• *The Issue of Avoidability*

The notion of avoidability did not figure significantly in the discussion of Civil War causation until the revisionists introduced it as
the pivotal element in their approach. They interjected the surprising
possibility that the most searing event in American history could
perhaps have been averted. Maybe the war was, after all, a blunder,
a terrible mistake.

This viewpoint had broad-ranging implications that resonated
strongly with the many Americans in the mid-twentieth century
who thought that wars, especially the First World War, achieved
very little, and who, during the height of the Cold War in the
1950s, wanted to believe that their country was harmonious and
consensual and had always been so. Though attractive and intriguing, the thesis of "the repressible conflict" and "the needless war"
nevertheless rested on a counterfactual assumption. The fact is that
the war was *not* avoided; contemporaries tried long and hard to
prevent it but could not find a way out. To suggest that they could

have or, in a moral sense, should have is speculative and ahistorical. And, with only an occasional exception, historians have now disengaged from this kind of discussion.

Still, an unwillingness to indulge in counterfactual speculation does not mean that historians have refused to consider alternative scenarios and outcomes in their attempts to explain the coming of the Civil War. In fact, the weighing of plausible options and different possibilities is the essence of good, imaginative historical analysis. Scholars can neither understand nor explain the actual course of events without considering what might have happened but did not. That approach is, however, quite different from asserting, as the revisionists had done, that events could or even should have turned out differently.

A refusal to acknowledge the avoidability of the war does not mean that this premise has to be replaced by a thoroughly deterministic explanation that views the war as inevitable and the sectional differences as utterly irreconcilable. In the first place, the war that ended up being unavoidable was not always so. There must have been a point of no return, a moment when armed conflict could no longer be prevented or postponed. Clearly, the turning point had not arrived in 1850, because the intersectional arrangement that Congress worked out that year had settled the matter short of war. However, was war unavoidable by 1857, as Kenneth M. Stampp has recently suggested? Or did it become inescapable once Lincoln's election was assured by the summer of 1860—or perhaps later, after the Confederacy's bombardment of Fort Sumter?

In the second place, the differences between the sections were not so irrepressible that they allowed for no similarity or compatibility whatsoever. If, however, the differences had been so extreme, then the wisest course of action would have been to admit the impossibility of any solution and to agree to dissolve the Union—to let the South leave in peace. The fact that the North did not want the South to go and that southerners felt deep ambivalence about seeking their independence from the United States indicated that the two sections were not completely distinct and incompatible entities. Although North and South may have found their differences irreconcilable on some vital issues, the people who lived in the two regions held many things in common. Had the situation been otherwise, it would have taken them a good deal less than "four score and seven years" to discover that they could not settle peacefully a problem whose existence the nation's founders had acknowledged during the formation of the Union in the 1780s.

The inclination among contemporary historians to set aside their predecessors' concerns does not mean that the vigorous debate and controversy that were evident earlier will be absent from now on. Rather, contentiousness will continue, but it will focus on different issues and problems. What these might be was unclear in 1962 when, in the second edition of his *Americans Interpret Their Civil War*, Thomas J. Pressly confessed that "a confusion of voices" characterized historical writing on the origins of the Civil War. With less need now to assign blame and guilt, to downplay the role of slavery, and to believe that war was avoidable, the discussion of Civil War causation has acquired sharper focus and greater precision. Although less flamboyant and agonized, the direction taken by recent historical scholarship guarantees that explanations of why and how civil war came to the United States will remain both intriguing and insightful.

*   *   *

Abraham Lincoln, in his second inaugural address of March 4, 1865, presented one of the most succinct and insightful accounts of why and how the war came. Although books and articles in the thousands have been written on this subject ever since, Lincoln's brief outline of a few hundred words in length—little more than a sketch, in fact—is surprisingly inclusive and, in many respects, quite remarkably perceptive, if not convincing. What better place, then, to begin this anthology of historical writing about the coming of the Civil War?

> On the occasion corresponding to this four years ago, all thoughts were anxiously directed to an impending civil-war. All dreaded it—all sought to avert it. While the inaugeral [*sic*] address was being delivered from this place, devoted altogether to *saving* the Union without war, insurgent agents were in the city seeking to *destroy* it without war—seeking to dissol[v]e the Union, and divide effects, by negotiation. Both parties deprecated war; but one of them would *make* war rather than let the nation survive; and the other would *accept* war rather than let it perish. And the war came.

One eighth of the whole population were colored slaves, not distributed generally over the Union, but localized in the Southern part of it. These slaves constituted a peculiar and powerful interest. All knew that this interest was, somehow, the cause of the war. To strengthen, perpetuate, and extend this interest was the object for which the insurgents would rend the Union, even by war; while the government claimed no right to do more than to restrict the territorial enlargement of it. Neither party expected for the war, the magnitude, or the duration, which it has already attained. Neither anticipated that the *cause* of the conflict might cease with, or even before, the conflict itself should cease. Each looked for an easier triumph, and a result less fundamental and astounding.

The address concluded with the famous paragraph beginning with these words: "With malice toward none; with charity for all; with firmness in the right, as God gives us the right, let us strive on to finish the work we are in. . . ."

Chronology

1828   *December*: South Carolina passes resolutions opposing the Tariff of Abominations, accompanied by John C. Calhoun's unsigned *South Carolina Exposition and Protest*.

1830   *Spring*: Daniel Webster of Massachusetts debates Robert Y. Hayne of South Carolina in the Senate over the nature of the Union.

1831   *January*: William Lloyd Garrison founds *The Liberator*. *August*: Nat Turner's Rebellion in Southampton County, Virginia. *November*: Virginia calls a convention to debate gradual emancipation.

1832   *November*: South Carolina adopts an ordinance nullifying the tariffs of 1828 and 1832.

1833   *March*: Congress passes both a compromise tariff and a "force" bill. *December*: American Anti-Slavery Society is founded in Philadelphia.

1834   *August*: Slavery is abolished in the British Empire.

1836   *March*: Texas declares its independence and, after a military victory at San Jacinto that avenged an earlier defeat at the Alamo, the republic is recognized by Mexico. *November*: Martin Van Buren (Democrat) is elected president over the Whig field of Daniel Webster, William H. Harrison, and Hugh Lawson White. *Summer*: House of Representatives debates and adopts "gag rule," requiring abolition petitions to be tabled.

1840   *November*: Newly founded Liberty party runs James G. Birney for president. The Whig candidate, William H. Harrison, wins the election.

1843   *Summer*: Senate debates and defeats Texas annexation treaty.

1844   *November*: James K. Polk (Democrat) wins presidency with only a plurality of the popular vote; Liberty party gets 62,000 votes.

1845   *December*: Texas is admitted to the Union as a slave state.

1846   *May*: United States makes war on Mexico. *August*: Wilmot Proviso is introduced in the House.

1847   *September*: U.S. forces enter Mexico City; hostilities end.

1848   *January*: Gold is discovered in California. *March*: Treaty of Guadalupe Hidalgo with Mexico is ratified by the Senate, 38–14. *November*: Zachary Taylor (Whig) is elected over Lewis Cass (Democrat) and Martin Van Buren (Free Soil).

1850   *February*: Henry Clay introduces his proposals for solving the problems arising from the recent acquisitions from Mexico. *March*: John C. Calhoun dies. *April*: Nashville Convention meets and fails to form a Southern Rights party. *July*: Taylor dies suddenly; Millard Fillmore assumes presidency. *September*: Five separate acts known as the Compromise of 1850 pass. *December*: Georgia calls a convention and gives the compromise a conditional endorsement known as the Georgia Platform.

1851   *February*: Shadrach, a fugitive slave, eludes federal authorities in their attempt to return him from Boston to his master; in *April* and *June*, Thomas Sims and Anthony Burns are turned over, despite public opposition in Boston.

1852   Harriet Beecher Stowe's *Uncle Tom's Cabin* is published. *November*: Franklin Pierce, a New Hampshire Democrat, becomes president; the last presidential campaign by the Whig party.

1854   *May*: Stephen A. Douglas's Kansas–Nebraska Act is passed by Congress; a group of thirty Anti-Nebraska congressmen forms the Republican party, although a public meeting in

Ripon, Wisconsin, in February first uses the name. *October*: Ostend Manifesto is issued by James Buchanan, James Mason, and Pierre Soulé.

During the year, American, or Know Nothing, party is founded.

1855   *October*: Free-state constitution for Kansas is drafted in Topeka. During the year, William Walker, trying to extend slavery into Central America, seizes control of Nicaragua.

1856   *May*: "Sack of Lawrence," Kansas; Pottawatomie Massacre by John Brown and followers in Kansas; Charles Summer is beaten senseless on the Senate floor by Representative Preston Brooks after his speech on "The Crime Against Kansas." *November*: John C. Frémont garners 114 electoral votes in the Republicans' first presidential campaign; Buchanan wins 45 percent of the popular vote and with 174 electoral votes becomes president

1857   *March*: *Dred Scott* decision is handed down by the Supreme Court. *August*: Economic panic is precipitated by lack of consumer demand. *December*: Proslavery Lecompton constitution is ratified in Kansas.

1858   *June–October*: Senatorial debates throughout Illinois between Abraham Lincoln and Stephen A. Douglas. *August*: Kansas voters reject the resubmitted Lecompton constitution and so the state fails to achieve statehood.

1859   *October*: John Brown's Raid at Harpers Ferry, Virginia.

1860   *April*: Delegates from the Lower South walk out of the Democratic convention in Charleston, later reassembling in Richmond to nominate Vice President John C. Breckinridge. *June*: Democrats meet again and select Stephen A. Douglas for president; Constitutional Unionists gather in Baltimore and choose John Bell of Tennessee for president; Republicans meet in Chicago and nominate Abraham Lincoln. *November*: Lincoln is elected president with 39 percent of the popular vote and 180 electoral votes. *December*: South Carolina secedes.

1861   *January*: Six states in the Lower South secede—Mississippi, Alabama, Georgia, Florida, Louisiana, and Texas; the steamer "Star of the West" is repulsed when it tries to supply Fort Sumter. *February*: Peace Conference in Washington—twenty-one states are represented; Confederate States of America is formed in Montgomery, Alabama. *March*: Lincoln is inaugurated. *April*: Fort Sumter surrenders after a federal attempt to resupply it is met with a Confederate bombardment; President Lincoln calls for seventy-five thousand militiamen and proclaims a blockade of southern ports; Virginia secedes. *May*: North Carolina, Tennessee, and Arkansas leave the Union. *July*: First major battle of the war is fought at Bull Run, just outside Washington—a Confederate victory. *September*: Kentucky's neutrality ends with the Union seizure of Paducah.

The Coming of the
American Civil War

Earlier Explanations

The Need for Justification

Alexander H. Stephens

A WAR FOR STATE RIGHTS

Alexander H. Stephens of Georgia had been one of the South's leading spokesmen in the U.S. Congress when, in 1861, he was chosen vice president of the Confederacy, despite his opposition to his own state's decision to secede from the Union. Though its second-highest official, he became increasingly critical of the new government as it assumed what he regarded as excessive and dangerous powers. He made his views widely known, much to the embarrassment of President Jefferson Davis and the rest of the Confederate administration.

The expansion of central authority at the expense of state and local government was, Stephens believed, the issue at the heart of the South's struggle against Washington before the war. This principle could not be abandoned when the same threat came from nearby Richmond. After the war, when Stephens compiled a massive two-volume treatise defending the South's course, he presented it as a battle to preserve "federation," or localism, against "consolidation," or centralism. The conflict therefore had occurred over two opposing political philosophies or, more specifically, clashing constitutional principles. Slavery was not the issue.

Stephens's apology was entitled *A Constitutional View of the Late War Between the States* (1868–1870). In his use of the phrase "war between the states," Stephens introduced a descriptive term that has often since been applied to the Civil War. The phrase is, however, quite erroneous, because the contest was waged not by states but by two organized governments, the Union and the Confederacy.

It is a postulate, with many writers of this day, that the late War was the result of two opposing ideas, or principles, upon the subject of African Slavery. Between these, according to their theory, sprung the "irrepressible conflict," in principle, which ended in the terrible conflict of arms. Those who assume this postulate, and so theorize upon it, are but superficial observers.

That the War had its origin in *opposing principles*, which, in their action upon the *conduct of men*, produced the ultimate collision

From Alexander H. Stephens, *A Constitutional View of the Late War Between the States* (Philadelphia, 1868), Vol. 1, pp. 9–12.

of arms, may be assumed as an unquestionable fact. But the opposing principles which produced these results in physical action were of a very different character from those assumed in the postulate. They lay in the organic Structure of the Government of the States. The conflict in principle arose from different and opposing ideas as to the nature of what is known as the General Government. The contest was between those who held it to be strictly Federal in its character, and those who maintained that it was thoroughly National. It was a strife between the principles of Federation, on the one side, and Centralism, or Consolidation, on the other.

Slavery, so called, was but *the question* on which these antagonistic principles, which had been in conflict, from the beginning, on divers *other questions,* were finally brought into actual and active collision with each other on the field of battle.

Some of the strongest Anti-slavery men who ever lived were on the side of those who opposed the Centralizing principles which led to the War. Mr. Jefferson was a striking illustration of this, and a prominent example of a very large class of both sections of the country, who were, most unfortunately, brought into hostile array against each other. No more earnest or ardent devotee to the emancipation of the Black race, upon humane, rational and Constitutional principles, ever lived than he was. Not even Wilberforce himself was more devoted to that cause than Mr. Jefferson was. And yet Mr. Jefferson, though in private life at the time, is well known to have been utterly opposed to the Centralizing principle, when *first* presented, on *this question,* in the attempt to impose conditions and restrictions on the State of Missouri, when she applied for admission into the Union, under the Constitution. He looked upon the movement as a political maneuver to bring this delicate subject (and one that lay so near his heart) into the Federal Councils, with a view, by its agitation in a forum where it did not properly belong, to strengthen the Centralists in their efforts to revive their doctrines, which had been so signally defeated on so many other questions. The first sound of their movements on this question fell upon his ear as a "fire bell at night." The same is true of many others. Several of the ablest opponents of that State Restriction, in Congress, were equally well known to be as decidedly in favor of emancipation as Mr. Jefferson was. Amongst these, may be named Mr. Pinckney and

Alexander H. Stephens. U.S. representative from Georgia, 1843–1859, 1873–1882; vice president of the Confederacy, 1861–1865; and governor of Georgia, 1882–1883. (*National Archives*)

Mr. Clay, from the South, to say nothing of those men from the North, who opposed that measure with equal firmness and integrity.

It is the fashion of many writers of the day to class all who opposed the Consolidationists in *this*, their *first* step, as well as all who opposed them in all their subsequent steps, on *this question*, with what they style the Pro-Slavery Party. No greater injustice could be done any public men, and no greater violence be done to the truth of History, than such a classification. Their opposition to that measure, or kindred subsequent ones, sprung from no attachment to Slavery; but, as Jefferson's, Pinckney's and Clay's, from their strong convictions that the Federal Government had no rightful or Constitutional control or jurisdiction over such questions; and that no such action, as that proposed upon them, could be taken by Congress without destroying the elementary and vital principles upon which the Government was founded.

By their acts, they did not identify themselves with the Pro-Slavery Party (for, in truth, no such Party had, at that time, or at any time in the History of the Country, any organized existence). They only identified themselves, or took position, with those who maintained the Federative character of the General Government.

In 1850, for instance, what greater injustice could be done any one, or what greater violence could be done the truth of History, than to charge Cass, Douglas, Clay, Webster and Fillmore, to say nothing of others, with being advocates of Slavery, or following in the lead of the Pro-Slavery Party, because of their support of what were called the adjustment measures of that year?

Or later still, out of the million and a half, and more, of the votes cast, in the Northern States, in 1860, against Mr. Lincoln, how many, could it, with truth, be said, were in favor of Slavery, or even that legal subordination of the Black race to the White, which existed in the Southern States?

Perhaps, not one in ten thousand! It was a subject, with which, they were thoroughly convinced, they had nothing to do, and could have nothing to do, under the terms of the Union, by which the States were Confederated, except to carry out, and faithfully perform, all the obligations of the Constitutional Compact, in regard to it.

They simply arrayed themselves against that Party which had virtually hoisted the banner of Consolidation. The contest, so commenced, which ended in the War, was, indeed, a contest between opposing principles; but not such as bore upon the policy or impolicy of African Subordination. They were principles deeply underlying all considerations of that sort. They involved the very nature and organic Structure of the Government itself. The conflict, on *this question* of Slavery, in the Federal Councils, from the beginning, was not a contest between the advocates or opponents of that peculiar Institution, but a contest, as stated before, between the supporters of a strictly Federative Government, on the one side, and a thoroughly National one, on the other.

It is the object of this work to treat of these opposing principles, not only in their bearings upon the *minor question* of Slavery, as it existed in the Southern States, and on which they were brought into active collision with each other, but upon others (now that this element of discord is removed) of far more transcendent importance, looking to the great future, and the preservation of that Constitutional Liberty which is the birthright of every American, as well as the solemnly-guaranteed right of all who may here, in this new world, seek an asylum from the oppressions of the old. . . .

Henry Wilson

A SLAVE POWER CONSPIRACY

Henry Wilson was elected to the U.S. Senate in 1854 after the American, or Know Nothing, party captured the legislature of his home state, Massachusetts. Although he had gained this high office with Know Nothing support, he was able nonetheless to maintain his credentials as a member of the new antislavery party, the Republicans. Having started out as a shoemaker and becoming known as "the cobbler of Natick," he was responsive to the demands of workingmen as well as to the dangers of an expanding system of slavery. He became vice president (1873–1875) during Grant's second term but died while in office.

Like many others in the Republican party, Wilson perceived the South's efforts during the 1850s to retain power and influence in the federal government as a conspiracy headed by the slaveholders, who began to be referred to as the Slave Power. The idea was widespread that the republic's values and institutions were being subverted by this conspiratorial interest. Wilson's three-volume vindication of the North's stand against this internal threat—*The History of the Rise and Fall of the Slave Power in America* (1872–1877)—never explicitly identifies the conspirators but merely asserts their existence. The only specifics about this putative conspiracy that Wilson offers appear toward the end of the

From *The History of the Rise and Fall of the Slave Power in America*, by Henry Wilson. Vol. 1, pp. 1–2; Vol. 3, pp. 127–35.

extract that follows. In the original, they are in Chapter Ten of the third volume.

God's Holy Word declares that man was doomed to eat his bread in the sweat of his face. History and tradition teach that the indolent, the crafty, and the strong, unmindful of human rights, have ever sought to evade this Divine decree by filching their bread from the constrained and unpaid toil of others. From inborn indolence, conjoined with avarice, pride, and lust of power, has sprung slavery in all its Protean forms, from the mildest type of servitude to the harsh and hopeless condition of absolute and hereditary bondage. Thus have grown and flourished caste and privilege, those deadly foes of the rights and well-being of mankind, which can exist only by despoiling the many for the benefit of the few.

American slavery reduced man, created in the Divine image, to property. It converted a being endowed with conscience, reason, affections, sympathies, and hopes, into a chattel. It sunk a free moral agent, with rational attributes and immortal aspirations, to merchandise. It made him a beast of burden in the field of toil, an outcast in social life, a cipher in the courts of law, and a pariah in the house of God. To claim himself, or to use himself for his own benefit or the benefit of wife or child, was deemed a crime. His master could dispose of his person at will, and of everything acquired by his enforced and unrequited toil.

This complete subversion of the natural rights of millions, by which they were "deemed, held, taken, reputed, and adjudged in law to be chattels personal to all intents, constructions, and purposes whatsoever," constituted a system antagonistic to the doctrines of reason and the monitions of conscience, and developed and gratified the most intense spirit of personal pride, a love of class distinctions, and the lust of dominion. Hence arose a commanding power, ever sensitive, jealous, proscriptive, dominating, and aggressive, which was recognized and fitly characterized as the Slave Power.

This slavery and this Slave Power, in their economical, social, moral, ecclesiastical, and political relations to the people and to the government, demoralizing the one and distracting the councils of the other, made up the vital issues of that "irrepressible conflict" which finally culminated in a civil war that startled the nations by its suddenness, fierceness, and gigantic proportions. . . .

Henry Wilson. U.S. senator from Massachusetts, 1854–1872, and vice president of the United States, 1873–1875. (*National Archives*)

*

No intelligent and adequate estimate of the Rebellion and its causes, immediate and remote, can be formed without special note of the small proportion of the people of the South who were at the outset in favor of that extreme measure. Even in the six States which first seceded, South Carolina possibly excepted, there was far from a majority who originally gave it their approval. In the remaining five the proportion was much smaller; though this large preponderance was overcome by able, adroit, and audacious management. By means illegitimate and indefensible, reckless of principle and of consequences, a comparatively few men succeeded in dragooning whole States into the support of a policy the majority condemned, to following leaders the majority distrusted and most cordially disliked. As no sadder and more suggestive commentary was ever afforded of the utter demoralization of slaveholding society, and of the helpless condition of a community that accepted slavery, and accommodated itself to the only conditions on which it could be maintained, it seems needful, to an intelligent apprehension of the subject, though it will be necessary to anticipate events somewhat, that notice should be taken here of the process by which this was done.

How, then, could such an object be accomplished? How could such a result be secured? How came it to pass that this comparatively small number could persuade whole States to support a policy that not only was, but was seen to be, suicidal? How could a class of men who despised the colored man because he was colored, and the poor whites because they were poor, inspire the latter with a willingness, an enthusiasm even, to take up arms, subject themselves to all the hardships and hazards of war, for the express purpose of perpetuating and making more despotic a system that had already despoiled them of so much, and was designed to make still more abject their degradation? A summary and substantial answer might be that it was by the adoption of the same principles and of the same policy by which the Slave Power had dominated and so completely controlled the nation for the preceding two generations; only aggravated and made more intolerant in the immediate communities where slavery was domiciled and had become the controlling social as well as political element. But there was an individuality and a specific character about this last and dying effort of slaveholding control that may justify and call for a more detailed account, even though it require the reproduction of some facts and features thereof of which mention has been already made. Nor does it seem amiss, in this connection, to introduce the words of another,—a foreigner, who thus records the impressions of one who made his observations uninfluenced at least by Northern prejudices and prepossessions.

The first item or element in the answer now sought must be looked for in the mental and moral condition of Southern society. Alluding to this point in his recent History of the Civil War in America, the Comte de Paris, says: "Notwithstanding all that has been said on the subject [slavery], our people, who fortunately have not had to wrestle with it, are not aware how much this subtle poison instils itself into the very marrow of society. . . . But the effects of the servile institution upon the dominant race present a spectacle not less sad and instructive to the historian and philosopher; for a fatal demoralization is the just punishment that slavery inflicts upon those who expect to find nothing in it but profit and power." Proceeding to demonstrate how this demoralization "is the inevitable consequence of slavery, and how, by an inexorable logic, the simple fact of the enslavement of the black corrupts, among the whites, the ideas and morals which are the very foundation of society," and showing that "it is among what are called good slave owners that we must inquire into the pretended moral perfection of slavery, in order to understand its flagrant immorality," he adds, with a pungent pathos that cannot but flush with shame the cheek of every thoughtful American, "What a deeply sorrowful spectacle for any one who wishes to study human nature to see every sense of righteousness and equity so far perverted in a whole population by the force of habit, that the greatest portion of the ministers of all denominations were not ashamed to sully Christianity by a cowardly approval of slavery; and men who bought and sold their fellow-beings took up arms for the express purpose of defending this odious privilege, in the name of liberty and property." Alluding to another phase of slaveholding society, he directs attention to the fact that "the servile institution, in violating the supreme law of humanity, which links indissolubly together those two words, labor and progress, and in making labor itself a means for brutalizing man, not only degraded the slave, but it also engendered depravity in the master; for the despotism of a whole race, like the absolute power of a single individual or an oligarchy, always ends by disturbing the reason and the moral sense of those who have once inhaled its intoxicating fragrance."

Speaking of the "falsehood" of slavery as having "become the basis of society," of the increase of its influence and power resulting from the prosperity produced by "the extraordinary impulse given to the cultivation of the sugar-cane and the cotton-plant," and of the change in Southern sentiment from regarding the system, with the fathers, as "a social sore" which "the enlightenment and patriotism of their successors" would "heal" to the opinion that regarded "the social system founded upon slavery as the highest state of perfection that modern civilization had reached," he thus sets forth his estimate of Southern society as it existed at the opening of the Rebellion: "In proportion as slavery thus increased in prosperity and power, its influence became more and more preponderant in the community which had adopted it. Like a parasitical plant, which, drawing to itself all the sap of the most vigorous tree, covers it gradually with a foreign verdure and poisonous fruits, so slavery was impairing the morals of the South, and the spirit of her institutions. The form of liberty existed, the press seemed to be free, the deliberations of legislative bodies were tumultuous, and every man boasted of his independence. But the spirit of true liberty, tolerance towards the minority and respect for individual opinion, had departed, and those deceitful appearances concealed the despotism of an inexorable master, slavery,—a master before whom the most powerful of slaveholders was himself but a slave, as abject as the meanest of his laborers.

"No one had a right to question its legitimacy, and like the *Eumenides* [a Greek religious cult], which the ancients feared to offend by naming them, so wherever the Slave Power was in the ascendant, people did not even dare to mention its name, for fear of touching upon too dangerous a subject. It was on this condition only that such an institution could maintain itself in a prosperous and intelligent community. It would have perished on the very day when the people should be at liberty to discuss it.

"Therefore, notwithstanding their boasted love of freedom, the people of the South did not hesitate to commit any violence in order to crush out, in its incipiency, any attempt to discuss the subject. Any one who had ventured to cast the slightest reflection upon the slavery system could not have continued to live in the South; it was sufficient to point the finger at any stranger and call him an Abolitionist, to consign him at once to the fury of the populace."

Dwelling at some length upon the plantation system and "the inconveniences felt in a region of country yet half wild," with a mention of some of the incidents and contingencies attending the working of "their large domains" by servile labor, he noted the division of Southern society into three classes, "at the foot of the ladder the negro bowed down upon the soil he had to cultivate; . . . at the top the masters, in the midst of an entirely servile population, more intelligent than educated, brave but irascible, proud but overbearing, eloquent but intolerant, devoting themselves to public affairs—the exclusive direction of which belonged to them—with all the ardor of their temperament.

"The third class—that of common whites, the most important on account of its numbers—occupied a position below the second, and far above the first, without, however, forming an intermediate link between them, for it was deeply imbued with all the prejudices of color. This was the *plebs romana,* the crowds of clients who parade with ostentation the title of citizen, and only exercise its privileges in blind subserviency to the great slaveholders, who were the real masters of the country If slavery had not existed in their midst, they would have been workers and tillers of the soil, and might have become farmers and small proprietors. But the more their poverty draws them nearer to the inferior class of slaves, the more anxious are they to keep apart from them, and they spurn work in order to set off more ostentatiously their quality of free-men. This unclassified population, wretched and restless, supplied Southern policy with the fighting vanguard which preceded the planter's invasion of the West with his slaves. At the beginning of the war the North believed that this class would join her in condemnation of the servile institution, whose ruinous competition it ought to have detested. But the North was mistaken in thinking that reason would overcome its prejudices. It showed, on the contrary, that it was ardently devoted to the maintenance of slavery. Its pride was even more at stake than that of the great slaveholders; for while the latter were always sure of remaining in a position far above the freed negroes, the former feared lest their emancipation should disgrace the middle white classes by raising the blacks to their level."

Without the adduction of other particulars, or the recognition of other elements, these make the improbability of the results now under consideration seem less than they would otherwise appear. For certainly it is sufficiently obvious that a society made up of such materials could not but present an inviting field for the machinations of the shrewd, unscrupulous, and designing. With ignorance so profound, with prejudices so unreasoning, and with passions so inflammable, it was not difficult to hoodwink and commit such people to purposes and plans not only dangerous to others but destructive to themselves. But there were other causes. There were auxiliaries that gave greatly increased potency to those elements of mischief. There were combination and careful and long-considered preparation. Indeed, division of labor and assignment of parts have seldom been more carefully attended to. "Each man," says the Comte, "had his part laid out. Some, delegated by their own States, constantly visited the neighboring States in order to secure that unanimity to the movement which was to constitute its strength; others were endeavoring to win over the powerful border States, such as Virginia, Kentucky, Missouri, as well as North Carolina and Tennessee, which stood aghast, terrified at the approach of the crisis brought on by their associates; some, again, were even pleading their cause in the North, in the hope of recruiting partisans among those Democrats whom they had forsaken at the last election; while others kept their seats in Congress in order to be able to paralyze its action; forming, at the same time, a centre whence they issued directions to their friends in the South to complete the dismemberment of the Republic. Jefferson Davis himself continued to take part in the deliberations of the Senate."

Corroborative of the above, and at the same time indicative of the actual method adopted by the conspirators, is the following letter which appeared in the "National Intelligencer," at Washington on the morning of January 11, 1861. It is introduced by the editor, with the remark that it was from "a distinguished citizen of the South who formerly represented his State with great distinction in the popular branch of Congress." It has since transpired that the writer was the Hon. L. D. Evans of Texas, formerly a member of the XXXIVth Congress, and subsequently a judge of the Supreme Court of his adopted State. A native of Tennessee and long resident in Texas, he ever remained true to the Union, and not only advised but encouraged and supported Governor Houston to resist the clamors of the revolutionists in their demands for an extra session of the legislature. Though overborne in this and compelled to leave the State, he rendered essential service to the Union cause and the administration of Mr. Lincoln. He writes:—

"I charge that on last Saturday night a caucus was held in this city by the Southern secession Senators from Florida, Georgia, Alabama, Mississippi, Louisiana, Arkansas, and Texas. It was then and there resolved in effect to assume to themselves the political power of the South and the control of all political and military operations for the present. They telegraphed to complete the plan of seizing forts, arsenals, and custom-houses, and advised the conventions now in session, and soon to assemble, to pass ordinances for immediate secession; but, in order to thwart any operations of the government here, the conventions of the seceding States are to retain their representatives in the Senate and the House.

"They also advised, ordered, or directed the assembling of a convention of delegates from the seceding States at Montgomery on the 4th of February. This can of course only be done by the revolutionary conventions usurping the powers of the people, and sending delegates over whom they will lose all control in the establishment of a provisional government, which is the plan of the dictators.

"This caucus also resolved to take the most effectual means to dragoon the legislatures of Tennessee, Kentucky, Mississippi, Arkansas, Texas, and Virginia into following the seceding States.

"Maryland is also to be influenced by such appeals to popular passion as have led to the revolutionary steps which promise a conflict with the State and Federal governments in Texas. They have possessed themselves of all the avenues of information in the South,—the telegraph, the press, and the general control of the postmasters. They also confidently rely upon defections in the army and navy.

"The spectacle here presented is startling to contemplate. Senators intrusted with the representative sovereignty of the States, and sworn to support the Constitution of the United States, while yet acting as the privy counsellors of the President, and anxiously looked to by their constituents to effect some practical plan of adjustment, deliberately conceive a conspiracy for the overthrow of the government through the military organizations, the dangerous secret order, the Knights of the Golden Circle, 'Committees of Safety,' Southern leagues, and other agencies at their command; they have instituted as thorough a military and civil despotism as ever cursed a maddened country.

"It is not difficult to foresee the form of government which a convention thus hurriedly thrown together at Montgomery will irrevocably fasten upon a deluded and unsuspecting people. It must essentially be 'a monarchy founded upon military principles' or it cannot endure. Those who usurp power never fail to forge strong chains. It may be too late to sound the alarm. Nothing may be able to arrest the action of revolutionary tribunals whose decrees are principally in 'secret sessions.' But I call upon the people to pause and reflect before they are forced to surrender every principle of liberty, or to fight those who are becoming their masters rather than their servants."

Abundant corroboration of these statements has since been found, revealing the fact of such a meeting and its action. Among the proofs is a letter, written by Senator Yulee, one of the conspirators, and found in Florida after the capture of Fernandina, giving an account of the meeting and its purposes, among which, as he expresses it, was the thought, that by retaining their seats in Congress, "we can keep the hands of Mr. Buchanan tied, and disable the Republicans from effecting any legislation which will strengthen the hands of the incoming administration."

The next morning Mr. Wilson met Mr. Evans, and, surmising him to have been the writer of the communication, inquired whether or not his surmise was correct. Receiving an affirmative answer, with the remark that the members of that secret conclave should be arrested, Mr. Wilson replied that they deserved expulsion and punishment for their treason, but he felt constrained to add, "There are too many of them, and to expel them will be to precipitate the revolution"; so perilous did he deem the situation, so really weak was the government, and so illy prepared to cope with its traitorous foes, and repel the dangers that threatened and surrounded it. Even such high-handed treason could be enacted with impunity, and that within the sacred precincts of the capitol. . . .

Frederick Douglass

A BATTLE OF PRINCIPLES AND IDEAS

Frederick Douglass was probably the preeminent African-American of the Civil War era. A slave in Maryland until about age twenty, he escaped in 1838 and became a leading figure in the campaign to abolish slavery. During the war he pressed the federal government to emancipate the slaves and to allow them to fight for their freedom in the Union army. In Reconstruction he was the leading spokesman for African-Americans, demanding that the Republican party remain responsible for ensuring the preservation of the gains that the nation—especially blacks—had made as a result of the war.

Douglass, of course, wrote no book of sectional vindication like those of Stephens, Wilson, and others. Instead he produced a classic autobiography, *The Life and Times of Frederick Douglass* (1881). All the same, speeches that he gave in the 1870s revealed very clearly a perspective on the war that took the form of a vindication. As the former Confederates regained control in the South and again became accepted, in effect legitimized, Douglass warned against the danger of forgetting what the North had fought for. Reminding his listeners about the war's objectives and achievements was the purpose of his speech of May 30, 1878, Decoration Day—the forerunner of Memorial Day—when flowers were placed on the graves of slain Union soldiers. Although it was a brutal physical combat, Douglass believed that the war had been fought over ideas and values and that the right ones had prevailed.

The Feelings of the Colored Race

My own feeling toward the old master class of the South is well known. Though I have worn the yoke of bondage, and have no love for what are called the good old times of slavery, there is in my heart no taint of malice toward the ex-slaveholders. Many of them were not sinners above all others, but were in some sense the slaves of the slave system, for slavery was a power in the State greater than the State itself. With the aid of a few brilliant orators and plotting conspirators, it sundered the bonds of the Union and inaugurated war. Identity of interest and the sympathies created by it produced an irresistible current toward the cataract of disunion

From Frederick Douglass, "There was a right side in the late war," from *The Frederick Douglass Papers*, Series One, Volume 4, edited by John Blassingame and John R. McKivigan. Yale University Press, 1991. Used by permission.

by which they were swept down. I have no denunciations for the past. The hand of friendship and affection which I recently gave my old master on his death-bed I would cordially extend to all men like him.

Speaking for my race as well as for myself, I can truthfully say that neither before the war, during the war, nor since the war have the colored people of the South shown malice or resentment toward the old slaveholding class, as a class, because of any or all the wrongs inflicted upon them during the days of their bondage. On the contrary, whenever and wherever this class has shown any disposition to respect the feelings and protect the rights of colored men, colored men have preferred to support them. No men from the East, West, North, or from any other quarter can so readily win the heart and control the political action of the colored people of the South as can the slaveholding class, if they are in the least disposed to be just to them and to faithfully carry out the provisions of the Constitution. They respect the old master class, but they hate and despise slavery.

The world has never seen a more striking example of kindness, forbearance, and fidelity than was shown by the slave population of the South during the war. To them was committed the care of the families of their masters while those masters were off fighting to make the slavery of these same slaves perpetual. The hearths and homes of those masters were left at their mercy. They could have killed, robbed, destroyed, and taken their liberty if they had chosen to do so, but they chose to remain true to the trust reposed in them, and utterly refused to take any advantage of the situation, to win liberty or destroy property. No act of violence lays to their charge. All the violence, crimes, and outrages alleged against the negro have originated since his emancipation.

Judging from the charges against him now, and assuming their truth, a sudden, startling, and most unnatural change must have been wrought in his character and composition. And, for one, I do not believe any such change has taken place. If the ex-master has lost the affection of the slave, it is his own fault. Men are not changed from lambs into tigers instantaneously, nor from tigers into lambs instantaneously. If the negro has lost confidence in the old master-class, it is due to the conduct of that class toward him since the war and since his emancipation. What has been said of the

Frederick Douglass. A slave in Maryland until his escape in 1838; orator and newspaper editor in the campaign to abolish slavery; and preeminent African-American leader during and after the Civil War. (*National Archives*)

kindly temper and disposition of the colored people of the South to the old master-class, may be equally said of the feelings of the North toward the whole South. There is no malice rankling here against the South—there was none before the war, there was none during the war, and there has been none since the war. The policy of pacification of President Hayes was in the line of Northern sentiment. No American citizen is stigmatized here as a "carpet-bagger," or "interloper," because of his Southern birth. He may here exercise the right of speech, the elective franchise, and all other rights of citizenship as those to the manor born. The Lamars, the Hills, the Gordons, and the Butlers of the South [all four were U.S. senators] may stump any or all the States of New-England, and sit in safety at the hearths and homes made desolate by a causeless rebellion in which they were leaders, without once hearing an angry word, or seeing an insulting gesture.

That so much cannot be said of the South is certainly no fault of the people of the North. We have always been ready to meet rebels more than half way and to hail them as fellow-citizens, countrymen, clansmen, and brothers beloved. As against the North there is no earthly reason for the charge of persecution and punishment of the South. She has suffered to be sure, but she has been the author of her own suffering. Her sons have not been punished, but have been received back into the highest departments of the very Government they endeavored to overthrow and destroy. They now dominate the House of Representatives, and hope soon to control the United States Senate, and the most radical of the radicals of the North will bow to this control, if it shall be obtained without violence and in the legitimate exercise of constitutional rights.

Distinctions That Must Be Preserved

Nevertheless, we must not be asked to say that the South was right in the rebellion, or to say the North was wrong. We must not be asked to put no difference between those who fought for the Union and those who fought against it, or between loyalty and treason. We must not be asked to be ashamed of our part in the war. That is much too great a strain upon Northern conscience and self-respect to be borne in silence. A certain sound was recently given to the trumpet of freedom by Gen. Grant when he told the veterans of Ohio, in a letter written from Milan, Italy, "That he trusted none of them would ever feel a disposition to apologize for the part they took in the late struggle for national existence, or for the cause for which they fought." I admit that the South believed it was right, but the nature of things is not changed by belief. The Inquisition was not less a crime against humanity because it was believed right by the Holy Fathers. The bread and wine are no less bread and wine, though to faith they are flesh and blood. I admit further, that viewed merely as a physical contest, it left very little for self-righteousness or glory on either side. Neither the victors nor the vanquished can hurl reproaches at each other, and each may well enough respect and honor the bravery and skill of the other. Each found in the other a foeman worthy of his steel. The fiery ardor and impetuosity of the one was only a little more than matched by the steady valor and patient fortitude of the other. Thus far we meet upon common ground, and strew choicest flowers upon the graves of the dead heroes of each respectively and equally. But this war will not consent to be viewed simply as a physical contest. It is not for this that the nation is in solemn procession about the graves of its patriot sons to-day. It was not a fight between rapacious birds and ferocious beasts, a mere display of brute courage and endurance, but it was a war between men, men of thought as well as action, and in dead earnest for something beyond the battle-field. It was not even a war of geography or topography or of race.

> "Lands intersected by a narrow frith
> Abhor each other.
> Mountains interposed make enemies of nations."

But the sectional character of this war was merely accidental, and its least significant feature. It was a war of ideas, a battle of principles and ideas which united one section and divided the other: a war between the old and new, slavery and freedom, barbarism and civilization; between a government based upon the broadest and grandest declaration of human rights the world ever heard or read, and another pretended government, based upon an open, bold, and shocking denial of all rights, except the right of the strongest.

The Significance of Decoration Day

Good, wise, and generous men at the North, in power and out of power, for whose good intentions and patriotism we must all have the highest respect, doubt the wisdom of observing this memorial day, and would have us forget and forgive, strew flowers alike and lovingly, on rebel and on loyal graves. This sentiment is noble and generous, worthy of all honor as such; but it is only a sentiment after all, and must submit to its own rational limitations. There was a right side and a wrong side in the late war, which no sentiment ought to cause us to forget, and while to-day we should have malice toward none, and charity toward all, it is no part of our duty to confound right with wrong, or loyalty with treason. If the observance of this memorial day has any apology, office, or significance, it is derived from the moral character of the war, from the far-reaching, unchangeable, and eternal principles in dispute, and for which our sons and brothers encountered hardship, danger, and death. Man is said to be an animal looking before and after. It is his distinction to improve the future by a wise consideration of the past. In looking back to this tremendous conflict, after-coming generations will find much at which to marvel. They will marvel that men to whom was committed the custody of the Government, sworn to protect and defend the Constitution and the Union of the States, did not crush this rebellion in its egg; that they permitted treason to grow up under their very noses, not only without rebuke or repulse, but rather with approval, aid, and comfort—vainly thinking thus to conciliate the rebels; that they permitted the resources of the Union to be scattered, and its forts and arsenals to be taken possession of without raising a voice or lifting a finger to prevent the crime. They will marvel that the men who, with broad blades and bloody hands sought to destroy the Government were the very men who had been through all its history the most highly favored by the Government. They will marvel at this as when a child stabs the breast that nursed it into life. They will marvel still more that, after the rebellion was suppressed, and treason put down by the loss of nearly a half a million of men, and after putting on the nation's neck a debt heavier than a mountain of gold, the Government has so soon been virtually captured by the [Democratic] party which sought its destruction. . . .

The Problem of Inevitability

Charles and Mary Beard

THE APPROACH OF THE IRREPRESSIBLE CONFLICT

The Beards' *Rise of American Civilization* (1929) is a classic of American historical literature. Although two volumes in length, it was intended not for specialists but for a general audience. Surveying the entire sweep of American history, it enabled the Beards to develop some of their insights and assumptions about the forces that, over the long term, drove and shaped historical events.

Like other Progressives in the first decades of the twentieth century, they were convinced that human will and intention did not determine the course of history. Rather, elemental and impersonal forces, in particular economic factors, were far more influential. So the Civil War, they believed, was brought on, not by the decisions of men or by moral imperatives over slavery, but by the pressure of economic interests and developments.

The following extract comes from the first chapter of Volume I, as well as from the first few pages of Chapter 2, where the authors refer to the Civil War as "the Second American Revolution." In the Beards' interpretation the conflict was essentially a contest between manufacturing interests in the North and southern planters, the outcome of which rearranged the nation's economic structure so decisively that it warranted being termed a revolution.

Charles A. Beard (1874–1948) was perhaps the most influential of all American historians. Besides his writing and his teaching at Columbia University, he was active in public life as a social reformer and dissenting intellectual. Among his many publications, the most important historical works are *An Economic Interpretation of the Constitution of the United States* (1913) and *Economic Origins of Jeffersonian Democracy* (1915). Mary Ritter Beard (1876–1958), also a social reformer, wrote *Women's Work in Municipalities* (1915) and *Women as a Force in History* (1946).

Had the economic systems of the North and the South remained static or changed slowly without effecting immense dislocations in the social structure, the balance of power might have been maintained indefinitely by repeating the compensatory tactics of 1787, 1820, 1833, and 1850; keeping in this manner the inherent antagonisms within the bounds of diplomacy. But nothing was stable in the economy of the United States or in the moral sentiments associated with its diversities.

Within each section of the country, the necessities of the productive system were generating portentous results. The periphery of the industrial vortex of the Northeast was daily enlarging, agriculture in the Northwest was being steadily supplemented by manufacturing, and the area of virgin soil open to exploitation by planters was diminishing with rhythmic regularity—shifting with mechanical precision the weights which statesmen had to adjust in their efforts to maintain the equilibrium of peace. Within each of the three sections also occurred an increasing intensity of social concentration as railways, the telegraph, and the press made travel and communication cheap and almost instantaneous, facilitating the centripetal process that was drawing people of similar economic status and parallel opinions into cooperative activities. Finally the intellectual energies released by accumulating wealth and growing leisure—stimulated by the expansion of the reading public and the literary market—developed with deepened accuracy the word-patterns of the current social persuasions, contributing with galvanic effect to the consolidation of identical groupings.

*

As the years passed, the planting leaders of Jefferson's agricultural party insisted with mounting fervor that the opposition, first of the Whigs and then of the Republicans, was at bottom an association of interests formed for the purpose of plundering productive management and labor on the land. And with steadfast insistence they declared that in the insatiable greed of their political foes lay the source of the dissensions which were tearing the country asunder.

"There is not a pursuit in which man is engaged (agriculture excepted)," exclaimed Reuben Davis of Mississippi in 1860, "which is not demanding legislative aid to enable it to enlarge its profits

and all at the expense of the primary pursuit of man— agriculture.
. . . Those interests, having a common purpose of plunder, have
united and combined to use the government as the instrument of
their operation and have thus virtually converted it into a consolidated empire. Now this combined host of interests stands arrayed
against the agricultural states; and this is the reason of the conflict
which like an earthquake is shaking our political fabric to its foundation." The furor over slavery is a mere subterfuge to cover other
purposes. "Relentless avarice stands firm with its iron heel upon the
Constitution." This creature, "incorporated avarice," has chained
"the agricultural states to the northern rock" and lives like a vulture
upon their prosperity. It is the effort of Prometheus to burst his
manacles that provokes the assault on slavery. "These states struggle
like a giant," continued Davis, "and alarm these incorporated interests, lest they may break the chain that binds them to usurpation;
and therefore they are making this fierce onslaught upon the slave
property of the southern states." . . .

*

But the planters were after all fighting against the census
returns, as the phrase of the day ran current. The amazing growth
of northern industries, the rapid extension of railways, the swift
expansion of foreign trade to the ends of the earth, the attachment
of the farming regions of the West to the centers of manufacture
and finance through transportation and credit, the destruction of
state consciousness by migration, the alien invasion, the erection of
new commonwealths in the Valley of Democracy, the nationalistic
drive of interstate commerce, the increase of population in the
North, and the southward pressure of the capitalistic glacier all
conspired to assure the ultimate triumph of what the orators were
fond of calling "the free labor system." This was a dynamic thrust
far too powerful for planters operating in a limited territory with
incompetent labor on soil of diminishing fertility. Those who swept
forward with it, exulting in the approaching triumph of machine
industry, warned the planters of their ultimate subjection.

To statesmen of the invincible forces recorded in the census
returns, the planting opposition was a huge, compact, and self-
conscious economic association bent upon political objects—the
possession of the government of the United States, the protection

of its interests against adverse legislation, dominion over the territories, and enforcement of the national fugitive slave law throughout the length and breadth of the land. No phrase was more often on the lips of northern statesmen than "the slave power." The pages of the Congressional Globe bristled with references to "the slave system" and its influence over the government of the country. But it was left for William H. Seward of New York to describe it with a fullness of familiar knowledge that made his characterization a classic.

Seward knew from experience that a political party was no mere platonic society engaged in discussing abstractions. "A party," he said, "is in one sense a joint stock association, in which those who contribute most direct the action and management of the concern. The slaveholders contributing in an overwhelming proportion to the capital strength of the Democratic party, they necessarily dictate and prescribe its policy. The inevitable caucus system enables them to do this with a show of fairness and justice." This class of slaveholders, consisting of only three hundred and forty-seven thousand persons, Seward went on to say, was spread from the banks of the Delaware to the banks of the Rio Grande; it possessed nearly all the real estate in that section, owned more than three million other "persons" who were denied all civil and political rights, and inhibited "freedom of speech, freedom of press, freedom of the ballot box, freedom of education, freedom of literature, and freedom of popular assemblies. . . . The slaveholding class has become the governing power in each of the slaveholding states and it practically chooses thirty of the sixty-two members of the Senate, ninety of the two hundred and thirty-three members of the House of Representatives, and one hundred and five of the two hundred and ninety-five electors of the President and Vice-President of the United States." . . .

Having described the gigantic operating structure of the slavocracy, Seward drew with equal power a picture of the opposing system founded on "free labor." He surveyed the course of economy in the North—the growth of industry, the spread of railways, the swelling tide of European immigration, and the westward roll of free farmers—rounding out the country, knitting it together, bringing "these antagonistic systems" continually into closer contact. Then he uttered those fateful words which startled conservative citizens from Maine to California—words of prophecy which proved to be brutally true—"the irrepressible conflict."

This inexorable clash, he said, was not "accidental, unnecessary, the work of interested or fanatical agitators and therefore ephemeral." No. "It is an irrepressible conflict between opposing and enduring forces." The hopes of those who sought peace by appealing to slave owners to reform themselves were as chaff in a storm. "How long and with what success have you waited already for that reformation? Did any property class ever so reform itself? Did the patricians in old Rome, the noblesse or clergy in France? The landholders in Ireland? The landed aristocracy in England? Does the slaveholding class even seek to beguile you with such a hope? Has it not become rapacious, arrogant, defiant?" All attempts at compromise were "vain and ephemeral." There was accordingly but one supreme task before the people of the United States—the task of confounding and overthrowing "by one decisive blow the betrayers of the Constitution and freedom forever." In uttering this indictment, this prophecy soon to be fulfilled with such appalling accuracy, Seward stepped beyond the bounds of cautious politics and read himself out of the little group of men who were eligible for the Republican nomination in 1860. Frantic efforts to soften his words by explanations and additions could not appease his critics. . . .

*

From what has just been said it must be apparent that the forces which produced the irrepressible conflict were very complex in nature and yet the momentous struggle has been so often reduced by historians to simple terms that a reexamination of the traditional thesis has become one of the tasks of the modern age. On the part of northern writers it was long the fashion to declare that slavery was the cause of the conflict between the states. Such for example was the position taken by James Ford Rhodes and made the starting point of his monumental work.

Assuming for the moment that this assertion is correct in a general sense, it will be easily observed even on a superficial investigation that "slavery" was no simple, isolated phenomenon. In itself it was intricate and it had filaments through the whole body economic. It was a labor system, the basis of planting, and the foundation of the southern aristocracy. That aristocracy, in turn, owing to the nature of its economic operations, resorted to public policies that were opposed to capitalism, sought to dominate the federal government, and, with the help of free farmers also engaged in agriculture, did at last dominate it. In the course of that political conquest, all the plans of commerce and industry for federal protection and subvention were overborne. It took more than a finite eye to discern where slavery as an ethical question left off and economics—the struggle over the distribution of wealth—began.

On the other hand, the early historians of the southern school, chagrined by defeat and compelled to face the adverse judgment of brutal fact, made the "rights of states"—something nobler than economics or the enslavement of Negroes—the issue for which the Confederacy fought and bled. That too like slavery seems simple until subjected to a little scrutiny. What is a state? At bottom it is a majority or perhaps a mere plurality of persons engaged in the quest of something supposed to be beneficial, or at all events not injurious, to the pursuers. And what are rights? Abstract, intangible moral values having neither substance nor form? The party debates over the economic issues of the middle period answer with an emphatic negative. If the southern planters had been content to grant tariffs, bounties, subsidies, and preferences to northern commerce and industry, it is not probable that they would have been molested in their most imperious proclamations of sovereignty.

But their theories and their acts involved interests more ponderable than political rhetoric. They threatened the country with secession first in defying the tariff of abominations and when they did secede thirty years later it was in response to the victory of a tariff and homestead party that proposed nothing more dangerous to slavery itself than the mere exclusion of the institution from the territories. It took more than a finite eye to discern where their opposition to the economic system of Hamilton left off and their affection for the rights of states began. The modern reader tossed about in a contrariety of opinions can only take his bearings by examining a few indubitable realities.

*

With reference to the popular northern view of the conflict, there stands the stubborn fact that at no time during the long gathering of the storm did Garrison's abolition creed rise to the dignity of a first rate political issue in the North. Nobody but agitators, beneath the contempt of the towering statesmen of the age, ever dared to advocate it. No great political organization even gave it the most casual indorsement.

When the abolitionists launched the Liberty party in the campaign of 1844 to work for emancipation, . . . the voters answered their plea for "the restoration of equality of political rights among men" in a manner that demonstrated the invincible opposition of the American people. Out of more than two and a half million ballots cast in the election, only sixty-five thousand were recorded in favor of the Liberty candidate. That was America's answer to the call for abolition; and the advocates of that policy never again ventured to appeal to the electorate by presenting candidates on such a radical platform.

No other party organized between that time and the clash of arms attempted to do more than demand the exclusion of slavery from the territories and not until the Democrats by repealing the Missouri Compromise threatened to extend slavery throughout the West did any party poll more than a handful of votes on that issue. It is true that Van Buren on a free-soil platform received nearly three hundred thousand votes in 1848 but that was evidently due to personal influence, because his successor on a similar ticket four years afterward dropped into an insignificant place.

Even the Republican party, in the campaign of 1856, coming hard on the act of defiance which swept away the Missouri compact, won little more than one-third the active voters to the cause of restricting the slavery area. When transformed after four more years into a homestead and high tariff party pledged merely to liberty in the territories, the Republicans polled a million votes fewer than the number cast for the opposing factions and rode into power on account of the divided ranks of the enemy. Such was the nation's reply to the anti-slavery agitation from the beginning of the disturbance until the cannon shot at Sumter opened a revolution.

Moreover not a single responsible statesman of the middle period committed himself to the doctrine of immediate and unconditional abolition to be achieved by independent political action. John Quincy Adams, ousted from the presidency by Jacksonian Democracy but returned to Washington as the Representative of a

Massachusetts district in Congress, did declare that it was the duty
of every free American to work directly for the abolition of slavery
and with uncanny vision foresaw that the knot might be cut with
the sword. But Adams was regarded by astute party managers as a
foolish and embittered old man and his prophecy as a dangerous
delusion.

Practical politicians who felt the iron hand of the planters at
Washington—politicians who saw how deeply intertwined with the
whole economic order the institution of slavery really was—could
discover nothing tangible in immediate and unconditional abolition
that appealed to reason or came within the range of common sense.
Lincoln was emphatic in assuring the slaveholders that no Republican had ever been detected in any attempt to disturb them. "We
must not interfere with the institution of slavery in the states where
it exists," he urged, "because the Constitution forbids it and the
general welfare does not require us to do so."

Since, therefore, the abolition of slavery never appeared in the
platform of any great political party, since the only appeal ever made
to the electorate on that issue was scornfully repulsed, since the
spokesman of the Republicans emphatically declared that his party
never intended to interfere with slavery in the states in any shape
or form, it seems reasonable to assume that the institution of slavery
was not the fundamental issue during the epoch preceding the
bombardment of Fort Sumter.

*

Nor can it be truthfully said, as southern writers were fond of
having it, that a tender and consistent regard for the rights of states
and for a strict construction of the Constitution was the prime
element in the dispute that long divided the country. As a matter
of record, from the foundation of the republic, all factions were for
high nationalism or low provincialism upon occasion according to
their desires at the moment, according to turns in the balance of
power. New England nullified federal law when her commerce was
affected by the War of 1812 and came out stanchly for liberty and
union, one and inseparable, now and forever, in 1833 when South
Carolina attempted to nullify a tariff act. Not long afterward, the
legislature of Massachusetts, dreading the overweening strength of
the Southwest, protested warmly against the annexation of Texas

and resolved that "such an act of admission would have no binding force whatever on the people of Massachusetts."

Equally willing to bend theory to practical considerations, the party of the slavocracy argued that the Constitution was to be strictly and narrowly construed whenever tariff and bank measures were up for debate; but no such piddling concept of the grand document was to be held when a bill providing for the prompt and efficient return of fugitive slaves was on the carpet. Less than twenty years after South Carolina prepared to resist by arms federal officers engaged in collecting customs duties, the champions of slavery and states' rights greeted with applause a fugitive slave law which flouted the precious limitations prescribed in the first ten Amendments to the Constitution—a law which provided for the use of all the powers of the national government to assist masters in getting possession of their elusive property—which denied to the alleged slave, who might perchance be a freeman in spite of his color, the right to have a jury trial or even to testify in his own behalf. In other words, it was "constitutional" to employ the engines of the federal authority in catching slaves wherever they might be found in any northern community and to ignore utterly the elementary safeguards of liberty plainly and specifically imposed on Congress by language that admitted of no double interpretation. . . .

*

In the spring of 1861 the full force of the irrepressible conflict burst upon the hesitant and bewildered nation and for four long years the clash of arms filled the land with its brazen clangor. For four long years the anguish, the calamities, and the shocks of the struggle absorbed the energies of the multitudes, blared in the headlines of the newspapers, and loomed impressively in the minds of the men and women who lived and suffered in that age.

Naturally, therefore, all who wrote of the conflict used the terms of war. In its records, the government of the United States officially referred to the contest as the War of the Rebellion, thus by implication setting the stigma of treason on those who served under the Stars and Bars. Repudiating this brand and taking for his shield the righteousness of legitimacy, one of the leading southern statesmen, Alexander H. Stephens, in his great history of the conflict, called it the War between the States. This, too, no less than

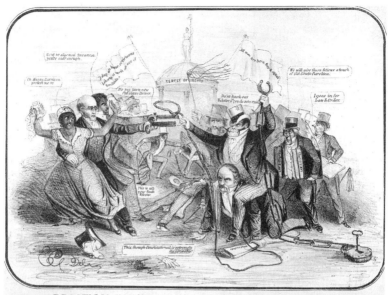

PRACTICAL ILLUSTRATION OF THE FUGITIVE SLAVE LAW.

Fugitive Slave Law, 1850. A contemporary cartoon showing how the federal law requiring the return of fugitives from the slaveholding states made a mockery of the ideals of liberty and of law and order. On the left, William Lloyd Garrison, the abolitionist, is protecting a female slave; on the right, Daniel Webster, the great Whig orator and spokesman for American nationalism, is being ridden by exultant but disreputable slaveowners. (*Chicago Historical Society*)

the title chosen by the federal government, is open to objections; apart from the large assumptions involved, it is not strictly accurate for, in the border states, the armed struggle was a guerrilla war and in Virginia the domestic strife ended in the separation of several counties, under the aegis of a new state constitution, as West Virginia. More recently a distinguished historian, Edward Channing, entitled a volume dealing with the period The War for Southern Independence—a characterization which, though fairly precise, suffers a little perhaps from abstraction.

As a matter of fact all these symbols are misleading in that they overemphasize the element of military force in the grand dénouement. War there was unquestionably, immense, wide-sweeping, indubitable, as Carlyle would say. For years the agony of it hung like a pall over the land. And yet with strange swiftness the cloud was lifted and blown away. Merciful grass spread its green mantle over the cruel scars and the gleaming red splotches sank into the hospitable earth.

It was then that the economist and lawyer, looking more calmly on the scene, discovered that the armed conflict had been only one phase of the cataclysm, a transitory phase; that at bottom the so-called Civil War, or the War between the States, in the light of Roman analogy, was a social war, ending in the unquestioned establishment of a new power in the government, making vast changes in the arrangement of classes, in the accumulation and distribution of wealth, in the course of industrial development, and in the Constitution inherited from the Fathers. Merely by the accidents of climate, soil, and geography was it a sectional struggle. If the planting interest had been scattered evenly throughout the industrial region, had there been a horizontal rather than a perpendicular cleavage, the irrepressible conflict would have been resolved by other methods and accompanied by other logical defense mechanisms.

In any event neither accident nor rhetoric should be allowed to obscure the intrinsic character of that struggle. If the operations by which the middle classes of England broke the power of the king and the aristocracy are to be known collectively as the Puritan Revolution, if the series of acts by which the bourgeois and peasants of France overthrew the king, nobility, and clergy is to be called the French Revolution, then accuracy compels us to characterize by the same term the social cataclysm in which the capitalists, laborers, and farmers of the North and West drove from power in the national government the planting aristocracy of the South. Viewed under the light of universal history, the fighting was a fleeting incident; the social revolution was the essential, portentous outcome.

To be sure the battles and campaigns of the epoch are significant to the military strategist; the tragedy and heroism of the contest furnish inspiration to patriots and romance to the makers of epics. But the core of the vortex lay elsewhere. It was in the flowing substance of things limned by statistical reports on finance, commerce, capital, industry, railways, and agriculture, by provisions of constitutional law, and by the pages of statute books—prosaic muniments which show that the so-called civil war was in reality a Second American Revolution and in a strict sense, the First.

The physical combat that punctuated the conflict merely hastened the inevitable. As was remarked at the time, the South was fighting against the census returns—census returns that told of accumulating industrial capital, multiplying captains of industry, expanding railway systems, widening acres tilled by free farmers. Once the planting and the commercial states, as the Fathers with faithful accuracy described them, had been evenly balanced; by 1860 the balance was gone.

Frank L. Owsley

THE IRREPRESSIBLE CONFLICT

Frank L. Owsley also accepted the idea of irrepressibility but, in his view, the issues were quite different from those emphasized by the Beards. The polemical piece that follows was contributed to *I'll Take My Stand* (1929), the antimodernist manifesto of the Nashville Agrarians, an influential group of scholars and writers centered on Vanderbilt University who were hostile to the urban, industrial way of life that was becoming characteristic of America in the twentieth century. As might be expected, Owsley's essay on the South and the Civil War argued that the conflict was between two societies—one was agrarian, the other industrial.

Owsley's interpretation seems to be similar to the Beards' approach. But the similarities are in fact superficial, because Owsley's use of the terms *agrarian* and *industrial* did not refer to economic interests and classes but to social structure and cultural values. An agricultural society was totally at odds, he believed, with one built upon industry and permeated by its values. And, of course, the agrarian way of life was eminently preferable to Owsley.

Although stated in extreme terms, Owsley's depiction of the sectional conflict in this essay was consistent with his more scholarly work, because he regarded the Old South as an essentially agrarian society shaped, not by the values and interests of the large planters, but by those of the small

landowners, often referred to as the "yeomanry" or, in Owsley's term, the "plain folk."

Frank L. Owsley (1890–1956) taught at Vanderbilt University for most of his life. His most famous books were *Plain Folk of the Old South* (1949); *King Cotton Diplomacy* (2nd ed., 1959) with Harriet C. Owsley; and *State Rights in the Confederacy* (1925).

The system of society which developed in the South . . . was close to the soil. It might be organized about the plantation with its wide fields and its slaves and self-sufficiency, or it might center around a small farm, ranging from a fifty-acre to a five-hundred-acre tract, tilled by the owner, undriven by competition, supplied with corn by his own toil and with meat from his own pen or from the fields and forests. The amusements might be the fine balls and house parties of the planter or the three-day break-down dances which David Crockett loved, or horse races, foot races, cock and dog fights, boxing, wrestling, shooting, fighting, log-rolling, house raising, or corn-shucking. It might be crude or genteel, but it everywhere was fundamentally alike and natural. The houses were homes, where families lived sufficient and complete within themselves, working together and fighting together. And when death came, they were buried in their own lonely peaceful graveyards, to await doomsday together.

This agrarian society had its own interests, which in almost all respects diverged from the interests of the industrial system of the North. The two sections, North and South, had entered the revolution against the mother country with the full knowledge of the opposing interests of their societies; knowing this difference, they had combined in a loose union under the Articles of Confederation. Finally, they had joined together under the Constitution fully conscious that there were thus united two divergent economic and social systems, two civilizations, in fact. The two sections were evenly balanced in population and in the number of states, so that at the time there was no danger of either section's encroaching upon the interests of the other. This balance was clearly understood. Without it a union would not have been possible. Even with the understanding that the two sections would continue to hold this even balance, the sections were very careful to define and limit the powers of the federal government lest one section with its peculiar interests should get control of the national government and use the powers of that government to exploit the other section. Specific powers were granted the federal government, and all not specifically granted were retained by the states.

But equilibrium was impossible under expansion and growth. One section with its peculiar system of society would at one time or another become dominant and control the national government and either exploit the other section or else fail to exercise the functions of government for its positive benefit. Herein lies the irrepressible conflict, the eternal struggle between the agrarian South and the commercial and industrial North to control the government either in its own interest or, negatively, to prevent the other section from controlling it in its interests. Lincoln and Seward and the radical Republicans clothed the conflict later in robes of morality by making it appear that the "house divided against itself" and the irrepressible conflict which resulted from this division marked a division between slavery and freedom.

Slavery . . . was part of the agrarian system, but only one element and not an essential one. To say that the irrepressible conflict was between slavery and freedom is either to fail to grasp the nature and magnitude of the conflict, or else to make use of deliberate deception by employing a shibboleth to win the uninformed and unthinking to the support of a sinister undertaking. Rob Roy MacGregor, one of the chief corruptionists of the present-day power lobby, said that the way the power companies crush opposition and win popular support is to pin the word "bolshevik" upon the leaders of those who oppose the power-lobby program. The leaders of the Northern industrial system could win popular support by tagging their opponents as "*enemies of liberty*" and themselves as "champions of freedom." This they did. Lincoln was a politician and knew all the tricks of a politician. Seward was a politician and knew every *in* and *out*. This is true of other leaders of the "party of high ideals" which assumed the name of Republican party. Doubtless, Lincoln, Seward, and others were half sincere in their idea of an irrepressible conflict, but their fundamental purpose was to win elections and get their party into power—the party of the industrial North—with an industrial program for business and a sop of free lands for the Western farmer.

The irrepressible conflict, then, was not between slavery and freedom, but between the industrial and commercial civilization of the North and the agrarian civilization of the South. The industrial North demanded a high tariff so as to monopolize the domestic markets, especially the Southern market, for the South, being agrarian, must purchase all manufactured goods. It was an exploitative principle, originated at the expense of the South and for the benefit of the North. After the South realized that it would have little industry of its own, it fought the protective tariff to the point of nullification in South Carolina and almost to the point of dissolving the Union. In this as in other cases Southerners saw that what was good for the North was fatal to the South.

The industrial section demanded a national subsidy for the shipping business and merchant marine, but, as the merchant marine was alien to the Southern agrarian system, the two sections clashed. It was once more an exploitation of one section for the benefit of the other.

The industrial North demanded internal improvements— roads, railroads, canals—at national expense to furnish transportation for its goods to Southern and Western markets which were already hedged around for the benefit of the North by the tariff wall. The South objected to internal improvements at national expense because it had less need of transportation than the North and because the burden would be heavier on the South and the benefits greater for the North—another exploitation of the Southern system. The North favored a government-controlled bank; but as corporate wealth and the quick turnover of money were confined to that section, such an institution would be for the sole benefit, the South believed, of the North. . . .

It is interesting to observe that all the favors thus asked by the North were of doubtful constitutional right, for nowhere in the Constitution were these matters specifically mentioned; it is further significant that all the powers and favors thus far demanded by the North were merely negatived by the South; no substitute was offered. The North was demanding positive action on the part of the federal government, and the South was demanding that no action be taken at all. In fact, it may be stated as a general principle that the agrarian South asked practically nothing of the federal government in domestic legislation. It might be imperialistic in its foreign policy, but its domestic policy was almost entirely negative. Even in the matter of public lands the South favored turning over these lands to the state within which they lay, rather than have them controlled by the federal government.

Had these differences, inherent in agrarian and industrial civilizations, been the only ones, it is obvious that conflict would have been inevitable and that two different political philosophies would have been developed to justify and rationalize the conflict which was foreshadowed in the very nature of the demands of the sections: centralization in the North and state rights in the South. But there was another and deadlier difference. There was the slavery system in the South. . . .

Slavery was no simple question of ethics; it cut across the categories of human thought like a giant question mark. It was a moral, an economic, a religious, a social, a philosophical, and above all a political question. It was no essential part of the agrarian civilization of the South—though the Southerners under attack assumed that it was. Without slavery the economic and social life of the South would have not been radically different. Perhaps the plantation life would not have been as pronounced without it, yet the South would long have remained agricultural—as it still is after sixty-five years of "freedom"! Certainly the South would have developed its political philosophy very much as it did. Yet the slavery question furnished more fuel to sectional conflict and created more bitterness than any or all the other elements of the two groups. . . .

*

Thus the two sections clashed at every point. Their economic systems and interests conflicted. Their social systems were hostile; their political philosophies growing out of their economic and social systems were as impossible to reconcile as it is to cause two particles of matter to occupy the same space at the same time; and their philosophies of life, growing out of the whole situation in each section, were as two elements in deadly combat. What was food for the one was poison for the other.

When the balance of power was destroyed by the rapid growth of the North, and the destruction of this balance was signalized in the election of Lincoln by a frankly sectional, hostile political party, the South, after a futile effort at obtaining a concession from Lincoln which would partly restore the balance of power, dissolved its partnership with the industrial North.

This struggle between an agrarian and an industrial civilization, then, was the irrepressible conflict, the house divided against itself, which must become according to the doctrine of the industrial section all the one or all the other. It was the doctrine of intolerance, crusading, standardizing alike in industry and in life. The South had to be crushed out; it was in the way; it impeded the progress of the machine. So Juggernaut drove his car across the South.

Avery O. Craven

THE REPRESSIBLE CONFLICT

Scholars describe Avery O. Craven's approach to Civil War causation as "revisionist," since he believed the sectional issues could be solved without resorting to war. Instead, he believed, extremists and agitators intervened and converted a manageable disagreement into an emotionally charged impasse in which pride and passion dictated war, not negotiation.

For Craven, the tragedy was not just that the situation got out of control but that the outcome was so undesirable—the centralized urban and industrial society of the late nineteenth century. This was the very kind of society that Owsley believed the South stood in opposition to. Craven, on the other hand, saw such a society as the unintended outcome, not the issue or the cause, of the war. Nevertheless, there is still a connection with the Owsley piece, for Craven does not assign blame for the war equally between extremists and agitators on both sides. Rather, he gives the clear impression that the South was simply minding its own business until provoked by overzealous northern reformers.

Avery O. Craven (1886–1980) taught at the University of Chicago. He wrote *Edmund Ruffin, Southerner* (1932); *The Repressible Conflict* (1939); *The Coming of Civil War* (1942); and *The Growth of Southern Nationalism, 1848–1861* (1953).

The move for an independent South which came to a climax in 1861 did not arise from permanent physical and social conditions.

Excerpts from Avery O. Craven, "The Repressible Conflict," in Craven, *An Historian and the Civil War*, University of Chicago Press, 1964. Used by permission.

It sprang rather from temporary emotional factors cultivated both without and within the section. Men fought because they had come to fear and hate—because they had at last accepted a distorted picture of both themselves and the people in other sections.

We have found little in the natural setup of the South to make a unity out of the varied states and regions stretching from Virginia to Texas. That had to be achieved through conflict. Nor have we found inherent differences great enough to make war "inevitable" or "irrepressible" between this section and other sections within the nation. That was to be an artificial creation of inflamed minds. Around the institution of slavery was engendered most of the bitterness which made war necessary. Yet slavery in itself . . . was not an all-inclusive institution. If it had not become a symbol first of sectional differences and then of southern depravity, or superiority, according to the point of view—it might have been faced as a national question and dealt with as successfully as the South American countries dealt with the same problem. Lincoln said he was fighting to save the Union and most certainly men of the South had been struggling for decades to save the Constitution on which that Union rested and was made possible. What we are slowly coming to realize is that war was the product, not so much of sectional differences as of emotions developed about differences, which by 1861 made it impossible to reason, to trust, or to compromise. Both sides believed the other to be composed of persons who could only be handled by force—fiends in human form whose lives need not be spared, whose homes could be pillaged and burned, and whose institutions must be destroyed. The North could say that it was fighting to save a Union which God had established as a great experiment in democracy and which Southerners would destroy and replace with chaos, aristocracy, and human bondage. That is the whole substance of Lincoln's Gettysburg Address. The South, on the other hand, could say that it was fighting to save the original Constitution and to defend rights granted under that Constitution; that Yankees would not respect either constitutions or rights—they would even, in John Brown fashion, stir racial wars.

Higher ideals and purposes have never actuated two belligerents. Worse qualities have never been attributed to enemies. Yet when the war had been over long enough for the historian to look back without passion or prejudice, he was to discover that in saving the Union the North had really achieved a nationalism, which in turn spelled centralization in the interests of industrialism and a new dominant section, which was to make colonial provinces of both South and West for the next generation or more, which was to crush the farmers of the nation and head them toward peasantry, and which was to create a new urban way of life which Spengler and his kind [Oswald Spengler wrote the controversial *The Decline of the West*, 2 vols., 1919, 1922.] believe to be the last stage in the decline of Western civilization. Workers talking of "wage slavery"; capitalists piling fortunes high while poverty and starvation stalk the streets; culture, a bought and borrowed thing, stored in museums, with intellectual sterility everywhere save in a few provincial corners! To such ends did three decades of quarreling and four years of bitter warfare make substantial contributions. . . .

For a generation southern men and women lived under such an attack. It began, as we have said, as a simple questioning of the justice of human slavery by a few earnest, if fanatical, humanitarians. It ended on the level of a high moral crusade, the justice of which few northern men questioned, and tended to include in its sweep of purpose the overthrow of the whole southern way of life. [William Lloyd] Garrison and [Wendell] Phillips and [Theodore] Parker became as well known in the South as in the North. In fact, one writer has recently evaluated Garrison in the antislavery impulse as more important for the hatred he stirred below Mason and Dixon's line than for the influence he wielded above it. Gradually the South became conscious and bitter. It turned in self-defense. A "refutation of the calumnies circulated against" the section appeared almost as soon as the attack was begun. It showed that emotions had been stirred and revealed the possibility of a sectional response. Edwin Holland asked his neighbors to present facts in refutation of charges made and referred to the "abundant testimony of the hostile and unfriendly spirit with which the most vital interests" of the South were discussed. He declared that "the North and East" were "or affected to be, totally ignorant of the actual state and character of our Negro population; they represent the condition of their bondage as a perpetual revolution of labor and severity, rendered still more deplorable by an utter destitution of all the comforts of life.

. . ." He charged "malignity of design" and "utter contempt of truth in such statements" and declared them uttered without "the most ordinary regard for our feelings."

By 1854 the Macon *Georgia Telegraph* could say that "the grand question . . . is what shall be done to protect the South from this everlasting enmity and turmoil, which tears the country to pieces . . . when any question arises which . . . affects the question of slavery." It felt the Union could stand anything but

> the insolent and insidious rust of a progressing, perverted, and corrupt public opinion, which we know has been manufactured with more than Jesuitical zeal and perseverance for a quarter of a century in a portion of this Confederacy. The pseudo ministry . . . of our country . . . take the child's young mind and preoccupy it by many species of lying and blasphemous outcry . . . and follow the child into manhood with this sort of teaching as regards Southern people, until lies and sophistry and false information about us have become ingrained into the very intellect and hearts of Northern people.

A more positive reply was offered in the ingenious "proslavery argument" which was evolved in the South from 1820 to 1860. From a half-apologetic defense of slavery as a necessary evil, it grew to an aggressive glorification of a way of life. The Bible, the Past, Nature, and Civilization were all appealed to, and when the task was completed the Southerner stood before the world a superior man in a superior society. An early group attempted to point out the benefits of slavery to the Negro himself. The Reverend J. C. Stiles showed that slavery had turned twice as many heathens into Christians as all other missionary efforts combined, and Reverend [Thornton] Stringfellow was certain that God had confined the institution to the South because of the superior qualities in its people for lifting ignorant Negroes to culture! Others pointed out the inability of the Negro to be of economic benefit to himself and society without the supervision and direction which slavery afforded. A few with a scientific bent, such as [John H.] Van Evrie and [Josiah C.] Nott, insisted on the unique origins of the Negro and his peculiar physical and mental traits which predestined him to servitude. The clergy, even then a bit skeptical of science, accepted the differences but explained them by the curse of God on Ham.

From such beginnings, the defense went on to ingenious refinements as men discovered that slaves were better off than factory
workers; that all labor, regardless of the system, was exploited; that
republican government could exist only where all white men were
free from drudgery; and that without slavery in agriculture all farmers were destined to a degrading peasantry. It reached its fullness in
the staunch belief that under slavery, the South had achieved a vastly
superior civilization toward which the rest of the world must move.
Here was a society without a labor conflict, without race conflict,
and without social agitation. There was no unemployment and no
old-age worries for its toilers. Culture and refinement prevailed, and
the ruin which urban life produced in "depravity of morals . . .
increase of want, and of crime," as Edward Fisher charged, was
lacking. Slavery had marked the beginning of man's upward climb,
as Professor [Thomas R.] Dew had early declared, and it now
marked its highest peak. When war broke, the Reverend J. H.
Thornwell could say:

> The parties in this conflict are not merely abolitionists and slavehold-
> ers; they are atheists, socialists, communists, red republicans, jacobins
> on the one side, and the friends of order and regulated freedom on
> the other. In one word, the world is the battle ground, Christianity
> and atheism the combatants, and the progress of humanity the stake.

What stands out in all this is the belief in the peculiar quality
and character of the South; the growing emotion involved in attack
and defense; the assumption of differences inherent and persistent.
There was a North, and there was a South. They represented entirely
different values and qualities. They were by nature enemies. And,
what is most significant, *moral* values were involved—things affecting humanity, civilization, God's purposes in this world. Those are
things for which men give their lives, for which holy wars are fought.
National consciousness is woven from fear and resentment as well
as from conviction and faith. Material realities shrink into insignif-
icance when brought into comparison.

Meanwhile the "average American" went about his busy way. The
nation had entered a new period of expansion which carried it across
the plains and mountains to the Pacific. The Indian and Mexican

learned anew the meaning of Manifest Destiny. Behind frontiers, old Wests found their lands and crops in competition with those ahead and readjustments forced upon them which ran back in waves even to the eastern seaboard. The old western demands for lands and better ways to improved markets thus gained new strength, especially in the region above the Ohio, and the banner of democracy was hoisted over every demand. Americans had a right to prosperity as well as to freedom and equality. In the deep South, cotton erected its kingdom to strengthen the hold of agriculture below Mason and Dixon's line, and in the Northeast the Industrial Revolution reached maturity great enough to produce a depression. The nation grew "fearfully"; inequality increased at an even greater rate.

Such expansion inevitably exaggerated the already great sectional division and conflict, and soon the sectional spokesmen, in the struggle for place and advantage, were making telling use of emotions generated in the slavery controversy. James McDowell, in 1832, had told the slaveholders of Virginia that "a Crusade, in the name of liberty, *but with the purpose of plunder,* will be preached against the States that protect it [slavery]—that they will be held up as the common enemies of man whom it will be a duty to overthrow and justice to despoil. . . ." Events now proved the soundness of his warning, but they also showed that he had seen only half of the truth. Southern leaders too would make use of slavery sentiments to forward their ends and to produce unity among their followers.

After 1840 few issues were allowed to stand on their own merits. Individuals and groups, consciously and unconsciously, used slavery to aid their interests. John C. Calhoun and John Quincy Adams, seeking political advantage, tangled slavery hopelessly with the western demand for the annexation of Texas. David Wilmot introduced his trouble-making Proviso as part of a political game which he and his friends were playing. The repeal clause in the Kansas-Nebraska Act was the afterthought of a mere handful of politicians and not a move in response to southern demands. The Appeal to Independent Democrats which [Salmon P.] Chase and his group used to stir the Northwest was false in its assertions and unfair in its purposes, but it was politically effective. The damaging section in the Dred Scott Decision was an *obiter dictum* [an *obiter dictum* is a statement in a judicial decision that is not germane to the case under consideration], forced, according to the late Professor [Frank] Hodder, by the political ambitions of dissenting judges. John Brown, who reduced rabid talk to action, is frankly considered insane by his most able biographer.

Yet these uncalled-for moves and this irresponsible leadership were the very things which lifted the crusade of a band of "crackpot reformers" in the North and an extravagant group of "fire-eaters" in the South to the proportions of a national conflict adjustable only by civil war. Texas and slavery combined begot the Wilmot Proviso, which, in turn, forced the crisis of 1850. The repeal of the Missouri Compromise begot the Republican party and ultimately the combination of a political party and a moral crusade. The Dred Scott *obiter dictum* justified the continuation of that party as a perpetual guard against the aggressions of the South. John Brown brought the race question to the fore and added the final emotional appeal needed to pound the divergent classes of the South into a working unity.

The politician thus gave an air of reality to the abstractions of those who had evolved the slavery question into a struggle of civilizations. In his hands the conflict between freedom and slavery became a sectional contest for lands, internal improvements, tariffs, and new areas for expansion. The continuation of material well-being and the existence of fundamental rights were linked with the spread or the restriction of the "peculiar institution." An emotional fervor and moral force, which only slavery could create, was thus thrown about a whole set of very practical and concrete problems. Two ways of life and two opposing sets of constitutional principles were thus forced into an irrepressible contest for supremacy. Yet, as a matter of fact, few actual gains or losses were involved. Texas would have progressed about as it did if slavery had never been mentioned. There were only two slaves in Kansas in 1860, and there never was the slightest chance of slavery's entering Kansas or Nebraska. All well-informed men knew that by 1857, and many were saying so at the very time Lincoln was making political capital out of proslavery danger. A dozen *obiter dicta* would not have spread slavery over the North, and a hundred John Browns could not have produced a general revolution among the slaves.

The combined efforts of reformer and politician gradually created the notion of the "slave power" and of "Black Republican-

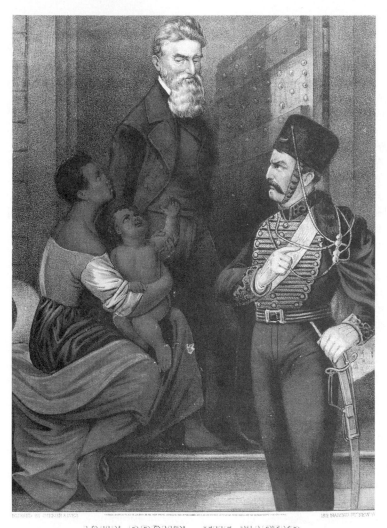

JOHN BROWN — THE MARTYR.

Meeting a Slave Mother and her Child on the steps of Charlestown Jail on his way to Execution.
Regarding them with a look of compassion, Captain Brown stooped and kissed the Child then met his fate.

Martyrdom of John Brown, 1959. A classical rendering of John Brown, crusader against tyranny and protector of the lowly slave, as he prepared for the gallows. Note the European, probably Russian, figures representing the military and religious bulwarks of tyranny—an attempt by the artist to give Brown's actions a far-reaching significance. (*Chicago Historical Society*) ism." Each of these creations was supposed to consist of a well-organized force and program. The one was determined to spread slavery throughout the land. The other was determined to wipe out the institution of slavery even at the cost of a race war. Both were fictions. Yet partisans were able to bring all the fears and apprehensions, all the noble purposes and sentiments aroused by the anti-slavery and the proslavery crusades, to their side and to pour all the bitter distortions of that conflict upon their opponents. They made a conscious North and a conscious South. Each could fight for God against the Devil and his human allies. One would struggle for Union and democracy, the other for self-rule and the Constitution untarnished. Sane men on both sides, and they constituted a majority even in 1861, were helpless before fanatics armed with such holy weapons. . . .

James G. Randall

THE BLUNDERING GENERATION

Another revisionist, perhaps the most distinguished, was James G. Randall. Distressed by the carnage of war and its obvious inability to solve political disputes, as was especially the case with World War I, Randall saw the period before the Civil War through the lens of the late 1930s, colored by the approach of yet another military conflagration.

His article, "The Blundering Generation" (1940), was Randall's most forceful statement of his view that the Civil War was needless. It happened, Randall argued, because of human failure, specifically the inability of the political leadership to act wisely and decisively. Randall's article, of which only an extract is printed here, was not so much a piece of historical research as an indictment of human incompetence and foolishness. Nonetheless, it was possibly the best known of the revisionists' output of books and articles from the 1930s to the 1950s.

James G. Randall (1881–1953), who taught at the University of Illinois at Urbana-Champaign, was one of the greatest of Lincoln scholars. His books on the Civil War president include *Lincoln the President*, 4 vols. (1945–1955); *Lincoln the Liberal Statesman* (1947); and *Constitutional Problems Under Lincoln* (rev. ed., 1951). With his student David Herbert

Randall, James G., "The Blundering Generation," *Mississippi Valley Historical Review*, XXVII (June, 1940), 3–28. Used by permission.

Donald, he published an influential textbook, *The Civil War and Recon-struction* (2d ed., 1969).

War causation tends to be "explained" in terms of great forces. Something elemental is supposed to be at work, be it nationalism, race conflict, or quest for economic advantage. With these forces predicated, the move toward war is alleged to be understandable, to be explained, and therefore to be in some sense reasonable. Thought runs in biological channels and nations are conceived as organisms. Such thought is not confined to philosophers; it is the commonest of mental patterns. A cartoonist habitually draws a nation as a person. In this manner of thinking Germany does so and so; John Bull takes this or that course, and so on. When thought takes so homely a form it is hardly called a philosophical concept; for that purpose the very same thing would appear under a Greek derivative or Freudian label. However labeled, it may be questioned whether the concept is any better than a poor figure of speech, a defective metaphor which is misleading because it has a degree of truth.

Ruritania—to be no more specific—does so and so in the sense that it has a government, the government acts for the nation, and for political purposes there is no other way in which the country can act. The doubtful part is to infer that there is one directing mind for Ruritania which is the distillation of all the millions of minds. Where government has a bogus quality such an inference is more doubtful than if government has a well grounded or estab-lished quality. Give certain conditions of forced leadership and sup-pressed thought, the oneness of executive action in a nation may in fact represent nothing at all in terms of consolidated will and intent distilled from the whole mass. What passes for mass thought these days is not so much distilled as it is translated from golden plates handed down on some ideological Hill of Cumorah and read through the magic of authoritarian Urim and Thummim. The ter-rifying fact is that such bogus thought can be manufactured; it can be produced wholesale and distributed at top speed; it can control a nation; it is the shabby mental *ersatz* of an abnormal period.

War-making is too much dignified if it is told in terms of broad national urges, of great German motives, or of compelling Russian ambitions. When nations stumble into war, or when peoples rub their eyes and find they have been dragged into war, there is at some point a psychopathic case. Omit the element of abnormality, or of bogus leadership, or inordinate ambition for conquest, and diagnosis fails. In the modern scene it fails also if one omits manipulation, dummies, bogeys, false fronts, provocative agents, made-up incidents, frustration of elemental impulses, negation of culture, propaganda that is false in intent, criminal usurpation, and terrorist violence. These are reflections on the present bedeviled age, but their pertinence to the subject at hand is seen in the fact that scholarly discussions in explanation of war on the economic or cultural basis frequently include the Civil War as a supposedly convincing example. The writer doubts seriously whether a consensus of scholars who have competently studied the Civil War would accept either the cultural motive or the economic basis as the effective cause.

If one were to explain how this or that group or individual got into the Civil War, he could rely on no one formula. He would have to make up a series of elements or situations of which the following are only a few that might be mentioned: the despairing plunge, the unmotivated drift, the intruding dilemma, the blasted hope, the self-fulfilling prediction, the push-over, the twisted argument, the frustrated leader, the advocate of rule or ruin, and the reform-your-neighbor prophet. Robert Toombs [U.S. senator from Georgia] said he would resist Stephen A. Douglas though he could see "nothing but . . . defeat in the future"; there is your despairing plunge. Young Henry Watterson, a Tennessee antislavery Unionist who fought for the Confederacy, is an example of the unmotivated drift. To many an individual the problem was not to fight with the side whose policies he approved of, but to be associated with the right set. Such an individual motive could not by a process of multiplication become in any reasonable sense a large-group motive. Yet it would be understandable for the individual. Usually in war time individuals have no choice of side, though in the American Civil War they sometimes did, especially on the border. Even where such choice was possible, the going to war by the individual in the sixties was due less to any broad "cause" or motive than to the fact that war existed, so that fighting was the thing to do. The obtaining of soldiers is not a matter of genuine persuasion as to issues. War participation is not a proof of war attitude.

The intruding dilemma was found in the great border and the great upper South where one of two ugly courses had to be chosen, though neither choice made sense in terms of objectives and interests in those broad regions. The self-fulfilling prediction is recognized in the case of those who, having said that war must come, worked powerfully to make it come. The blasted hope, *i.e.* the wish for adjustment instead of butchery, was the experience of most of the people, especially in the border and upper South. The frustrated leader is seen in the Unionist who came to support secession, or in such northerners as Thurlow Weed and William H. Seward who sought compromise and then supported war. The plea that "better terms" could be had out of the Union, which implied a short secession gesture though uttered by determined secessionists, was the crafty argument for secession to be used in addressing Unionists. This might be dubbed the twisted argument. The push-over is seen in the whole strategy of secession leaders by which anti-secession states and Union-loving men were to be dragged in by the accelerated march of events.

These are things which belong as much to the "explanation" of the Civil War as any broad economic or cultural or elemental factor. It should be remembered how few of the active promoters of secession became leaders of the Confederacy; their place in the drama was in the first act, in the starting of trouble. Nor should sectional preference cause one to forget how large a contribution to Union disaster, and how little to success, was given by northern radicals during the war. Clear thinking would require a distinction between causing the war and getting into the war. Discussion which overlooks this becomes foggy indeed. It was small minorities that caused the war; then the regions and sections got into it. No one seems to have thought of letting the minorities fight it out. Yet writers who descant upon the causation of the war write grandly of vast sections, as if the fact of a section being dragged into the slaughter was the same as the interests of that section being consciously operative in its causation. Here lies one of the chief fallacies of them all.

In writing of human nature in politics Graham Wallas [in *Human Nature in Politics*, 1909] has shown the potent effect of irrational attitudes. He might have found many a Civil War example. None of the "explanations" of the war make sense, if fully analyzed.

The war has been "explained" by the choice of a Republican president, by grievances, by sectional economics, by the cultural wish for southern independence, by slavery, or by events at [Fort] Sumter. But these explanations crack when carefully examined. The election of Lincoln fell so far short of swinging southern sentiment against the Union that secessionists were still unwilling to trust their case to an all-southern convention or to cooperation among southern states. In every election from 1840 to 1852 Lincoln voted for the same candidate for whom many thousands of southerners voted. Lincoln deplored the demise of the Whig party and would have been only too glad to have voted in 1856 for another Harrison, another Taylor, or another Fillmore. Alexander Stephens stated that secessionists did not desire redress of grievances and would obstruct such redress. Prophets of sectional economics left many a southerner unconvinced; it is doubtful how far their arguments extended beyond the sizzling pages of *DeBow's Review* and the agenda of southern commercial congresses. The tariff was a potential future annoyance rather than an acute grievance in 1860. What existed then was largely a southern tariff law. Practically all tariffs are one-sided. Sectional tariffs in other periods have existed without producing war. Southern independence on broad cultural lines is probably more of a modern thesis than a contemporary motive of sufficient force to have carried the South out of the Union on any cooperative, all-southern basis.

It was no part of the Republican program to smash slavery in the South, nor did the territorial aspect of slavery mean much politically beyond agitation. Southerners cared little about actually taking slaves into existing territories; Republicans cared so little in the opposite sense that they avoided the prohibition of slavery in those territorial laws that were passed with Republican votes in February and March, 1861. Things said of "the South" often failed to apply to southerners, or of "the North" to northerners. Thwarted "Southern rights" were more often a sublimation than a definite entity. "The North" in the militant pre-war sense was largely an abstraction. The Sumter affair was not a cause, but an incident resulting from pre-existing governmental deadlock; Sumter requires explanation, and that explanation carries one back into all the other alleged factors. In contemporary southern comments on Lincoln's course at Sumter one finds not harmony but a jangling of discordant voices. Virginia resented Lincoln's action at Sumter for a reason opposite to that of South Carolina; Virginia's resentment was in the anti-secessionist sense. By no means did all the North agree with Lincoln's course as to Sumter. Had Lincoln evacuated Sumter without an expedition, he would have been supported by five and a half of seven cabinet members, Chase taking a halfway stand and Blair alone taking a positive stand for an expedition. What Lincoln refused as to Sumter was what the United States government had permitted in general as to forts and arsenals in the South. Stronger action than at Sumter was taken by Lincoln at [Fort] Pickens without southern fireworks. There is no North-versus-South pattern that covers the subject of the forts. Nor is the war itself to be glibly explained in rational North-versus-South terms.

Let one take all the factors—the Sumter maneuver, the election of Lincoln, abolitionism, slavery in Kansas, cultural and economic differences—and it will be seen that only by a kind of false display could any of these issues, or all of them together, be said to have caused the war if one omits the elements of emotional unreason and overbold leadership. If one word or phrase were selected to account for the war, that word would not be slavery, or state-rights, or diverse civilizations. It would have to be such a word as fanaticism (on both sides), or misunderstanding, or perhaps politics. To Graham Wallas misunderstanding and politics are the same thing.

The fundamental or the elemental is often no better than a philosophical will o' the wisp. Why do adventitious things, or glaringly abnormal things, have to be elementally or cosmically accounted for? If, without proving his point, the historian makes war a thing of "inevitable" economic conflict, or cultural expression, or *Lebensraum* [literally, "living space," a term used by German leaders of the first half of the twentieth century to justify their nation's territorial expansion], his generalizations are caught up by others, for it would seem that those historians who do the most generalizing, if they combine effective writing with it, are the ones who are most often quoted. The historian's pronouncements are taken as the statement of laws whether he means them so or not; he is quoted by sociologists, psychologists, behaviorists, misbehaviorists, propagandists, and what not; he becomes a contributor to those "dynamic" masses of ideas, or ideologies, which are among the sorriest plagues of the present age. As to wars, the ones that have not happened are perhaps best to study. Much could be said about such wars. As much could be said in favor of them as of actual wars. Cultural and economic difficulties in wars that have not occurred are highly significant. The notion that you must have war when you have cultural variation, or economic competition, or sectional difference is an unhistorical misconception which it is stupid in historians to promote. Yet some of the misinterpretations of the Civil War have tended to promote it. . . .

Recent Explanations

Political and Institutional Origins of the Sectional Conflict

David Herbert Donald

AN EXCESS OF DEMOCRACY: THE AMERICAN CIVIL WAR AND THE SOCIAL PROCESS

In this essay, written in 1956, David Herbert Donald argued that, in the middle of the nineteenth century, the United States lacked institutional structure and social cohesion. This deficiency made it very difficult for the government to exercise authority and control as well as for the citizenry to develop attachments and connections to the society as a whole. When the sectional crisis erupted, Donald argues, the institutions that might have checked or moderated it did not exist.

This insight is a version of the "repressible conflict" approach of the revisionists because it suggests that, had viable institutions existed, the sectional dispute might have been solvable. The author even indicates such a possibility. On the other hand, the lack of structure in the society was not something that could be remedied. Rather, it was part of the actual situation that already existed; in effect, it was a given. Nevertheless, the relative formlessness of American society at the time is a feature to be considered in explaining both the ease with which the southern states resorted to secession and the inability of the federal government to effect a settlement of the dispute. For a response to this article, see Phillip S. Paludan's essay on the Civil War as a crisis in law and order, page 300.

David Herbert Donald's many books on the Civil War era, besides the collection of essays entitled *Lincoln Reconsidered* from which this selection is taken, include a biography of Charles Sumner, published in two volumes (1960, 1970); *The Politics of Reconstruction, 1863–1867* (1967); *Liberty and Union* (1978); and *Civil War and Reconstruction* (1969), with James G. Randall. He has won the Pulitzer Prize for biography twice—for the first volume of his Sumner biography in 1961 and for a life of the southern novelist Thomas Wolfe, entitled *Looking Homeward,* in 1988. Prior to his retirement in 1991, he taught at Harvard University.

From *Lincoln Reconsidered* by David Herbert Donald. Copyright © 1956 by David Herbert Donald. Reprinted by permission of Alfred A. Knopf, Inc.

The Civil War, I believe, can best be understood neither as the result of accident nor as the product of conflicting sectional interests, but as the outgrowth of social processes which affected the entire United States during the first half of the nineteenth century.

It is remarkable how few historians have attempted to deal with American society as a whole during this critical period. Accustomed to looking upon it as a pre-war era, we have stressed divisive elements and factors of sectional conflict. Contemporary European observers, on the whole, had a better perspective. Some of these foreign travelers looked upon the American experiment with loathing; others longed for its success; but nearly all stressed the basic unity of American culture, minimizing the ten per cent of ideas and traits which were distinctive to the individual sections and stressing the ninety per cent of attitudes and institutions which all Americans shared.

It is time for us to emulate the best of these European observers and to draw a broad picture of the common American values in the early nineteenth century. Any such analysis would have to start with the newness of American life. Novelty was the keynote not merely for the recently settled regions of the West but for all of American society. Though states like Virginia and Massachusetts had two hundred years of history behind them, they, too, were affected by social changes so rapid as to require each generation to start anew. In the Northeast the rise of the city shockingly disrupted the normal course of societal evolution. Boston, for example, grew from a tidy, inbred city of 40,000 in 1830 to a sprawling, unmanageable metropolis of 178,000 by 1860; New York leaped from 515,000 to 805,000 in the single decade of the 1850's. This kind of urban life was as genuinely a frontier experience as settling on the Great Plains; to hundreds of thousands of European-born immigrants and American farm boys and girls, moving to the big city was an enormously exhilarating and unsettling form of pioneering. In the Old South the long-settled states of the Eastern coast were undergoing a parallel evolution, for the opening of rich alluvial lands along the Gulf Coast offered bonanzas as surely as did the gold mines of California. In the early nineteenth century all sections of the United States were being transformed with such rapidity that stability and security were everywhere vanishing values; nowhere could a father safely predict what kind of world his son would grow up in.

Plenty was another characteristic of this new American society. From the richness of the country's basic resources, Americans, as David M. Potter has observed, ought to be called "The People of Plenty." The lands begged to be developed. Immigrants from less privileged lands found it almost impossible to credit the abundance which everywhere surrounded them. As settlers in the Wabash Valley sang:

> Way down upon the Wabash
> Such lands were never known.
> If Adam had passed over it,
> This soil he'd surely own.
> He'd think it was the Garden
> He played in when a boy,
> And straight he'd call it Eden
> In the State of Illinois.

Mineral wealth surpassed men's dreams. And there was nothing to divert Americans from the exploitation of their resources. As [Alexis de] Tocqueville pointed out, the absence of strong neighbors to the north and the south gave the United States a peculiar position among the nineteenth-century powers; she alone could devote her entire energies to the creation of wealth, instead of wasting them upon arms and warlike preparations. Some Americans made their fortunes in manufacturing; others in cotton and rice plantations; still others in the mines and lands of the West. Not everybody got rich, of course, but everybody aspired to do so. Both the successful and those less fortunate were equally ruthless in exploiting the country's natural resources, whether of water power, of fertile fields, of mineral wealth, or simply of human labor.

Rapid social mobility was another dominant American trait. Though some recent sociological studies have correctly warned us that the Horatio Alger stories represent a myth rather than a reality of American society and that, even in the early nineteenth century, education, family standing, and inherited wealth were valuable assets, we must not forget that there was nevertheless an extraordinary opportunity in the United States for poor boys to make good. Surely in no other Western society of the period could a self-taught merchant's apprentice have founded the manufacturing dynasty of the Massachusetts Lawrences; or a semi-literate ferryboatman named Vanderbilt have gained control of New York City's transportation system; or the son of a London dried-fish shopkeeper named Benjamin have become Senator from Louisiana; or a self-taught prairie lawyer have been elected President of the nation.

Such vertical mobility was not confined to any class or section in the United States. Though most of us are willing to accept the rags-to-riches version of frontier society, we often fail to realize that everywhere in America the early nineteenth century was the day of the self-made man. The Boston Brahmins, as Cleveland Amory has wittily pointed out, were essentially *nouveaux riches;* the Proper Bostonians' handsome houses on Beacon Hill, their affectations of social superiority, their illusions of hearing ancestral voices concealed the fact that most of them derived from quite humble origins, and within the last generation or two. In the South there were, of course, a few fine old families—but not nearly so many as the F.F.V.'s [First Families of Virginia] fondly fancied—but these were not the leaders of Southern society. The typical figure of the ante-bellum South is not Robert E. Lee but tight-fisted Thomas Sutpen, William Faulkner's fictional character, whose unscrupulous rise from hardscrabble beginnings to the planter class is traced in *Absalom, Absalom.*

*

A new society of plenty, with abundant opportunities for self-advancement, was bound to leave its hallmark upon its citizens, whether they lived in North, South, or West. The connection between character and culture is still an essentially unexplored one, but it is surely no accident that certain widely shared characteristics appeared among Americans in every rank of life. In such a society, richly endowed with every natural resource, protected against serious foreign wars, and structured so as to encourage men to rise, it was inevitable that a faith in progress should be generally shared. The idea of progress is not, of course, an American invention, and no claim is even suggested here that nineteenth-century Americans were unique. Indeed, the American experience is merely a special case of the sweeping social transformation which was more slowly changing Europe as well. But American circumstances did make for a particularly verdant belief that betterment, whether economic, social, or moral, was just around the corner. Surely Mark Twain's Colonel Beriah Sellers is, if not a unique American type, the representative American citizen of his age.

Confidence in the future encouraged Americans in their tendency to speculate. A man of even very modest means might anticipate making his fortune, not through exertions of his own, but through the waves of prosperity which seemed constantly to float American values higher and higher. A small initial capital could make a man another John Jacob Astor. "I have now a young man in my mind," wrote C. C. Andrews from Minnesota in 1856, "who came to a town ten miles this side of St. Paul, six months ago, with $400. He commenced trading, and has already, by good investments and the profits of his business, doubled his money." It was no wonder that Americans rejected the safe investment, the "sure thing," to try a flier into the unknown. In some cases the American speculative mania was pathological. A writer in November 1849 described the frenzied state of mind of Californians:

> The people of San Francisco are mad, stark mad. . . . A dozen times or more, during the last few weeks, I have been taken by the arm by some of the *millionaires* —so they call themselves, I call them madmen—of San Francisco, looking wondrously dirty and out at elbows for men of such magnificent pretensions. They have dragged me about, through the mud and filth almost up to my middle, from one pine box to another, called mansion, hotel, bank, or store, as it may please the imagination, and have told me, with a sincerity that would have done credit to the Bedlamite, that these splendid . . . structures were theirs, and they, the fortunate proprietors, were worth from two to three hundred thousand dollars a year each.

But one does not have to turn to the gold rush of California to learn what abundance can do to social values. A sympathetic contemporary Southerner, Joseph G. Baldwin, described "The Flush Times in Mississippi and Alabama," when the virgin lands in that region were first opened to settlement.

> . . . the new era had set in—the era of the second great experiment of independence: the experiment, namely, of credit without capital, and enterprise without honesty. . . . Every cross-road and every avocation presented an opening,—through which a fortune was seen by the adventurer in near perspective. Credit was a thing of course.

To refuse it—if the thing was ever done—were an insult for which a bowie-knife were not a too summary or exemplary means of redress . . . prices rose like smoke. Lots in obscure villages were held at city prices; lands, bought at the minimum cost of government, were sold at from thirty to forty dollars an acre. . . . . Society was wholly unorganized: there was no restraining public opinion: the law was well-nigh powerless—and religion scarcely was heard of except as furnishing the oaths and *technics* of profanity. . . .

Allowance must of course be made for a writer of imaginative fiction, but there is a basic truth in Baldwin's observations. In nineteenth-century America all the recognized values of orderly civilization were gradually being eroded. Social atomization affected every segment of American society. All too accurately Tocqueville portrayed the character of the new generation of Southerners: "The citizen of the Southern states becomes a sort of domestic dictator from infancy; the first notion he acquires in life is that he was born to command, and the first habit he contracts is that of ruling without resistance. His education tends, then, to give him the character of a haughty and hasty man—irascible, violent, ardent in his desires, impatient of obstacles." William H. Herndon, Lincoln's law partner, graphically depicted the even cruder settlers in the West:

These men could shave a horse's main [*sic*] and tail, paint, disfigure and offer him for sale to the owner in the very act of inquiring for his own horse. . . . They could hoop up in a hogshead a drunken man, they being themselves drunk, put in and nail down the head, and roll the man down New Salem hill a hundred feet or more. They could run down a lean, hungry wild pig, catch it, heat a ten-plate stove furnace hot, and putting in the pig, could cook it, they dancing the while a merry jig.

Even the most intimate domestic relations were drastically altered in nineteenth-century America. For centuries the Western tradition had been one in which females were subordinate to males, and in which the wife found her full being only in her husband. But in the pre–Civil War United States such a social order was no longer possible. In Massachusetts, for example, which in 1850 had 17,480 more females than males, many women could no longer look to their normal fulfilment in marriage and a family; if they were from the lower classes they must labor to support themselves, and if they were from the upper classes they must find satisfaction in charitable deeds and humanitarian enterprises. It is not altogether surprising that so many reform movements had their roots in New England. In the West, on the other hand, women were at a great premium; however old or ugly, they found themselves marriageable. One reads, for example, of a company of forty-one women who traveled from the East to frontier Iowa. Before their steamship could reach the wharf, the shore was crowded with men using megaphones to make proposals of marriage. "Miss with the blue ribbon in your bonnet, will you take me?" "Hallo thar, gal, with a cinnamon shawl; if agreeable we will jine." It was, consequently, extremely difficult to persuade these ladies that, after marriage, they had no legal existence except as chattels of their husbands. Not surprisingly, woman's suffrage, as a practical movement, flourished in the West.

Children in such a society of abundance were an economic asset. A standard toast to wedding couples was: "Health to the groom, and here's to the bride, thumping luck, and big children." Partly because they were so valuable, children were well cared for and given great freedom. Virtually every European traveler in the nineteenth century remarked the uncurbed egotism of the American child: "Boys assume the air of full grown coxcombs." "Parents have no command over their children." "The children's faces were dirty, their hair uncombed, their disposition evidently untaught, and all the members of the family, from the boy of six years of age up to the owner (I was going to say master) of the house, appeared independent of each other." "The lad of fourteen . . . struts and swaggers and smokes his cigar and drinks rum; treads on the toes of his grandfather, swears at his mother and sister, and vows that he will run away . . . the children govern the parents."

This child was father of the American man. It is no wonder that Tocqueville, attempting to characterize nineteenth-century American society, was obliged to invent a new word, "individualism." This is not to argue that there were in pre–Civil War America no men of orderly, prudent, and conservative habits; it is to suggest that rarely in human history has a people as a whole felt itself so completely unfettered by precedent. In a nation so new that, as President James K. Polk observed, its history was in the future, in a land of such abundance, men felt under no obligation to respect the lessons of the past. Even in the field of artistic and literary endeavor acceptance of classical forms or acquiescence in the dictates of criticism was regarded as evidence of inferiority. Ralph Waldo Emerson set the theme for nineteenth-century Americans: "Let me admonish you, first of all, to go alone; to refuse the good models, even those which are sacred in the imagination of men. . . . Imitation cannot go above its model. The imitator dooms himself to hopeless mediocrity. . . . Yourself a newborn bard of the Holy Ghost, cast behind you all conformity. . . ."

Every aspect of American life witnessed this desire to throw off precedent and to rebel from authority. Every institution which laid claim to prescriptive right was challenged and overthrown. The Church, that potent instrument of social cohesion in the colonial period, was first disestablished, and then strange new sects, such as the Shakers, Mormons, and Campbellites, appeared to fragment the Christian community. The squirearchy, once a powerful conservative influence in the Middle States and the South, was undermined by the abolition of primogeniture and entails and then was directly defied in the Anti-Rent War of New York. All centralizing economic institutions came under attack. The Second Bank of the United States, which exercised a healthy restraint upon financial chaos, was destroyed during the Jackson period, and at the same time the Supreme Court moved to strike down vested monopoly rights.

Nowhere was the American rejection of authority more complete than in the political sphere. The decline in the powers of the Federal government from the constructive centralism of George Washington's administration to the feeble vacillation of James Buchanan's is so familiar as to require no repetition here. With declining powers there went also declining respect. Leonard D. White's scholarly works on American administrative history accurately trace the descending status and the decreasing skill of the Federal government employees. The national government, moreover, was not being weakened in order to bolster the state governments, for they too were decreasing in power. The learned historians of Massachusetts during these years, Oscar and Mary Handlin, find the theme of their story in the abandonment of the idea of "Commonwealth," in the gradual forgetting of the ideal of the purposeful state which had once concerted the interests of all its subordinate groups. By the 1850's the authority of all government in America was at a low point; government to the American was, at most, merely an institution with a negative role, a guardian of fair play.

Declining power of government was paralleled by increased popular participation in it. The extension of the suffrage in America has rarely been the result of a concerted reform drive, such as culminated in England in 1832 and in 1867; rather it has been part of the gradual erosion of all authority, of the feeling that restraints and differentials are necessarily anti-democratic, and of the practical fact that such restrictions are difficult to enforce. By the mid-nineteenth century in most American states white manhood suffrage was virtually universal.

All too rarely have historians given sufficient attention to the consequences of the extension of the franchise in America, an extension which was only one aspect of the general democratic rejection of authority. Different appeals must necessarily be made to a broad electorate than to an *élite* group. Since the rival parties must both woo the mass of voters, both tended to play down issues and to stand on broad equivocal platforms which evaded all subjects of controversy. Candidates were selected not because of their demonstrated statesmanship but because of their high public visibility. The rash of military men who ran for President in the 1840's and 1850's was no accident. If it is a bit too harsh to say that extension of the suffrage inevitably produced leaders without policies and parties without principles, it can be safely maintained that universal democracy made it difficult to deal with issues requiring subtle understanding and delicate handling. Walter Bagehot, that shrewd English observer, was one of the few commentators who accurately appreciated the changes that universal suffrage brought to American life. Writing in October 1861, he declared:

> The steadily augmenting power of the lower orders in America has naturally augmented the dangers of the Federal Union . . . a dead level of universal suffrage runs, more or less, over the whole length of the United States . . . it places the entire control over the political action of the whole State in the hands of common labourers, who are of all classes the least instructed—of all the most aggressive—of all the most likely to be influenced by local animosity—of all the most likely to exaggerate every momentary sentiment—of all the least likely to be capable of a considerable toleration for the constant oppositions of opinion, the not infrequent differences of interests,

and the occasional unreasonableness of other States. . . . The unpleasantness of mob government has never before been exemplified so conspicuously, for it never before has worked upon so large a scene.

One does not, of course, have to accept the Tory accent to recognize the validity of Bagehot's analysis. Simply because Americans by the middle of the nineteenth century suffered from an excess of liberty, they were increasingly unable to arrive at reasoned, independent judgments upon the problems which faced their society. The permanent revolution that was America had freed its citizens from the bonds of prescription and custom but had left them leaderless. Inevitably the reverse side of the coin of individualism is labeled conformity. Huddling together in their loneliness, they sought only to escape their freedom. Fads, fashions, and crazes swept the country. Religious revivalism reached a new peak in the 1850's. Hysterical fears and paranoid suspicions marked this shift of Americans to "other-directedness." Never was there a field so fertile before the propagandist, the agitator, the extremist.

*

These dangerously divisive tendencies in American society did not, of course, go unnoticed. Tocqueville and other European observers were aware of the perils of social atomization and predicted that, under shock, the Union might be divided. Nor were all Americans indifferent to the drift of events. Repeatedly in the Middle Period conservative statesmen tried to check the widespread social disorganization. Henry Clay, for example, attempted to revive the idea of the national interest, superior to local and individual interests, by binding together the sections in his American System: the West should produce the nation's food; the South its staples; and the East its manufactures. The chief purpose of Daniel Webster's great patriotic orations was to stimulate a national feeling based on shared traditions, values, and beliefs. Taking as his twin maxims "The best authority for the support of a particular provision in government is experience . . ." and "Because a thing has been wrongly done, it does not therefore follow that it can now be undone . . . ," Webster tried to preserve the Union from shocks and rapid change. John C. Calhoun, too, argued for uniting "the most opposite and conflicting interests . . . into one common attachment to the country" through protecting the rights of minorities. With suitable guarantees to vested sectional interests (notably to slavery), Calhoun predicted that "the community would become a unity, by becoming a common center of attachment of all its parts. And hence, instead of faction, strife, and struggle for party ascendancy, there would be patriotism, nationality, harmony, and a struggle only for supremacy in promoting the common good of the whole."

Nor did conservative statesmanship die with the generation of Webster, Clay, and Calhoun. Down to the very outbreak of the Civil War old Whigs like John Jordan Crittenden, John Bell, and Edward Everett argued for adjustment of sectional claims to the national interest. Abraham Lincoln, another former Whig, tried to check the majoritarianism of his fellow countrymen by harking back to the Declaration of Independence, which he termed the "sheet anchor of our principles." In the doctrine that all men are created equal Lincoln found justification for his belief that there were some rights upon which no majority, however large or however democratic, might infringe. Majority rule, he maintained, could no more justify the extension of slavery to the territories than majority rule could disenfranchise the Irish, or the Catholics, or the laboring men of America. Soberly he warned that in a country like America, where there was no prescriptive right, the future of democratic government depended upon the willingness of its citizens to admit moral limits to their political powers.

None of these attempts to curb the tyranny of the majority were successful; all went too strongly against the democratic current of the age. American society was changing so rapidly that there was no true conservative group or interest to which a statesman could safely appeal. Webster, it is clear, would have preferred to find his following among yeoman farmers, holding approximately equal wealth; instead he was obliged to rely upon the banking, manufacturing, and speculative interests of the Northeast, the hard, grasping, *arriviste* element of society, a group which had itself risen through the democratic process. These special interests used Webster to secure tariffs, banking acts, and internal improvement legislation favorable to themselves, but they selfishly dropped him when he talked of subordinating their local particularism to the broad national interest.

Similarly Calhoun sought a conservative backing in the plantation aristocracy, the same aristocracy which in a previous generation had produced George Washington, James Madison, and John Marshall. But while Calhoun prated of a Greek democracy, in which all white men, freed by Negro slavery of the burdens of menial labor, could deliberate upon statesmanlike solutions to the nation's problems, the conservative aristocracy upon which his theories depended was vanishing. Political and economic leadership moved from Virginia, first to South Carolina, then to Mississippi. The educated, cosmopolitan plantation owners of the 1780's disappeared; in their place emerged the provincial Southron, whose sentiments were precisely expressed by an up-country South Carolinian: "I'll give you my notion of things; I go first for Greenville, then for Greenville District, then for the up-country, then for South Carolina, then for the South, then for the United States; and after that I don't go for anything. I've no use for Englishmen, Turks and Chinese." These slave-masters of the new cotton kingdom endorsed Calhoun and his doctrines so long as their own vested interests were being protected; after that, they ignored his conservative philosophy.

Possibly in time this disorganized society might have evolved a genuinely conservative solution for its problems, but time ran against it. At a stage when the United States was least capable of enduring shock, the nation was obliged to undergo a series of crises, largely triggered by the physical expansion of the country. The annexation of Texas, the war with Mexico, and the settlement of California and Oregon posed inescapable problems of organizing and governing this new empire. Something had to be done, yet any action was bound to arouse local, sectional hostilities. Similarly in 1854 it was necessary to organize the Great Plains territory, but, as Stephen A. Douglas painfully learned, organizing it without slavery alienated the South, organizing it with slavery offended the North, and organizing it under popular sovereignty outraged both sections.

As if these existential necessities did not impose enough strains upon a disorganized society, well-intentioned individuals insisted upon adding others. The quite unnecessary shock administered by the Dred Scott decision in 1857 is a case in point; justices from the antislavery North and the proslavery South, determined to settle the slavery issue once and for all, produced opinions which in fact settled nothing but only led to further alienation and embitterment. Equally unnecessary, of course, was the far ruder shock which crazy John Brown and his little band administered two years later when they decided to solve the nation's problems by taking the law into their own hands at Harpers Ferry.

These crises which afflicted the United States in the 1850's were not in themselves calamitous experiences Revisionist historians have correctly pointed out how little was actually at stake: slavery did not go into New Mexico or Arizona; Kansas, after having been opened to the peculiar institution for six years, had only two Negro slaves; the Dred Scott decision declared an already repealed law unconstitutional; John Brown's raid had no significant support in the North and certainly roused no visible enthusiasm among Southern Negroes. When compared to crises which other nations have resolved without great discomfort, the true proportions of these exaggerated disturbances appear.

But American society in the 1850's was singularly ill equipped to meet any shocks, however weak. It was a society so new and so disorganized that its nerves were rawly exposed. It was, as Henry James noted, a land which had "no sovereign, no court, no personal loyalty, no aristocracy, no church, no clergy, no army, no diplomatic service, no country gentlemen, no palaces, no castles, nor manors, nor old country houses, nor parsonages, nor thatched cottages, nor ivied ruins; no cathedrals, nor abbeys, nor little Norman churches; no great universities nor public schools . . . ; no literature, no novels, no museums, no pictures, no political society"—in short, which had no resistance to strain. The very similarity of the social processes which affected all sections of the country—the expansion of the frontier, the rise of the city, the exploitation of great natural wealth—produced not cohesion but individualism. The structure of the American political system impeded the appearance of conservative statesmanship, and the rapidity of the crises in the 1850's prevented conservatism from crystallizing. The crises themselves were not world-shaking, nor did they inevitably produce war. They were, however, the chisel strokes which revealed the fundamental flaws in the block of marble, flaws which stemmed from an excess of democracy.

Arthur Bestor

THE AMERICAN CIVIL WAR AS A CONSTITUTIONAL CRISIS

When historians have claimed that the sectional conflict really centered on constitutional issues, they have often downplayed the significance of slavery as a cause, as Alexander H. Stephens did. Moreover, explanations of the dispute that have stressed constitutional differences have frequently seemed less plausible because there must have been something more involved than debates about legal technicalities. Besides, legal technicalities can always be worked out.

In Arthur Bestor's view, the debate did, in fact, revolve around slavery. But the South's "peculiar institution" was discussed at the time as a constitutional question, that is, whether the U.S. Constitution protected or proscribed slavery. It could be argued that, if this was so, then the slavery issue was more negotiable than if the morality of the system were at stake. But, in Bestor's view, this way of treating the matter actually posed a problem as intractable and fundamental as the moral dilemma because disputes about the Constitution are disputes about the system of government—the polity itself. If the Civil War was, in fact, a constitutional crisis, then, in Bestor's opinion, the situation confronting the American polity was about as serious as could be imagined.

Arthur Bestor (born 1908) taught at the University of Washington at Seattle. He wrote another important article on constitutional issues in the antebellum era—"State Sovereignty and Slavery," *Journal of the Illinois Historical Society* (Summer 1961)—as well as a work in cultural history, *Backwoods Utopias* (1950).

Within the span of a single generation—during the thirty-odd years that began with the annexation of Texas in 1845 and ended with the withdrawal of the last Union troops from the South in 1877—the United States underwent a succession of constitutional crises more severe and menacing than any before or since. From 1845 on, for some fifteen years, a constitutional dispute over the expansion of slavery into the western territories grew increasingly tense until a paralysis of normal constitutional functioning set in. Abruptly, in

Arthur Bestor, "The American Civil War as a Constitutional Crisis," *American Historical Review,* January 1964, vol. 69, No. 2, pp. 327–41, 344–51. Reprinted by permission of the author.

1860–1861, this particular constitutional crisis was transformed into another: namely, that of secession. Though the new crisis was intimately linked with the old, its constitutional character was fundamentally different. The question of how the Constitution ought to operate as a piece of working machinery was superseded by the question of whether it might and should be dismantled. A showdown had come, and the four-year convulsion of Civil War ensued. Then, when hostilities ended in 1865, there came not the hoped for dawn of peace, but instead a third great constitutional struggle over Reconstruction, which lasted a dozen years and proved as harsh and divisive as any cold war in history. When the nation finally emerged from three decades of corrosive strife, no observer could miss the profound alterations that its institutions had undergone. Into the prodigious vortex of crisis and war every current of American life had ultimately been drawn.

So all-devouring was the conflict and so momentous its effects, that to characterize it (as I have done) as a series of constitutional crises will seem to many readers an almost irresponsible use of language, a grotesque belittling of the issues. Powerful economic forces, it will be pointed out, were pitted against one another in the struggle. Profound moral perplexities were generated by the existence of slavery, and the attacks upon it had social and psychological repercussions of incredible complexity. The various questions at issue penetrated into the arena of politics, shattering established parties and making or breaking the public careers of national and local leaders. Ought so massive a conflict be discussed in terms of so rarified an abstraction as constitutional theory?

To ask such a question, however, is to mistake the character of constitutional crises in general. When or why or how should they arise if not in a context of social, economic, and ideological upheaval? A constitution, after all, is nothing other than the aggregate of laws, traditions, and understandings—in other words, the complex of institutions and procedures—by which a nation brings to political and legal decision the substantive conflicts engendered by changes in all the varied aspects of its societal life. In normal times, to be sure, routine and recurrent questions of public policy are not thought of as constitutional questions. Alternative policies are discussed in terms of their wisdom or desirability. Conflicts are resolved by the ordinary operation of familiar constitutional machinery. A decision is reached that is essentially a political decision, measuring, in some rough way, the political strength of the forces that are backing or opposing some particular program of action, a program that both sides concede to be constitutionally possible, though not necessarily prudent or desirable.

When controversies begin to cut deep, however, the constitutional legitimacy of a given course of action is likely to be challenged. Questions of policy give place to questions of power; questions of wisdom to questions of legality. Attention shifts to the Constitution itself, for the fate of each particular policy has come to hinge upon the interpretation given to the fundamental law. In debating these constitutional questions, men are not evading the substantive issues. They are facing them in precisely the manner that the situation now requires. A constitutional dispute has been superadded to the controversies already present.

Should the conflict become so intense as to test the adequacy of existing mechanisms to handle it at all, then it mounts to the level of a constitutional crisis. Indeed the capability of producing a constitutional crisis is an ultimate measure of the intensity of the substantive conflicts themselves. If, in the end, the situation explodes into violence, then the catastrophe is necessarily a constitutional one, for its very essence is the failure and the threatened destruction of the constitutional framework itself.

The secession crisis of 1860–1861 was obviously an event of this kind. It was a constitutional catastrophe in the most direct sense, for it resulted in a civil war that destroyed, albeit temporarily, the fabric of the Union.

There is, however, another sense—subtler, but perhaps more significant—in which the American Civil War may be characterized as a constitutional crisis. To put the matter succinctly, the very form that the conflict finally took was determined by the pre-existing form of the constitutional system. The way the opposing forces were arrayed against each other in war was a consequence of the way the Constitution had operated to array them in peace. Because the Union could be, and frequently had been, viewed as no more than a compact among sovereign states, the dissolution of the compact was a conceivable thing. It was constitutional theorizing, carried on from the very birth of the Republic, which made secession the ultimate recourse of any group that considered its vital interests threatened.

Since the American system was a federal one, secession, when it finally occurred, put the secessionists into immediate possession of fully organized governments, capable of acting as no *ad hoc* insurrectionary regime could possibly have acted. Though sometimes described as a "Rebellion" and sometimes as a "Civil War," the American conflict was, in a strict sense, neither. It was a war between pre-existing political entities. But it was not (to use a third description) a "War between the States," for in war the states did not act severally. Instead, the war was waged between two federations of these states: one the historic Union, the other a Confederacy that, though newly created, was shaped by the same constitutional tradition as its opponent. In short, only the pre-existing structure of the American Constitution can explain the actual configuration even of the war itself.

The *configurative* role that constitutional issues played is the point of crucial importance. When discussed in their own terms and for their own sakes, constitutional questions are admittedly theoretical questions. One may indeed say (borrowing a phrase that even academicians perfidiously employ) that they are academic questions. Only by becoming involved with other (and in a sense more "substantive") issues, do they become highly charged. But when they do become so involved, constitutional questions turn out to be momentous ones, for every theoretical premise draws after it a train of practical consequences. Abstract though constitutional issues may be, they exert a powerful shaping effect upon the course that events will in actuality take. They give a particular direction to forces already at work. They impose upon the conflict as a whole a unique, and an otherwise inexplicable, pattern or configuration.

To speak of a configuration of forces in history is to rule out, as essentially meaningless, many kinds of questions that are popularly supposed to be both answerable and important. In particular, it rules out as futile any effort to decide which one of the various forces at work in a given historical situation was "*the* most important cause" of the events that followed, or "*the* decisive factor" in bringing them about, or "*the* crucial issue" involved. The reason is simple. The steady operation of a single force, unopposed and uninterrupted, would result in a development so continuous as to be, in the most literal sense, eventless. To produce an event, one force must impinge upon at least one other. The event is the consequence of their interaction. Historical explanation is, of necessity, an explanation of such interactions.

If interaction is the crucial matter, then it is absurd to think of assigning to any factor in history an intrinsic or absolute weight, independent of its context. In the study of history, the context is all-important. Each individual factor derives its significance from the position it occupies in a complex structure of interrelationships. The fundamental historical problem, in short, is not to measure the relative weight of various causal elements, but instead to discover the pattern of their interaction with one another. . . .

No single factor, whatever its nature, can account for the distinctive form that the mid-nineteenth-century American crisis assumed. Several forces converged, producing a unique configuration. Men were debating a variety of issues simultaneously, and their various arguments intertwined. Each conflict tended to intensify the others, and not only to intensify them but also to alter and deflect them in complicated ways. The crisis was born of interaction. . . .

When the historical record is as vast as the one produced by the mid-nineteenth-century American crisis—when arguments were so wearisomely repeated by such multitudes of men—it is sheer fantasy to assume that the issues discussed were not the real issues. The arguments of the period were public ones, addressed to contemporaries and designed to influence their actions. If these had not touched upon genuine issues, they would hardly have been so often reiterated. Had other lines of argument possessed a more compelling force, they would certainly have been employed.

The only tenable assumption, one that would require an overwhelming mass of contrary evidence to rebut, is that men and women knew perfectly well what they were quarreling about. And what do we find? They argued about economic measures—the tariff, the banking system, and the Homestead Act—for the obvious reason that economic interests of their own were at stake. They argued about slavery because they considered the issues it raised to be vital ones—vital to those who adhered to the ideal of a free society and vital to those who feared to disturb the *status quo*. They argued about the territories because they felt a deep concern for the kind of social order that would grow up there. They argued about the Constitution because they accepted its obligations (whatever they considered them to be) as binding.

These are the data with which the historian must reckon. Four issues were mentioned in the preceding paragraph: the issue of economic policy, the issue of slavery, the issue of the territories, and the issue of constitutional interpretation. At the very least, the historian must take all these into account. Other factors there indubitably were. To trace the interaction of these four, however, will perhaps suffice to reveal the underlying pattern of the crisis and to make clear how one of these factors, the constitutional issue, exerted a configurative effect that cannot possibly be ignored.

Conflicts over economic policy are endemic in modern societies. They formed a recurrent element in nineteenth-century American political conflict. To disregard them would be an even greater folly than to assume that they determined, by themselves, the entire course of events. Between a plantation economy dependent upon the sale of staples to a world market and an economy in which commerce, finance, and manufacturing were rapidly advancing, the points of conflict were numerous, real, and important. At issue were such matters as banks and corporations, tariffs, internal improvements, land grants to railroads, and free homesteads to settlers. In a general way, the line of division on matters of economic policy tended, at midcentury, to coincide with the line of division on the question of slavery. To the extent that it did so (and it did so far less clearly than many economic determinists assume), the economic conflict added its weight to the divisive forces at work in 1860–1861.

More significant, perhaps, was another and different sort of relationship between the persistent economic conflict and the rapidly mounting crisis before the Civil War. To put the matter briefly, the constitutional theories that came to be applied with such disruptive effects to the slavery dispute had been developed, in the first instance, largely in connection with strictly economic issues. Thus the doctrine of strict construction was pitted against the doctrine of loose construction as early as 1791, when Alexander Hamilton originated the proposal for a central bank. And the doctrine of nullification was worked out with ingenious thoroughness in 1832 as a weapon against the protective tariff. Whatever crises these doctrines precipitated proved to be relatively minor ones so long as the doctrines were applied to purely economic issues. Within this realm, compromise always turned out to be possible. The explosive force of irreconcilable constitutional theories became apparent only when the latter were brought to bear upon the dispute over slavery.

Inherent in the slavery controversy itself (the second factor with which we must reckon) were certain elements that made compromise and accommodation vastly more difficult than in the realm of economic policy. To be sure, slavery itself had its economic aspect. It was, among other things, a labor system. The economic life of many regions rested upon it. The economic interests that would be affected by any tampering with the institution were powerful interests, and they made their influence felt.

Nevertheless, it was the noneconomic aspect of slavery that made the issues it engendered so inflammatory. As Ulrich B. Phillips puts it, "Slavery was instituted not merely to provide control of labor but also as a system of racial adjustment and social order." The word "adjustment" is an obvious euphemism; elsewhere Phillips speaks frankly of "race control." The effort to maintain that control, he maintains, has been "the central theme of Southern history." The factor that has made the South "a land with a unity despite its diversity," Phillips concludes, is "a common resolve indomitably maintained—that it shall be and remain a white man's country."

It was this indomitable resolve—say rather, this imperious demand—that lay at the heart of the slavery controversy, as it lies at the heart of the struggle over civil rights today. To put the matter bluntly, the demand was that of a master race for a completely free hand to deal as it might choose with its own subject population. The word "sovereignty" was constantly on the lips of southern politicians. The concept they were invoking was one that Blackstone had defined as "supreme, irresistible, absolute, uncontrolled authority." This was the kind of authority that slaveholders exercised over their chattels. What they were insisting on, in the political realm, was that the same species of power should be recognized as belonging to the slaveholding states when dealing with their racial minorities. "State Sovereignty" was, in essence, the slaveowner's authority writ large.

If slavery had been a static system, confined geographically to the areas where the institution was an inheritance from earlier days, then the demand of the slaveholding states for unrestricted, "sovereign" power to deal with it was a demand to which the majority of Americans would probably have reconciled themselves for a long time. In 1861, at any rate, even Lincoln and the Republicans were prepared to support an ironclad guarantee that the Constitution would never be amended in such a way as to interfere with the institution within the slaveholding states. An irrepealable amendment to that effect passed both houses of Congress by the necessary two-thirds vote during the week before Lincoln's inauguration. The incoming President announced that he had "no objection" to the pending amendment, and three states (two of them free) actually gave their ratifications in 1861 and 1862. If the problems created by slavery had actually been, as slave-owners so vehemently maintained, of a sort that the slaveholding states were perfectly capable of handling by themselves, then the security offered by this measure might well have been deemed absolute.

As the historical record shows, however, the proposed amendment never came close to meeting the demands of the proslavery forces. These demands, and the crisis they produced, stemmed directly from the fact that slavery was *not* a static and local institution; it was a prodigiously expanding one. By 1860 the census revealed that more than half the slaves in the nation were held in bondage *outside* the boundaries of the thirteen states that had composed the original Union. The expansion of slavery meant that hundreds of thousands of slaves were being carried beyond the territorial jurisdictions of the states under whose laws they had originally been held in servitude. Even to reach another slaveholding state, they presumably entered that stream of "Commerce . . . among the several States," which the Constitution gave Congress a power "to regulate." If they were carried to United States territories that had not yet been made states, their presence there raised questions about the source and validity of the law that kept them in bondage.

Territorial expansion, the third factor in our catalogue, was thus a crucial element in the pattern of interaction that produced the crisis. The timing of the latter, indeed, indicates clearly the role that expansion played. Slavery had existed in English-speaking America for two centuries without producing any paralyzing convulsion. The institution had been brought to an end in the original states of the East and North by unspectacular exercises of legislative or judicial authority. Federal ordinances barring slavery from the Old Northwest had operated effectually yet inconspicuously since 1787. At many other points federal authority had dealt with slavery, outlawing the foreign slave trade on the one hand and providing for the return of fugitive slaves on the other. Prior to the 1840s constitutional challenges to its authority in these matters had been few and unimportant. Indeed, the one true crisis of the period, that of 1819–1821 over Missouri, was rooted in expansionism, precisely as the later one was to be. The nation was awaking to the fact that slavery had pushed its way northward and westward into the virgin lands of the Louisiana Purchase. Only when limits were drawn for it across the whole national domain did the crisis subside.

Suddenly, in the election of 1844, the question of territorial expansion came to the fore again. Events moved rapidly. Within the space of precisely a decade, between the beginning of 1845 and the end of 1854, four successive annexations added a million and a quarter square miles to the area under undisputed American sovereignty. Expansion itself was explosive; its interaction with the smoldering controversy over slavery made the latter issue explosive also.

The annexation of Texas in 1845, the war with Mexico that followed, and the conquests in the Southwest which that war brought about gave to the campaign against slavery a new and unprecedented urgency. Within living memory the plains along the Gulf of Mexico had been inundated by the westward-moving tide of slavery. Alabama and Mississippi, to say nothing of Arkansas and Missouri, furnished startling proof of how quickly and ineradicably the institution could establish itself throughout great new regions. Particularly telling was the example of Texas. There slavery had been carried by American settlers to nominally free soil beyond the boundaries of the United States; yet in the end the area itself was being incorporated in the Union. To guard against any possible repetition of these developments, antislavery forces reacted to the outbreak of the Mexican War by introducing and supporting the Wilmot Proviso. Originally designed to apply simply to territory that might be acquired from Mexico, it was quickly changed into an all-encompassing prohibition: "That there shall be neither slavery nor involuntary servitude in any territory on the continent of America which shall hereafter be acquired by or annexed to the United

States . . . in any . . . manner whatever." The steadfast refusal of the Senate to accept the proviso did not kill it, for the prospect of continuing expansion kept the doctrine alive and made it the rallying point of antislavery sentiment until the Civil War.

This prospect of continuing expansion is sometimes forgotten by historians who regard the issue of slavery in the territories as somehow bafflingly unreal. Since 1854, it is true, no contiguous territory has actually been added to the "continental" United States. No one in the later 1850s, however, could know that this was to be the historic fact. There were ample reasons to expect otherwise. A strong faction had worked for the annexation of the whole of Mexico in 1848. Filibustering expeditions in the Caribbean and Central America were sporadic from 1849 to 1860. As if to spell out the implications of these moves, the notorious Ostend Manifesto of 1854 had announced (over the signatures of three American envoys, including a future President) that the United States could not "permit Cuba to be Africanized" (in plainer language, could not allow the slaves in Cuba to become free of white domination and control), and had defiantly proclaimed that if Spain should refuse to sell the island, "then, by every law, human and divine, we shall be justified in wresting it from Spain if we possess the power." This was "higher law" doctrine with a vengeance. . . .

The issues raised by territorial expansion were, however, not merely prospective ones. Expansion was a present fact, and from 1845 onward its problems were immediate ones. Population was moving so rapidly into various parts of the newly acquired West, most spectacularly into California, that the establishment of civil governments within the region could hardly be postponed. Accordingly, within the single decade already delimited (that is, from the beginning of 1845 until the end of 1854), state or territorial forms of government were actually provided for every remaining part of the national domain, except the relatively small enclave known as the Indian Territory (now Oklahoma). The result was an actual doubling of the area of the United States within which organized civil governments existed. This process of political creation occurred not only in the new acquisitions, but it also covered vast areas, previously acquired, that had been left unorganized, notably the northern part of the old Louisiana Purchase. There, in 1854, the new territories of Kansas and Nebraska suddenly appeared on the map. With equal suddenness these new names appeared in the newspapers, connected with ominous events.

The process of territorial organization brought into the very center of the crisis a fourth factor, the last in our original catalogue, namely, the constitutional one. The organization of new territories and the admission of new states were, after all, elements in a constitution-making process. Territorial expansion drastically changed the character of the dispute over slavery by entangling it with the constitutional problem of devising forms of government for the rapidly settling West. Slavery at last became, in the most direct and immediate sense, a constitutional question, and thus a question capable of disrupting the Union. It did so by assuming the form of a question about the power of Congress to legislate for the territories.

This brings us face to face with the central paradox in the pre–Civil War crisis. Slavery was being attacked in places where it did not, in present actuality, exist. The slaves, close to four million of them, were in the states, yet responsible leaders of the antislavery party pledged themselves not to interfere with them there. In the territories, where the prohibition of slavery was being so intransigently demanded and so belligerently resisted, there had never been more than a handful of slaves during the long period of crisis. Consider the bare statistics. The census of 1860, taken just before the final descent into Civil War, showed far fewer than a hundred slaves in all the territories, despite the abrogation of restrictions by the Kansas-Nebraska Act and the Dred Scott decision. Especially revealing was the situation in Kansas. Though blood had been spilled over the introduction of slavery into that territory, there were actually only 627 colored persons, slave or free, within its boundaries on the eve of its admission to statehood (January 29, 1861). The same situation obtained throughout the West. In 1846, at the time the Wilmot Proviso was introduced, the Union had comprised twenty-eight states. By the outbreak of the Civil War, more than two and a third million persons were to be found in the western areas beyond the boundaries of these older twenty-eight states, yet among them were only 7,687 Negroes, free or slave. There was much truth in the wry observation of a contemporary: "The whole

Kansas–Nebraska Act, 1854. This map illustrates the vastness of the area that Stephen Douglas's legislation opened up to slavery. In addition, the map reveals how extensive was the territory whose status had not yet been determined.

controversy over the Territories . . . related to an imaginary negro in an impossible place."

The paradox was undeniable, and many historians treat it as evidence of a growing retreat from reality. Thus James G. Randall writes that the "larger phases of the slavery question . . . seemed to recede as the controversies of the fifties developed." In other words, "while the struggle sharpened it also narrowed." The attention of the country was "diverted from the fundamentals of slavery in its moral, economic, and social aspects," and instead "became concentrated upon the collateral problem as to what Congress should do with respect to slavery in the territories." Hence, "it was this narrow phase of the slavery question which became, or seemed, central in the succession of political events which actually produced the Civil War." As Randall sees it, the struggle "centered upon a political issue which lent itself to slogan making rather than to political analysis."

Slogan making, to be sure, is an important adjunct of political propaganda, and slogans can easily blind men to the relatively minor character of the tangible interests actually at stake. Nevertheless, a much more profound force was at work, shaping the crisis in this peculiar way. This configurative force was the constitutional system itself. The indirectness of the attack upon slavery, that is to say, the attack upon it in the territories, where it was merely a future possibility, instead of in the states, where the institution existed in force, was the unmistakable consequence of certain structural features of the American Constitution itself.

A centralized national state could have employed a number of different methods of dealing with the question of slavery. Against most of these, the American Constitution interposed a barrier that was both insuperable and respected. By blocking every form of frontal attack, it compelled the adoption of a strategy so indirect as to appear on the surface almost timid and equivocal. In effect, the strategy adopted was a strategy of "containment." Lincoln traced it to the founding fathers themselves. They had, he asserted, put into effect a twofold policy with respect to slavery: "restricting it from the new Territories where it had not gone, and legislating to cut off its source by the abrogation of the slave trade." Taken together, these amounted to "putting the seal of legislation against its spread." The second part of their policy was still in effect, but the first, said Lincoln, had been irresponsibly set aside. To restore it was his avowed object:

> I believe if we could arrest the spread [of slavery] and place it where Washington, and Jefferson, and Madison placed it, it would be in the course of ultimate extinction, and the public mind would, as for eighty years past, believe that it was in the course of ultimate extinction. The crisis would be past.

Whether or not slavery could have been brought to an end in this manner is a totally unanswerable question, but it requires no answer. The historical fact is that the defenders of slavery regarded the policy of containment as so dangerous to their interests that they interpreted it as signifying "that a war must be waged against slavery until it shall cease throughout the United States." On the other hand, the opponents of slavery took an uncompromising stand in favor of this particular policy because it was the only one that the

Constitution appeared to leave open. To retreat from it would be to accept as inevitable what Lincoln called "the perpetuity and nationalization of slavery." . . .

Of all the ambiguities in the written Constitution the most portentous proved in fact to be the ones that lurked in the clause dealing with territory: "The Congress shall have Power to dispose of and make all needful Rules and Regulations respecting the Territory or other Property belonging to the United States." At first glance the provision seems clear enough, but questions were possible about its meaning. Eventually they were raised, and when raised they turned out to have so direct a bearing upon the problem of slavery that they would not [go] down. What did the Constitution mean by mingling both "Territory" and "other Property," and speaking first of the power "to dispose of" such property? Was Congress in reality given a power to govern, or merely a proprietor's right to make regulations for the orderly management of the real estate he expected eventually to sell? If it were a power to govern, did it extend to all the subjects on which a full-fledged state was authorized to legislate? Did it therefore endow Congress with powers that were not federal powers at all but municipal ones, normally reserved to the states? In particular, did it bestow upon Congress, where the territories were concerned, a police power competent to deal with domestic relations and institutions like slavery? . . .

In whose hands, then, had the Constitution placed the power of decision with respect to slavery in the territories? This was, in the last analysis, the constitutional question that split the Union. To it, three mutually irreconcilable answers were offered.

The first answer was certainly the most straightforward. The territories were part of the "Property belonging to the United States." The Constitution gave Congress power to "make all needful Rules and Regulations" respecting them. Only a definite provision of the Constitution, either limiting this power or specifying exceptions to it, could destroy the comprehensiveness of the grant. No such limitations or exceptions were stated. Therefore, Congress was fully authorized by the Constitution to prohibit slavery in any or all of the territories, or to permit its spread thereto, as that body, in exercise of normal legislative discretion, might decide.

This was the straightforward answer; it was also the traditional answer. The Continental Congress had given that answer in the

Ordinance of 1787, and the first Congress under the Constitution had ratified it. For half a century thereafter the precedents accumulated, including the precedent of the Missouri Compromise of 1820. Only in the 1840s were these precedents challenged.

Because this was the traditional answer, it was (by definition, if you like) the conservative answer. When the breaking point was finally reached in 1860–1861 and four identifiable conflicting groups offered four constitutional doctrines, two of them accepted this general answer, but each gave it a peculiar twist.

Among the four political factions of 1860, the least well-organized was the group that can properly be described as the genuine conservatives. Their vehicle in the election of 1860 was the Constitutional Union party, and a rattletrap vehicle it certainly was. In a very real sense, however, they were the heirs of the old Whig party and particularly of the ideas of Henry Clay. Deeply ingrained was the instinct for compromise. They accepted the view just stated, that the power of decision with respect to slavery in a particular territory belonged to Congress. But they insisted that one additional understanding, hallowed by tradition, should likewise be considered constitutionally binding. In actually organizing the earlier territories, Congress had customarily balanced the prohibition of slavery in one area by the erection elsewhere of a territory wherein slaveholding would be permitted. To conservatives, this was more than a precedent; it was a constitutional principle. When, on December 18, 1860, the venerable John J. Crittendon offered to the Senate the resolutions summing up the conservative answer to the crisis, he was not in reality offering a new plan of compromise. He was, in effect, proposing to write into the Constitution itself the understandings that had governed politics in earlier, less crisis-ridden times. The heart of his plan was the re-establishment of the old Missouri Compromise line, dividing free territories from slave. An irrepealable amendment was to change this from a principle of policy into a mandate of constitutional law.

That Congress was empowered to decide the question of slavery for the territories was the view not only of the conservatives, but also of the Republicans. The arguments of the two parties were identical, up to a point; indeed, up to the point just discussed. Though territories in the past had been apportioned between freedom and slavery, the Republicans refused to consider this policy as anything more than a policy, capable of being altered at any time. The Wilmot Proviso of 1846 announced, in effect, that the time had come to abandon the policy. Radical though the proviso may have been in a political sense, it was hardly so in a constitutional sense. The existence of a congressional power is the basic constitutional question. In arguing for the existence of such a power over slavery in the territories, the Republicans took the same ground as the conservatives. In refusing to permit mere precedent to hamper the discretion of Congress in the *use* of that power, they broke with the conservatives. But the distinction they made between power and discretion, that is, between constitutional law and political policy, was neither radical nor unsound.

One innovation did find a place in antislavery, and hence in Republican, constitutional doctrine. Though precedent alone ought not to hamper the discretion of Congress, specific provisions of the Constitution could, and in Republican eyes did, limit and control that discretion. With respect to congressional action on slavery in the territories, so the antislavery forces maintained, the due process clause of the Fifth Amendment constituted such an express limitation. "Our Republican fathers," said the first national platform of the new party in 1856, "ordained that no person shall be deprived of life, liberty, or property, without due process of law." To establish slavery in the territories "by positive legislation" would violate this guarantee. Accordingly the Constitution itself operated to "deny the authority of Congress, of a Territorial Legislation [*sic*], of any individual, or association of individuals, to give legal existence to Slavery in any Territory of the United States." The Free Soil platform of 1848 had summed the argument up in an aphorism: "Congress has no more power to make a SLAVE than to make a KING; no more power to institute or establish SLAVERY, than to institute or establish a MONARCHY." As a doctrine of constitutional law, the result was this: the federal government had full authority over the territories, but so far as slavery was concerned, Congress might exercise this authority in only one way, by prohibiting the institution there.

The conservatives and the Republicans took the constitutional system as it stood, a combination of written text and historical precedent, and evolved their variant doctrines therefrom. By contrast, the two other factions of 1860—the northern Democrats under Stephen A. Douglas, and the southern Democrats whose senatorial leader was Jefferson Davis and whose presidential candidate was John C. Breckinridge—appealed primarily to constitutional theories above and beyond the written document and the precedents. If slogans are meaningfully applied, these two factions (each in its own way) were the ones who, in 1860, appealed to a "higher law."

For Douglas, this higher law was the indefeasible right of every community to decide for itself the social institutions it would accept and establish. "Territorial Sovereignty" (a more precise label than "popular sovereignty") meant that this right of decision on slavery belonged to the settlers in a new territory fully as much as to the people of a full-fledged state. At bottom the argument was one from analogy. The Constitution assigned responsibility for national affairs and interstate relations to the federal government; authority over matters of purely local and domestic concern were reserved to the states. So far as this division of power was concerned, Douglas argued, a territory stood on the same footing as a state. It might not yet have sufficient population to entitle it to a vote in Congress, but its people were entitled to self-government from the moment they were "organized into political communities." Douglas took his stand on what he regarded as a fundamental principle of American political philosophy: "that the people of every separate political community (dependent colonies, Provinces, and Territories as well as sovereign States) have an inalienable right to govern themselves in respect to their internal polity."

Having thus virtually erased the constitutional distinction between a territory and a state—a distinction that was vital (as we shall see) to the state sovereignty interpretation—Douglas proceeded to deal with the argument that since a territorial government was a creation of Congress, the powers it exercised were delegated ones, which Congress itself was free to limit, to overrule, or even to exercise through direct legislation of its own. He met the argument with an ingenious distinction. "Congress," he wrote, "may institute governments for the Territories," and, having done so, may "invest them with powers which Congress does not possess and cannot exercise under the Constitution." He continued: "The powers which Congress may thus *confer* but cannot *exercise,* are such as relate to the domestic affairs and internal polity of the Territory."

Their source is not to be sought in any provision of the written Constitution, certainly not in the so-called territorial clause but in the underlying principle of self-government.

Though Douglas insisted that the doctrine of popular sovereignty embodied "the ideas and principles of the fathers of the Revolution," his appeal to history was vitiated by special pleading. In his most elaborate review of the precedents (the article in *Harper's Magazine* from which quotations have already been taken), he passed over in silence the Northwest Ordinance of 1787, with its clear-cut congressional ban on slavery. Douglas chose instead to dwell at length upon the "Jeffersonian Plan of government for the Territories," embodied in the Ordinance of 1784. This plan, it is true, treated the territories as virtually equal with the member states of the Union, and thus supported (as against subsequent enactments) Douglas's plea for the largest measure of local self-government. When, however, Douglas went on to imply that the "Jeffersonian Plan" precluded, in principle, any congressional interference with slavery in the territories, he was guilty of outright misrepresentation. Jefferson's original draft (still extant in his own hand) included a forthright prohibition of slavery in all the territories. The Continental Congress, it is true, refused at the time to adopt this particular provision, a fact that Douglas mentioned, but there is no evidence whatever to show that they believed they lacked the power to do so. Three years later, the same body exercised this very power by unanimous vote of the eight states present.

Disingenuousness reached its peak in Douglas's assertion that the Ordinance of 1784 "stood on the statute book unrepealed and irrepealable . . . when, on the 14th day of May, 1787, the Federal Convention assembled at Philadelphia and proceeded to form the Constitution under which we now live." Unrepealed the ordinance still was, and likewise unimplemented, but irrepealable it was not. Sixty days later, on July 13, 1787, Congress repealed it outright and substituted in its place the Northwest Ordinance, which Douglas chose not to discuss.

Despite these lapses, Douglas was, in truth, basing his doctrine upon one undeniably important element in the historic tradition of American political philosophy. In 1860 he was the only thoroughgoing advocate of local self-determination and local autonomy. He could justly maintain that he was upholding this particular aspect of the constitutional tradition not only against the conservatives and the Republicans, but also (and most emphatically) against the southern wing of his own party, which bitterly repudiated the whole notion of local self-government, when it meant that the people of a territory might exclude slavery from their midst.

This brings us to the fourth of the parties that contested the election of 1860, and to the third and last of the answers that were given to the question of where the Constitution placed the power to deal with slavery in the territories.

At first glance there would appear to be only two possible answers. Either the power of decision lay with the federal government, to which the territories had been ceded or by which they had been acquired; or else the decision rested with the people of the territories, by virtue of some inherent right of self-government. Neither answer, however, was acceptable to the proslavery forces. By the later 1850s they were committed to a third doctrine, state sovereignty.

The theory of state sovereignty takes on a deceptive appearance of simplicity in most historical accounts. This is because it is usually examined only in the context of the secession crisis. In that situation the corollaries drawn from the theory of state sovereignty were, in fact, exceedingly simple. If the Union was simply a compact among states that retained their ultimate sovereignty, then one or more of them could legally and peacefully withdraw from it, for reasons which they, as sovereigns, might judge sufficient. Often overlooked is the fact that secession itself was responsible for reducing the argument over state sovereignty to such simple terms. The right to secede was only one among many corollaries of the complex and intricate doctrine of the sovereignty of the states. In the winter and spring of 1860–1861, this particular corollary, naked and alone, became the issue on which events turned. Earlier applications of the doctrine became irrelevant. As they dropped from view, they were more or less forgotten. The theory of state sovereignty came to be regarded simply as a theory that had to do with the perpetuity of the Union.

The simplicity of the theory is, however, an illusion. The illusion is a consequence of reading history backward. The proslavery constitutional argument with respect to slavery in the territories cannot possibly be understood if the fifteen years of debate prior to

1860 are regarded simply as a dress rehearsal for secession. When applied to the question of slavery, state sovereignty was a positive doctrine, a doctrine of power, specifically, a doctrine designed to place in the hands of the slaveholding states a power sufficient to uphold slavery and promote its expansion *within* the Union. Secession might be an ultimate recourse, but secession offered no answer whatever to the problems of power that were of vital concern to the slaveholding states so long as they remained in the Union and used the Constitution as a piece of working machinery.

As a theory of how the Constitution should operate, as distinguished from a theory of how it might be dismantled, state sovereignty gave its own distinctive answer to the question of where the authority lay to deal with matters involving slavery in the territories. All such authority, the theory insisted, resided in the sovereign states. But how, one may well ask, was such authority to be exercised? The answer was ingenious. The laws that maintained slavery—which were, of course, the laws of the slaveholding states—must be given extraterritorial or extrajurisdictional effect. In other words, the laws that established a property in slaves were to be respected, and if necessary enforced, by the federal government, acting as agent for its principals, the sovereign states of the Union.

At the very beginning of the controversy, on January 15, 1847, five months after the introduction of the Wilmot Proviso, Robert Barnwell Rhett of South Carolina showed how that measure could be countered, and proslavery demands supported, by an appeal to the *mystique* of the sovereignty of the several states:

> Their sovereignty, unalienated and unimpaired . . . , exists in all its plenitude over our territories; as much so, as within the limits of the States themselves. . . . The only effect, and probably the only object of their reserved sovereignty, is, that it secures to each State the right to enter the territories with her citizens, and settle and occupy them with their property—with whatever is recognised as property by each State. The ingress of the citizen, is the ingress of his sovereign, who is bound to protect him in his settlement.

Nine years later the doctrine had become the dominant one in proslavery thinking, and on January 24, 1856, Robert Toombs of Georgia summed it up succinctly: "Congress has no power to limit, restrain, or in any manner to impair slavery: but, on the contrary, it is bound to protect and maintain it in the States where it exists, and wherever its flag floats, and its jurisdiction is paramount." In effect, the laws of slavery were to become an integral part of the laws of the Union, so far as the territories were concerned.

Four irreconcilable constitutional doctrines were presented to the American people in 1860. There was no consensus, and the stage was set for civil war. The issues in which the long controversy culminated were abstruse. They concerned a seemingly minor detail of the constitutional system. The arguments that supported the various positions were intricate and theoretical. But the abstractness of constitutional issues has nothing to do, one way or the other, with the role they may happen to play at a moment of crisis. The sole question is the load that events have laid upon them. Thanks to the structure of the American constitutional system itself, the abstruse issue of slavery in the territories was required to carry the burden of well-nigh all the emotional drives, well-nigh all the political and economic tensions, and well-nigh all the moral perplexities that resulted from the existence in the United States of an archaic system of labor and an intolerable policy of racial subjection. To change the metaphor, the constitutional question of legislative authority over the territories became, so to speak, the narrow channel through which surged the torrent of ideas and interests and anxieties that flooded down from every drenched hillside upon which the storm cloud of slavery discharged its poisoned rain.

Michael F. Holt

PARTY DYNAMICS AND THE COMING OF THE CIVIL WAR

One of the most conspicuous features of the coming of the war was the political turmoil that accompanied it. The system of party politics, established in the 1830s, that consisted of the Whigs and the Democrats as the major protagonists broke down. The Whig party dissolved in the early

Michael F. Holt, "Party Breakdown and the Coming of the Civil War," in Holt, *The Political Crisis of the 1850s,* pp. 9–16, 184–99. Copyright © 1978. Reprinted by permission of John Wiley & Sons Inc.

1850s, and the American, or Know Nothing, party replaced it. But almost immediately, the Know Nothings gave way to a new, northern party, the Republicans. Meanwhile, the Democrats split apart along sectional lines after 1858.

But why did this collapse and realignment occur when it did? After all, sectional disputes and the slavery question had been acknowledged features in national political life for several decades before the Jacksonian party system broke down in the 1850s. Rejecting the more traditional view that the issue of slavery destroyed the parties, Michael F. Holt claims that the rivalry between the Whigs and Democrats had become moribund as the issues that had divided them earlier began to disappear. Needing new issues to revitalize their party organizations, political leaders saw the slavery question as a very real alternative. So they seized upon it and manipulated it—with disastrous consequences. In a sense, this approach contains some of the ingredients of the "repressible conflict" position, with the politicians seeming to blunder and become shortsighted.

Michael F. Holt (born 1940), who teaches at the University of Virginia, has written *Forging of a Majority: The Formation of the Republican Party in Pittsburgh, 1848–1860* (1969) and *The Political Crisis of the 1850s* (1978), from which this excerpt is taken.

Party Consensus and the Demise of the Whigs

Historians have long looked to politics for the origins of the Civil War, and they have offered two major interpretations of political developments between 1845 and 1860. Both are primarily concerned with the breakdown of the old party system and the rise of the Republicans and not with the second aspect of the crisis—the loss of faith in politicians, the desire for reform, and their relationship to republican ideology. By spelling out my reservations about and disagreements with these interpretations, the assumptions behind and, I hope, the logic of my own approach to the political crisis of the 1850s will become clearer.

The standard interpretation maintains that intensifying sectional disagreements over slavery inevitably burst into the political arena, smashed the old national parties, and forced the formation of new, sectionally oriented ones. The Second Party System [the political era from the 1830s until the 1850s, in which the Whigs and the Democrats were the major parties] was artificial, some historians contend, since it could survive only by avoiding divisive sectional issues and by confining political debate to sectionally neutral economic questions on which the national parties had coherent stands. Once sectional pressure was reaggravated by the events of the late 1840s and early 1850s, those fragile structures shattered and were replaced. "On the level of politics," writes Eric Foner, "the coming of the Civil War is the intrusion of sectional ideology into the political system, despite the efforts of political leaders of both parties [Whigs and Democrats] to keep it out. Once this happened, political competition worked to exacerbate, rather than to solve, social and sectional conflicts."

There is much to be said for this interpretation. The Republican party did rise to dominance in the North largely because of an increase of Northern hostility toward the South, and its ascendance worsened relations between the sections. Attributing the political developments prior to its rise to the same sectional force that caused the rise has the virtue of simplicity. But that argument distorts a rapidly changing and very complex political situation between 1845 and 1860. There were three discrete, sequential political developments in those years that shaped the political crisis that led to war— the disappearance of the Whig party and with it of the old framework of two-party competition, a realignment of voters as they switched party affiliation, and a shift from a nationally balanced party system where both major parties competed on fairly even terms in all parts of the nation to a sectionally polarized one with Republicans dominant in the North and Democrats in the South. Although related, these were distinct phases, occurring with some exceptions in that order, and they were caused by different things. Although the inflammation of sectional antagonism between 1855 and 1860 helped to account for the new sectional alignment of parties, sectional conflict by itself caused neither the voter realignment of middecade nor the most crucial event of the period—the death of the Whig party, especially its death at the state level. It bears repeating that the demise of the Whig party, and with it of the traditional framework of two-party competition at the local, state, and national levels, was the most critical development in this sequence. Its disappearance helped foster popular doubts about the legitimacy of politics as usual, raised fears that powerful conspiracies were undermining republicanism, allowed the rise of the Republican party in the North, and created the situation in the lower South that produced secession there and not elsewhere.

The theory that the Second Party System was artificial and was shattered once the slavery issue arose, like the larger theory of the war's causation it reflects, founders on the problem of timing. There is considerable evidence that sectional conflict over slavery characterized the Second Party System throughout its history. Slavery was not swept under the rug; it was often the stuff of political debate. Proponents of the traditional interpretation, indeed, have often confused internal divisions within the national parties with their demise. Although they point to different dates when the rupture was fatal, they have assumed that once the national parties were split into Northern and Southern wings over slavery, the parties were finished. Yet the Whig and Jacksonian parties, like almost all political organizations at any time, had frequently been divided— over slavery as well as other issues. They functioned for years in that condition. To establish the existence of sectional splits within the national parties is not to answer the vexed question of why those divisions were fatal in the 1850s and not in the 1830s and 1840s. If it was the sectional conflict that destroyed the old party system, the crucial question is why the parties were able to manage that conflict at some times and not at others. For a number of reasons, the easy reply that the volatile slavery issue simply became more explosive in the 1850s than earlier is not an adequate answer to this question.

The second major interpretation of the politics of the 1850s also has its merits and liabilities. Arguing that traditional historians have viewed events in the 1850s with the hindsight knowledge that the Civil War occurred, a new group of political historians insist that the extent to which sectionalism affected political behavior, especially popular voting behavior at the grass-roots level, has been exaggerated. Local social tensions, especially ethnic and religious tensions, motivated voters in the 1850s, they contend, not national issues like slavery, which was of so much concern to national political elites. What applies to Congress and national leaders, these new political historians say in effect, does not apply to the local level of politics. Prohibitionism, nativism, and anti-Catholicism produced the voter realignment in which the Whigs disappeared and new parties emerged in the North.

By focusing on voting behavior, this ethnocultural interpretation presents a compelling analysis of why an anti-Democratic majority was created in many parts of the North. Explaining why Northern voters realigned between 1853 and 1856, however, does not answer why the Republican party appeared or why party politics were sectionally polarized at the end of the decade. Prophets of the ethnocultural thesis, moreover, have done little to explain Southern politics, yet developments in Dixie where Catholics and immigrants were few were just as important as events in the North in leading to war. Nor do voting studies really explain the crucial first phase— the death of the Whig party. Party reorganization accompanied voter realignment in the 1850s, and ethnocultural tensions alone do not explain why new parties were necessary. Why didn't anti-Democratic voters simply become Whigs? This question has a particular urgency when one realizes that in the 1840s ethnocultural issues had also been present and that the Whigs and Democrats had aligned on opposite sides of them. The problem with stressing ethnocultural issues, as with stressing sectionalism, is why those issues could be contained within, indeed could invigorate, old party lines at one time yet could help to destroy them at another.

The fundamental weakness of previous interpretations of why the old two-party system broke down is their misunderstanding of how and why it worked. They have not adequately explored either the relationship between political parties and issues or the impact of the federal system with its divided responsibilities among local, state, and national governments on the parties and the party system. Whether historians stress sectionalism or ethnocultural issues, their central assumption seems to be that issues arising from the society at large caused political events. The Second Party System functioned because it dealt with "safe" economic questions, but once those issues were replaced or displaced by new disruptive matters the parties broke down and realignment followed. Yet what made the Second Party System work in the end was not issues *per se* or the presence of safe issues and absence of dangerous ones. In the end what made the two-party system operate was its ability to allow political competition on a broad range of issues that varied from time to time and place to place. If the genius of the American political system has been the peaceful resolution of conflict, what has supported two-party systems has been the conflict itself, not its resolution. As long as parties fought with each other over issues or took opposing stands even when they failed to promote opposing programs, as long as they defined alternative ways to secure repub- lican ideals, voters perceived them as different and maintained their loyalty to them. Party health and popular faith in the political process depended on the perception of party difference, which in turn depended on the reality—or at least the appearance—of interparty conflict. As long as parties seemed different from each other, voters viewed them as viable vehicles through which to influence government.

Politicians had long recognized that group conflict was endemic to American society and that the vitality of individual parties depended on the intensity of their competition with opposing parties. Thomas Jefferson had perceived in 1798 that "in every free and deliberating society, there must, from the nature of man, be opposite parties, and violent dissensions and discords." "Seeing that we must have somebody to quarrel with," he wrote John Taylor, "I had rather keep our New England associates for that purpose, than to see our bickerings transferred to others." Even more explicit in their recognition of what made parties work were the founders of New York's Albany Regency in the 1820s. They deplored the lack of internal discipline and cohesion in the Jeffersonian Republican party once the Federalists disappeared, and they moved quickly to remedy it. Although any party might suffer defeats, they realized, "it is certain to acquire additional strength . . . by the attacks of adverse parties." A political party, indeed, was "most in jeopardy when an opposition is not sufficiently defined." During "the contest between the great rival parties [Federalists and Jeffersonians] each found in the strength of the other a powerful motive of union and vigor." Significantly, those like Daniel Webster who deplored the emergence of mass parties in the 1820s and 1830s also recognized that strife was necessary to perpetuate party organization and that the best way to break it down was to cease opposition and work for consensus. Politicians in the 1840s and 1850s continued to believe that interparty conflict was needed to unify their own party and maintain their voting support. Thus an Alabama Democrat confessed that his party pushed a certain measure at the beginning of the 1840 legislative session explicitly as "the best means for drawing the party lines as soon as possible" while by 1852, when opposition to that state's Democracy appeared to disintegrate, another warned perceptively, "I think the only danger to the Democratic party is that it will become too much an omnibus in this State. We have nothing to fear from either the Union, or Whig party or both combined. From their friendship and adherence much." Many of the important decisions in the 1840s and 1850s reflected the search by political leaders for issues that would sharply define the lines between parties and thus reinvigorate the loyalty of party voters.

If conflict sustained the old two-party system, what destroyed it was the loss of the ability to provide interparty competition on *any* important issue at *any* level of the federal system. Because the political system's vitality and legitimacy with the voters depended on the clarity of the definition of the parties as opponents, the blurring of that definition undid the system. What destroyed the Second Party System was consensus, not conflict. The growing congruence between the parties on almost all issues by the early 1850s dulled the sense of party difference and thereby eroded voters' loyalty to the old parties. Once competing groups in society decided that the party system no longer provided them viable alternatives in which they could carry on conflict with each other, they repudiated the old system by dropping out, seeking third parties that would meet their needs, or turning to nonpartisan or extrapolitical action to achieve their goals. Because the collapse of the Second Party System was such a vital link in the war's causation, therefore, one arrives at a paradox. While the Civil War is normally viewed as the one time when conflict prevailed over consensus in American politics, the prevalence of consensus over conflict in crucial parts of the political system contributed in a very real way to the outbreak of war in the first place. . . .

*

Party Conflict and the Rise of the Republicans

The sectionalization of American politics was emphatically *not* simply a reflection or product of basic popular disagreements over black slavery. Those had long existed without such a complete polarization developing. Even though a series of events beginning with the Kansas-Nebraska Act greatly increased sectional consciousness, it is a mistake to think of sectional antagonism as a spontaneous and self-perpetuating force that imposed itself on the political arena against the will of politicians and coerced parties to conform to the lines of sectional conflict. Popular grievances, no matter how intense, do not dictate party strategies. Political leaders do. Some one has to politicize events, to define their political relevance in terms of a choice between or among parties, before popular grievances can have political impact. It was not events alone that caused Northerners and Southerners to view each other as enemies of the basic rights they both cherished. Politicians who pursued very traditional partisan strategies were largely responsible for the ultimate breakdown of the political process. Much of the story of the coming of the Civil War is the story of the successful efforts of Democratic politicians in the South and Republican politicians in the North to keep the sectional conflict at the center of political debate and to defeat political rivals who hoped to exploit other issues to achieve election.

For at least thirty years political leaders had recognized that the way to build political parties, to create voter loyalty and mobilize support, and to win elections was to find issues or positions on issues that distinguished them from their opponents and that therefore could appeal to various groups who disliked their opponents by offering them an alternative for political action—in sociological terms, to make their party a vehicle for negative reference group behavior. Because of the American ethos, the most successful tactic had been to pose as a champion of republican values and to portray the opponent as antirepublican, as unlawful, tyrannical, or aristocratic. Jackson, Van Buren, and Polk, Antimasons and Whigs, had all followed this dynamic of the political system. Stephen A. Douglas and William H. Seward had pursued the same strategy in their unsuccessful attempt to rebuild the disintegrating Second Party System with the Kansas-Nebraska Act in 1854. After faith in the old parties had collapsed irreparably, when the shape of future political alignments was uncertain, Republican politicians quite consciously seized on the slavery and sectional issue in order to build a new party. Claiming to be the exclusive Northern Party that was necessary to halt slavery extension and defeat the Slave Power conspiracy was the way they chose to distinguish themselves from Democrats, whom they denounced as pro-Southern, and from the Know Nothings, who had chosen a different organizing principle — anti-Catholicism and nativism—to construct their new party.

To say that Republican politicians agitated and exploited sectional grievances in order to build a winning party is a simple description of fact. It is not meant to imply that winning was their only objective or to be a value judgment about the sincerity or insincerity of their personal hatred of black slavery. Some undoubt- edly found slavery morally intolerable and hoped to use the national government to weaken it by preventing its expansion, abolishing it in federal enclaves like the District of Columbia, and undermining it within Southern states by whatever means were constitutionally possible, such as opening the mails to abolitionist literature and prohibiting the interstate slave trade. The antislavery pedigree of Republican leaders, however, was in a sense irrelevant to the triumph of the Republican party. The leaders were divided over the policies they might pursue if they won control of the national government, and leadership views were often far in advance of those held by their electorate. Much more important was the campaign they ran to obtain power, their skill in politicizing the issues at hand in such a way as to convince Northern voters that control of the national government by an exclusive Northern party was necessary to resist Slave Power aggressions. The Republicans won more because of what they were against than because of what they were for, because of what they wanted to stop, not what they hoped to do.

As the presidential campaign of 1856 approached, Republican success remained uncertain. Although the bolt of the North Amer- icans in February had reduced American or Know Nothing support primarily to the slave states, the Americans campaigned vigorously for Millard Fillmore in those areas of the North that were most in doubt and that the Republicans had to carry in order to win— Illinois, Indiana, and especially the Middle Atlantic states. There is ample evidence that the Democrats secretly funded the Know Noth- ing campaign to keep their opponents divided. The Americans officially renounced secrecy in 1856 and softened their most pro- scriptive positions, but they still called for an increase in the naturalization period, denounced foreign and Catholic interference in politics, and proclaimed that only Americans ruling America could purify politics and restore the nation to early republican ideals. Vilifying the Democrats as tools of the papal plot, they also de- nounced corruption and fraud in the Pierce administration and cried that true reform could be achieved only by expelling Democrats from power. But the Americans also condemned the Republicans as proforeign and raised the fatal charge that Frémont was Catholic. Always superpatriotic in their rhetoric, the Americans added the potent issue of Unionism to their arsenal. The Republicans were abolitionist fanatics whose victory would provoke secession, they charged, while the Democrats were dominated by secessionist fire-eaters from the South. Only an American victory could assure the permanency of the Union and with it of the republican experiment.

The major challenge to the Republicans, however, came from the Democrats, whose strength in the South they could not rival. The Democrats could win merely by preserving their majorities in a few of the Northern states they had swept in 1852, and in the 1855 state elections they had begun to make a comeback from the disaster of 1854 in New Jersey, Pennsylvania, Indiana, Illinois, and Wisconsin. Opposition to Know Nothingism and prohibitionism had bolstered the Democrats in 1855, and in 1856 they stressed their long-time defense of religious and ethnic minorities and of personal freedom from the attacks of intolerant bigots and self-righteous moral reformers who, they argued, were prominent in both the American and Republican parties. The secret machinations of Know Nothingism constituted a conspiracy against republican government, they complained, and for the remainder of the decade they charged that Know Nothings controlled the Republican party. To improve their chances in all-important Pennsylvania, the Democrats selected James Buchanan as their presidential candidate. The national Democratic platform endorsed the Kansas-Nebraska Act, lauded the principle of congressional noninterference as the proper solution to the problem of slavery in the territories, and insisted that new states be admitted with or without slavery, as their constitutions prescribed. Thus it drew a sharp line between the Democrats and the Republicans who denounced the Act, demanded congressional prohibition of slavery from all territories, and often vowed to prevent the entry of any more slave states no matter what their constitutions said. The Republican advantage was not as great as it seemed, however; after the initial shock of 1854, many long-time Democratic voters in the North seemed disposed to see how the doctrine of self-government actually worked in Kansas. To reinforce their loyalty, Democrats defended popular sovereignty as a perfect manifestation of government by the people and a logical extension of traditional Democratic states rights principles that would preserve a heterogeneous society. Equally important,

Northern Democrats continued to promise that popular sovereignty would bar slavery expansion just as surely as congressional prohibition.

To offset the Republican appeal on the slavery issue even more, the Democrats launched a two-pronged attack. Like the Americans, they labeled the Republicans as dangerous sectionalists whose victory would disrupt the Union. All Union-loving Democrats and former Whigs, they contended, must vote for Buchanan to prevent that catastrophe, because Fillmore could not possibly win. More insidious, but equally effective, the Democrats viciously race-baited the Republicans. Castigating them as "Black Republican Abolitionists" and "nigger lovers" who cared much more about blacks than Northern whites, they charged that the Republicans would abolish slavery in the South and thus inundate the North with a horde of freed blacks who would rob white workers of their jobs, ruin their neighborhoods, and even marry their daughters. "To elevate the African race in this country to complete equality of political and economic condition with the white man, is the one aim of the party that supports Fremont," wrote one Democratic paper in a mild version of this appeal, and later it pronounced the single issue in the contest to be "the white race or the Negro race."

The Republicans thus faced two foes who not only offered compelling versions of their own as how best to save republican principles and the Union, but who also exploited palpably powerful prejudices. To counteract them, the Republicans had to develop a persuasion that could win the widest possible support from a Northern constituency that was racist and overwhelmingly believed federal abolition in the states unconstitutional and dangerous to the Union. The most delicate problem was black slavery, and historians have disagreed about what the Republican position on it was and how central that stand was to their appeal. Evidence exists in Republican platforms, pamphlets, speeches, and editorials to support widely varying interpretations of what the party stood for and, by inference from that rhetoric, why Northerners supported it. Some historians, for example, argue that the Republicans were abolitionists dedicated to eradicating slavery as soon as it was constitutionally feasible, while others insist that humanitarian or moral antipathy to the institution, if not outright abolitionism, was the moving force behind the party. They point out that the 1856 Republican national platform condemned slavery as a "relic of barbarism" and a patent violation of the Declaration of Independence's proclamation that "all men are created equal and have inalienable rights to life, liberty, and the pursuit of happiness." Together with other assaults on slavery's inhumanity, demands that it be extinguished, and paeans to freedom and liberty, these can provide evidence that Republicans sincerely wanted to remedy the plight of the black slave.

Yet juxtaposed to demands that slavery be ended and freedom extended were constant Republican denials that the federal government had any right to interfere with slavery within Southern states or that Republicans had any intention of doing so. Similarly, along with enlightened talk of the equality of all men appeared blatant racism or at least strained arguments that concern for the black, free or slave, had nothing to do with the Republican party, evidence that seems to refute assertions that moral antipathy to black slavery or humanitarianism was the basic force behind Republicanism. "NO NEGRO EQUALITY IN THE NORTH," pledged a Republican banner at an Illinois rally in 1860. A Pittsburgh orator and future Radical Republican congressman proclaimed in 1856 that "he cared nothing for the 'nigger'; it was not the mission of the Republican party to preach rebellion—he had a higher mission to preach—deliverance to the white man." The Hartford *Courant* tingingly defended the party's free-soil principles that same year: "The Republicans mean to preserve all of this country that they can from the pestilential presence of the black man." Less insultingly, a Pennsylvania Republican editor declared in 1855 that "the real question at issue between the North and South in the present contest, is not a sentimental difference growing out of the oppression of the negro," while Seward echoed in 1860, "The motive of those who have protested against the extension of slavery [has] always been concern for the welfare of the white man, not an unnatural sympathy with the negro."

Historians have tried to reconcile these contradictory appeals in various ways. Some simply admit that the party was a heterogeneous coalition ranging from radicals to conservatives on the slavery issue whose rhetoric reflected the diverse views of its different elements. Others have excused the Republicans' racist remarks as an attempt to defend the party from Democratic charges that it cared more about blacks than whites. In reality, they argue, the

Republicans were more favorable to black rights than Democrats, as their voting records against discriminatory laws in Northern state legislatures demonstrate. Still others have accepted the racism of some Republicans and the reluctance of the vast majority to interfere with slavery in the South by arguing that the Republicans were essentially a free-soil party, not an abolitionist or antislavery party. Opposition to slavery extension, which sprang from a number of sources, constituted the party's central thrust. Many sincerely believed that slavery had to expand to survive and that restricting it would bring about its ultimate destruction. Others wanted to protect the free labor system of the North by preserving areas for its expansion, while some wanted to keep blacks out of the territories for racist reasons. Many Republicans, finally, desired to stop the growth of Southern political power.

Prohibition of slavery expansion was the specific policy most frequently voiced by the Republicans and one with which everyone in the party agreed, if for different reasons. Northern hostility to slavery extension was authentic and deep-seated. Yet to assert that free-soilism constituted the core of Republicanism is to miss the essence of the Republican appeal. Prevention of slavery extension was the issue the Republicans seized on to politicize their message, but it was not the heart of that message. It was a goal of the party, but not the party's fundamental purpose. As Charles Sumner admitted when congratulating Henry J. Raymond, who wrote the address from the Republicans' national organizational meeting in February 1856, an address that focused on the need to keep Kansas free:

> For a long time my desire has been to make an issue with the slave oligarchy; & provided this can be had I am indifferent to the special point selected. Of course, at this moment Kansas is the inevitable point. In protecting this territory against tyranny we are driven to battle with the tyrants, who are the oligarchs of slavery.

The words of Sumner, who was much more sympathetic to blacks than most Republicans, suggest that the majority of the party disliked white slaveholders more than black slavery or even slavery extension. The Republicans, in fact, presented themselves basically as an anti-Southern or antislaveholder party. What was at stake, they cried, was not the future shape of Western society but the present condition of the American republic. Skillfully they portrayed the sectional conflict in terms of the republican ideology that had suffused American politics since the time of the Revolution. This was not a case of a new sectional ideology overwhelming a political system that had previously been nonideological or of new antagonisms toward black slavery displacing old concerns about banks, monopolies, and executive tyranny. This was a case of the Republicans consciously applying the traditional republican idiom to the issue they had selected to define their party and using that idiom to explain what the sectional conflict meant to Northern whites who were generally apathetic about the plight of blacks or were hostile to them. "Convince the laboring class that [slavery] is at war with our republican institutions and opposed to their interests," advised an Indiana Republican in 1856. In one form, the Republicans' case did focus on black slavery. Arguing that the Founding Fathers had envisioned the eventual extinction of the institution, they maintained that Southern attempts to extend and perpetuate it perverted the original purposes of the republic from freedom to slavery. Yet their most effective argument was much more general and traditional and had little to do with the institution of slavery itself. Identifying the Slave Power conspiracy as the major threat to republican liberty, equality, and self-government, the Republicans promised, as parties had since the 1820s, that voting for them was the best way to preserve the republican institutions of whites from despotism, unrestrained power, and privilege. Thus a Republican Congressman demanded in June 1856: "Are we to have a government of the people, a real representative Republican Government? or are the owners of slave property, small in number but with the power in their hands, and strongly entrenched in every power, to rule us with arbitrary and undisputed sway?"

The key to unraveling the paradoxes in Republican rhetoric, the juxtaposition of egalitarianism and racism, of pledges not to interfere with slavery in the South alongside calls to end slavery and join a great crusade for freedom, is to remember that the word "slavery" had long had a definite meaning aside from the institution of black slavery in the South. It was in this sense that many Republicans used the word. Slavery implied subordination to tyranny, the loss of liberty and equality, the absence of republicanism. Slavery resulted when republican government was overthrown or usurped, and that, charged Republicans, was exactly what the Slave Power was trying to do. Hence the slavery that many Republicans objected to most was not the bondage of blacks in the South but the subjugation of Northern whites to the despotism of a tiny oligarchy of slaveholders bent on destroying their rights, a minority who controlled the Democratic party and through it the machinery of the federal government. Thus one Republican complained privately in 1857, "The Slave power will not submit. The tyrants of the lash will not withhold until they have put padlocks on the lives of freemen. The Union which our fathers formed seventy years ago is not the Union today . . . the sons of the Revolutionary fathers are becoming *slaves* or *masters*." Thus a Chicago Republican congressman, after reciting a litany of supposed Slave Power aggressions against the North, later recalled, "All these things followed the taking possession of the Government and lands by the slave power, until we [in the North] were the slaves of slaves, being chained to the car of this Slave Juggernaut." Thus the black abolitionist Frederick Douglass perceptively observed, "The cry of Free Men was raised, not for the extension of liberty to the black man, but for the protection of the liberty of the white."

The basic objective of Republican campaigns from 1856 to 1860, therefore, was to persuade Northerners that slaveholders meant to enslave them through their control of the national government and to enlist Northern voters behind the Republican party in a defensive phalanx to ward off *that* slavery, and not in an offensive crusade to end black slavery, by driving the Slave Power from its control of the national government. For such a tactic to succeed, the Republicans required two things. First, to make an asset and not a liability of their existence as an exclusive Northern party, they needed events to increase Northern antagonism toward the South so that men believed the South, and not foreigners and Catholics or the Republicans themselves, posed the chief threat to the republic. More important, they had successfully to identify the Democratic party as an agent or lackey of the South. Because the Republicans campaigned only in the North, because Northern voters chose among Northern candidates instead of between Northerners and Southerners, only by making Northern Democrats surrogates for the Slave Power could they make their case that Republicans alone, and not simply any Northern politicians, were needed to resist and overthrow the slavocracy. Because they dared not promise overt action against slaveholders except for stopping slavery expansion, in other words, Republicans could not exploit Northern anger, no matter how intense it was, unless they could convince Northern voters that supporting the Republicans and defeating Northern Democrats was an efficacious and constitutional way to defeat the Slave Power itself.

By the summer of 1856 it was much easier to identify the Democracy with the South than it had been earlier. For one thing, the results of the congressional elections of 1854 and 1855 had dramatically shifted the balance of sectional power within the Democratic party, a result that was plainly evident when the 34th Congress met during 1856. From 1834 to 1854 the Democratic congressional delegation had usually been reasonably balanced between North and South. In the 33rd Congress, Northern Democrats had even outnumbered Southern Democrats in the House by a margin of 91 to 67. But in 1856 there were only 25 Northerners as compared to 63 Southerners, and even though Northern Democratic representation would increase after the 1856 elections, the sectional balance would never be restored before the Civil War. The South seemed to dominate the Democracy, and that fact was especially difficult to hide during a presidential election year. Because the Democrats, unlike the Republicans, met in a common national convention with Southerners and campaigned in both sections, Democrats could not deny their Southern connection. The Democratic platform endorsing the Kansas-Nebraska Act strengthened that identification, thereby flushing out regular Northern Democrats who had tried to evade the Nebraska issue in 1854 and 1855 and infuriating anti-Nebraska Democrats who had clung to the party in hopes of reversing its policy but who now bolted to the Republicans.

What made the Democratic platform commitment especially damaging in the North were events in Kansas itself. Many Northern voters sincerely revered the principle of self-determination by local majority rule, and because they had been assured by Northern Democrats that nonslaveholders would move to Kansas in greater numbers than slaveholders, they anticipated that popular sovereignty would produce free soil in the West. If their expectations had been fulfilled, if popular sovereignty had worked as Stephen Douglas envisioned it, the course of American history might have been different. But things did not go according to plan in Kansas, and it became a whip that Republicans used to flay the Democracy. To understand why, one must differentiate between what actually happened on the plains of Kansas and what political propagandists said was happening.

Although there was much publicity about groups in the Northeast and Deep South, like the New England Emigrant Aid Company, which organized to send settlers to Kansas to control it for free or slave states, most people who went there came from the Midwest and border slave states. Their main interest was acquiring land and making money. Insofar as they cared at all about the slavery issue, the vast majority, including nonslaveholding Missourians, wanted to keep both black slaves and free blacks out of the territory. There was much turmoil and some violence typical of a frontier situation, but most of this concerned disputed land claims, competition for lucrative government contracts, and rivalry for the location of county seats, not slavery. A minority of the settlers from free states, however, had been sent from New England by antislavery societies, and some of them were authentic abolitionists. Unlike most settlers, the New Englanders opposed slavery on moral grounds, denounced the exclusion of free blacks, and insisted that blacks be granted equal rights. Their presence frightened nonslaveholding Southerners, who wished Kansas to be free, into following the small group of slaveholders in the territory because they feared that the New Englanders would make Kansas an abolitionist sanctuary for fugitive slaves.

The New Englanders also scared slaveholders in neighboring Missouri, who wildly exaggerated the number and influence of the abolitionists. When popular sovereignty received its first real test in the election of a territorial legislature on March 30, 1855, Missourians, led by U.S. Senator David R. Atchison, poured across the border to vote and secure a proslavery government for Kansas. At that early date, when few Northern settlers had arrived, the proslavery men would probably have won the election without the Missourians' interference, but the invasion of the "Border Ruffians" made a mockery of local self-government. The territorial governor threw out some of the fraudulent returns and put a few antislavery men in the legislature, but the proslavery men were in firm control. They then passed a series of incredible laws that stripped antislavery men of basic constitutional rights. Officeholding in Kansas was limited to men who would take an oath that they favored slavery. Asserting that slavery was illegal in the territory was declared a felony. Harboring a fugitive slave was punishable by ten years' imprisonment, inciting a slave to escape or circulating abolitionist literature became a capital offense. As if to practice what they preached, the proslavery men then expelled antislavery representatives from the legislature. Vowing that "we owe no allegiance to the tyrannical enactments of this spurious legislature," Northern settlers responded by organizing their own government at Topeka in opposition to the "bogus legislature" at Lecompton. That government brazenly declared Kansas a free state and elected its own governor and legislature. Kansans were polarized not so much by attitudes toward slavery or blacks as by allegiance to rival governments, for many who supported the Lecompton legislature wanted to keep slavery out of Kansas. Its laws were so unjust, however, that by the end of 1855 a majority of the people in the territory aligned with the Topeka regime.

The ostensible division of Kansas between Northerners and Southerners over the question of slavery extension, when the real division was over the legitimacy of the territorial legislature, gave Republicans in the East a marvelous opportunity. Friction between the two camps, both of which were heavily armed, was inevitable, because neither recognized the laws of the other government as binding or its officials as legal. Efforts by the agents of one government to enforce laws against settlers who paid fealty to the other, even for the many crimes that had nothing to do with slavery, took on the aura of a war between antislavery and proslavery factions, a conflict that Republican propagandists distorted far beyond reality. When the Lecompton government sent a posse to arrest several free state leaders in the town of Lawrence and when that posse, which included Missourians, burned some buildings and destroyed two printing presses but killed no one in the town on May 21, 1856, Republicans labeled it "The Sack of Lawrence." "The War Actually Begun—Triumph of the Border Ruffians—Lawrence in Ruins—Several Persons Slaughtered—Freedom Bloodily Subdued," hyperbolized the Eastern Republican press. Ignoring more serious atrocities like the fanatical John Brown's brutal massacre at Pottawatomie Creek of five nonslaveholding Southerners affiliated with the territorial government, Republicans shrieked that Kansas was bleeding because lawless slaveholders were butchering defenseless Northern settlers in their effort to force slavery on the territory. What gave Kansas such partisan value to Republicans was that President Pierce denounced the Topeka government as revolutionary, officially recognized the proslavery legislature as the only legal authority in the territory, and pledged to use federal force to uphold its laws. The national Democratic administration was seemingly helping the South and the Missouri Border Ruffians to impose slavery on the unwilling settlers of Kansas. The Democracy had apparently aligned itself with the anti-Republican forces, which violated the law, trampled majority rule, and deprived citizens of basic liberties. The Republican Seward made the case explicit in a Senate speech when he likened Pierce to King George III, a despotic tyrant who oppressed Kansans just as the British monarch had subjugated American colonists.

If the prolonged imbroglio in Kansas helped the Republicans by arousing the North against the South and the Democratic party, so did a much briefer but related incident in Washington. On May 19 and 20, 1856, Charles Sumner, the Republican Senator from Massachusetts, delivered a carefully rehearsed speech called "The Crime against Kansas" in which he insultingly excoriated slavery, the South, and several individual senators, among them South Carolina's Andrew Pickens Butler. On May 22, the day after the so-called "Sack of Lawrence" a cousin of Butler who was determined to avenge the family name, Representative Preston S. Brooks of South Carolina, strode into the Senate chamber, accosted Sumner who was seated at his desk, and in less than a minute beat him senseless with a gutta percha cane. Sumner's bloody head wounds were so severe that he could not attend the Senate regularly for over three years, but the immediate sectional reaction to Brooks's dramatic act was more important than Sumner's lingering personal agony. Throughout the South, Democratic newspapers praised Brooks for chastising an insolent Yankee abolitionist, and he was sent scores of new canes from admiring Southerners to replace the one he had splintered on Sumner's head. For Republicans Sumner became a martyr, an actual victim of naked Southern aggression who personified the plight of the entire North. Nothing else could have given so much credibility to the Republican charge that the arrogant slavocracy meant to subjugate and enslave Northern whites just as they had their black slaves. The assault, proclaimed Republicans, clearly demonstrated the need of Northerners to unite behind a party with backbone, which could resist the impudent Southerners. "The remedy for ruffianism resides in a united North," asserted one Massachusetts Republican paper. "Old party names must be forgotten, old party ties surrendered."

"Bleeding Kansas" and "Bleeding Sumner" electrified the North. More than anything else in 1856 they accounted for the Republicans' success in enlisting diverse and often mutually hostile Northern voters behind their standard. Together they had created an issue "that properly directed, might carry the election by storm," wrote one observer at the end of May, while a New Yorker testified, "The feeling all over our State, in relation to Kansas affairs and the assault on Sumner, is more intense and determined than I thought it would be." By June Republicans were exulting that "the outrage upon Sumner & the occurrences in Kansas have helped us vastly." At the same time, Southern Know Nothings recognized that Northern anger doomed all hopes of maintaining the national American party at full strength. Thus a Virginian despaired to a Northern Fillmore man, "Recent events in Kansas and Washington seem to be driving the masses of your people into the arms of the Republican party and forcing a coalition between them and the Americans who disapprove of Mr. F[illmore]'s nomination."

Kansas and Sumner provided Republican propagandists with an invincible combination. Both were direct clashes between Northern whites and Southern whites in which the Northerners could be cast as the victims of aggression. Neither directly involved black slavery or black rights. The race question was acutely embarrassing for Republicans, and the more they could ignore blacks—free and slave—the more they could keep their appeal lily white, the more they liked it. In addition, the incidents could be politicized in the broadest terms employing the idiom of republicanism, for they presaged the actual enslavement of Northern whites. "Did you ever see such infernal, outrageous, liberty-crushing, persecuting, tyrannical, I can't find any word to express it but damnable, proceedings as those engineered by Pierce & Douglas in Kansas? It makes my blood boil," wrote an Indiana Republican. Similarly, a Massachusetts Yankee fumed that the fate of Northerners in Kansas showed that "the *Missouri Savages* seem determined to prevent their settlement in the Territory except as servants or slaves of the South . . . what has taken place in Kansas and at Washington within the last few months is a disgrace to the country and a reproach to our republican form of government." The incidents, in sum, had much wider resonance in the North than any attacks on the institution of black slavery or even slavery extension could have had. "The antislavery sentiment in New Jersey is not a moving power among the people," wrote one Republican. "The Sumner outrage is however severely condemned and has had its effect." The Republican national platform in 1856 illustrated perfectly the balance of campaign themes. It denounced slavery as immoral, demanded that Congress prevent its expansion and admit Kansas immediately as a free state, and devoted the bulk of its space to cataloging and protesting the violation of the rights of Northern white settlers in Kansas by the despotic proslavery legislature, which was aided by the Democratic administration.

Kansas and Sumner provided the main ammunition in 1856, but in that campaign and for the remainder of the decade the Republicans utilized the republican idiom in other ways against Southerners and Democrats. To complement their argument that slavery expansion must be stopped to preserve the opportunities of free labor, for example, Republicans portrayed planters as supercilious aristocrats contemptuous of the common man while the Republicans were an egalitarian party that protected the poor from the privileged. "The contest ought not to be considered a *sectional* one but the war of a *class*—the slaveholders—against the laboring people of *all classes*," wrote the border state Republican and former Jacksonian Francis P. Blair to his son in 1856. Seward iterated in 1860 that "it is an eternal question between classes—between the few privileged and the many underprivileged—the eternal question between aristocracy and democracy." Over and over, as well, Republicans denounced the apparent usurpation of the national government from the people by a tiny minority of planters. Pledging "to resist the spread of Slavery and the aggressions of the Slave Power, and to secure a free government for a free people," a Republican association in Buffalo announced:

> We require for our country a government of the people, instead of a government by an oligarchy; a government maintaining before the

world the rights of men rather than the privilege of masters. . . . We insist that there shall be no Slavery outside the Slave States, and no domination over the action of the National Government by the Slave Power.

Similarly, a Republican meeting in Hartford castigated "the maladministration and abuse of powers" by the Democratic administration, which was controlled by "the nullification dynasty."

The way to restore the government to the people, the Republicans argued, was to revive the republican doctrine of majority rule. Whereas the Know Nothings had promised to return power to the people by ousting hack politicians from office and the Democrats did so by calling for local self-determination, the Republicans argued that if people were free and equal in a republic, then only majority rule fairly represented the equal rights of all. Because the North was a majority section in the nation, the North and not the South ought to control the government. Protesting as undemocratic and un-American the idea that 20 million free whites in the North should be ruled by slaves and their 350,000 masters, a Pennsylvania Republican meeting demanded "the reestablishment of the rule of the majority." When confronted with threats of Southern secession if the Republicans won in 1860, a Pittsburgh editor scornfully replied, "This is the merest rant. It is an insulting demand to the majority to disband and give up their cherished views and purposes." The Republicans' success in translating the sectional conflict politically into a fundamental principle of republican government is attested to by the postwar memoirs of General Ulysses S. Grant, who had been largely apolitical before the war. Referring to the major Southern and Northern candidates in the 1860 election, he tersely summarized, "The contest was really between Mr. Breckinridge and Mr. Lincoln; between minority rule and rule by the majority."

Even though the Republican organization was still embryonic in 1856, the party's appeal was so compelling and its tactics for combining with the North Americans so skillful that Frémont almost won the presidential election. The Republicans carried every free state except California, Illinois, Indiana, Pennsylvania, and New Jersey. Buchanan and his running mate John C. Breckinridge of Kentucky carried those states as well as all the slave states except Maryland, thereby securing election, even though they garnered only 45 percent of the popular vote in the three-way race. Frémont won 33 percent of the popular vote (45 percent in the North) and Fillmore 21 percent. Fillmore carried only Maryland, but he ran very strongly in other slave states, especially Kentucky, Tennessee, Louisiana, and Florida. More important to the result, Fillmore won about 165,000 votes in the free states that Frémont failed to carry and almost 400,000 in the entire North. Together the Frémont and Fillmore votes totaled more than Buchanan's in California, New Jersey, and Illinois and almost equaled it in Pennsylvania and Indiana. As important, although the Democratic vote declined in the Northeast from 1852, except in Buchanan's home state of Pennsylvania, the Democrats gained over 100,000 votes in the Midwest. Immigrant revulsion from the Know Nothing stigma of Republicanism, continued faith among farmers in popular sovereignty, racial fears stirred up by the Democratic campaign, and genuine fears for the Union probably accounted for that accession.

The basic lesson of the election for the Republicans was that they would have to improve their fortunes in the lower North. If they had carried Pennsylvania and either Illinois or Indiana, they could have won. Specifically, the Republicans would have to offset the continuing appeal of the Democrats in that region and especially to capture those anti-Democratic voters who had supported Fillmore instead of Frémont. Die-hard nativists and anti-Catholics had backed Fillmore, but both Fillmore and Buchanan had benefited from the cry that Republican victory would disrupt the Union. The voters the Republicans had to add to their coalition in order to win the presidency were more conservative than those they had already drawn to the fold. They had not yet been persuaded that the national Democratic party was a mere tool of the Slave Power, that the Slave Power's aggressions posed the greatest danger to the Union by undermining its republican basis, and that the preservation of the Union of the Founding Fathers therefore required the replacement of the Democratic regime by the Republican party. To triumph, in sum, the Republicans had both to broaden their appeal to include Fillmore Americans and to strengthen their basic case against the South and the Democratic party.

On the other hand, despite the Republicans' impressive performance in 1856, their status as the second party in a new two-party system was by no means secure. It was still uncertain what shape political strife would permanently assume, and many former

Whigs in the North still hoped to recreate a bisectional opposition party that combined Northerners and Southerners, something the Republicans could never do by running as an anti-Southern party. With a fifth of the popular vote, the American party remained a potential base for a new nonsectional opposition party that might replace the Republicans if the need for an exclusive Northern party disappeared. Many Know Nothings and former Whigs had backed Frémont in 1856 only because blatant Slave Power aggressions against Northern rights and the threat of slavery extension into Kansas had seemed to dictate its necessity. If those supposed aggressions stopped, if the menace of a Slave Power plot appeared to recede, and if different nonsectional issues arose that could be used against the Democracy, then the rationale of the Republican party would dissolve and the way might be opened for a very different anti-Democratic party. Because that threat soon materialized, more was involved in the history of the Republican party between Frémont's defeat and Abraham Lincoln's victory than merely expanding its 1856 base. Republicans had to fight a vigorous holding action to prevent erosion of that base. . . .

Kenneth M. Stampp

THE IRREPRESSIBLE CONFLICT

In the following essay, Kenneth M. Stampp critiques the viewpoint, so persistent in studies of the causes of the Civil War, that a military conflict was avoidable. Proponents of this approach have often engaged in what is called counterfactual argument, in effect speculating about what might have averted war. This technique is useful, even necessary at times, because asking the question "What if?" provides the historian with an imaginary scenario that offers insight and perspective about why and how the event that actually happened did so.

To test the "repressible conflict" hypothesis, Stampp reduces speculation to specifics by demonstrating that the only set of possibilities that could have prevented war was not in fact available to the protagonists.

Kenneth M. Stampp, "The Irrepressible Conflict," in Stampp, *The Imperiled Union,* pp. 220–26, 227, 230–32, 234–36, 237–45. Copyright © 1980. Reprinted by permission of Oxford University Press.

The author then suggests an alternative approach. Because this approach is rather imprecisely defined but is certainly not economic or cultural, it is appropriate to include it in this section on politics and institutions.

Kenneth M. Stampp (born 1912) taught at the University of California at Berkeley. He has written extensively on the Civil War era. Among his most important books are *The Peculiar Institution* (1956); *And the War Came: The North and the Secession Crisis, 1860–1861* (1950); *The Era of Reconstruction, 1865–1877* (1965); and *America in 1857: A Nation on the Brink* (1990). This extract is from *The Imperiled Union* (1980), a collection of his own essays.

Perhaps no military conflict in history has produced more anguished writing about whether it was evitable or inevitable than the American Civil War. The problem, of course, is one that can never be solved conclusively even by the most exhaustive research, because it involves metaphysical questions about free will and psychological questions about the limits of human choice. Yet historians do sometimes indulge in "counterfactual history"—informed speculation about how things would have been if certain other things had or had not happened—and that essentially is the kind of history that revisionists have written. They were interested not only in explaining why the Civil War occurred but in showing how, by a different course of action, it could have been avoided and how much better off the country would have been if its history had been one of continued peace.

The Civil War settled the issues of the sectional conflict at a cost of more than half a million lives. The revisionists' alternative to the war was compromise, delay, patience, and the avoidance of recrimination and confrontation in order to maintain a milieu of political tranquility in which sectional differences could have been rationally resolved. Their conviction that evolutionary forces would soon have ended slavery peacefully was a basic premise of their case. In his account of the crisis, James Buchanan contended that, "If left to the wise ordinances of a superintending Providence, which never acts rashly, [slavery] would have been gradually extinguished in our country . . . without bloodshed. . . ." [The historian Charles W.] Ramsdell, though relying on economic and geographic forces rather than Providence, made this the moral of his argument that slavery had extended to its natural limits. "[Can] we say with conviction," he asked, "that this war accomplished anything of lasting good that could not and would not have been won by the peaceful processes of social evolution? Is there not ground for the tragic conclusion that it accomplished little which was not otherwise attainable?" E. Merton Coulter [another historian] made the point concisely: "The Civil War was not worth the cost. . . . What good the war produced would have come with time in an orderly way; the bad would not have come at all."

Precisely when slavery's peaceful end would have come no revisionist could say, but most of them guessed that it could have lasted no longer than another generation, or no later than the end of the nineteenth century. In any event, when emancipation came, it would not have cost the life of one soldier for every six slaves freed—a per capita cost that [David M.] Potter quite understandably found rather staggering. On the other hand, the postponement of emancipation for a generation, while saving the lives of soldiers, would have exacted its own price. It would have meant that the four million slaves of 1860, as well as their descendants, would have remained in bondage until the forces anticipated by the revisionists moved white masters in their own good time to grant freedom to their black laborers. How to balance the lives of half a million soldiers against the prolonged bondage of four million slaves is a question with profound moral implications; how one resolves it will doubtless depend in part on one's judgment of slavery itself. Clearly, the revisionists believed that the survival of black bondage for another generation would not have been too high a price for avoiding the bloodshed of the Civil War. Given their characteristic view of southern slavery, their resolution of this moral dilemma was logical enough.

In considering the plausibility of the case for a repressible conflict, one must note that the writings of historians who advanced it were not always models of measured and temperate discourse. Some revisionists wrote with a passion that approached the intensity of those antebellum orators whose verbal excesses they so roundly condemned. More important than style, however, was a logical inconsistency that lay at the heart of their argument. Revisionists advanced a highly deterministic explanation of how slavery would have been abolished if the Civil War had not occurred. Unalterable conditions and uncontrollable trends—the realities of western soil and climate, the impact of the laws of supply and demand on cotton and slave prices, "the processes of social evolution," and the resulting realization of rational Southerners that slavery was a burden—would have led inevitably to the ultimate adaptation of southern agriculture to a free-labor system. Yet, revisionists rejected the deterministic concept of an irrepressible conflict as an explanation of the Civil War itself. They discerned no logical, fundamental forces operating to bring on this great and tragic event, only the unnecessary, irrational behavior of a blundering generation of politicians and agitators. But if one generation of Northerners could produce a needless war over issues irrationally perceived, might not another generation of Southerners have defied all the presumably sound reasons for abandoning slavery and preserved it for irrational—say, for example, racist—reasons? Revisionists, though apparently assuming that history normally follows a rational course, by their analysis of the sectional crisis, themselves made a substantial case for irrational behavior as a historical force. Thereby, they compromised their optimistic hypothesis that slavery, in a logical progression, was destined "within a comparatively short time" to be abolished without war.

*

Assuming that historians of the repressible conflict were justified in their optimistic belief that sectional problems were amenable to resolution without violence, the problem still remains of determining how the antebellum crises could have been avoided while the benevolent forces of peaceful change did their work. The revisionist answer was clear enough: abolitionists should not have carried on their agitation; Free-Soilers should have trusted [Stephen A.] Douglas's principle of popular sovereignty to keep slavery out of the territories; Republicans should not have made political issues of the repeal of the Missouri Compromise, the Kansas question, or the Dred Scott decision; in short, Northerners should have avoided provoking Southerners and left the resolution of the slavery issue to them. Apart from its transparent one-sidedness, this exercise in counterfactual history contains a serious analytical flaw. To question the necessity of certain specific incidents in antebellum sectional relations is one thing; to object wholly to the temper of an age is quite another.

A plausible analysis of antebellum politics and of the options that were reasonably open to that generation must begin with the assumption that an antislavery movement would exist in the northern states. That such a movement did exist was hardly the unfortunate result of some perverse historical accident, such as the emergence of a William Lloyd Garrison, or the outbreak of an epidemic of acute neuroses in the northern population, as the portraits of abolitionists in revisionist literature would seem to suggest. Characterizations of them as "pious cranks" troubled with "maladjustments, inferiority complexes, and repressed desires" may describe accurately a few of the more bizarre figures attracted to the movement, but not the members or leaders in general. No historian has demonstrated convincingly that neurotics were proportionally more numerous among abolitionists than among their critics. Nor has a persuasive case been made for the hypothesis that abolitionist leaders were a displaced elite, victims of the industrial revolution, losing status and finding an outlet for their discontents in a crusade against slavery. The idea that abolitionists responded not to an objective, external social problem but to their own internal psychic problems and status anxieties is not adequate to describe a group with as varied personalities and economic, social, and cultural backgrounds as Garrison, Wendell Phillips, Arthur and Lewis Tappan, Theodore Dwight Weld, James G. Birney, Sarah and Angelina Grimké, Gerrit Smith, James Russell Lowell, Theodore Parker, and Thomas Wentworth Higginson. . . .

Abolitionism, of course, was always a movement of a minority, for even in an era of reform most men and women were absorbed in the problems of their own daily lives and were either indifferent to reformers or regarded them as disturbing nuisances. Nationalists disliked abolitionists for disregarding constitutional restraints and endangering the Union; practical men of business viewed them as a threat to their rich southern trade; and conservative clergymen feared them as a disruptive force in the churches. Above all, the racism that was nearly universal in nineteenth-century America, by fostering anxieties about the consequences of liberating millions of black slaves, severely limited the abolitionist appeal. Indeed, as historians have amply demonstrated, the abolitionists themselves, though far in advance of their contemporaries, were by no means free of race prejudice. To appreciate the importance of racism as a deterrent to abolitionism one needs merely to consider how much stronger the movement would have been if the South's slave population had been white rather than black. . . .

Both contemporaries and historians criticized abolitionists more often for their commitment to "immediatism" than for any other alleged shortcoming. Only impractical, irresponsible fools, they charged, would ignore all the social problems of emancipation, the need for a period of gradual transition, and call for slavery's immediate end. But this criticism was an oversimplification of the abolitionist goal and took it out of the context of the times. Immediatism, as abolitionists usually understood the term, was not a naïve program to abolish slavery in a day; rather, it meant that the process of abolishing slavery, a sin, should commence at once, though its completion would probably take some time. It also meant a rejection of the gradualism that would postpone even the commencement of emancipation until some future date.

To this antebellum generation of reformers, familiar with religious revivalism, with the spectacle of mass responses to the sermons of preachers such as Charles G. Finney, and with the miraculous experience of conversion and the instant renunciation of sin, the goal of immediatism did not seem unrealistic. In the early years of their crusade, abolitionists dared hope that their tactic of "moral suasion"—trying to convince slaveholders that slavery was sinful and imperiled their salvation—might, like a great revival, bring masses of slaveholders to an immediate decision to emancipate their slaves. In any case, moral suasion was the only tactic open to them, for the federal government had no power to interfere with slavery in the southern states, and the abolitionists, committed as they were to peaceful methods, did not countenance a slave insurrection. They never addressed their appeals to the slaves themselves, only to white masters, and the danger of slave rebellions if emancipation were not adopted was a persistent theme in their literature. . . .

*

If abolitionism of a moralistic, immediate type is accepted as a logical and quite inescapable product of antebellum society, and slavery as an exotic aberration, the task of historians who would make a case for a repressible conflict is not to wish away the abolitionists but to explain how an atmosphere favorable to political tranquillity, compromise, and patient delay might have been maintained in spite of the irritant of an antislavery crusade. This would require a rather radical reformulation of the problem as revisionists customarily perceived it, for much of the responsibility for avoiding sectional confrontation would be transferred from the North to the South. In effect, antebellum Southerners asked for the tolerant acceptance of an institution which, however vital it may have been economically, was a moral anachronism in their age, until they found a convenient and safe way to give it up. They asked a great deal of their generation, and their best hope of avoiding a national crisis— of keeping the conflict repressible—was to defuse the antislavery movement by minimizing its appeal to the northern public, and thus to soften the impact of some quite compelling ideological forces. To consider how this might have been possible involves another exercise in counterfactual history, one premised on the existence of *both* southern slavery and northern antislavery.

The first requirement was that Southerners avoid aggressively proslavery postures which would diminish the traditional expectation that through a natural progression slavery would give way to a free-labor system. The fact that many post-Revolutionary Southerners conceded the evils of slavery and assumed at least a vague antislavery stance encouraged northern reformers to be temperate and patient. However, the gradual change to a less apologetic tone— a change that antedated abolitionism—eventually altered perceptions of the possibility for emancipation without intervention from the outside.

During the eighteenth century some Southerners had defended slavery occasionally on racial and religious grounds; during the Missouri controversy they justified it more vigorously; and during the following decade their defense accelerated until, in 1832, Thomas R. Dew of Virginia published the first book-length treatise upholding slavery as a positive good. As the defense became increasingly sweeping, invoking biblical authority, historical experience, scientific evidence, and racist concepts, southern intellectuals romanticized slavery into an ideal paternal relationship beneficial to both master and slave. Reacting to these changed circumstances, a northern reformer expressed dismay at "the sentiments openly expressed . . . that slavery is not an evil . . . [and] that it is criminal toward the South . . . to indulge even a hope that the chains of the captive may some day or other, no matter how remote the time, be broken." The positive-good hypothesis, an aggressive vindication of slavery about which many Southerners themselves had uneasy feelings, by shocking northern reformers into organized activity, played a major role in undermining sectional peace. It was, in the terminology of revisionism, an irresponsible blunder that needlessly heightened tensions between North and South.

A second basic condition for the preservation of political tranquillity was a southern program to reform the institution of slavery in those aspects where it was most exposed to sensational abolitionist attacks. To this end, and at the cost of compromising somewhat the property rights of slaveholders, southern legislatures should have given legal protection to slave marriages, prohibited the breakup of slave families when estates were sold for debt or divided among heirs, reduced the brutal aspects of the slave trade, given slaves greater protection from violent assault, defined the rape of a slave woman as a crime, given slaves a stronger position in courts of law, regulated more strictly their labor and living conditions, and repealed the laws against teaching them to read and write, thus shifting the emphasis in the legal codes from slaves as property to slaves as persons. Reforms such as these would not have made bondage acceptable to abolitionists, but they would have blunted their attack by depriving them of some of their most effective propaganda weapons. The vulnerable slave woman, exposed to her master's lust, faced with the dissolution of her family at her master's will, required to engage in heavy field labor; the slave coffles driven to the plantations of the Southwest by unfeeling traders; the physical punishment inflicted by some callous masters—these were the materials from which abolitionists constructed their accounts of slavery. By improving the condition of the slave the southern states would not only have reduced the abolitionist appeal but checked the growing sense that without external pressure nothing would ever change. . . .

A third essential requirement for avoiding an irrepressible conflict was acceptance of a federal policy of confining slavery to the fifteen states that recognized it at the time of the Mexican War. Nothing alarmed Northerners more than the aggressive demand of southern politicians that the western territories be opened to slavery; nothing lent more credence to the abolitionist charge that a Slave

Power conspired to make slavery a national institution. The fact that much of the northern opposition to slavery expansion was less an expression of moral feelings than of race prejudice does not in the least diminish its importance as a political force. Traditionally, historians of the repressible conflict placed the onus on the North for agitating what they thought was an issue without substance; but Daniel E. Somes, a congressman from Maine, shifted the responsibility to those who probably most deserved to bear it. "You say it is a mere abstraction for which we are contending," he told Southerners. "And yet you regard this abstraction of so much importance to you that you say you are willing to dissolve the Union . . . to secure it. If it is an abstraction with us, of course it must be an abstraction with you." For this alleged abstraction, this issue without substance, southern politicians waged a bitter fight against the adoption of the Wilmot Proviso. In 1854 they secured the repeal of the Missouri Compromise before they would permit the passage of legislation to organize the territories of Kansas and Nebraska, thus provoking an unprecedented uprising of the northern people, encouraging the formation of the purely sectional Republican party, and doing severe damage to the conservative national Democratic party.

By the 1850s many southern politicians and editors supported Calhoun's doctrine that the Constitution protected slavery in all the territories; and in 1857 they rallied behind the Supreme Court's decision in the Dred Scott case, which denied that slavery could be barred by either Congress or a territorial legislature. Subsequently, when Douglas claimed that, in spite of the Court's decision, the people of a territory could exclude slavery simply by refusing to protect it, southern politicians proposed a remedy so extravagant as to suggest not merely irresponsibility but a flight from reality. They demanded that Congress adopt a code protecting slavery in all the territories and, in 1860, that the Democratic party incorporate their demand in its national platform. The reckless southern agitation of the slavery expansion issue was a blunder whose consequences included the fragmentation of national political organizations and the destruction beyond repair of the conditions essential to continued sectional peace.

A fourth requirement was that Southerners set an example of temperate response to antislavery criticism and of open-mindedness to moderate proposals for eventual manumission. Instead, southern defenders of slavery sought to prevent discussion altogether; they seemed prepared, if necessary, to violate the federal Bill of Rights and thus to threaten the liberties not only of black slaves but of white freemen as well. Southern laws designed to protect the white community from slave insurrections were interpreted so broadly as to prevent all discussion of slavery in the schools and colleges, in the press, or in public meetings. "The expression of Black Republican opinions in our midst is incompatible with our honor and safety as a people," wrote a North Carolina editor during the presidential campaign of 1856. "Let our schools and seminaries of learning be scrutinized, and if Black Republicans be found in them, let them be driven out. That man is neither a fit nor a safe instructor of our young men, who even inclines to . . . Black Republicanism." By constructing an "intellectual blockade," as Clement Eaton called it, proslavery Southerners gave northern reformers additional reason to despair that slavery would ever be abolished by internal forces alone.

One of the most serious tactical blunders southern politicians ever made was supporting the passage of a Gag Rule to prevent congressional discussion of petitions and memorials relating to slavery. Between 1836 and 1844, while the rule was in effect, the right of petition was seriously compromised, and abolitionists could argue plausibly that the Slave Power would even subvert the Constitution to preserve their evil institution. Rather than reducing agitation, the Gag Rule increased the flood of petitions and enabled abolitionists to present their cause to the country in a manner most favorable to them. Meanwhile, angry southern congressmen made wild threats and uttered indiscreet remarks that provided more grist for the abolitionists' mill. . . .

*

Having flouted every requirement for the preservation of an atmosphere conducive to compromise and political tranquillity, politicians of the Deep South committed the ultimate blunder of attempting secession after the election of the first Republican President, Abraham Lincoln. Their action was swift and impetuous—all seven states had seceded within less than three months after the election—and they gave Congress no opportunity to consider a compromise plan. As early as December 13, 1860, thirty southern congressmen signed a letter to the southern people declaring, "The argument is exhausted. All hope of relief in the Union . . . is extinguished. . . . We are satisfied the honor, safety and independence of the Southern people require the organization of a Southern Confederacy." Before the end of January nearly all the congressmen from the Deep South had resigned, and northern and border-state moderates had no one with whom to discuss a compromise and the restoration of peace and political tranquillity.

Since only one of the seceding states submitted its ordinance of secession to popular ratification, the debate among historians whether the secession conventions represented the will of the people will doubtless go on indefinitely. Yet, granted that the people might have changed their minds six months or a year later, there is little reason to doubt that secession was the will of a substantial majority at the time the decision was made. The majority for secession was overwhelming in every secession convention, the closest vote being 61–39 in Alabama. Texas was the only state to provide for a popular referendum, and there secession was approved by a plurality of approximately three to one.

Northern and southern conservatives argued in vain that secession was a reckless act, that, so far from giving the South greater security, secession would heighten the dangers it faced and threaten the supreme disaster of defeat in war. They reminded secessionists that Lincoln was not an abolitionist, that he acknowledged slavery to be a local institution over which the federal government had no jurisdiction, and that he recognized his duty to enforce the fugitive-slave law. Secession, they warned, would prevent slaveholders from recovering fugitives, for the federal government would no longer be obligated to assist them; it would strengthen the abolitionists, for love of the Union would cease to be an inhibiting force; and it would deprive the seceding states of all the territories, for none would be open to them. The conservatives insisted that Lincoln's election was not a threat to the South, for as a minority President with less than 40 percent of the popular vote his position would be weak. The new Congress would have an anti-Republican majority; hence the Republican legislative program would be effectively blocked, and Lincoln's appointments would require the approval of a hostile Senate. Finally, the conservatives described the Republicans as internally divided, a loose coalition of discordant elements which

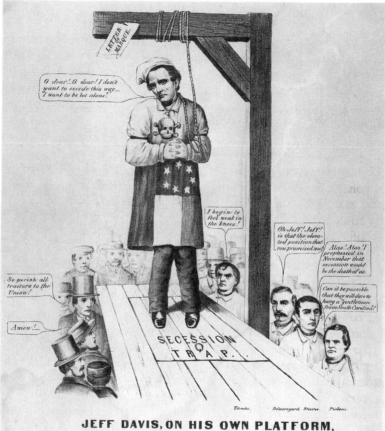

JEFF DAVIS, ON HIS OWN PLATFORM,
or the last "act of secession".

"Secession Trap" cartoon, 1861. Ridiculing Jefferson Davis as a pitiful figure who was falling into the "secession trap," this cartoon aimed to puncture the illusion that withdrawal from the Union was a grand and courageous move that would save the South. The anxious southern political leaders to the right of the platform are, from top to bottom, Robert Toombs of Georgia; P. G. T. Beauregard, who commanded the bombardment of Fort Sumter; Alexander H. Stephens of Georgia; and Francis W. Pickens, governor of South Carolina. (*Chicago Historical Society*) might fall apart before the next presidential campaign. How, then, could secession be viewed as anything but the last and greatest blunder of an irrational and irresponsible generation of southern politicians? . . .

*

The alternative case for a repressible conflict presented here has the merit of taking into account some of the fundamental conditions of northern antebellum society that traditional revisionists chose to ignore. But in a different way it, too, is flawed. While accepting northern antislavery tendencies as an inescapable force in sectional relations, it is premised on an assumption that Southerners were exposed to no comparable social pressures—that they were free to choose between the acts they committed, which brought on a profound crisis and Civil War, and a more rational, controlled, and peaceable course. In short, like the old revisionist interpretation, it is one-sided, for it fails to recognize the predicament of the South.

In a slave society, especially one in which racial and cultural differences separated masters and slaves, certain intrinsic stresses existed that added another factor to the antebellum political equation and made southern behavior as understandable and predictable as the rise of abolitionism in the North. These southern stresses, together with the circumstances that produced northern antislavery, make untenable either the revisionist concept or the alternative concept of a repressible conflict. They bring us back to Seward's "irrepressible conflict between opposing and enduring forces," but not to the clash of economic interests seen by [Charles A.] Beard, or even to the clash of cultures variously described by, among others, [Edward] Channing, [Allan] Nevins, and [Eugene D.] Genovese. Slavery produced in the South not a unique culture in any primordial sense, but a special set of problems.

Slavery, of course, was at bottom a labor system, and property in slaves constituted the largest capital investment of most masters. That the South's nearly 400,000 slaveholders should have been reluctant to surrender this vast interest may not have been admirable, but it was hardly irrational. James H. Hammond of South Carolina was being coldly realistic when he posed his well-known rhetorical question: "[Were] ever any people, civilized or savage, persuaded by arguments, human or divine, to surrender, voluntarily, two billion dollars?" That a proslavery argument should have been devised to defend an interest of such magnitude was not surprising, and it is logical to assume that a substantial number of slaveholders, by accepting its validity, truly believed in the morality of slavery and thus insulated themselves from the abolitionist assault.

As a justification of a viable labor system and large capital investment the proslavery argument was in part a product of the practical realities of southern economic life. However, in its most common form, it was not a defense of slavery in general but, more specifically, of the subordination of black slaves to white masters. The racial dimension of southern bondage explains, perhaps better than the economic interests involved, the violent and sometimes irrational response to antislavery attacks. Slavery thus injected not one but two ineluctable realities into southern life: first, the large economic interest is represented, and, second, the emotion-laden race issue which deeply concerned slaveholders and nonslaveholders alike. In 1860, black slaves constituted nearly one-third of the southern population. In two states (South Carolina and Mississippi) they outnumbered the whites; in four others (Florida, Georgia, Alabama, and Louisiana) the number of slaves and of whites was about equal. If racism was a powerful force in the northern states, which contained a scant quarter-million free blacks, it was a force of overwhelming proportions in the southern states, where one-third as many whites lived with a quarter-million free blacks and four million black slaves.

Given the almost universal conviction, heavily stressed in the proslavery argument, that blacks were not only physically but intellectually and emotionally different from and inferior to whites, and that assimilation would be a racial disaster, slavery had great significance as a system of control. Slavery was—so went the conventional wisdom—the only sure way to maintain the supremacy of the white race. Phillips identified white Southerners as "a people with a common resolve indomitably maintained—that [the South] shall be and remain a white man's country. The consciousness of a function in these premises, whether expressed with the frenzy of a demagogue or maintained with a patrician's quietude, is the cardinal test of a Southerner and the central theme of Southern history." This statement may border on hyperbole, but it was inspired by the knowledge that many white Southerners, nonslaveholders not the least among them, made the preservation of white supremacy a central concern of their lives. Accordingly, an attack on slavery was a threat not only to the southern economy but to the entire white race.

However, if Southerners preserved slavery in part to govern an alien race, they relied on a system with some serious built-in dangers. The volatile ingredient inherent in a slave society was the unpredictable behavior of the slaves, who were controlled primarily by force or the threat of force. Individual acts of violence against whites were not uncommon; organized conspiracies and insurrections occurred infrequently, but the danger was ever present. Southerners never forgot the Santo Domingo insurrection of the 1790s, in which most of the white population was exterminated, or the Gabriel conspiracy in Richmond in 1800, or the Denmark Vesey conspiracy in Charleston in 1822, or the Nat Turner insurrection in Southampton County, Virginia, in 1831, in which nearly sixty whites lost their lives. In the South the white population had to be forever on guard—to maintain special patrols, to restrict the movements of slaves, to prohibit them from gathering in large numbers unless whites were present, to give whites despotic power over slaves, and almost never to question a white man for his treatment of a slave. The antebellum South was a land troubled by a nagging dread of slave insurrections; indeed, it is impossible to understand the psychology of white Southerners, or the events of the sectional conflict, without taking this fact into account.

If the fear of slave violence was a constant, at certain times, when a conspiracy was discovered, or more commonly, when rumors of a conspiracy were afloat, the fear bordered on the pathological, if it did not explode into pure hysteria. John Randolph once told his fellow congressmen: "I speak from facts when I say, that the night bell never tolls for fire in Richmond, that the mother does not hug the infant more closely to her bosom. I have been witness to some of the alarms in the capital of Virginia." In 1822, a group of Charlestonians sent a memorial to the state legislature asserting that there was "only [one] principle that can maintain slavery, the 'principle of fear.' . . . We should always act as if we had an enemy in the very bosom of the state, prepared to rise upon and surprise the whites, whenever an opportunity afforded."

These candid statements of the anxieties that were endemic in the antebellum South tell a great deal about the sources of the

American sectional conflict. In the name of white supremacy and to protect the South from the horrors of Santo Domingo, as well as to secure the slaveholders' economic interests, the agitation of abolitionists *had* to be suppressed, the Gag Rule enforced, the mails censored, the "intellectual blockade" maintained. These were the inescapable imperatives of southern life as surely as abolitionism was an unavoidable product of intellectual currents in the nineteenth-century North. Without these imperatives John Brown's raid on Harpers Ferry might have been dismissed as a ridiculous event, at most a minor irritant, and would not have induced the acute slave-conspiracy hysteria that swept the South during the crucial presidential election of 1860.

A significant number of Southerners seemed not to have found the proslavery argument a fully convincing defense of their peculiar institution, and consequently the pressure on them in this tension-ridden society was all the more severe. Many, perhaps most, slaveholders accepted the system because the slaves were black, but great numbers of them were tormented by the accusation that they were parties to a betrayal of the principles embodied in the Declaration of Independence. Those who were troubled by moral uncertainties seldom resolved their problem by surrendering their investments and abandoning a profitable labor system, and certainly their private doubts made them love their abolitionist critics none the more. Rather, they united with those who firmly believed in the morality of slavery in a desperate attempt to escape the threat of abolitionism from without and to minimize the danger of slave rebellion from within. As a last resort they sought both security and tranquillity through independence.

The historians of the repressible conflict thus failed to reconcile their case not only with the essential reality of a northern antislavery movement but with certain inescapable facts of southern slave society. Economic interests, racial beliefs, and fear of slave insurrections impelled Southerners to make demands and take actions that precipitated a series of sectional confrontations culminating in the secession crisis of 1860–61. The Republican party of the 1850s was not an abolitionist party, as most Southerners seemed to think, and slavery in the southern states was never a clear issue in the politics of that decade. But the party was vaguely antislavery; its ranks contained an articulate minority of strong-minded abolitionists;

and, for both racist and moral reasons, it was firmly committed to keeping slavery out of the territories. This is what gave substance to the southern perception of the Republican party as a threat to its peculiar institution. The interplay of these proslavery and antislavery forces, not the irresponsible blunders of northern or southern politicians, or economic conflict, or irreconcilable cultural differences, brought on the irrepressible conflict about which Seward spoke.

There still remains the question of the evitability or inevitability of the Civil War itself—a question that will probably continue to be, as it is now, unanswerable. It may well be that the country reached a point sometime in the 1850s when it would have been almost impossible to avoid a violent resolution of the sectional crisis. During that decade, northern antislavery and southern proslavery radicals became increasingly militant and prone to anticipate an ultimate resort to armed conflict; and the point of no return may have been reached in 1857 with the Dred Scott decision, the Kansas crisis, Douglas's break with the Buchanan administration, and the severe economic panic of that year. This, of course, is sheer speculation, for, as Seward would have reminded us, to make a case for an irrepressible conflict is not to prove the inevitability of war. But somehow the war came, and it seems no less tragic because it resulted from conditions and events more substantial than the irresponsible acts of a blundering generation. The irrepressible conflict of antebellum years made the war, if not inevitable, at least an understandable response to its stresses by men and women no more or less wise than we.

Social and Economic Origins
of the Sectional Conflict

Elizabeth Fox-Genovese and Eugene D. Genovese

THE SOUTHERN SLAVEHOLDERS
AGAINST THE MODERN WORLD

The attack on slavery in the southern United States did not occur in isolation. In the following essay, the Genoveses employ a Marxist approach and a broad-ranging comparative perspective to show that the sectional conflict in America was part of a much larger process under way in the nineteenth century.

During this era, they contend, slaveholders elsewhere in the New World were under siege, as were the large landowners in Europe. Slaveholders were being challenged by rival economic interests and world views. In essence, there was a struggle for dominance between contending classes—between the landed aristocracy, some of whom were slaveowners, and the industrial and commercial bourgeoisie. Invariably, this contest resulted in violence and, in the case of the United States, civil war.

Elizabeth Fox-Genovese (born 1941) teaches at Emory University and is the author of *Within the Plantation Household: Black and White Women of the Old South* (1988). Eugene D. Genovese (born 1930) is Distinguished Scholar-in-Residence at the University Center in Georgia. He has had a major impact on the study of the slave system in the South through such books as *The Political Economy of Slavery* (1965), *The World the Slaveholders Made* (1969), *Roll, Jordan, Roll: The World the Slaves Made* (1974), and *From Rebellion to Revolution: Afro-American Slave Revolts in the Making of the New World* (1979). Together, the Genoveses have written a collection of essays entitled *Fruits of Merchant Capital* (1983), from which the following essay is taken.

Americans have, with reason, long brooded over slavery as if it were our own national equivalent of original sin. For slavery rent the world's most noble republic and disgraced the world's most promising democracy; it precipitated a war, often literally though not metaphorically fratricidal, that proved ghastly in itself and terrifying in its implications for the future of humanity; and it left a legacy of racism that has brought mortification and unremitting agony to southerners and northerners, whites and blacks. Yet, the burden of slavery fell not upon our country alone, not upon the slaveholding countries of the Western Hemisphere alone, but upon the world.

An advanced state of economic integration and international struggle for power marked the world of the nineteenth century. During that extraordinary era of bourgeois ascendancy and world conquest, European capitalists and workers, nationalists, liberals, and democrats, imperialists and racists permeated and recast the world at large. The slaveholders of the Old South, like those of the Caribbean and South America and like the residual landholding classes of Europe, deeply influenced the capitalist world in which we still live, much as the resistance of slaves and peasants deeply influenced both that world and the revolutionary societies that have arisen to challenge it.

Slavery burdened not merely the United States but the entire world with the creation of powerful landholding classes based on unfree labor. These classes enormously strengthened opposition to the revolutionary tidal wave of bourgeois liberalism and democracy, although slavery had reemerged in the modern world largely under bourgeois auspices. The spread of capitalism in Europe had created a mass market for cotton, sugar, tobacco, and other plantation staples. The growth of a capitalist shipping industry had made possible the magnitude of the slave trade, and other capitalist sectors had provided not only the capital but the commodities necessary to sustain the African connection and service the American plantations. Plantation slavery arose in the Americas as part of the process of international capitalist development.

The specific conditions of plantation life and organization, however, provided fertile ground for the emergence of retrograde ruling classes. And for the moment it makes little difference whether we view these new landed classes as variant capitalist classes, as incipient new aristocracies, as some kind of hybrid, or as social classes of a new type. Clearly, they began by advancing world economic development and ended by threatening to stifle it. Initially, these ruling classes brought millions of Africans and other self-sufficient peoples into commodity production for a world market, provided commodities needed to sustain capitalist expansion in Europe, created new markets for burgeoning European industry, and accumulated capital, some of which spurred European industry directly and more of which indirectly contributed to market formation and commercial expansion.

Yet, in the end they built no technologically advanced, economically progressive, politically and militarily self-reliant nations of their own; much less did they create anything their warmest admirers could recognize as a great culture or civilization. Their initial dynamism became frozen in place. In one country after another, sad decline followed stagnation, at least relative to the progressive capitalist sectors of the world. Retrogression followed an orgy of prosperity: the West Indies became cultural as well as economic wrecks; Brazil lost its chance to become a great power; and the American South became this country's least dynamic and prosperous region—to put it charitably. The great slaveholding countries moved from a central position in the worldwide advance of capitalism, with its unprecedented standards of living even for the masses, to a periphery of misery, poverty, discouragement, and general embarrassment. But, of course, for the slaves whose blood and toil had created the original wealth, those countries had never been anything else.

The underdevelopment and backwardness that still grip most of the old slaveholding countries have provided burden enough for today's world to bear. But much more remains at stake. The slaveholders of the Americas in effect reinforced the political role of the declining landholding classes of Europe, first in opposing the spread of bourgeois liberalism and then, after their own defeat by the bourgeoisie, in opposing the spread of democracy. The influence of the slaveholders and the European landed classes was uniformly reactionary, although by no means uniform in specific content or intensity. In Europe, in Latin America, and, to a lesser extent, even in the United States, these classes significantly retarded the great movements for recognition of autonomy of the individual and the legitimate participation of the masses in political life.

The intervention of these landed classes on the side of reaction came at a fateful moment in the history of Europe and America—at the very moment at which the bourgeoisie itself, faced with threats

A gathering of slaves near Baton Rouge, Louisiana. The dress and appearance of the slaves as well as their number indicate that this was an unusually large and prosperous plantation. (*Illinois State Historical Library*)

from the Left, was being forced to recognize the contradiction between its historic commitment to individual freedom and its early, if always uneasy, flirtation with democracy and equality. Jacobinism [the Jacobins were the radicals led by Robespierre in the French Revolution], after all, was quintessentially a bourgeois movement, but by the middle of the nineteenth century any form of Jacobinism looked like socialism, communism, or anarchy to a bourgeoisie increasingly frightened by mass politics.

Even the most liberal bourgeoisies—those of England, France, and the United States—which continued to adhere to some form of democratic commitment, turned outward in an attempt to solve what they condescendingly called "the social question" at home at the expense of colonial peoples. The legacy of the old colonialism and its ideologically essential racism served their strategy well, as did the remnants of the old landed classes directly. We need not follow [the economist] Joseph Schumpeter in attributing modern imperialism to the atavistic tendencies of the old landholding elites to recognize the importance of their role.

By 1861 the slaveholders were determined to defend their property and power. In this respect they stood alongside the slave-holding planters of Brazil and Cuba, alongside the Russian lords— elegantly delineated by Pushkin, Turgenev, Dostoevski, and Tolstoi and unforgettably satirized by Gogol—lords who, with the support of such brutal rulers as Catherine the Great, had slowly reduced their serfs to a status close to that of slaves, and who set a high standard of pitiless brutality in the suppression of peasant revolts. And as late as 1861 the southern slaveholders also stood alongside such dying but still deadly landholding classes as those of Poland, Hungary, Italy, and Japan, which commanded unfree or only technically free labor in regimes even then looked upon as barbarous by both the bourgeois and working classes of western Europe.

The southern slaveholders were not transplanted boyars or Junkers or Polish lords or even Brazilian *senhores de engenho* [sugar planters]. Each of these classes had its own traditions, sensibilities, characteristics, notions of civilized life, and peculiar relation to labor; each had its own internal divisions. The slaveholders of Virginia were not quite the same as those of Louisiana, any more than the *senhores de engenho* of the sugar-growing Brazilian Northeast were quite the same as the *fazendeiros* [planters] of the coffee-growing Brazilian South. And yet, they did, in a broad sense, represent variations on one side of a great historical divide.

These classes mounted, in different degrees, stubborn opposition to the emerging forces of the modern world. Some of them were remnants of a world that was steadily being overthrown by the expansion of world capitalism. Others, including the American slaveholders, had their class origins in that very expansion. But all, to the extent that they could create and consolidate their political power, had increasing difficulty in living in a world of emerging cities, industries, mechanization, international finance, and the participation of the masses in politics.

From an economic point of view, these landed classes commanded regimes that, however profitable in the narrow sense, lacked the development possibilities of regimes based on free labor and, therefore, the military possibilities for survival in a world of increasingly competitive nation-states. The Junkers learned that hard lesson during the Napoleonic wars, although not until Bismarck's time did they learn it well enough. The Russian lords learned it, to the extent that they learned it at all, during the Crimean War and the peasant rebellions that came before and after it. The Brazilians had their own national disaster during the Paraguayan War and the unraveling of their social and political structure. And the Japanese suffered the humiliation of the so-called opening by the West. The nineteenth century, in short, demonstrated from one end of the world to the other that the path of safety and survival for old ruling classes as well as for new nations was the path of accommodation to the irresistible advance of nationalism and industrial capitalism. Whether in a death struggle or a reluctant compromise, the great landholders who survived as individuals, as families, or as whole classes did so at the price of surrendering their traditional ways of life as well as their political autonomy, not merely to new men but to a new class based on the property relations of money and markets.

The passing of the great landed classes, however slow, partial, or disguised, marked the final victory and consolidation of a worldwide system of capitalist production and, with it, of a new world view or, rather, a new complex of antagonistic world views. In a sense, the economic struggle between contending economic systems had long ago been settled. The decisive struggles had become political, ideological, and moral. From the sixteenth century onward, the new system of capitalist production, spreading across the world from northwestern Europe, embraced something much more important, something more decisive, than international commerce. International commerce had played an important role in the ancient world and in the great empires of China and India. And it was particularly notable in the magnificent expansion of Islam across the Mediterranean basin into Spain and black Africa and eastward to China, Central Asia, and Indonesia. Without a vigorous and well-organized commercial system, the great Muslim caliphates of the eighth and ninth centuries and beyond, with their brilliant contributions to art, science, philosophy, and law, would have been impossible. Yet none of these commercially developed civilizations succeeded in creating an integrated worldwide system of production and exchange; nor did they even try.

The spread of capitalism in early-modern Europe marked the rise of a new mode of production—that is, of new social relations based on personal freedom and on a revolutionary and apparently self-revolutionizing technology associated with those relations. And it also marked a revolution in human values, the decisive feature of which was precisely the freedom of labor—that is, the transformation of labor-power into a commodity. That freedom liberated human beings to work for themselves and to accumulate wealth; it also forced the laboring poor out of their traditional dependence on the protection, such as it was, of lords and patrons and placed them under the stern whip of marketplace necessity.

This new mode of production gave rise to a new theory of property. The right of the individual to property both in his own person and his labor-power constituted not merely its economic but also its moral foundation. Once that theory of property took root, the very definition of the rights and duties of the individual in relation to the state changed dramatically, and so did the content of race relations.

True, the Christian tradition had long established the principle of equality before God and the responsibility of the individual for his actions. The Christian ethic had long stressed that, while men must render unto Caesar the things that are Caesar's, men must also assume full responsibility for rendering unto God the things that are God's; and God's things included the moral sanctity of individual life and the immortality of the soul. But this great tradition, itself so revolutionary and heroic, did not destroy the principle of property in man, and the specific history of the Catholic Church had actually reinforced and legitimized the principle of class subordination. It is in this sense that David Brion Davis, in his excellent book *The Problem of Slavery in the Age of Revolution,* refers to the new bourgeois idea of freedom, especially in its Hegelian form, as bearing only superficial resemblance to the Christian idea, although the early emergence of the Christian idea of freedom in Western civilization decisively prepared the ground for the emergence of the secular bourgeois idea during the Enlightenment.

The spread of capitalism revolutionized thought as well as material life. Liberalism, in those eighteenth and nineteenth-century forms which today are usually associated with free-market conservatives, became the dominant ideology of the bourgeoisie. This new ruling class took its stand on the freedom of the individual and on some form of political representation. In time, new bourgeois nation-states, most notably Germany and Japan, would assume a more authoritarian political stance. But even there, industrial capitalism carried with it an expanded commitment to individual freedom and to broadened political participation.

In short, the forward movement of capitalist relations of production required a new definition of the rights and responsibilities of the individual and, as John C. Calhoun, George Fitzhugh, and other leading southerners understood, posed a powerful challenge to all previous ideas of an organic society within which some men assumed major responsibility for the lives and well-being of others. The bourgeoisie and the older landed classes eventually contended over the nature and destiny of human life. For centuries, political leaders deliberately obscured this issue and arranged compromises to deal with its manifestations. In the end, two irreconcilable world views met in combat, sometimes quickly or peacefully resolved and sometimes, as in the United States, resolved by a brutal test of physical strength.

But this struggle was not to be so clean-cut, if only because the wonderful new freedom bestowed upon the laboring classes carried with it a good dose of hunger, neglect, deprivation, misery, and death. The roots of the working-class democratic and socialist movement lay in the attempt of artisans and craftsmen to resist the destruction of their independent way of life and their absorption into the marketplace of labor. But by the middle of the nineteenth century, the struggle of the artisans and craftsmen had irrevocably been lost; its impulses and ideas of equality, fraternity, and democracy had passed into the working-class movement, most militantly into its socialist contingent.

Accordingly, the old landed classes faced ideological and political challenge both from bourgeois liberalism and from a proletarian socialism with origins in bourgeois thought but increasingly independent of it. Recall, therefore, the dire warnings of Calhoun, Fitzhugh, James Hammond, G. F. Holmes, Henry Hughes, and others that the bourgeoisie would rue the day it destroyed the landed classes and with them, a great bulwark against lower-class radicalism. And, in fact, in many countries the bourgeoisies did unite with their old landowning enemies to turn back the challenge from the Left. Still, in this unequal partnership, the bourgeoisie steadily strengthened its position as senior partner, and the landowners steadily surrendered their old way of life to become, in effect, a mere appendage of the capitalist class. The old organic relations among men disappeared, sometimes quickly, sometimes slowly as in the more patriarchal areas of the New South in which paternalism lingered well into the twentieth century, if only as an echo of a bygone era.

Even in such countries as Germany, Japan, and Italy, the upper-class coalition agreed upon the essential bourgeois principles of freedom of labor, at least in the marketplace sense, while it took a hard line against the democratic and egalitarian impulses that had themselves arisen within the earlier bourgeois revolutions.

Thus, even the most admirable and genuinely paternalistic of the old landed classes generally surrendered the best of their traditions, most notably, the organic view of society and the idea that men were responsible for each other, while they retained the worst of their traditions, most notably, their ever deepening arrogance and contempt for the laboring classes and darker races. These vices they offered as a gift to a triumphant bourgeoisie, which had acquired enough of the same already. The postbellum South provided a striking, if qualified, example of this worldwide reactionary tendency. The Calhouns and Fitzhughs might have been startled to learn that the great conservative coalition they had called for could come into being only after the destruction of their beloved plantation-slave regime. But it could not have been other; nor, despite appearances, was it other in Germany or Japan. In every case, the terms of the coalition had to include, as sine qua non, acceptance of bourgeois property relations and the hegemony of the marketplace, albeit qualified by authoritarianism and state regulation of the economy. In the United States the price was relatively low: the postbellum South suffered political reaction and economic stagnation, and the nation as a whole suffered from the strengthening of the conservative elements in its political life. But, on balance, the United States, more than any other country with the possible exception of England, successfully blended the classic bourgeois commitment to individual freedom with the more radical currents of democracy and mass participation in politics; and, in addition, it provided a high standard of material comfort.

To present the southern slaveholders as one of many landed classes arrayed against the progressive currents of the eighteenth and especially nineteenth centuries implies no identity or equation. As a class, the southern slaveholders had their own extraordinary virtues as well as vices and could not escape being American in their inheritance of traditions of freedom and democracy; indeed with justice they claimed to have helped shape those traditions. The constitutions of states like Mississippi ranked among the country's most democratic, and South Carolina's conservatism made it an exception among the slave states. The slave states maintained a degree of freedom of speech, assembly, and the press that might have been the envy of the people of much of Europe, a degree of freedom unheard-of in the rest of the world. Even most of the poorer white men had some access to politics and some effect on the formation of social policy. And if the white literacy rate and general educational standard opened the South to just abolitionist criticism, they still compared favorably with those of most other countries.

Hence, many learned and able historians have stressed the "Americanness" of the Old South and viewed its deviations from national norms as a mere regional variation on a common theme. And let it be conceded that by many useful criteria even the most reactionary elements of the slaveholding class had more in common with northern Americans of all classes than with the Russian boyars or Prussian Junkers.

This interpretation nonetheless loses sight of slavery's overwhelming impact on the South, of the dangerous political role it was playing in American national life, and of the fundamental historical tendency it represented. If world-historical processes of the nineteenth century are viewed as a coherent whole, then that cranky and sometimes insincere reactionary George Fitzhugh was right in seeing the slaveholding South as part of a great international counterrevolutionary movement against the spread of a bourgeois world order. The great problem for the most progressive, liberal, and democratically inclined slaveholders and other proslavery southerners was that the slavery question could not be isolated as a regional peculiarity occasioned by a special problem of racial adjustment.

Consider the basic question of political freedom. Foreign travelers often supported southern claims to being a liberal-spirited and tolerant people. What northern state, for example, was sending Jews to the United States Senate? The only drawback concerned abolitionist propaganda that threatened to unleash anarchy and blood-shed. And here, southern intolerance was neither paranoid nor ir-rational nor blindly Neanderthal; it represented a local version of the elementary principle of self-preservation. And here, the slaves themselves ruined their masters. No matter that they rose in insur-rection rarely and in small numbers. As the medieval scholastics insisted, existence proves possibility. However infrequent and mili-tarily weak the appearance of a Gabriel Prosser, a Denmark Vesey, or a Nat Turner, they and others like them did exist, and so, there-fore, did the danger of slave revolt. White southerners would have been mad to teach significant numbers of their slaves to read and write, to permit abolitionist literature to fall into their hands, to take an easy view of politicians, clergymen, and editors who so much as questioned the morality and justice of the very foundation of their social order and domestic peace. The economic, social, and political consequences of slavery ill served the mass of whites too, and agitation of the slavery question threatened to open a class struggle among whites. To that extent the slaveholders' actions were overdetermined.

On national terrain, slave-state politicians fought for the gag rule and thereby threatened the sacred right of petition. They had to advocate tampering with the mails, had to defend a measure of lynch law against people who talked too much, had to proclaim boldly that a free press could not safely be allowed to be too free, and had to offend northern sensibilities by demanding a fugitive-slave law that bluntly doubted the scrupulousness of the vaunted jury system. The slaveholders demonstrated time and time again that, despite their honest protestations of respect for freedom and even democracy, the exigencies of their social system were dragging them irresistibly toward political and social policies flagrantly ty-rannical, illiberal, and undemocratic, at least by American standards. No matter how much and how genuinely they tried to stand by their cherished Jeffersonian traditions, they were compelled, step by step, down the road charted by their most extreme theorists, for their commitment to survival as a ruling class as well as a master race left them less and less choice.

It was not necessary for the slaveholders and their supporters to embrace Fitzhugh's extreme doctrines; indeed, it is doubtful that they ever could or would have. Yet, the thoughtful Calhoun tried to reform the federal Constitution to make it safe for slavery, and younger politicians during the 1850s made desperate attempts to bully northern consent to increasingly unpalatable measures. From a northern perspective, slaveholding southerners, drunk with their near-absolute power over human beings, had become tyrannical, intransigent, and incapable of reasoned compromise. From a southern perspective, even friendly and moderate northerners were willing to acquiesce in measures that would threaten southern property and social order and, to make matters worse, were increasingly willing to view slavery as a kind of moral leprosy. Both sides were right in their own terms, for slavery had, as Tocqueville and others had warned, separated two great white American peoples even more deeply in moral perspective than in material interest. And moral separation, quite as readily as material, threatened confrontation and war once made manifest on political terrain.

We end then with the paradox that the southern slaveholders, who might have qualified for inclusion among the world's most liberal and even democratic ruling classes, qualified in the eyes of their northern fellow Americans as a grossly reactionary and undemocratic force, much as the hardened and retrograde landowners of Europe so qualified in the eyes of the liberal bourgeoisie. The southern slaveholders were doing in American terms what the English colonial slaveholders were doing when they threw their weight against parliamentary reform, what the French slaveholders in the colonies and the aristocrats at home were doing when they supported the counterrevolution, what the Prussian Junkers were doing when they demolished the liberal movement of 1848, and what the Russian boyars were doing when they suicidally refused to limit the imperial power. . . .

Barrington Moore, Jr.

THE AMERICAN CIVIL WAR: THE LAST CAPITALIST REVOLUTION

Barrington Moore, Jr.'s contribution to the debate on the causes of the Civil War is a chapter from his massive study of the transition to modern society by the major nations of the world today, *Social Origins of Dictatorship and Democracy* (1965). In Moore's view the Civil War established the United States as a liberal capitalist society, characterized by democratic values and a market economy. This path was similar to that taken by France and Britain, but it differed from the more conservative course of Bismarck's Germany and contrasted sharply with the transitions in Russia and China in the twentieth century.

Like Beard, Moore saw the Civil War as a conflict between classes and interests that happened to focus on the moral issue of slavery and to assume the particular form of a dispute between geographic regions. Unlike Beard, however, he employed some of the categories of Marxist analysis, though their application is far from strict. The upshot is a depiction of the Civil War in a comparative historical framework and in the context of social and economic developments in Europe and America during the nineteenth century.

Barrington Moore, Jr. (born 1913), is a sociologist who taught at Harvard University. His other influential books include *Political Power and Social Theory* (1965); *A Critique of Pure Tolerance*, with Robert Paul Wolff (1965); *Injustice: The Social Bases of Obedience and Revolt* (1978); and *Authority and Inequality Under Capitalism and Socialism* (1987).

Plantation and Factory: An Inevitable Conflict?

The main differences between the American route to modern capitalist democracy and those followed by England and France stem from America's later start. The United States did not face the problem of dismounting a complex and well-established agrarian society of either the feudal or the bureaucratic forms. From the very beginning commercial agriculture was important, as in the Virginian tobacco plantations, and rapidly became dominant as the country was settled. The political struggles between a precommercial landed aristocracy and a monarch were not part of American history. Nor has American society ever had a massive class of peasants comparable to those in Europe and Asia. For these reasons one may argue that American history contains no revolution comparable to the Puritan and French Revolutions nor, of course, the Russian and Chinese twentieth-century revolutions. Still there have been two great armed upheavals in our history, the American Revolution and the Civil War, the latter one of the bloodiest conflicts in modern history up to that time. Quite obviously, both have been significant elements in the way the United States became the world's leading industrial capitalist democracy by the middle of the twentieth century. The Civil War is commonly taken to mark a violent dividing point between the agrarian and industrial epochs in American history. . . . I shall discuss its causes and consequences from the standpoint of whether or not it was a violent breakthrough against an older social structure, leading to the establishment of political democracy, and on this score comparable to the Puritan and French Revolutions. More generally I hope to show where it belongs in the genetic sequence of major historical upheavals that we can begin arbitrarily with the sixteenth-century peasant wars in Germany, that continues through the Puritan, French, and Russian Revolutions, to culminate in the Chinese Revolution and the struggles of our own time.

The conclusion, reached after much uncertainty, amounts to the statement that the American Civil War was the last revolutionary offensive on the part of what one may legitimately call urban or bourgeois capitalist democracy. Plantation slavery in the South, it is well to add right away, was not an economic fetter upon industrial capitalism. If anything, the reverse may have been true; it helped to promote American industrial growth in the early stages. But slavery was an obstacle to a political and social democracy. There are ambiguities in this interpretation. Those that stem from the character of the evidence are best discussed as the analysis proceeds. Others lie deeper and, as I shall try to show . . . , would not disappear no matter what evidence came to light. . . .

The American Revolution can be trotted out from time to time as a good example of the American (or sometimes Anglo-Saxon) genius for compromise and conciliation. For this, the Civil War will not do; it cuts a bloody gash across the whole record.

Why did it happen? Why did our vaunted capacity for settling our differences fail us at this point? Like the problem of human evil and the fall of Rome for Saint Augustine, the question has long possessed a deep fascination for American historians. An anxious if understandable concern seems to underlie much of the discussion. For some time, it often took the form of whether or not the war was avoidable. The present generation of historians has begun to show impatience with this way of putting the problem. To many the question seems merely a semantic one, since if either side had been willing to submit without fighting there would have been no war. To call it a semantic problem dodges the real issue: why was there an unwillingness to submit on either side or both?

It may be helpful to put the question in less psychological terms. Was there in some objective sense a mortal conflict between the societies of the North and the South? The full meaning of this question will emerge more clearly from trying to answer it on the basis of specific facts than through theoretical discussion at this point. Essentially we are asking whether the institutional requirements for operating a plantation economy based on slavery clashed seriously at any point with the corresponding requirements for operating a capitalist industrial system. I assume that, in principle at any rate, it is possible to discover what these requirements really were in the same objective sense that a biologist can discover for any living organism the conditions necessary for reproduction and survival, such as specific kinds of nourishment, amounts of moisture, and the like. It should also be clear that the requirements or structural imperatives for plantation slavery and early industrial capitalism extend far beyond economic arrangements as such and certainly into the area of political institutions. Slave societies do not have the same political forms as those based on free labor. But, to return to our central question, is that any reason why they have to fight?

One might start with a general notion to the effect that there is an inherent conflict between slavery and the capitalist system of formally free wage labor. Though this turns out to be a crucial part of the story, it will not do as a general proposition from which the Civil War can be derived as an instance. As will appear shortly, cotton produced by slave labor played a decisive role in the growth not only of American capitalism but of English capitalism too. Capitalists had no objection to obtaining goods produced by slavery as long as a profit could be made by working them up and reselling them. From a strictly economic standpoint, wage labor and plantation slavery contain as much of a potential for trading and complementary political relationships as for conflict. We can answer our question with a provisional negative: there is no abstract general reason why the North and South had to fight. Special historical circumstances, in other words, had to be present in order to prevent agreement between an agrarian society based on unfree labor and a rising industrial capitalism.

For clues as to what these circumstances might have been, it is helpful to glance at a case where there was an agreement between these two types of subsocieties within a larger political unit. If we know what makes an agreement possible, we also know something about circumstances that might make it impossible. Once again the German record is helpful and suggestive. Nineteenth-century German history demonstrates quite clearly that advanced industry can get along very well with a form of agriculture that has a highly repressive system of labor. To be sure, the German Junker [large landowners in Prussia who played a dominant role in Bismarck's Germany] was not quite a slave owner. And Germany was not the United States. But where precisely did the decisive differences lie? The Junkers managed to draw the independent peasants under their wing and to form an alliance with sections of big industry that were happy to receive their assistance in order to keep the industrial workers in their place with a combination of repression and paternalism. The consequence in the long run was fatal to democracy in Germany.

German experience suggests that, if the conflict between North and South had been compromised, the compromise would have been at the expense of subsequent democratic development in the United States, a possibility that, so far as I am aware, no revisionist historian has explored. It also tells us where we might look with profit. Why did Northern capitalists have no need of Southern "Junkers" in order to establish and strengthen industrial capitalism in the United States? Were political and economic links missing in the United States that existed in Germany? Were there other and different groups in American society, such as independent farmers, in the place of peasants? Where and how were the main groups aligned in the American situation? It is time now to examine the American scene more closely. . . .

Toward an Explanation of the Causes of the War

The alignment of the main social groupings in American society in 1860 goes a long way toward explaining the character of the war, or the issues that could and could not come to the surface—more bluntly what the war could be about. It tells us what was likely *if* there was to be a fight; by itself the alignment does not account very well for *why* there actually was a fight. . . . [We shall now] discuss . . . the question of whether or not there was an inherent mortal conflict between North and South.

Let us take up the economic requirements of the two systems one by one in order of 1) capital requirements, 2) requirements for labor, and 3) those connected with marketing the final product.

Though the point is open to some dispute, it is possible to detect definite expansionist pressures in the plantation economy. Fresh virgin lands were necessary for the best profits. Thus there was some pressure on the side of capital requirements. There are corresponding indications that the labor supply was tight. More slaves would have been very helpful. Finally, to make the whole system work, cotton, and to a lesser extent other staples, had to fetch a good price in the international market.

Northern industry required a certain amount of assistance from the government in what might be called overhead costs of capital construction and the creation of a favorable institutional environment: a transportation system, a tariff, and a sufficiently tight currency so that debtors and small men generally did not have undue advantages. (Some inflation, on the other hand, that would keep prices moving up would probably be rather welcome, then as now.) On the side of labor, industry needed formally free wage laborers, though it is not easy to prove that free labor is necessarily superior to slavery in a factory system, except for the fact that someone has to have money in order to buy what industry produces. But perhaps that is a sufficient consideration. Finally, of course, growing industry did need an expanding market, provided still in those days quite largely by the agricultural sector. The West furnished much of this market and may be regarded as part of the North for the sake of this crude model.

It is difficult to perceive any really serious structural or "mortal" conflict in this analysis of the basic economic requirements, even though I have deliberately tried to bias the model in that direction. Here it is indispensable to remember, as revisionist historians of the Civil War correctly point out, that any large state is full of conflicts of interest. Tugging and hauling and quarreling and grabbing, along with much injustice and repression, have been the ordinary lot of human societies throughout recorded history. To put a searchlight on these facts just before a violent upheaval like the Civil War and call them the decisive causes of the war is patently misleading. To repeat, it would be necessary to show that compromise was impossible in the nature of the situation. From the analysis so far this does not seem to be the case. The most one can say along this line is that an increase in the area of slavery would have hurt the free farmers of the West badly. Although the areas where each kind of farming would pay were determined by climate and geography, no one could be sure where they were without trying. Still this factor alone does not seem sufficient to account for the war. Northern industry would have been as happy with a plantation market in the West as with any other, if such considerations were all that mattered, and the conflict could very likely have been ironed out. The other points of potential and actual conflict seem less serious. Northern requirements in the area of capital construction, the demand for internal improvements, a tariff, etc., cannot be regarded as threatening a crushing burden for the Southern economy. To be sure quite a number of marginal planters would have suffered, a factor of some importance. But if Southern society was run by the more successful planters, or if this influence was no more than very important, the smaller fry could have been sacrificed for the sake of a deal. In the question of slave labor versus free there was no real economic conflict because the areas were geographically distinct. Every account that I have come upon indicates that Northern labor was either lukewarm or hostile to the antislavery issue.

In addition to the conflict between free farmers in the West and the plantation system, about the strongest case one can make in strictly economic terms is that for the South secession was not an altogether unreasonable proposal mainly because the South did not need much that the North really had to offer. In the short run the North could not buy much more cotton than it did already. The most that the North could have offered would have been to reopen the slave trade. There was talk about taking over Cuba for slavery, and even some desultory action. As quite recent events have shown, under other circumstances such a move might be an extremely popular one in all parts of the country. At that time it seems to have been both impractical and impolitic.

To sum up, the strictly economic issues were very probably negotiable. Why, then, did the war happen? What was it about? The apparent inadequacy of a strictly economic explanation—I shall argue in a moment that the fundamental causes were still economic ones—has led historians to search for others. Three main answers are distinguishable in the literature. One is that the Civil War was fundamentally a moral conflict over slavery. Since large and influential sections of the public in both the North and the South refused to take a radical position either for or against slavery, this explanation runs into difficulties, in effect the ones that Beard and others tried to circumvent in their search for economic causes. The second answer tries to get around both sets of difficulties by the proposition that *all* the issues were really negotiable and that the blunderings of politicians brought on a war that the mass of the population in the North and in the South did not want. The third answer amounts to an attempt to push this line of thought somewhat further by analyzing how the political machinery for achieving consensus in American society broke down and allowed the war to erupt. In this effort, however, historians tend to be driven back toward an explanation in terms of moral causes.

Each of the explanations, including that stressing economic factors, can marshal a substantial body of facts in its support. Each has hit at a portion of the truth. To stop at this observation is to be satisfied with intellectual chaos. The task is to relate these portions of the truth to each other, to perceive the whole in order to understand the relationship and significance of partial truths. That such a search is endless, that the discovered relations are themselves only partial truths, does not mean that the search ought to be abandoned.

To return to the economic factors, it is misleading, if at times necessary, to take them separately from others with the traditional labels political, moral, social, etc. Similarly, it is a necessity for the sake of comprehensible exposition to break the issues down one by one in some other series—such as slavery as such, slavery in the territories, tariff, currency, railroads and other internal improvements, the alleged Southern tribute to the North. At the same time, the breakdown into separate categories partially falsifies what it describes because individual people were living through all these things at once, and persons who were apathetic about one issue could become excited about another. As the connection among issues became apparent, the concern spread among articulate people. Even if each individual issue had been negotiable, a debatable point, collectively and as a unit they were almost impossible to negotiate. And they were a unit, and so perceived by more than a few contemporaries, because they were manifestations of whole societies.

Let us begin the analysis afresh with this viewpoint in mind. Primarily for economic and geographical reasons, American social structure developed in different directions during the nineteenth century. An agrarian society based on plantation slavery grew up in the South. Industrial capitalism established itself in the Northeast and formed links with a society based on farming with family labor in the West. With the West, the North created a society and culture whose values increasingly conflicted with those of the South. The focal point of the difference was slavery. Thus we may agree with [Allan] Nevins that moral issues were decisive. But these issues are incomprehensible without the economic structures that created and supported them. Only if abolitionist sentiment had flourished in the South, would there be grounds for regarding moral sentiments as an independent factor in their own right.

The fundamental issue became more and more whether the machinery of the federal government should be used to support one society or the other. That was the meaning behind such apparently unexciting matters as the tariff and what put passion behind the Southern claim that it was paying tribute to the North. The question of power at the center was also what made the issue of slavery in the territories a crucial one. Political leaders knew that the admission of a slave state or a free one would tip the balance one way or another. The fact that uncertainty was an inherent part of the situation due to unsettled and partly settled lands to the West greatly magnified the difficulties of reaching a compromise. It was more and more necessary for political leaders on both sides to be alert to any move or measure that might increase the advantages of the other. In this larger context, the thesis of an attempted Southern veto on Northern progress makes good sense as an important cause of the war.

This perspective also does justice, I hope, to the revisionist thesis that it was primarily a politician's war, perhaps even an agitator's war, if the terms are not taken to be merely abusive epithets. In a complex society with an advanced division of labor, and especially in a parliamentary democracy, it is the special and necessary task of politicians, journalists, and only to a somewhat lesser extent clergymen to be alive and sensitive to events that influence the distribution of power in society. They are also the ones who provide the arguments, good and bad alike, both for changing the structure of society and for maintaining things as they are. Since it is their job to be alert to potential changes, while others keep on with the all-absorbing task of making a living, it is characteristic of a democratic system that politicians should often be clamorous and intensify division. The modern democratic politician's role is an especially paradoxical one, at least superficially. He does what he does so that most people do not have to worry about politics. For that same reason he often feels it necessary to arouse public opinion to dangers real and unreal.

From this standpoint too, the failure of moderate opinion to halt the drift to war becomes comprehensible. Men of substance in both North and South furnished the core of moderate opinion. They were the ones who in ordinary times are leaders in their own community—"opinion makers," a modern student of public opinion would be likely to call them. As beneficiaries of the prevailing order, and mainly interested in making money, they wanted to suppress the issue of slavery rather than seek structural reforms, a very difficult task in any case. The Clay-Webster Compromise of 1850 was a victory for this group. It provided for stricter laws in the North about the return of fugitive slaves and for the admission of several new states to the union: California as a free state, New Mexico and Utah at some future date with or without slavery as their constitutions might provide at the time of admission. Any attempt to drag the slavery issue out into the open and seek a new solution made large numbers of these groups cease being moderates. That is what happened when Senator Stephen A. Douglas put an end to the

Compromise of 1850 only four years later by reopening the question of slavery in the territories. Through proposing in the Kansas-Nebraska Act that the settlers decide the issue for themselves one way or the other, he converted, at least for the time being, wide sections of Northern opinion from moderation to views close to abolitionism. In the South, his support was not much more than lukewarm.

By and large the moderates had the usual virtues that many people hold are necessary to make democracy work: willingness to compromise and see the opponent's viewpoint, a pragmatic outlook. They were the opposite of doctrinaires. What all this really amounted to was a refusal to look facts in the face. Trying mainly to push the slavery issue aside, the moderates were unable to influence or control the series of events generated by the underlying situation. Crises such as the struggles over "bleeding Kansas," the financial panic of 1857, John Brown's melodramatic attempt to put himself at the head of a slave insurrection, and many others eroded the moderate position, leaving its members increasingly disorganized and confused. The practicality that tries to solve issues by patiently ignoring them, an attitude often complacently regarded as the core of Anglo-Saxon moderation, revealed itself as totally inadequate. An attitude, a frame of mind, without a realistic analysis and program is not enough to make democracy work even if a majority share this outlook. Consensus by itself means little; it depends what the consensus is about.

Finally, as one tries to perceive American society as a whole in order to grasp the causes and meaning of the war, it is useful to recall that searching for the sources of dissension necessarily obscures a major part of the problem. In any political unity that exists for a long time, there must be causes to produce the unity. There have to be reasons why men seek accommodation for their inevitable differences. It is difficult to find a case in history where two different regions have developed economic systems based on diametrically opposite principles and yet remained under a central government that retained real authority in both areas. I cannot think of any. In such a situation there would have to be very strong cohesive forces to counteract the divisive tendencies. Cohesive forces appear to have been weak in the midnineteenth century in the United States, though there is always the risk of exaggerating their weakness because the Civil War did happen.

Trade is an obvious factor that can generate links among various sections of a country. The fact that Southern cotton went mainly to England is almost certainly a very important one. It meant that the link with the North was so much the weaker. English partiality to the Southern cause during the war itself is well known. But it will not do to put too much weight on the direction of trade as an aspect of disunity. As pointed out earlier, Northern mills were beginning to use more cotton. When the Western market fell off sharply after the crash of 1857, New York merchants relied for a time more heavily on their Southern connections. In a word, the situation in trade was changing; had the war been averted, historians who look first for economic causes would have had no difficulty in finding an explanation.

Though the fact that cotton still linked the South with England more than with the North was significant, two other aspects of the situation may have been more important. One has already been mentioned: the absence of any strong radical working-class threat to industrial capitalist property in the North. Secondly, the United States had no powerful foreign enemies. In this respect, the situation was entirely different from that facing Germany and Japan, who both experienced their own versions of political modernization crises somewhat later, 1871 in Germany, 1868 in Japan. For this combination of reasons, there was not much force behind the characteristic conservative compromise of agrarian and industrial elites. There was little to make the owners of Northern mills and Southern slaves rally under the banner of the sacredness of property.

To sum up with desperate brevity, the ultimate causes of the war are to be found in the growth of different economic systems leading to different (but still capitalist) civilizations with incompatible stands on slavery. The connection between Northern capitalism and Western farming helped to make unnecessary for a time the characteristic reactionary coalition between urban and landed elites and hence the one compromise that could have avoided the war. (It was also the compromise that eventually liquidated the war.) Two further factors made compromise extremely difficult. The future of the West appeared uncertain in such a way as to make the distribution of power at the center uncertain, thus intensifying and magnifying all causes of distrust and contention. Secondly, as just noted, the main forces of cohesion in American society, though growing stronger, were still very weak. . . .

Gavin Wright

THE ECONOMICS OF COTTON, SLAVERY, AND THE CIVIL WAR

In this essay Gavin Wright, an economist, examines the role of economic considerations in the South's decision to secede. By contrast with the overarching interpretations of the Beards, the Genoveses and Moore, the economic questions that Wright tackles are more specific and focused, and they also lend themselves to statistical analysis.

After discussing such issues as soil exhaustion and the economic need for territorial expansion, the profitability of slavery, and the diminishing supply of slaves, Wright concludes that, by all measurable indicators, cotton prices were remarkably high in the late 1850s, and so were slave prices. Therefore, southern slaveowners wanted to resist at all costs any threat to the South's current and future prosperity, based as it was on the lucrative trade in cotton and slaves. Assumptions that slavery would die out in the near future were unrealistic. So, according to Wright, historians are mistaken in thinking that the slave system was in economic crisis before the Civil War. Also unsound are assertions that, because slavery was unviable, the effort to restrict its expansion and growth was overzealous, and possibly even needless.

Gavin Wright (born 1943) teaches at Stanford University. In addition to *The Political Economy of the Cotton South* (1978), from which this excerpt is taken, he has written the prize-winning *Old South, New South: Revolutions in the Southern Economy Since the Civil War* (1986).

Economic interpretations of the Civil War have come and gone over the years. They appear most often nowadays in partnership with loosely defined concepts like "modernization," whose links to economic structure are rather distant and diffuse. But the concerns over economic prospects and economic threats were so immediate and so prominent in the political debates of the 1850s that it is difficult to believe that the role of economics was so remote. This . . . [essay] argues that the current dissatisfaction with economic

Reprinted from THE POLITICAL ECONOMY OF THE COTTON SOUTH, *Households, Markets, and Wealth in the Nineteenth Century,* by Gavin Wright, by permission of W. W. Norton & Company, Inc. Copyright © 1978 by W. W. Norton & Company, Inc.

analyses of the war stems from an inappropriate conception of what an economic interpretation should be. No reasonable historical explanation should characterize individuals as motivated solely by the pursuit of economic gain. Nor is it reasonable to view the sections as though they were negotiating and fighting over aggregate economic costs and benefits, because the political leadership had neither the means nor the desire to calculate and pursue such collective goals. Instead, the main task of an economic interpretation should be to show how the structure of economic interests and incentives encouraged individuals to mobilize politically, and how an underlying logic of interests and coalitions led political representatives to pursue certain lines of action.

This is an ambitious program, which is by no means completed here. But . . . [a preliminary analysis suggests the following]: In both North and South, politics were heavily influenced by the interests of propertyholders. However, there were decisive differences in the processes by which property values were determined in the two regions, and in the resulting incentives for economic and political behavior. In the North, property rights in labor were prohibited, and, hence, efforts to augment property values focused on land: land clearing and improvement, promotion of canals and railroads to improve access to markets, attracting immigrants through vigorous recruitment and offers of credit, schools, roads, etc. In the South one could own slaves, and for this reason much of the same drive toward property accumulation was channeled along very different lines. In the North energies went toward raising the value of particular farms and local areas because land is not moveable; in the South there was relatively little a slaveowner could do to raise the value of individual slaves, though he could hope to accumulate slave property over time by fostering high fertility and low mortality. Slaves were moveable personal property; the value of an owner's slave property was determined not by his individual behavior and local development, but by regional slave markets and world cotton markets, and this value was essentially uniform in all parts of the slave South at any moment. As prices rose to levels well above the costs of replacement, concern for slave property values moved mainly into the realm of regional psychology, distinctively sensitive to expectations and fears about the economic and political future. Seen in this light, Southern political behavior did make economic

Sale of Slaves and Stock.

The Negroes and Stock listed below, are a Prime Lot, and belong to the ESTATE OF THE LATE LUTHER McGOWAN, and will be sold on Monday, Sept. 22nd, 1852, at the Fair Grounds, in Savannah, Georgia, at 1:00 P. M. The Negroes will be taken to the grounds two days previous to the Sale, so that they may be inspected by prospective buyers.

On account of the low prices listed below, they will be sold for cash only, and must be taken into custody within two hours after sale.

No.	Name.	Age.	Remarks.	Price.
1	Lunesta	27	Prime Rice Planter,	$1,275.00
2	Violet	16	Housework and Nursemaid,	900.00
3	Lizzie	30	Rice, Unsound,	300.00
4	Minda	27	Cotton, Prime Woman,	1,200.00
5	Adam	28	Cotton, Prime Young Man,	1,100.00
6	Abel	41	Rice Hand, Eyesight Poor,	675.00
7	Tanney	22	Prime Cotton Hand,	950.00
8	Flementina	39	Good Cook, Stiff Knee,	400.00
9	Lanney	34	Prime Cottom Man,	1,000.00
10	Sally	10	Handy in Kitchen,	675.00
11	Maccabey	35	Prime Man, Fair Carpenter,	980.00
12	Dorcas Judy	25	Seamstress, Handy in House,	800.00
13	Happy	60	Blacksmith,	575.00
14	Mowden	15	Prime Cotton Boy,	700.00
15	Bills	21	Handy with Mules,	900.00
16	Theopolis	39	Rice Hand, Gets Fits,	575.00
17	Coolidge	29	Rice Hand and Blacksmith,	1,275.00
18	Bessie	69	Infirm, Sews,	250.00
19	Infant	1	Strong Likely Boy	400.00
20	Samson	41	Prime Man, Good with Stock,	975.00
21	Callie May	27	Prime Woman, Rice,	1,000.00
22	Honey	14	Prime Girl, Hearing Poor,	850.00
23	Angelina	16	Prime Girl, House or Field,	1,000.00
24	Virgil	21	Prime Field Hand,	1,100.00
25	Tom	40	Rice Hand, Lame Leg,	750.00
26	Noble	11	Handy Boy,	900.00
27	Judge Lesh	55	Prime Blacksmith,	800.00
28	Booster	43	Fair Mason, Unsound,	600.00
29	Big Kate	37	Housekeeper and Nurse,	950.00
30	Melie Ann	19	Housework, Smart Yellow Girl,	1,250.00
31	Deacon	26	Prime Rice Hand,	1,000.00
32	Coming	19	Prime Cotton Hand,	1,000.00
33	Mabel	47	Prime Cotton Hand,	800.00
34	Uncle Tim	60	Fair Hand with Mules,	600.00
35	Abe	27	Prime Cotton Hand,	1,000.00
36	Tennes	29	Prime Rice Hand and Cocahman,	1,250.00

There will also be offered at this sale, twenty head of Horses and Mules with harness, along with thirty head of Prime Cattle. Slaves will be sold separate, or in lots, as best suits the purchaser. Sale will be held rain or shine.

Notice of a slave sale, 1852. This list shows how slaves were described as merchandise for sale and how a dollar value was estimated and then attached to each of them. It also indicates that they were to be sold "separate, or in lots" and therefore without any consideration for whether they were related to each other. (*Chicago Historical Society*) sense in immediate and not just in long-run terms. It will be helpful to begin with a discussion of some of the standard economic interpretations and why they are unsatisfactory.

Direct Economic Conflicts Between North and South

One historical tradition, dating back to the work of Charles and Mary Beard, draws a distinction between slavery and economic issues, treating the first as a moral issue, the second primarily as the conflict between agrarian and industrial interests. It is not easy to find North-South issues on economic policy that are separable from slavery, and one suspects that Beard's emphasis on the tariff as the nub of discontent arises at least partially by default. Southern rhetoricians generally complained about the tariff and other allegedly biased federal subsidies to Northern business and shipping interests, but one must remember that those men, too, had a difficult time finding overt examples of the Northern "oppression" that they complained of so strenuously. Most recent writers have simply been unwilling to believe that such issues as the tariff, banking, and internal improvements can bear the weight of explaining the bloody conflict of the 1860s. Not only was neither region unified on these matters, but each one seems to have been greatly defused and compromised by the 1850s. A survey of federal legislation of sectional interest passed during that decade shows no general trend for or against either region, and something of an increase in Southern influence on Congressional committees and the Supreme Court. To be sure, such economic disputes as the nullification crisis of 1832 may have contributed in a general way to the rise of regional consciousness in the South, but even for this case, [William W.] Freehling has shown that slavery was lurking not far below the surface.

However, there is no good reason why economic interpretations of the war should eschew the economics of slavery. There is one potential economic cause of regional conflict that continues to have a following: the claim that the slave economy depended upon continued acquisition of fresh land, and that this expansionism was on an inevitable collision course with the desires of free white Northern settlers. The doctrine that slavery had to expand or die was of course part of the rhetoric of some politicians in the 1850s; it received scholarly support from the British economist J. E. Cairnes [in 1863], and in recent times has been defended by such dissimilar writers as Eugene Genovese and the economists [Alfred] Conrad and [John R.] Meyer. This is a tempting hypothesis on several counts, among which is that it seems to flow naturally from the very definition of slavery as capitalized labor. Whereas in the free labor economy of the North, westward expansion threatened to hurt eastern business by driving up the wages of labor, in the South planters were in a position to capture the benefits of more expensive labor, in the form of higher slave prices. Thus, the North was economically of two minds about territorial expansion, but the South had an interest in expansion that unified east and west.

The problem with this logically sound argument is that it just doesn't work. Whatever the importance of expansion to slaveholders, there is no evidence to indicate that they were "feeling the pinch" of land shortage in the 1850s. Supplies of untouched cotton land were vast within the 1860 boundaries of the slave states, as Cairnes himself recognized: "For nearly a quarter of a century— ever since the annexation of Texas—the territory at the disposal of the South has been much greater than its available slave force has been able to cultivate; and its most urgent need has now become, not more virgin soils on which to employ its slaves, but more slaves for the cultivation of its virgin soils." If we ask what microeconomic pressures might have been generated by land shortage, we find that, in fact, improved acreage was growing more rapidly than population in every cotton state; the rise in land values reflected these ongoing improvements and the prosperity of the cotton boom—only the relatively small fraction of the population that owned no land before the boom could view this rising wealth as an economic squeeze in any objective sense. And in light of the evidence of rising average land values, can we reasonably believe that Southerners were politically agitated over soil exhaustion in the midst of the spectacular cotton yields of the late 1850s?

In short, the land-expansion hypothesis as argued by Cairnes and his followers is an economic *Hamlet* without the prince. At most, it could explain the emergence of sectional conflict over a much longer time period, but not the intensification of these conflicts during the 1850s. Even for the longer period, it is not clear that slaveholders on balance stood to gain from a more rapid westward expansion of Southern agriculture, because of the unique place of American cotton in the world markets. Any slaveowner could find a buyer for his slaves if he chose to; the relevant question is whether westward expansion tended, as Cairnes believed, to raise the price of slaves. For this calculation, one has to set the effects of additional land on productivity against the effects of additional cotton on the cotton price. One simulation experiment estimates the positive elasticity at .32 (percentage change in output/percentage change in land), the negative elasticity between −.439 and −.495 during the period 1830 to 1860. Such a calculation can only be the roughest approximation to the actual net effects, but when one recalls that it neglects entirely any effects on southeastern land values or free labor supplies, it becomes still more difficult to maintain that the South had reason to be any more unified on expansion than the North.

Now one may argue that these economic effects were not all equally visible at the time, but the effects of policies on the price of cotton were certainly not outside the attention of planters. For example, in 1829 when Senator Robert Hayne of South Carolina delivered his first speech opposing the tariff and advocating a cheap land-sales policy, he was criticized at home on precisely these grounds, for "supporting a measure infinitely more destructive [than the tariff] to the interests of his constituents." In the 1830s and 1840s the South showed no unity on the issues of territorial expansion and the distribution of public lands. A study by Dean Yarwood of the lines of cleavage in the Congress of 1850 shows that "the question of the disposition of western lands was an entirely separate dimension" from the North-South sectional split. (This was not true in 1860, by which time the crisis had deepened to the point where the votes on almost every issue divided on sectional lines.) As late as 1854, the South divided on the Homestead Act along east-west and party lines (and according to whether or not a state had public lands within its boundaries), almost as markedly as the North. Again and again the South seems not to have been united on any economic policies, even those connected with slavery, but only on the issue of slavery *qua* slavery; it was the sectional crisis over slavery that conveyed regional unity onto economic legislation and other issues.

Having found these actual economic conflicts insubstantial, many writers, including Yarwood, conclude that it must have been the apprehension of future policies on economics and slavery that led the South to secede. This argument is difficult to refute, but it is rendered suspect by the fact that it often seems to be reached by precisely this process of logical elimination. It is true enough that the Republican platform of 1860 contained an economic program not altogether to Southern liking; but none of these proposals was new, and it was, after all, the South's bolting of the Democratic party in 1860 that made Lincoln's election inevitable. One can find statements reflecting all sorts of apprehensions and fears, but there is also an abundance of contradictory testimony, and unless it can be shown that these fears manifested themselves in actual behavior or pressures or incentives, or in some way reflected a perception of real trends, the argument is unconvincing. . . .

The Profitability of Slavery Once More

If the profitability of slavery is accepted, explanations based specifically on the notion that slaveowners were losing money can be ruled out. But this agreement does not take us far, and the precise meaning of the statement "slavery was profitable" makes a great deal of difference. Following Conrad and Meyer, a number of studies have attempted to estimate the rate of return on investment in slave property by comparing the market price of slaves to a hypothetical stream of returns over a hypothetical future. As [Yasuhichi] Yasuba and [Richard] Sutch argued, this is no test of the viability of slavery, but only a measure of the appropriateness of the capitalization of the income stream—a test that can never be conclusive, once we recall that the income stream is a hypothetical expected one. Yasuba's analysis is depicted in [the diagram on page 161]: in each year the price of slaves is determined by the interaction of a demand curve with an inelastic supply curve, because, after the closing of the African slave trade, the aggregate slave labor supply could not be increased in response to higher prices, except over time. The observed slave price was in fact well above the long-run cost of rearing new slaves, and the difference between the two accrued as a capitalized rent to the owner of the slave at the time of birth. Slave prices rose steadily over time, to levels far above the rearing cost, and indeed were never higher than on the eve of the Civil War.*

*For simplicity, the diagram abstracts from the dimension of *time,* but of course each year's rearing costs must be appropriately compounded to reflect the interval between birth and prime age (if this is the standard).

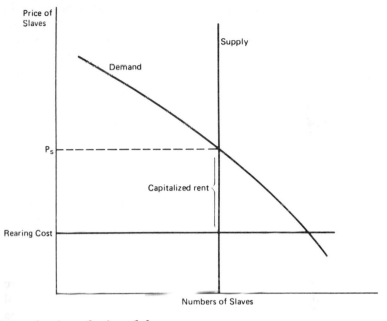

Determination of price of slaves.

The point is not just that the real proof of profitability is the high slave prices themselves, but that the rising profitability is *embodied* in the higher prices. In the abstract, there is little point in sharply differentiating between the slaveholders' interest in annual earnings on his crops and in the value of his slave property, because slave prices will reflect the expected stream of future earnings from the use of slave labor. For similar reasons, economists frequently use the change in land values as a measure of the benefits of transportation improvements. In reality, of course, there was great variability among slaveholders in realized earnings and presumably in expectations as well; but the capital gains from rising slave prices were sufficient to make financial successes of all but the most incompetent slaveowners. The fact is that virtually every slaveholder who was careful enough to keep his slaves alive made at least a normal profit during the 1850s from capital gains alone. One may argue that these slave prices were too high, and that they would have had to fall, . . . but there is no gainsaying the historical fact that up to the moment of secession, slaveholders' wealth had continued to grow to levels that were truly staggering in comparison with the average wealth of any other significant group in the population. Some historians continue to advance the absurd proposition that slaveholders were being "squeezed" by high slave prices, and that the development created a divergence of interest between "young, rising slaveholders" and "older, established" slaveholders. Slaves were bought and slaves were sold, but slaveholders as a class were being enriched, and even the smallest holder would find his financial portfolio dominated by the value of his slave property. Of course, the higher prices meant that nonslaveholders had more difficult access to the slaveowning class: but this was at most an opportunity foregone or deferred, and however resentful they might have felt about their position, these were not the men who made the secessionist revolution.

Once we understand that the essence of the profitability of slavery was the financial value of slave property, certain things fall into place. One implication is that profitability was enjoyed by every slaveholder, large and small, in every part of the South. The reasons for the high prices have to do with trends in cotton, but the capital gains extended to owners who had nothing to do with cotton— because, unlike land and unlike free labor, slaves were moveable and saleable and their value was determined in an efficient region-wide market independently of local crops, local productivity, and local development. To some historians it may seem self-evident that profitability studies that emphasize regional distinctions and variations are more sophisticated than an aggregate analysis, but in this case the most fundamental elements of the profitability are aggregate in their very nature. The value of slave property was a great unifying factor for the South, and an economic interest, largely separate from the interest in the success of southern agriculture, developed around these values. Edward Phifer, a close student of slaveowners' thinking, makes the following observation:

> One thing which has tended to lead scholars astray in their analysis of the economics of slavery has been their failure to probe the mind of the slaveholder. What must be understood is that the slaveholder was not at heart an investor; he was a speculator. His primary interest

was not in yearly income on an investment; his primary interest was in appreciation. . . . [T]hrough capital accumulation he hoped to endow his progeny for generations to come.

In context, it is clear that Phifer does not mean to suggest that slaveholders were looking for a quick sale, nor that they had no concern for yearly output: the situation envisaged is perhaps similar to homeownership today—most families buy one house to live in and do not frequently buy and sell in response to fluctuations in price; yet these households maintain an active and sometimes intense interest in the value of their homes.

Phifer was writing about Burke County, North Carolina: does his statement merely reflect the outlook of those in the slave-breeding states of the Old South? Certainly the relative importance of capital gains was not the same everywhere, but there is evidence that the differences between Southeast and Southwest were not great in this respect, and it is a fundamental error to believe that southwestern slaveowners had a countervailing interest in low slave prices. As we shall see, their political behavior reveals an equally intense concern for maintaining slave values. Across the South, slaveholders formed a class of great wealth with a distinctive unity of economic interest—not necessarily on policies concerning the economics of slavery, but in slavery itself. One notes the contrast with the farmers' movement of the late nineteenth century, for which unity was impossible because farmers' financial situations and economic interests varied widely, depending on crops, location, distance to markets, etc. The slave South had a unifying economic interest that transcended differences such as these. It is difficult to think of historical cases that are remotely comparable, and so perhaps it should not be altogether surprising that the resulting political behavior reflects a different logic from that which we are used to.

The evidence does support the view that secession was essentially a slaveholders' movement. Ralph A. Wooster has exhaustively tracked down 1,780 of the 1,859 delegates to the fifteen secession conventions of 1860–61. He found that delegates voting for secession were more likely to be slaveholders than those voting against, but this difference was not nearly as decisive as the striking correlation between the proportion of slaves in a county's population and the likelihood of that county's voting for secession. However, there is little basis in Wooster's evidence for a claim that large slaveholders were more likely to favor secession than small. Almost all of the opposition to secession came from counties with very few slaves. Granted that each state had a political setting of its own and that, in some of these, certain nonslaveholding areas may have cast the key votes; nonetheless, when the issue came down to a vote, it was clear enough where the slaveholders stood.

Making Economic Sense of the Politics of Slavery

The task of explaining the apparently irrational policies of secession and the regional aggressiveness that led up to secession remains. To understand the logic of this behavior, we have to remember that the price of slaves did not reflect an observable intrinsic value of slave labor, but an expectation of future returns. With slave values so far above cost-determined levels, it is no exaggeration to say that the determination of slave prices was essentially a psychological matter, albeit a psychology influenced by trends in cotton prices and production. The value of slave property was highly sensitive to changes in expectations, not so much in erratic year-to-year movements as in slower changes in long-term expectations about the future. [Robert W.] Fogel and [Stanley L.] Engerman's calculations contain the important implication that three-fourths of the slave price rise in the lower South between the late 1840s and the late 1850s is attributable to changes in expectations. The two distinctive dimensions of slave values—their psychological nature and their region-wide character—are essential to understanding the political behavior of slaveowners. They imply that every political discussion of slavery was an event that could affect the value of every slave-holders' property. Slaveholders had to worry, not just about the objective reality of Northern threats to slavery, but about the fears of these attacks harbored by their fellow owners.

This is very different from an argument based on slaveholder pessimism about the economic and political future. In light of the high and rising slave prices, so heavily weighted by expectations and confidence, it is difficult to credit interpretations based on a "mood of despair," a "sense of desperation," or even an "uneasiness about economic prospects" at the time of secession. If it is thought unreasonably abstract and simplified to subsume all Southern expectations into one "index of sanguinity," it should also be recorded that every systematic survey of opinion in the 1850s finds that expectations were favorable. A wide range of opinions may be found, but "in sheer numbers the optimists dwarf the pessimists," and the majority entered secession contemplating the "Great and Increased Prosperity of the South and the Brilliant Future Which Is Opening Upon Her." Genovese argues that slaveowners were not moved as much by narrow economic interest as by their commitment to maintaining a whole complex of social relationships; but it is difficult to distinguish broad from narrow motives when the two agree, as they do in this case, and it seems clear that most slaveowners did not feel pressured to choose between class preservation and immediate economic interests. As Professor [C. F.] McCay of South Carolina wrote on the eve of the Civil War: "Never before has the planting been more profitable than in the last few years . . . the planters have been everywhere rich, prosperous and happy."

The only dark cloud on the horizon was the threat of interference with slavery by the North. But slave prices reflected expectations with respect to the political as well as the economic future of slavery. Undoubtedly some slaveowners believed that Lincoln or a more radical successor meant to tamper with slavery; but to the extent that they did so believe, the evidence suggests that they did not fear Lincoln would be successful. They believed, in other words, that secession would succeed, and many believed that it would succeed peacefully. The main pillar under these beliefs was King Cotton thinking—the notion that the South, "safely entrenched behind her cotton bags . . . can defy the world—for the civilized world depends on the cotton of the South." Secessionist convention debate revealed widespread acceptance of the idea that the North could not possibly risk war on cotton, and, if she did, England would have to intervene on the side of the South. Some historians seem to believe that these arguments were largely concocted by secessionist agitators who did not really believe them, but even if this were so, the assurances were effective. Channing asserts that the overwhelming majority of South Carolinians believed in the imminence of a peaceful acquiescence by the North. As Mrs. Caroline Gilman wrote to her daughters in 1860, "Civil War was *foreign to the original plan.*"

The explanation for secession, then, is simply that slaveholders owned extremely valuable property and were not only enjoying prosperity but expected their good fortune to continue; the only serious threat to this situation was Northern interference with slavery; and it was widely believed that a straightforward safeguard against such interference was available—peaceful secession. On the basis of this evidence, we cannot and do not wish to rule out the contention that events were influenced by the actions of an elite minority, which consciously desired separation for irrational reasons or which did harbor long-run fears about the viability of slavery in the Union. But if this is the case, we can still say that the social basis for the success of their movement was the optimistic outlook of the majority. These judgments were of course mistaken, but they were based on a rational reading of the objective situation, and were supported by the extreme fears often voiced in England about the implications of a cutoff of cotton supply, and by the assurances of noninterference that flowed in from the "very highest political circles of the North." They also rested on the accurate perception that the North had no strong economic reasons to fight a war over slavery. Explaining the postsecession response of the North is more of a challenge to an economic historian than explaining secession itself.

But it is misleading to focus only on the prosperous year of 1860, because the political crisis of that year was only the culmination of years of bitter intersectional conflict. We still have to explain why Southerners went to extremes in insisting on absolute guarantees of their rights by the federal government everywhere in the Union. Why did they help to create an antislavery monster by brazenly chasing a handful of runaway slaves around the country, when the fugitive issue was acknowledged to be "not of the slightest consequence" as a practical matter? Why were they bent on squashing the slightest murmur of antislavery sentiment in the South? With so much to conserve, why weren't they more conservative?

Even these extremes of Southern behavior may be viewed as consistent with the basically economic motive of maintaining the value of slave property, when we remember that the value of slave property was so thoroughly dependent on expectations and confidence. Such a financial asset involves external effects of region-wide scope: even if *I* attach no importance whatsoever to fugitive slave legislation as it affects my own slaves, if I think that *you* (any nontrivial number of slaveowners or buyers) attach some importance to it, then the issue affects me financially and I have good reason to become a political advocate of strong guarantees. Thus, slaveowner concern for symbolic issues and remote territorial affairs need not reflect exaggerated fears of a general breakdown of slave discipline or hypersensitivity to inferred slights on their character, but immediate financial concern for the value of their property. Consider, for example, the following quotation from the *Charleston Mercury* (October 11, 1860), on the effects of the election of a Republican president:

> . . . thousands of slaveholders will despair of the institution. While the conditions of things in the [border] states will force their slaves on the markets of the cotton states, the timid of the cotton states will also sell their slaves. The general distrust, must affect purchasers. The consequence must be, slave property must be greatly depreciated. . . . We suppose, that taking in view all these things, it is not extravagant to estimate, that the submission of the South to the administration of the Federal Government under Messrs. Lincoln and Hamlin, must reduce the value of slaves in the South, one hundred dollars each.

Note that the writer makes no assertion about what Lincoln would do, and obviously believes that actual difficulties would be faced only on the border: but the $100 loss would be felt by every single slaveholder.

The closest analogy today is the behavior of homeowners. A house is typically the largest asset owned by a family—indeed families are usually heavily in debt if they buy a house—and here also the value of the property depends on the opinions and prejudices of others. In this case as well, prejudice and intolerance are intensified by market forces. *I* may not really care whether a black family moves next door, but, if I feel that others care, I will be under financial pressure to share their views or at least to act as though I do. The main differences between the housing case and slavery are that many owners held more than one slave, and that for slavery these were not "neighborhood effects" limited to a small geographic area but system-wide externalities, so that a threat to slavery anywhere was a threat to slaveowners everywhere. The effect was to greatly exacerbate the response to any threat.

Once this mechanism is understood, it begins to make economic sense for the South to have been so concerned with the letter of the law, and it becomes more understandable that slavery could not stand criticism on moral grounds. The strength of the argument is that it is not based on an exclusively economic nor exclusively rational conception of motivation and behavior. Fears, racism, misperceptions, and long-run strategic calculations all undoubtedly did exist. The point is that economic forces served to intensify every other motive for the South's insistence on guarantees of the rights of slaveholders and even the quest for a virtual moral endorsement of slavery by the North. The argument does not imply that Southern politicians were scrutinizing slave prices in their every action; but the widespread concern over property values created a situation in which an ambitious politician could easily mobilize a constituency by strongly insisting on absolute guarantees for slaveowners' rights. And was it coincidental that the suppression of internal antislavery opinion coincided, not just with the rise of abolitionism, but with the first great boom in cotton and slave prices in the mid-1830s? . . .

Cultural and Ideological Origins of the Sectional Conflict

Eric Foner

POLITICS, IDEOLOGY, AND THE ORIGINS OF THE CIVIL WAR

In his *Free Soil, Free Labor, Free Men* (1970), Eric Foner made an important contribution to the debate over the origins of the Civil War. The following essay distills the argument in his book, which is that the stance of the newly formed Republican party toward slavery and the South was so firmly held and internally consistent that it amounted, in essence, to an ideology. A worldview of this kind could not easily yield or compromise, as the South eventually realized.

The ramifications of Foner's insight about the Republicans are twofold. First, American political parties are not by nature pragmatic and opportunistic. They can be programmatic and principled and still win national elections. Second, ideas and issues were so powerful in the 1850s that the political system proved unable to manage them. The problem did not stem from the failure of the politicians or the political system to perform their assigned task of settling disputes. Rather, the disagreement in this case was so fundamental and intense that it defied resolution. Foner's contention that the ideological conflicts of the 1850s shattered the political parties is contested by Michael F. Holt's piece on pp. 90–113.

Besides *Free Soil, Free Labor, Free Men*, Eric Foner (born 1943) has written the prize-winning *Reconstruction: America's Unfinished Revolution, 1863–1877* (1988); *Nothing But Freedom: Emancipation and Its Legacy* (1983); and a collection of his own essays, *Politics and Ideology in the Age of the Civil War* (1980). He teaches at Columbia University.

It has long been an axiom of political science that political parties help to hold together diverse, heterogeneous societies like our own. Since more major parties in American history have tried, in Seymour

Eric Foner, "Politics, Ideology, and the Origins of the Civil War," from *Nation Divided: Essays on the Civil War & Reconstruction,* edited by George M. Fredrickson, 1975 Burgess Publishers. Reprinted with permission of Eric Foner.

Lipset's phrase, to "appear as plausible representatives of the whole society," they have been broad coalitions cutting across lines of class, race, religion, and section. And although party competition requires that there be differences between the major parties, these differences usually have not been along sharp ideological lines. In fact, the very diversity of American society has inhibited the formation of ideological parties, for such parties assume the existence of a single line of social division along which a majority of the electorate can be mobilized. In a large, heterogeneous society, such a line rarely exists. There are, therefore, strong reasons why, in a two-party system, a major party—or a party aspiring to become "major"—will eschew ideology, for the statement of a coherent ideology will set limits to the groups in the electorate to which the party can hope to appeal. Under most circumstances, in other words, the party's role as a carrier of a coherent ideology will conflict with its role as an electoral machine bent on winning the largest possible number of votes.

For much of the seventy years preceding the Civil War, the American political system functioned as a mechanism for relieving social tensions, ordering group conflict, and integrating the society. The existence of national political parties, increasingly focused on the contest for the Presidency, necessitated alliances between political elites in various sections of the country. A recent study of early American politics notes that "political nationalization was far ahead of economic, cultural, and social nationalization"—that is, that the national political system was itself a major bond of union in a diverse, growing society. But as North and South increasingly took different paths of economic and social development and as, from the 1830s onward, antagonistic value systems and ideologies grounded in the question of slavery emerged in these sections, the political system inevitably came under severe disruptive pressures. Because they brought into play basic values and moral judgments, the competing sectional ideologies could not be defused by the normal processes of political compromise, nor could they be contained within the existing inter-sectional political system. Once parties began to reorient themselves on sectional lines, a fundamental necessity of democratic politics—that each party look upon the other as a legitimate alternative government—was destroyed.

When we consider the causes of the sectional conflict, we must ask ourselves not only why civil war came when it did, but why it did not come sooner. How did a divided nation manage to hold itself together for as long as it did? In part, the answer lies in the unifying effects of inter-sectional political parties. On the level of politics, the coming of the Civil War is the story of the intrusion of sectional ideology into the political system, despite the efforts of political leaders of both parties to keep it out. Once this happened, political competition worked to exacerbate, rather than to solve, social and sectional conflicts. For as Frank Sorauf has explained:

> The party of extensive ideology develops in and reflects the society in which little consensus prevails on basic social values and institutions. It betokens deep social disagreements and conflicts. Indeed, the party of ideology that is also a major, competitive party accompanies a politics of almost total concern. Since its ideology defines political issues as including almost every facet of life, it brings to the political system almost every division, every difference, every conflict of any importance in society.

"Parties in this country," wrote a conservative northern Whig in 1855, "heretofore have helped, not delayed, the slow and difficult growth of a consummated nationality." Rufus Choate was lamenting the passing of a bygone era, a time when "our allies were everywhere . . . there were no Alleghenies nor Mississippi rivers in our politics." Party organization and the nature of political conflict had taken on new and unprecedented forms in the 1850s. It is no accident that the breakup of the last major inter-sectional party preceded by less than a year the breakup of the Union or that the final crisis was precipitated not by any "overt act," but by a presidential election.

From the beginning of national government, of course, differences of opinion over slavery constituted an important obstacle to the formation of a national community. "The great danger to our general government," as Madison remarked at the Constitutional Convention, "is the great southern and northern interests of the continent, being opposed to each other." "The institution of slavery and its consequences," according to him, was the main "line of discrimination" in convention disputes. As far as slavery was concerned, the Constitution amply fulfilled Lord Acton's [a famous nineteenth-century British historian] dictum that it was an effort to avoid settling basic questions. Aside from the Atlantic slave trade, Congress was given no power to regulate slavery in any way—the framers' main intention seems to have been to place slavery completely outside the national political arena. The only basis on which a national politics could exist—the avoidance of sectional issues— was thus defined at the outset.

Although the slavery question was never completely excluded from political debate in the 1790s, and there was considerable Federalist grumbling about the three-fifths clause of the Constitution after 1800, the first full demonstration of the political possibilities inherent in a sectional attack on slavery occurred in the Missouri controversy of 1819–21. These debates established a number of precedents which forecast the future course of the slavery extension issue in Congress. Most important was the fact that the issue was able for a time to completely obliterate party lines. In the first votes on slavery in Missouri, virtually every northerner, regardless of party, voted against expansion. It was not surprising, of course, that northern Federalists would try to make political capital out of the issue. What was unexpected was that northern Republicans, many of whom were aggrieved by Virginia's long dominance of the Presidency and by the Monroe administration's tariff and internal improvements policies, would unite with the Federalists. As John Quincy Adams observed, the debate "disclosed a secret: it revealed the basis for a new organization of parties. . . . Here was a new party really formed . . . terrible to the whole Union, but portentously terrible to the South." But the final compromise set another important precedent: enough northern Republicans became convinced that the Federalists were making political gains from the debates and that the Union was seriously endangered to break with the sectional bloc and support a compromise which a majority of northern Congressmen—Republicans and Federalists—opposed. As for the Monroe administration, its semiofficial spokesman, the *National Intelligencer,* pleaded for a return to the policy of avoiding sectional issues, even to the extent of refusing to publish letters which dealt in any way with the subject of slavery.

The Missouri controversy and the election of 1824, in which four candidates contested the Presidency, largely drawing support from their home sections, revealed that in the absence of two-party competition, sectional loyalties would constitute the lines of political division. No one recognized this more clearly than the architect of the second party system, Martin Van Buren. In his well-known letter to Thomas Ritchie of Virginia, Van Buren explained the need for a revival of national two-party politics on precisely this ground: "Party attachment in former times furnished a complete antidote for sectional prejudices by producing counteracting feelings. It was not until that defense had been broken down that the clamor against Southern Influence and African Slavery could be made effectual in the North." Van Buren and many of his generation of politicians had been genuinely frightened by the threats of disunion which echoed through Congress in 1820; they saw national two-party competition as the alternative to sectional conflict and eventual disunion. Ironically, as Richard McCormick has made clear, the creation of the second party system owed as much to sectionalism as to national loyalties. The South, for example, only developed an organized, competitive Whig party in 1835 and 1836 when it became apparent that Jackson, the southern President, had chosen Van Buren, a northerner, as his successor. Once party divisions had emerged, however, they stuck, and by 1840, for one of the very few times in American history, two truly inter-sectional parties, each united behind a single candidate, competed for the Presidency.

The 1830s witnessed a vast expansion of political loyalties and awareness and the creation of party mechanisms to channel voter participation in politics. But the new mass sense of identification with politics had ominous implications for the sectional antagonisms which the party system sought to suppress. The historian of the Missouri Compromise has observed that "if there had been a civil war in 1819–1821 it would have been between the members of Congress, with the rest of the country looking on in amazement." This is only one example of the intellectual and political isolation of Washington from the general populace which James Young has described in *The Washington Community*. The mass, non-ideological politics of the Jackson era created the desperately needed link between governors and governed. But this very link made possible the emergence of two kinds of sectional agitators: the abolitionists, who stood outside of politics and hoped to force public opinion and through it, politicians—to confront the slavery issue, and political agitators, who used politics as a way of heightening sectional self-consciousness and antagonism in the populace at large.

Because of the rise of mass politics and the emergence of these sectional agitators, the 1830s was the decade in which long-standing, latent sectional divisions were suddenly activated, and previously unrelated patterns of derogatory sectional imagery began to emerge into full-blown sectional ideology. Many of the anti-slavery arguments which gained wide currency in the 1830s had roots stretching back into the eighteenth century. The idea that slavery degraded white labor and retarded economic development, for example, had been voiced by Benjamin Franklin. After 1800, the Federalists, increasingly localized in New England, had developed a fairly coherent critique, not only of the social and economic effects of slavery, but of what Harrison Gray Otis called the divergence of "manners, habits, customs, principles, and ways of thinking" which separated northerners and southerners. And, during the Missouri debates, almost every economic, political, and moral argument against slavery that would be used in the later sectional debate was voiced. In fact, one recurring argument was not picked up later—the warning of northern Congressmen that the South faced the danger of slave rebellion if steps were not taken toward abolition. (As far as I know, only Thaddeus Stevens of Republican spokesmen in the 1850s would explicitly use this line of argument.)

The similarity between Federalist attacks on the South and later abolitionist and Republican arguments, coupled with the fact that many abolitionists—including Garrison, Phillips, the Tappans, and others—came from Federalist backgrounds, has led James Banner to describe abolitionism as "the Massachusetts Federalist ideology come back to life." Yet there was a long road to be traveled from Harrison Gray Otis to William H. Seward, just as there was from Thomas Jefferson to George Fitzhugh. For one thing, the Federalist distrust of democracy, social competition, and the Jeffersonian cry of "equal rights," their commitment to social inequality, hierarchy, tradition, and order prevented them from pushing their anti-slavery views to their logical conclusion. And New England Federalists were inhibited by the requirements of national party organization and competition from voicing anti-slavery views. In the 1790s, they maintained close ties with southern Federalists, and after 1800 hope of reviving their strength in the South never completely died. Only a party which embraced social mobility and competitive individualism, rejected the permanent subordination of any "rank" in society, and was unburdened by a southern wing could develop a fully coherent anti-slavery ideology.

An equally important reason why the Federalists did not develop a consistent sectional ideology was that the South in the early part of the nineteenth century shared many of the Federalists' reservations about slavery. The growth of an anti-slavery ideology, in other words, depended in large measure on the growth of pro-slavery thought, and, by the same token, it was the abolitionist assault which brought into being the coherent defense of slavery. The opening years of the 1830s, of course, were ones of crisis for the South. The emergence of militant abolitionism, Nat Turner's rebellion, the Virginia debates on slavery, and the nullification crisis suddenly presented assaults to the institution of slavery from within and outside the South. The reaction was the closing of southern society in defense of slavery, "the most thorough-going repression of free thought, free speech, and a free press ever witnessed in an American community." At the same time, southerners increasingly abandoned their previous, highly qualified defenses of slavery and embarked on the formulation of the pro-slavery argument. By 1837, as is well known, John C. Calhoun could thank the abolitionists on precisely this ground:

> This agitation has produced one happy effect at least; it has compelled us at the South to look into the nature and character of this great institution, and to correct many false impressions that even we had entertained in relation to it. Many in the South once believed that it was a moral and political evil; that folly and delusion are gone; we see it now in its true light, and regard it as the most safe and stable basis for free institutions in the world.

The South, of course, was hardly as united as Calhoun asserted. But the progressive rejection of the Jeffersonian tradition, the suppression of civil liberties, and the increasing stridency of the defense of slavery all pushed the South further and further out of the inter-sectional mainstream, setting it increasingly apart from the rest of the country. Coupled with the Gag Rule and the mobs which broke up abolitionist presses and meetings, the growth of pro slavery thought was vital to a new anti-slavery formulation which emerged in the late 1830s and which had been absent from both the Federalist attacks on slavery and the Missouri debates—the idea of the Slave Power. The Slave Power replaced the three-fifths clause as the symbol of southern power, and it was a far more sophisticated and complex formulation. Abolitionists could now argue that slavery was not only morally repugnant, it was incompatible with the basic democratic values and liberties of white Americans. As one abolitionist declared, "We commenced the present struggle to obtain the freedom of the slave; we are compelled to continue it to preserve our own." In other words, a process of ideological expansion had begun, fed in large measure by the sequence of response and counterresponse between the competing sectional outlooks. Once this process had begun, it had an internal dynamic which made it extremely difficult to stop. This was especially true because of the emergence of agitators whose avowed purpose was to sharpen sectional conflict, polarize public opinion, and develop sectional ideologies to their logical extremes.

As the 1840s opened, most political leaders still clung to the traditional basis of politics, but the sectional, ideological political agitators formed growing minorities in each section. In the South, there was a small group of outright secessionists and a larger group, led by Calhoun, who were firmly committed to the Union but who viewed sectional organization and self-defense, not the traditional reliance on inter-sectional political parties, as the surest means of protecting southern interests within the Union. In the North, a small radical group gathered in Congress around John Quincy Adams and Congressmen like Joshua Giddings, William Slade, and Seth Gates—men who represented areas of the most intense abolitionist agitation and whose presence confirmed Garrison's belief that, once public opinion was aroused on the slavery issue, politicians would have to follow step. These radicals were determined to force slavery into every congressional debate. They were continually frustrated but never suppressed, and the reelection of Giddings in 1842 after his censure and resignation from the House proved that in some districts party discipline was no longer able to control the slavery issue.

The northern political agitators, both Congressmen and Liberty party leaders, also performed the function of developing and popularizing a political rhetoric, especially focused on fear of the Slave Power, which could be seized upon by traditional politicians and large masses of voters if slavery ever entered the center of political conflict.

In the 1840s, this is precisely what happened. As one politician later recalled, "Slavery upon which by common consent no party issue had been made was then obtruded upon the field of party action." It is significant that John Tyler and John C. Calhoun, the two men most responsible for this intrusion, were political outsiders, men without places in the national party structure. Both of their careers were blocked by the major parties but might be advanced if tied to the slavery question in the form of Texas annexation. Once introduced into politics, slavery was there to stay. The Wilmot Proviso, introduced in 1846, had precisely the same effect as the proposal two decades earlier to restrict slavery in Missouri—it completely fractured the major parties along sectional lines. As in 1820, opposition to the expansion of slavery became the way in which a diverse group of northerners expressed their various resentments against a southern-dominated administration. And, as in 1821, a small group of northern Democrats eventually broke with their section, reaffirmed their primary loyalty to the party, and joined with the South to kill the Proviso in 1847. In the same year, enough southerners rejected Calhoun's call for united sectional action to doom his personal and sectional ambitions.

But the slavery extension debates of the 1840s had far greater effects on the political system than the Missouri controversy had had. Within each party, they created a significant group of sectional politicians—men whose careers were linked to the slavery question and who would therefore resist its exclusion from future politics. And in the North, the 1840s witnessed the expansion of sectional political rhetoric—as more and more northerners became familiar with the "aggressions" of the Slave Power and the need to resist them. At the same time, as anti-slavery ideas expanded, unpopular and divisive elements were weeded out, especially the old alliance of anti-slavery with demands for the rights of free blacks. Opposition to slavery was already coming to focus on its lowest common denominators—free soil, opposition to the Slave Power, and the union.

The political system reacted to the intrusion of the slavery question in the traditional ways. At first, it tried to suppress it. This is the meaning of the famous letters opposing the immediate annexation of Texas issued by Clay and Van Buren on the same spring day in 1844, probably after consultation on the subject. It was an agreement that slavery was too explosive a question for either party to try to take partisan advantage of it. The agreement, of course, was torpedoed by the defeat of Van Buren for the Democratic nomination, a defeat caused in part by the willingness of his

Democratic opponents to use the Texas and slavery questions to discredit Van Buren—thereby violating the previously established rules of political conduct. In the North from 1844 onward, both parties, particularly the Whigs, tried to defuse the slavery issue and minimize defection to the Liberty party by adopting anti-southern rhetoric. This tended to prevent defections to third parties, but it had the effect of nurturing and legitimating anti-southern sentiment within the ranks of the major parties themselves. After the 1848 election in which northern Whigs and Democrats vied for title of "free soil" to minimize the impact of the Free Soil party, William H. Seward commented, "Antislavery is at length a respectable element in politics."

Both parties also attempted to devise formulas for compromising the divisive issue. For the Whigs, it was "no territory"—an end to expansion would end the question of the spread of slavery. The Democratic answer, first announced by Vice President Dallas in 1847 and picked up by Lewis Cass, was popular sovereignty or non-intervention: giving to the people of each territory the right to decide on slavery. As has often been pointed out, popular sovereignty was an exceedingly vague and ambiguous doctrine. It was never precisely clear what the powers of a territorial legislature were to be or at what point the question of slavery was to be decided. But politically such ambiguity was essential (and intentional) if popular sovereignty were to serve as a means of settling the slavery issue on the traditional basis—by removing it from national politics and transferring the battleground from Congress to the territories. Popular sovereignty formed one basis of the compromise of 1850, the last attempt of the political system to expel the disease of sectional ideology by finally settling all the points at which slavery and national politics intersected.

That compromise was possible in 1850 was testimony to the resiliency of the political system and the continuing ability of party loyalty to compete with sectional commitments. But the very method of passage revealed how deeply sectional divisions were embedded in party politics. Because only a small group of Congressmen—mostly northwestern Democrats and southern Whigs—were committed to compromise on every issue, the "omnibus" compromise measure could not pass. The compromise had to be enacted serially with the small compromise bloc, led by Stephen A. Douglas of Illinois, aligned with first one sectional bloc, then the other, to pass the individual measures.

His role in the passage of the compromise announced the emergence of Douglas as the last of the great Unionist, compromising politicians, the heir of Clay, Webster, and other spokesmen for the center. And his career, like Webster's, showed that it was no longer possible to win the confidence of both sections with a combination of extreme nationalism and the calculated suppression of the slavery issue in national politics. Like his predecessors, Douglas called for a policy of "entire silence on the slavery question," and throughout the 1850s, as Robert Johannsen has written, his aim was to restore "order and stability to American politics through the agency of a national, conservative Democratic party." Ultimately, Douglas failed—a traditional career for the Union was simply not possible in the 1850s—but it is equally true that in 1860 he was the only presidential candidate to draw significant support in all parts of the country.

It is, of course, highly ironic that it was Douglas's attempt to extend the principle of popular sovereignty to territory already guaranteed to free labor by the Missouri Compromise which finally shattered the second party system. We can date exactly the final collapse of that system—February 15, 1854—the day a caucus of southern Whig Congressmen and Senators decided to support Douglas's Nebraska bill, despite the fact that they could have united with northern Whigs in opposition both to the repeal of the Missouri Compromise and the revival of sectional agitation. But in spite of the sectionalization of politics which occurred after 1854, Douglas continued his attempt to maintain a national basis of party competition. In fact, from one angle of vision, whether politics was to be national or sectional was the basic issue of the Lincoln-Douglas debates of 1858. The Little Giant presented local autonomy—popular sovereignty for states and territories—as the only "national" solution to the slavery question, while Lincoln attempted to destroy this middle ground and force a single, sectional solution on the entire Union. There is a common critique of Douglas's politics, expressed perhaps most persuasively by Allan Nevins, which argues that, as a man with no moral feelings about slavery, Douglas was incapable of recognizing that this moral issue affected millions of northern voters. This, in my opinion, is a serious misunderstanding of Douglas's politics. What he insisted was not that there was no moral question involved in slavery but that it was not the function of the politician to deal in moral judgments. To Lincoln's prediction that the nation could not exist half slave and half free, Douglas replied that it had so existed for seventy years and could continue to do so if northerners stopped trying to impose their own brand of morality upon the South.

Douglas's insistence on the separation of politics and morality was expressed in his oft-quoted statement that—in his role as a politician—he did not care if the people of a territory voted slavery "up or down." As he explained in his Chicago speech of July 1858, just before the opening of the great debates:

> I deny the right of Congress to force a slave-holding state upon an unwilling people. I deny their right to force a free state upon an unwilling people. I deny their right to force a good thing upon a people who are unwilling to receive it. . . . It is no answer to this argument to say that slavery is an evil and hence should not be tolerated. You must allow the people to decide for themselves whether it is a good or an evil.

When Lincoln, therefore, said the real purpose of popular sovereignty was "to educate and mould public opinion, at least northern public opinion, to not care whether slavery is voted down or up," he was, of course, right. For Douglas recognized that moral categories, being essentially uncompromisable, are unassimilable in politics. The only solution to the slavery issue was local autonomy. Whatever a majority of a state or territory wished to do about slavery was right—or at least should not be tampered with by politicians from other areas. To this, Lincoln's only possible reply was the one formulated in the debates—the will of the majority must be tempered by considerations of morality. Slavery was not, he declared, an "*ordinary* matter of domestic concern in the states and territories." Because of its essential immorality, it tainted the entire nation, and its disposition in the territories, and eventually in the entire nation, was a matter of national concern to be decided by a national, not a local, majority. As the debates continued, Lincoln increasingly moved to this moral level of the slavery argument: "Everything that emanates from [Douglas] or his coadjutors, carefully excludes the thought that there is anything wrong with slavery.

Abraham Lincoln, 1858. This very formal portrait shows the aspiring Illinois Republican. Lincoln and his party were using the debates with Douglas to influence the state elections of 1858 in hopes of denying the Democrats a majority in the legislature and thereby preventing Douglas from being returned to the Senate. (*University Libraries, University of Nebraska–Lincoln*)

All their arguments, if you will consider them, will be seen to exclude the thought. . . . If you do admit that it is wrong, Judge Douglas can't logically say that he don't care whether a wrong is voted up or down."

In order to press home the moral argument, moreover, Lincoln had to insist throughout the debates on the basic humanity of the black; while Douglas, by the same token, logically had to define blacks as subhuman, or at least, as the Dred Scott decision had insisted, not part of the American "people" included in the Declaration of Independence and the Constitution. Douglas's view of the black, Lincoln declared, conveyed "no vivid impression that the Negro is a human, and consequently has no idea that there can be any moral question in legislating about him." Of course, the standard of morality which Lincoln felt the nation should adopt regarding slavery and the black was the sectional morality of the Republican party.

By 1860, Douglas's local majoritarianism was no more acceptable to southern political leaders than Lincoln's national and moral majoritarianism. The principle of state rights and minority self-determination had always been the first line of defense of slavery from northern interference, but southerners now coupled it with the demand that Congress intervene to establish and guarantee slavery in the territories. The Lecompton fight had clearly demonstrated that southerners would no longer be satisfied with what Douglas hoped the territories would become—free, Democratic states. And the refusal of the Douglas Democrats to accede to southern demands was the culmination of a long history of resentment on the part of northern Democrats, stretching back into the 1840s, at the impossible political dilemma of being caught between increasingly anti-southern constituency pressure and loyalty to an increasingly pro-southern national party. For their part, southern Democrats viewed their northern allies as too weak at home and too tainted with anti-southernism after the Lecompton battle to be relied on to protect southern interests any longer.

As for the Republicans, by the late 1850s they had succeeded in developing a coherent ideology which, despite internal ambiguities and contradictions, incorporated the fundamental values, hopes, and fears of a majority of northerners. As I have argued elsewhere, it rested on a commitment to the northern social order, founded on

Stephen A. Douglas, circa 1859. This picture shows the senior Senator from Illinois around the time of the debates with Lincoln. Probably the pivotal figure in American politics in the 1850s, Douglas would be the Democratic presidential candidate in 1860, but, a year later at age forty-eight, he was dead of acute rheumatism and multiple complications. (*Library of Congress*)

the dignity and opportunities of free labor, and to social mobility, enterprise, and "progress." It gloried in the same qualities of north-ern life—materialism, social fluidity, and the dominance of the self-made man—which twenty years earlier had been the source of widespread anxiety and fear in Jacksonian America. And it defined the South as a backward, stagnant, aristocratic society, totally alien in values and social order to the middle-class capitalism of the North.

Some elements of the Republican ideology had roots stretching back into the eighteenth century. Others, especially the Republican emphasis on the threat of the Slave Power, were relatively new. Northern politics and thought were permeated by the Slave Power idea in the 1850s. The effect can perhaps be gauged by a brief look at the career of the leading Republican spokesman of the 1850s, William H. Seward. As a political child of upstate New York's burned-over district and anti-masonic crusade, Seward had long believed that the Whig party's main political liability was its image as the spokesman of the wealthy and aristocratic. Firmly committed to egalitarian democracy, Seward had attempted to reorient the New York State Whigs into a reformist, egalitarian party, friendly to immigrants and embracing political and economic democracy, but he was always defeated by the party's downstate conservative wing. In the 1840s, he became convinced that the only way for the party to counteract the Democrats' monopoly of the rhetoric of democracy and equality was for the Whigs to embrace anti-slavery as a party platform.

The Slave Power idea gave the Republicans the anti-aristocratic appeal with which men like Seward had long wished to be associated politically. By fusing older anti-slavery arguments with the idea that slavery posed a threat to northern free labor and democratic values, it enabled the Republicans to tap the egalitarian outlook which lay at the heart of northern society. At the same time, it enabled Republicans to present anti-slavery as an essentially conservative reform, an attempt to reestablish the anti-slavery principles of the founding fathers and rescue the federal government from southern usurpation. And, of course, the Slave Power idea had a far greater appeal to northern self-interest than arguments based on the plight of black slaves in the South. As the black abolitionist Frederick Douglass noted, "The cry of Free Men was raised, not for the extension of liberty to the black man, but for the protection of the liberty of the white."

By the late 1850s, it had become a standard part of Republican rhetoric to accuse the Slave Power of a long series of transgressions against northern rights and liberties and to predict that, unless halted by effective political action, the ultimate aim of the conspiracy—the complete subordination of the national government to slavery and the suppression of northern liberties—would be accomplished. Like other conspiracy theories, the Slave Power idea was a way of ordering and interpreting history, assigning clear causes to otherwise inexplicable events, from the Gag Rule to Bleeding Kansas and the Dred Scott decision. It also provided a convenient symbol through which a host of anxieties about the future could be expressed. At the same time, the notion of a black Republican conspiracy to overthrow slavery and southern society had taken hold in the South. These competing conspiratorial outlooks were reflections, not merely of sectional "paranoia," but of the fact that the nation was every day growing apart and into two societies whose ultimate interests were diametrically opposed. The South's fear of black Republicans, despite its exaggerated rhetoric, was based on the realistic assessment that at the heart of Republican aspirations for the nation's future was the restriction and eventual eradication of slavery. And the Slave Power expressed northerners' conviction, not only that slavery was incompatible with basic democratic values, but that to protect slavery, southerners were determined to control the federal government and use it to foster the expansion of slavery. In summary, the Slave Power idea was the ideological glue of the Republican party—it enabled them to elect in 1860 a man conservative enough to sweep to victory in every northern state, yet radical enough to trigger the secession crisis.

Did the election of Lincoln pose any real danger to the institution of slavery? In my view, it is only possible to argue that it did not if one takes a completely static—and therefore ahistorical—view of the slavery issue. The expansion of slavery was not simply an issue; it was a fact. By 1860, over half the slaves lived in areas outside the original slave states. At the same time, however, the South had become a permanent and shrinking minority within the nation. And in the majority section, anti-slavery sentiment had expanded at a phenomenal rate. Within one generation, it had moved from the commitment of a small minority of northerners to the motive force behind a victorious party. That sentiment now demanded the exclusion of slavery from the territories. Who could tell what its demands would be in ten or twenty years? The incoming President had often declared his commitment to the "ultimate extinction" of slavery. In Alton, Illinois, in the heart of the most pro-slavery area of the North, he had condemned Douglas because "he looks to no end of the institution of slavery." A Lincoln administration seemed likely to be only the beginning of a prolonged period of Republican hegemony. And the succession of generally weak, one-term Presidents between 1836 and 1860 did not obscure the great expansion in the potential power of the Presidency which had taken place during the administration of Andrew Jackson. Old Hickory had clearly shown that a strong-willed President, backed by a united political party, had tremendous power to shape the affairs of government and to transform into policy his version of majority will.

What was at stake in 1860, as in the entire sectional conflict, was the character of the nation's future. This was one reason Republicans had placed so much stress on the question of the expansion of slavery. Not only was this the most available issue concerning slavery constitutionally open to them, but it involved the nation's future in the most direct way. In the West, the future was tabula rasa, and the future course of western development would gravely affect the direction of the entire nation. Now that the territorial issue was settled by Lincoln's election, it seemed likely that the slavery controversy would be transferred back into the southern states themselves. Secessionists, as William Freehling has argued, feared that slavery was weak and vulnerable in the border states, even in Virginia. They feared Republican efforts to encourage the formation of Republican organizations in these areas and the renewal of the long-suppressed internal debate on slavery in the South itself. And, lurking behind these anxieties, may have been fear of anti-slavery debate reaching the slave quarters, of an undermining of the masters' authority, and, ultimately, of slave rebellion itself. The slaveholders knew, despite the great economic strength of King Cotton, that the existence of slavery as a local institution in a larger free economy demanded an inter-sectional community consensus, real or enforced. It was this consensus which Lincoln's election seemed to undermine, which is why the secession convention of South Carolina declared, "Experience has proved that slaveholding states cannot be safe in subjection to non-slaveholding states."

More than seventy years before the secession crisis, James Madison had laid down the principles by which a central government and individual and minority liberties could coexist in a large and heterogeneous Union. The very diversity of interests in the nation, he argued in the Federalist Papers, was the security for the rights of minorities, for it ensured that no one interest would ever gain control of the government. In the 1830s, John C. Calhoun recognized the danger which abolitionism posed to the South—it threatened to rally the North in the way Madison had said would not happen—in terms of one commitment hostile to the interests of the minority South. Moreover, Calhoun recognized, when a majority interest is organized into an effective political party, it can seize control of all the branches of government, overturning the system of constitutional checks and balances which supposedly protected minority rights. Only the principle of the concurrent majority—a veto which each major interest could exercise over policies directly affecting it—could reestablish this constitutional balance.

At the outset of the abolitionist crusade, Calhoun had been convinced that, while emancipation must be "resisted at all costs," the South should avoid hasty action until it was "certain that it is the real object, not by a few, but by a very large portion of the non-slaveholding states." By 1850, Calhoun was convinced that "Every portion of the North entertains views more or less hostile to slavery." And by 1860, the election returns demonstrated that this anti-slavery sentiment, contrary to Madison's expectations, had united in an interest capable of electing a President, despite the fact that it had not the slightest support from the sectional minority. The character of Lincoln's election, in other words, completely overturned the ground rules which were supposed to govern American politics. The South Carolina secession convention expressed secessionists' reaction when it declared that once the sectional Republican party, founded on hostility to southern values and interests, took over control of the federal government, "the guarantees of the Constitution will then no longer exist."

Thus the South came face to face with a conflict between its loyalty to the nation and loyalty to the South—that is, to slavery, which, more than anything else, made the South distinct. David Potter has pointed out that the principle of majority rule implies the existence of a coherent, clearly recognizable body of which more than half may be legitimately considered as a majority of the whole. For the South to accept majority rule in 1860, in other words, would have been an affirmation of a common nationality with the North. Certainly, it is true that in terms of ethnicity, language, religion—many of the usual components of nationality—Americans, North and South, were still quite close. On the other hand, one important element, community of interest, was not present. And perhaps most important, the preceding decades had witnessed an escalation of distrust—an erosion of the reciprocal currents of good will so essential for national harmony. "We are not one people," declared the New York *Tribune* in 1855. "We are two peoples. We are a people for Freedom and a people for Slavery. Between the two, conflict is inevitable." We can paraphrase John Adams's famous comment on the American Revolution and apply it to the coming of the Civil War—the separation was complete, in the minds of the people, before the war began. In a sense, the Constitution and national political system had failed in the difficult task of creating a nation—only the Civil War itself would accomplish it.

James M. McPherson

THE DISTINCTIVENESS OF THE OLD SOUTH

The protagonists in the American Civil War were two regions of the nation whose differences were ultimately irreconcilable short of war. Although this statement is unexceptionable, there remains the question of whether those differences were intrinsically significant or whether they became so because of human agency or later circumstances. James M. McPherson examines this problem and concludes that the contrasts were deep-seated and persistent.

The following essay discusses many aspects of life in the two regions. But the author singles out as the crucial area of difference their divergent norms as to how society should be structured and organized—specifically, the folk culture of the South as opposed to the North's more bureaucratic, impersonal model. This emphasis justifies the inclusion of the essay in this section on cultural and ideological approaches to Civil War causation.

James M. McPherson, "Southern Exceptionalism: A New Look at an Old Question," *Civil War History*, vol. 29, No. 3 (September 1983). Reprinted with permission of The Kent State University Press.

In passing, it is worth noting that wars do not necessarily result from conflicts between nations or groups that are utterly different from each other. Rather, similarities and subtle distinctions often generate friction leading to war.

James M. McPherson of Princeton University (born 1936) is the author of the Pulitzer Prize–winning *Battle Cry of Freedom: The Civil War Era* (1988), as well as *The Struggle for Equality: Abolitionists in the Civil War and Reconstruction* (1964) and a collection of essays, *Abraham Lincoln and the Second American Revolution* (1990).

The notion of American Exceptionalism has received quite a drubbing since the heyday of the exceptionalist thesis among the consensus school of historians in the 1950s. Interpreters of the American experience then argued that something special about the American experience—whether it was abundance, free land on the frontier, the absence of a feudal past, exceptional mobility and the relative lack of class conflict, or the pragmatic and consensual liberalism of our politics—set the American people apart from the rest of mankind. Historians writing since the 1950s, by contrast, have demonstrated the existence of class and class conflict, ideological politics, land speculation, and patterns of economic and industrial development similar to those of Western Europe which placed the United States in the mainstream of modern North Atlantic history, not on a special and privileged fringe.

If the theme of American Exceptionalism has suffered heavy and perhaps irreparable damage, the idea of Southern Exceptionalism still flourishes—though also subjected to repeated challenges. In this essay, "Southern Exceptionalism" refers to the belief that the South has "possessed a separate and unique identity . . . which appeared to be out of the mainstream of American experience." Or as Quentin Compson (in William Faulkner's *Absalom, Absalom!*) expressed it in a reply to his Canadian-born college roommate's question about what made Southerners tick: "You can't understand it. You would have to be born there."

The questions of whether the South was indeed out of the mainstream and if so, whether it has recently been swept into it, continue to be vital issues in Southern historiography. The clash of viewpoints can be illustrated by a sampling of titles or subtitles of books that have appeared in recent years. On one side we have: *The*

Enduring South; The Everlasting South; The Idea of the South; The Lasting South; and *The Continuity of Southern Distinctiveness*—all arguing, in one way or another, that the South was and continues to be different. On the other side we have: *The Southerner as American; The Americanization of Dixie; Epitaph for Dixie; Southerners and Other Americans; The Vanishing South;* and *Into the Mainstream.* Some of these books insist that "the traditional emphasis on the South's differentness . . . is wrong historically." Others concede that while the South may once have been different, it has ceased to be or is ceasing to be so. There is no unanimity among this latter group of scholars about precisely when or how the South joined the mainstream. Some emphasize the civil rights revolution of the 1960s; others the bulldozer revolution of the 1950s; still others the Chamber of Commerce Babbittry of the 1920s; and some the New South crusade of the 1880s. As far back as 1869 the Yankee novelist John William De Forest wrote of the South: "We shall do well to study this peculiar people, which will soon lose its peculiarities." As George Tindall has wryly remarked, the Vanishing South has "staged one of the most prolonged disappearing acts since the decline and fall of Rome."

Some historians, however, would quarrel with the concept of a Vanishing South because they believe that the South as a separate, exceptional entity never existed—with of course the ephemeral exception of the Confederacy. But a good many other historians insist that not only did a unique "South" exist before the Civil War, but also that its sense of a separate identity that was being threatened by the North was the underlying cause of secession. . . .

Many antebellum Americans certainly thought that North and South had evolved separate societies with institutions, interests, values, and ideologies so incompatible, so much in deadly conflict that they could no longer live together in the same nation. Traveling through the South in the spring of 1861, London *Times* correspondent William Howard Russell encountered this Conflict of Civilizations theme everywhere he went. "The tone in which [Southerners] alluded to the whole of the Northern people indicated the clear conviction that trade, commerce, the pursuit of gain, manufacture, and the base mechanical arts, had so degraded the whole race" that Southerners could no longer tolerate association with them, wrote Russell. "There is a degree of something like ferocity in the Southern mind [especially] toward New England which exceeds belief." A South Carolinian told Russell: "We are an agricultural people, pursuing our own system, and working out our own destiny, breeding up women and men with some other purpose than to make them vulgar, fanatical, cheating Yankees." Louis Wigfall of Texas, a former U.S. senator, told Russell: "We are a peculiar people, sir! . . . We are an agricultural people. . . . We have no cities—we don't want them. . . . We want no manufactures: we desire no trading, no mechanical or manufacturing classes. . . . As long as we have our rice, our sugar, our tobacco, and our cotton, we can command wealth to purchase all we want. . . . But with the Yankees we will never trade—never. Not one pound of cotton shall ever go from the South to their accursed cities."

Such opinions were not universal in the South, of course, but in the fevered atmosphere of the late 1850s they were widely shared. "Free Society!" exclaimed a Georgia newspaper. "We sicken at the name. What is it but a conglomeration of greasy mechanics, filthy operatives, small-fisted farmers, and moon-struck theorists . . . hardly fit for association with a southern gentleman's body servant." In 1861 the *Southern Literary Messenger* explained to its readers: "It is not a question of slavery alone that we are called upon to decide. It is free society which we must shun or embrace." In the same year Charles Colcock Jones, Jr.—no fire-eater, for after all he had graduated from Princeton and from Harvard Law School—spoke of the development of antagonistic cultures in North and South: "In this country have arisen two races [i.e., Northerners and Southerners] which, although claiming a common parentage, have been so entirely separated by climate, by morals, by religion, and by estimates so totally opposite to all that constitutes honor, truth, and manliness, that they cannot longer exist under the same government."

Spokesmen for the free-labor ideology—which had become the dominant political force in the North by 1860—reciprocated these sentiments. The South, said Theodore Parker, was "the foe to Northern Industry—to our mines, our manufactures, and our commerce. . . . She is the foe to our institutions—to our democratic politics in the State, our democratic culture in the school, our democratic work in the community, our democratic equality in the family." Slavery, said William H. Seward, undermined "intelligence, vigor, and energy" in both blacks and whites. It produced "an

exhausted soil, old and decaying towns, wretchedly neglected roads
. . . an absence of enterprise and improvement." Slavery was therefore "incompatible with all . . . the elements of the security, welfare,
and greatness of nations." The struggle between free labor and
slavery, between North and South, said Seward in his most famous
speech, was "an irrepressible conflict between two opposing and
enduring forces." The United States was therefore two nations, but
it could not remain forever so: it "must and will, sooner or later,
become either entirely a slaveholding nation, or entirely a free-labor
nation." Abraham Lincoln expressed exactly the same theme in his
House Divided speech. Many other Republicans echoed this argument that the struggle, in the words of an Ohio congressman, was
"between systems, between civilizations."

These sentiments were no more confined to fire-breathing
Northern radicals than were Southern exceptionalist viewpoints confined to fire-eaters. Lincoln represented the mainstream of his party,
which commanded a majority of votes in the North by 1860. The
dominant elements in the North and in the lower South believed
the United States to be composed of two incompatible civilizations.
Southerners believed that survival of their special civilization could
be assured only in a separate nation. The creation of the Confederacy
was merely a political ratification of an irrevocable separation that
had already taken place in the hearts and minds of the people.

The proponents of an assimilationist rather than exceptionalist
interpretation of Southern history might object that this concept of
a separate and unique South existed *only* in hearts and minds. It was
a subjective reality, they might argue, not an objective one. Objec-
tively, they would insist, North and South were one people. They
shared the same language, the same Constitution, the same legal
system, the same commitment to republican political institutions,
an interconnected economy, the same predominantly Protestant religion and British ethnic heritage, the same history, the same shared
memories of a common struggle for nationhood.

Two recent proponents of the objective similarity thesis are
Edward Pessen and the late David Potter. In a long article entitled
"How Different from Each Other Were the Antebellum North and
South?" Pessen concludes that they "were far more alike than the
conventional scholarly wisdom has led us to believe." His evidence
for this conclusion consists mainly of quantitative measures of the

distribution of wealth and of the socioeconomic status of political officeholders in North and South. He finds that wealth was distributed in a similarly unequal fashion in both sections, that voting requirements were similar, and that voters in both sections elected a similarly disproportionate number of men from the upper economic strata to office. The problem with this argument, of course, is that it could be used to prove many obviously different societies to be similar. France and Germany in 1914 and in 1932 had about the same distribution of wealth and similar habits of electing men from the upper strata to the Assembly or the Reichstag. England and France had a comparable distribution of wealth during most of the eighteenth century. Turkey and Russia were not dissimilar in these respects in the nineteenth century. And so on.

David Potter's contention that commonalities of language, religion, law, and political system outweighed differences in other areas is more convincing than the Pessen argument. But the Potter thesis nevertheless begs some important questions. The same similarities prevailed between England and her North American colonies in 1776, but they did not prevent the development of a separate nationalism in the latter. It is not language or law alone that are important, but the uses to which they are put. In the United States of the 1850s, Northerners and Southerners spoke the same language, to be sure, but they were increasingly using this language to revile each other. Language became an instrument of division, not unity. The same was true of the political system. So also of the law: Northern states passed personal liberty laws to defy a national Fugitive Slave Law supported by the South; a Southern-dominated Supreme Court denied the right of Congress to exclude slavery from the territories, a ruling that most Northerners considered an infamous distortion of the Constitution. As for a shared commitment to Protestantism, this too had become a divisive rather than unifying factor, with the two largest denominations—Methodist and Baptist—having split into hostile Southern and Northern churches over the question of slavery, and the third largest—Presbyterian—having split partly along sectional lines and partly on the question of slavery. As for a shared historical commitment to republicanism, by the 1850s this too was more divisive than unifying. Northern Republicans interpreted this commitment in a free-soil context, while most Southerners continued to insist that one of the most cherished tenets of republican liberty was the right of property—including property in slaves.

There is another dimension of the Potter thesis—or perhaps it would be more accurate to call it a separate Potter thesis—that might put us on the right track to solving the puzzle of Southern exceptionalism. After challenging most notions of Southern distinctiveness, Potter concluded that the principal characteristic distinguishing the South from the rest of the country was the persistence of a "folk culture" in the South. This gemeinschaft society, with its emphasis on tradition, rural life, close kinship ties, a hierarchical social structure, ascribed status, patterns of deference, and masculine codes of honor and chivalry, persisted in the South long after the North began moving toward a gesellschaft society with its impersonal, bureaucratic meritocratic, urbanizing, commercial, industrializing, mobile, and rootless characteristics. Above all, the South's folk culture valued tradition and stability and felt threatened by change; the North's modernizing culture enshrined change as progress and condemned the South as backward.

A critic of this gemeinschaft-gesellschaft dichotomy might contend that it was more myth than reality. One might respond to such criticism by pointing out that human behavior is often governed more by myth—that is, by people's perceptions of the world— than by objective reality. Moreover, there *were* real and important differences between North and South by the mid-nineteenth century, differences that might support the gemeinschaft-gesellschaft contrast.

The North was more urban than the South and was urbanizing at a faster rate. In 1820, 10 percent of the free-state residents lived in urban areas compared with 5 percent in the slave states; by 1860 the figures were 26 percent and 10 percent, respectively. Even more striking was the growing contrast between farm and non-farm occupations in the two sections. In 1800, 82 percent of the Southern labor force worked in agriculture compared with 68 percent in the free states. By 1860 the Northern share had dropped to 40 percent while the Southern proportion had actually increased slightly, to 84 percent. Southern agriculture remained traditionally labor-intensive while Northern agriculture became increasingly capital-intensive and mechanized. By 1860 the free states had nearly twice the value of farm machinery per acre and per farm worker as the slave states.

And the pace of industrialization in the North far outstripped that in the South. In 1810 the slave states had an estimated 31 percent of the capital invested in manufacturing in the United States; by 1840 this had declined to 20 percent and by 1860 to 16 percent. In 1810 the North had two and a half times the amount per capita invested in manufacturing as the South; by 1860 this had increased to three and a half times as much.

A critic of the inferences drawn from these data might point out that in many respects the differences between the free states east and west of the Appalachians were nearly or virtually as great as those between North and South, yet these differences did not produce a sense of separate nationality in East and West. This point is true—as far as it goes. While the western free states at midcentury did have a higher proportion of workers employed in non-farm occupations than the South, they had about the same percentage of urban population and the same amount per capita invested in manufacturing. But the crucial factor was *the rate of change.* The West was urbanizing and industrializing more rapidly than either the Northeast or the South. Therefore while North and South as a whole were growing relatively farther apart, the eastern and western free states were drawing closer together. This frustrated Southern hopes for an alliance with the Old Northwest on grounds of similarity of agrarian interests. From 1840 to 1860 the rate of urbanization in the West was three times greater than in the Northeast and four times greater than in the South. The amount of capital invested in manufacturing grew twice as fast in the West as in the Northeast and nearly three times as fast as in the South. The same was true of employment in non-farm occupations. The railroad-building boom of the 1850s tied the Northwest to the Northeast with links of iron and shifted the dominant pattern of inland trade from a North-South to an East-West orientation. The remarkable growth of cities like Chicago, Cincinnati, Cleveland, and Detroit with their farm-machinery, food-processing, machine-tool, and railroad-equipment industries foreshadowed the emergence of the industrial Midwest and helped to assure that when the crisis of the Union came in 1861 the West joined the East instead of the South.

According to the most recent study of antebellum Southern industry, the Southern lag in this category of development resulted not from any inherent economic disadvantages—not shortage of capital, nor low rates of return, nor non-adaptability of slave labor—but from the choices of Southerners who had money to invest it in agriculture and slaves rather than in manufacturing. In the 1780s Thomas Jefferson had praised farmers as the "peculiar deposit for substantial and genuine virtue" and warned against the industrial classes in cities as sores on the body politic. In 1860 many Southern leaders still felt the same way; as Louis Wigfall put it in the passage quoted earlier, "we want no manufactures; we desire no trading, no mechanical or manufacturing classes."

Partly as a consequence of this attitude, the South received only a trickle of the great antebellum stream of immigration. Fewer than one-eighth of the immigrants settled in slave states, where the foreign-born percentage of the population was less than a fourth of the North's percentage. The South's white population was ethnically more homogeneous and less cosmopolitan than the North's. The traditional patriarchal family and tight kinship networks typical of gemeinschaft societies, reinforced in the South by a relatively high rate of cousin marriages, also persisted much more strongly in the nineteenth-century South than in the North.

The greater volume of immigration to the free states contributed to the faster rate of population growth there than in the South. Another factor in this differential growth rate was out-migration from the South. During the middle decades of the nineteenth century, twice as many whites left the South for the North as vice versa. These facts did not go unnoticed at the time; indeed, they formed the topic of much public comment. Northerners cited the differential in population growth as evidence for the superiority of the free-labor system; Southerners perceived it with alarm as evidence of their declining minority status in the nation. These perceptions became important factors in the growing sectional self-consciousness that led to secession.

The most crucial demographic difference between North and South, of course, resulted from slavery. Ninety-five percent of the country's black people lived in the slave states, where blacks constituted one-third of the population in contrast to their one percent of the Northern population. The implications of this for the economy and social structure of the two sections, not to mention their ideologies and politics, are obvious and require little elaboration here. Two brief points are worth emphasizing, however. First, historians in recent years have discovered the viability of Afro-American culture under slavery. They have noted that black music, folklore, speech patterns, religion, and other manifestations of this culture influenced white society in the South. Since the Afro-American culture was preeminently a folk culture with an emphasis on oral tradition and other non-literate forms of ritual and communication, it reinforced the persistence of a traditional, gemeinschaft, folk-oriented society in the South.

Second, a number of recent historians have maintained that Northerners were as committed to white supremacy as Southerners. This may have been true, but the scale of concern with this matter in the South was so much greater as to constitute a different order of magnitude and to contribute more than any other factor to the difference between North and South. And of course slavery was more than an institution of racial control. Its centrality to many aspects of life focused Southern politics almost exclusively on defense of the institution—to the point that, in the words of the *Charleston Mercury* in 1858, "on the subject of slavery . . . the North and South . . . are not only two Peoples, but they are rival, hostile Peoples."

The fear that slavery was being hemmed in and threatened with destruction contributed to the defensive-aggressive style of Southern political behavior. This aggressiveness sometimes took physical form. Southern whites were more likely to carry weapons and to use them against other human beings than Northerners were. The homicide rate was higher in the South. The phenomenon of dueling persisted longer there. Bertram Wyatt-Brown attributes this to the unique Southern code of honor based on traditional patriarchal values of courtesy, status, courage, family, and the symbiosis of shame and pride. The enforcement of order through the threat and practice of violence also resulted from the felt need to control a large slave population.

Martial values and practices were more pervasive in the South than in the North. Marcus Cunliffe has argued to the contrary, but the evidence confutes him. Cunliffe's argument is based mainly on two sets of data: the prevalence of militia and volunteer military companies in the free as well as in the slave states; and the proportion of West Pointers and regular army officers from the two sections. Yet the first set of data do not support his thesis, and the second contradicts it. Cunliffe does present evidence on the popularity of military companies in Northern cities, but nowhere does he estimate the comparative numbers of such companies in North and South or the number of men in proportion to population who belonged to them. If such comparative evidence could be assembled, it would probably support the traditional view of a higher concentration of such companies in the South. What Northern city, for example, could compare with Charleston, which had no fewer than twenty-two military companies in the late 1850s—one for every two hundred white men of military age? Another important quasi-military institution in the South with no Northern counterpart escaped Cunliffe's attention—the slave patrol, which gave tens of thousands of Southerners a more practical form of military experience than the often ceremonial functions of volunteer drill companies could do.

As for the West Point alumni and regular army officers it is true, as Cunliffe points out, that about 60 percent of these were from the North and only 40 percent from the South in the late antebellum decades. What he fails to note is that the South had only about 30 percent of the nation's white population during this era, so that on a proportional basis the South was overrepresented in these categories. Moreover, from 1849 to 1861 all of the secretaries of war were Southerners, as were the general in chief of the army, two of the three brigadier generals, all but one commander of the army's geographical departments on the eve of the Civil War, the authors of the two manuals on infantry tactics and of the artillery manual used at West Point, and the professor who taught tactics and strategy at the military academy.

Other evidence supports the thesis of a significant martial tradition in the South contrasted with a concentration in different professions in the North. More than three-fifths of the volunteer soldiers in the Mexican War came from the slave states—on a per capita basis, four times the proportion of free-state volunteers. Seven of the eight military "colleges" (not including West Point and Annapolis) listed in the 1860 census were in the slave states. A study of the occupations of antebellum men chronicled in the *Dictionary of American Biography* found that the military profession claimed twice the percentage of Southerners as of Northerners, while this ratio was reversed for men distinguished in literature, art, medicine, and education. In business the per capita proportion of Yankees was three times as great, and among engineers and inventors it was six times as large. When Southerners labeled themselves a nation of warriors and Yankees a nation of shopkeepers—a common comparison in 1860—or when Jefferson Davis told a London *Times* correspondent in 1861 that "we are a military people," they were not just whistling Dixie.

One final comparison of objective differences is in order—a comparison of education and literacy in North and South. Contemporaries perceived this as a matter of importance. The South's alleged backwardness in schooling and its large numbers of illiterates framed one of the principal free-soil indictments of slavery. This was one area in which a good many Southerners admitted inferiority and tried to do something about it. But in 1860, after a decade of school reform in the South, the slave states still had only half the North's proportion of white children enrolled in public and private schools, and the length of the annual school term in the South was only a little more than half as long as in the North. Of course education did not take place solely in school. But other forms of education—in the home, at church, through lyceums and public lectures, by apprenticeship, and so on—were also more active in North than South. According to the census of 1860, per capita newspaper circulation was three times greater in the North, and the number of library volumes per white person was nearly twice as large.

The proportion of illiterate white people was three times greater in the South than in the North; if the black population is included, as indeed it should be, the percentage of illiterates was seven or eight times as high in the South. In the free states, what two recent historians have termed an "ideology of literacy" prevailed—a commitment to education as an instrument of social mobility, economic prosperity, progress, and freedom. While this ideology also existed in the South, especially in the 1850s, it was much weaker there and made slow headway against the inertia of a rural folk culture. "The Creator did not intend that every individual human being should be highly cultivated," wrote William Harper of South Carolina. "It is better that a part should be fully and highly educated and the rest utterly ignorant." Commenting on a demand by Northern workingmen for universal public education, the *Southern Review* asked: "Is this the way to produce producers? To make every child in the state a literary character would not be a good qualification for those who must live by manual labor."

The ideology of literacy in the North was part of a larger ferment which produced an astonishing number of reform movements that aroused both contempt and fear in the South. Southern whites viewed the most dynamic of these movements—abolitionism—as a threat to their very existence. Southerners came to distrust the whole concept of "progress" as it seemed to be understood in the North. *DeBow's Review* declared in 1851: "Southern life, habits, thoughts, and aims, are so essentially different from those of the North, that here a different character of books . . . and training is required." A Richmond newspaper warned in 1855 that Southerners must stop reading Northern newspapers and books and stop sending their sons to colleges in the North, where "every village has its press and its lecture room, and each lecturer and editor, unchecked by a healthy public opinion, opens up for discussion all the received dogmas of faith," where unwary youth are "exposed to the danger of imbibing doctrines subversive of all old institutions." Young men should be educated instead in the South "where their training would be moral, religious, and conservative, and they would never learn, or read a word in school or out of school, inconsistent with orthodox Christianity, pure morality, the right of property, and sacredness of marriage."

In all of the areas discussed above—urbanization, industrialization, labor force, demographic structure, violence and martial values, education, and attitudes toward change—contemporaries accurately perceived significant differences between North and South, differences that in most respects were increasing over time. The question remains: were these differences crucial enough to make the South an exception to generalizations about antebellum America?

This essay concludes by suggesting a tentative answer to the question: perhaps it was the *North* that was "different," the North that departed from the mainstream of historical development; and perhaps therefore we should speak not of Southern exceptionalism but of Northern exceptionalism. This idea is borrowed shamelessly from C. Vann Woodward, who applied it, however, to the post–Civil War United States. In essays written during the 1950s on "The Irony of Southern History" and "The Search for Southern Identity," Woodward suggested that, unlike other Americans but like most people in the rest of the world, Southerners had experienced poverty, failure, defeat, and had a skepticism about "progress" that grows out of such experiences. The South thus shared a bond with the rest of humankind that other Americans did not share. This theme of Northern exceptionalism might well be applied also to the antebellum United States—not for Woodward's categories of defeat, poverty, and failure, but for the categories of a persistent folk culture discussed in this essay.

At the beginning of the republic the North and South were less different in most of these categories than they became later. Nearly all Northern states had slavery in 1776, and the institution persisted in some of them for decades thereafter. The ethnic homogeneity of Northern and Southern whites was quite similar before 1830. The proportion of urban dwellers was similarly small and the percentage of the labor force employed in agriculture similarly large in 1800. The Northern predominance in commerce and manufacturing was not so great as it later became. Nor was the contrast in education and literacy as great as it subsequently became. A belief in progress and commitments to reform or radicalism were no more prevalent in the North than in the South in 1800—indeed, they may have been less so. In 1776, in 1800, even as late as 1820, similarity in values and institutions was the salient fact. Within the next generation, difference and conflict became prominent. This happened primarily because of developments in the North. The South changed relatively little, and because so many Northern changes seemed threatening, the South developed a defensive ideology that resisted change.

In most of these respects the South resembled a majority of the societies in the world more than the changing North did. Despite the abolition of legal slavery or serfdom throughout much of the western hemisphere and western Europe, much of the world— like the South—had an unfree or quasi-free labor force. Most societies in the world remained predominantly rural, agricultural, and labor-intensive; most, including even several European countries, had illiteracy rates as high or higher than the South's 45 percent; most like the South remained bound by traditional values and networks of family, kinship, hierarchy, and patriarchy. The North— along with a few countries in northwestern Europe—hurtled forward eagerly toward a future that many Southerners found distasteful if not frightening; the South remained proudly and even defiantly rooted in the past.

Thus when secessionists protested in 1861 that they were acting to preserve traditional rights and values, they were correct. They fought to protect their constitutional liberties against the perceived Northern threat to overthrow them. The South's concept of republicanism had not changed in three-quarters of a century; the North's had. With complete sincerity the South fought to preserve its version of the republic of the founding fathers—a government of limited powers that protected the rights of property and whose constituency comprised an independent gentry and yeomanry of the white race undisturbed by large cities, heartless factories, restless free workers, and class conflict. The accession to power of the Republican party, with its ideology of competitive, egalitarian, free-labor capitalism, was a signal to the South that the Northern majority had turned irrevocably toward this frightening, revolutionary future. Indeed, the Black Republican party appeared to the eyes of many Southerners as "essentially a revolutionary party" composed of "a motley throng of Sans culottes . . . Infidels and freelovers, interspersed by Bloomer women, fugitive slaves, and amalgamationists." Therefore secession was a preemptive counter-revolution to prevent the Black Republican revolution from engulfing the South. "*We* are not revolutionists," insisted James D. B. DeBow and Jefferson Davis during the Civil War. "We are resisting revolution. . . . We are not engaged in a Quixotic fight for the rights of man; our struggle is for inherited rights. . . . We are upholding the true doctrines of the Federal Constitution. We are conservative."

Union victory in the war destroyed the Southern vision of America and insured that the Northern vision would become the American vision. Until 1861, however, it was the North that was out of the mainstream, not the South. Of course the Northern states, along with Britain and a few countries in northwestern Europe, were cutting a new channel in world history that would doubtless have become the mainstream even if the American Civil War had not happened. But it did happen, and for Americans it marked the turning point. A Louisiana planter who returned home sadly after the war wrote in 1865: "Society has been completely changed by the war. The [French] revolution of '89 did not produce a greater change in the 'Ancien Regime' than has this in our social life." And

four years later George Ticknor, a retired Harvard professor, concluded that the Civil War had created a "great gulf between what
happened before in our century and what has happened since, or
what is likely to happen hereafter. It does not seem to me as if I
were living in the country in which I was born." From the war
sprang the great flood that wrenched the stream of American history
into a new channel and transferred the burden of exceptionalism
from North to South.

Kenneth S. Greenberg

ANGLOPHOBIA, SOUTHERN NATIONALISM, AND THE SECTIONAL CONFLICT

The South's feeling of separateness was sufficiently developed by the
1850s that, in the view of some historians, among them Kenneth S.
Greenberg, it amounted to something akin to national identity. In the
selection that follows, he argues that the South's identity was assuming
a national form as the section saw itself confronted by threats from New
England in the mid-nineteenth century. These threats recalled those the
American colonies had faced in the 1770s, which had resulted in national
independence.

In Greenberg's opinion, this emerging national identity was reflected
in the South's political culture—the set of assumptions that shape and
inform the conduct of public life. Unlike ideology, which is formulated
self-consciously, political culture is informal, consisting of the unwritten
rules of public discourse and behavior. If there was a distinctive southern
identity before the Civil War, its essential ingredients most likely resided
in the region's instinctual political culture. The existence of such a heightened sense of separate identity would suggest that the sections were far
apart culturally and ideologically, though this does not mean that war
was the only possible outcome.

Kenneth S. Greenberg (born 1947) teaches at Suffolk University and
is the author of *Masters and Statesmen: The Political Culture of American
Slavery* (1985), from which this selection is excerpted.

Greenberg, Kenneth S., *Masters and Statesmen: The Political Culture of American
Slavery,* pp 107–21, 125–35. Reprinted by permission of The Johns Hopkins University Press, Baltimore/London, 1985.

Nations are conceived in love and hate. The sense of identity that holds a nation together is a mixture of shared faiths, ideals, and customs as well as of common fears and enemies. Often, at the moment of birth fear of a common enemy is the dominant unifying force—fear of the corrupt, old regime or of the foreign oppressor. The United States has been no exception. Despite the similar customs and beliefs that might have bound the colonies together before 1776, fear of English oppression precipitated the final union. Eighty-five years later a similar fear pushed the Southern states into a new Confederate nation.

What is most striking about America's two experiences with nation-creation—in 1776 and in 1861—is not the existence of a fear of oppression but rather the remarkable historical connection between the objects of that fear. During the antebellum period traditional Southern anxieties about England, inherited from the republican ideology of the revolutionary period and reinforced by later events, underwent a slow transformation into a fear of New England and the North. The nature of this Anglophobia and its change into "New" Anglophobia must be closely analyzed if we are to understand the full dimensions of Confederate nationhood.

One must begin, of course, by recognizing that Anglophobia and Anglophilia—the hatred and love of England and things English—peacefully coexisted in the minds of many Americans, Northern and Southern, throughout the nineteenth century. This ambivalent response to the old colonial mother country is precisely what one should expect from a relatively young nation struggling for a distinct identity despite its largely derivative cultural heritage. Young American writers both imitated and tried to reject the models offered by English authors; Americans demanded a uniquely American literature even as they continued to read and copy the works of great English writers; American travelers found themselves drawn to and repulsed by their experience of English society. Even one of the central myths accepted by many nineteenth-century Americans, a myth embedded in numerous antebellum writings, depended on a double image of English society. The North, so the myth explains, had been settled by Puritan Roundheads, whereas the South was peopled by Cavaliers—the supporters of the monarchy in the English Civil War. "Under the stimulus of this divided heritage," suggests historian William R. Taylor in his elaboration of this set of ideas, "the North had developed a leveling, go-getting utilitarian society and the South had developed a society based on the values of the English gentry." This way of describing English society and its extension into America necessarily stimulated ambivalent responses. England could be conceived of as the cause of either of two opposite societies.

Yet to recognize that Americans had ambivalent attitudes toward England is not to denigrate the importance or power of these ideas. It would be improper to conclude that all Americans simultaneously loved and hated England, and hence the attitudes had no real significance because they canceled each other out. As is often true with ambivalent attitudes, different circumstances cause a people to emphasize one side of the ambivalence or the other in specific contexts. For example, it seems clear that certain portions of Southern society, especially the large planters of the coast, developed aristocratic pretensions that pushed them to imitate the English gentry. Many wealthy Southerners sent their sons to be educated at Eton, Oxford, and the Middle Temple. Two hundred and twenty-five of the 350 Americans who were admitted to the Inns of Court in London before 1860 came from Southern states, including 89 from South Carolina and 76 from Virginia. Similarly, some wealthy planters delighted in tracing their ancestry to the English upper classes; some built their houses after English models; and some bought their books in England. Yet . . . it was often these same men, as well as many other less wealthy Southerners, who used Anglophobic images and ideas to explain a variety of critical problems faced by their society.

The Revolution stimulated a host of negative attitudes toward England in every section of the emerging new nation. In the style of traditional republican thought, Americans repeatedly wrote not only of specific grievances, but of a subversive conspiracy of power-hungry men, as well as of a more general moral decline of an increasingly corrupt English society. Southerners shared the general fear that the tax acts and other British oppressions leading up to 1776 resulted from a conspiracy of power-hungry British ministers who threatened England's delicate mixed government. Many Southerners gradually came to feel that within the structure of English government they could not protect themselves against the abuses of these powerful men. They frequently described their situation as

South Carolina Declaration of Independence, December 20, 1860. In this official declaration, the delegates to the secession convention acknowledged how closely they were emulating their forebears' secession from the British Empire in 1776. (*Chicago Historical Society*) approaching slavery. Others came to see this conspiracy as symptomatic of a more general moral corruption eating away at English society. Henry Laurens, Edmund Jennings, and Landon Carter advised Americans to avoid English schools for fear that colonial youth might become tainted with the corruption. William Lee described Englishmen as "immersed in riches, luxury and dissipation." Henry Laurens bemoaned "the wretched state of female virtue in this kingdom [England]!" Thomas Jefferson and James Madison placed England in the general category of decadent, artificial, urban, hierarchical Europe, in contrast to a more egalitarian, rural, and natural America. Even if few Southerners understood the full logic of such arguments, the general image of powerful conspirators in control of a decadent, corrupt English society threatening to enslave Americans probably achieved wide acceptance.

The experience of the revolutionary war in the South added another dimension to the images of a power-hungry and corrupt English society. Many Southern states witnessed some of the most bitter fighting of the Revolution. The British occupation of Charleston and Savannah and the fighting in the Carolina back country left memories of brutality that would not easily fade. The South Carolinians John C. Calhoun, Andrew Pickens Butler, Preston Brooks, and Wade Hampton all grew up on stories of English butchery. Calhoun's 1843 campaign biography proudly noted that he had been named after his maternal uncle "whom the Tories had murdered in cold blood, and in his own yard, after destroying his house by fire." As a boy, John Randolph of Virginia wore an "ABRACADABRA" around his neck "to keep off the Ague and the British.". . .

Although the English threat to American slavery had always been a part of Southern Anglophobia, it became increasingly important beginning in the 1820s, especially as the abolition movements in England and then in America began to win wider popular attention. As early as the 1820 congressional debate over the extension of slavery into Missouri, William Smith of South Carolina charged that the North and Great Britain were involved in a conspiracy to abolish slavery. Smith maintained that the attack on the extension of slavery was only part of a larger and more insidious plot to destroy the institution. Such an idea seemed to win additional confirmation by events that followed in the wake of the discovery of the 1822 Denmark Vesey slave conspiracy.

Denmark Vesey had been accused of organizing an elaborate slave rebellion in Charleston. The rebellion, in fact, never took place but South Carolinians reacted to the discovery of the plot with considerable panic. Confronted with evidence of their vulnerability to secret conspiracy, Carolinians embarked on a series of measures to strengthen their security. Among other things, the Vesey plot seemed to reveal that slave contact with free black sailors—especially those who could bring word of the successful slave rebellion in Santo Domingo—had been a source of insurrectionary inspiration. One of the conspirators even admitted that he gave letters to black sailors in an attempt to win support for the rebellion from the Santo Domingo government. In response to such information the state legislature passed a law requiring free black employees on board a vessel entering Carolina ports to be imprisoned until the vessel departed. If the ship's captain failed to pay for the detention and ultimately failed to remove the prisoner, the black would become a slave. It was the first of many so-called Negro Seamen laws enacted in the South throughout the antebellum period. Georgia passed a similar law in 1829, North Carolina in 1830–31, Florida in 1832, Louisiana in 1842, and Alabama in 1839.

What is interesting about the Negro Seamen laws is that they placed England and the Northern states together in the position of attacking slavery. Free black sailors in Southern ports generally came from Great Britain or other American states where slavery had been abolished. Hence, soon after the South Carolina law went into effect, the owners of a Northern vessel assailed the statute in court. Simultaneously, England challenged the law through diplomatic channels. English diplomacy first took the form of a protest note from Ambassador Stratford Canning to Secretary of State John Quincy Adams. Adams, recognizing the merits of the English case, first worked quietly through Carolina congressmen, but failing to win satisfaction, he submitted the English protests directly to Governor John L. Wilson. The South Carolina Senate framed a defiant reply for Wilson: "The duty of the state to guard against insubordination or insurrection . . . is paramount to all *laws,* all *treaties,* all *constitutions.*" These words captured the spirit of South Carolina's reaction to English and Northern interference, even though the language proved too harsh to win the concurrence of both houses of the legislature.

The Negro Seamen controversy illustrates interesting connections among Anglophobia, New Anglophobia, republicanism, and the defense of slavery. First of all, the controversy was not a simple, insignificant, or isolated event in Southern history. Even when it first exploded, the dispute touched a raw nerve in Carolina society. Because of its connection with its fear of slave insurrection, the dispute became a major obsession of the South Carolina Association, a self-created, extralegal organization founded by the wealthiest and most influential members of the planter gentry in the wake of the Vesey insurrection. In fact, this private organization single-handedly undertook the defense of the laws in the courts and successfully lobbied for their enforcement in practice. The Negro Seamen acts provided the first opportunity for a large portion of the Carolina planter gentry openly to defy the federal government. The lesson of their success did not go unnoticed. But beyond this, the controversy continued to fester throughout the antebellum period as other states adopted these measures of "self-defense" and defied pressures from the courts and federal government. The Carolina example of resistance spread through the South.

Even more significant for the development of Southern nationalism, the Negro Seamen controversy presented Southerners with their first clear example of a Northern and English alliance to subvert slavery. They had always looked with suspicion at the Anglophilia of some in the North, but here was evidence of clear cooperation—a cooperation directed at undermining slavery. Here, for the first time, just ten years after the War of 1812, they confronted New Englander John Quincy Adams in alliance with England against the South's vital institution. He must have known immediately that he had hit a sensitive spot. Adams noted that, when the subject came up in a dinner conversation, Carolina Senator Robert Y. Hayne showed "so much excitement and temper that it became painful and necessary to change the topic." But it was a sensitive spot that Adams would repeatedly touch during his political career. Nearly twenty years later, in 1842, Adams as a congressman sponsored resolutions requesting the State Department to furnish documents related to the Seamen acts. The request for information was part of his continuing battle against these laws. Carolina Congressman Isaac E. Holmes denounced the resolution and accused Adams of "throwing a firebrand . . . which was to create a conflagration that might endanger the Republic, . . . he was calling on this union . . . to trample upon those rights which the states deemed most essential, and which they would not yield." Adams's antislavery agitation only seemed to threaten the Union and to benefit England.

The significance of the apparent association between the New Englander Adams and old England can be seen in South Carolina's reaction to the abortive attempt by Adams's home state, Massachusetts, to destroy the Negro Seamen acts. In 1844 Massachusetts sent a representative, Samuel Hoar, to Charleston in order to test once again in court the legality of the controversial legislation. The Carolina legislature, fully aware of the connection among England, Adams, and Massachusetts, simply labeled Hoar "the emissary of a foreign government" and asked Governor James Henry Hammond to expel him from the state. Even before the governor could act, however, Hoar was driven back to Massachusetts by the threat of mob violence—no doubt the work of the South Carolina Association. Louisiana treated its own "visitor" from Massachusetts with similar ceremony. When Southern states expelled Massachusetts emissaries as foreign agents their citizens had moved far down the road to a new national identity. By 1850, William Henry Trescot simply lumped together England and Massachusetts as opponents of the Negro Seamen acts. "England and Massachusetts," he wrote, "Lord Palmerston and Governor Briggs—both think the law of South Carolina imprisoning colored seamen a very unfeeling measure." The only difference between the two, he concluded with obvious implication, was that England, being a foreign power, could not so easily send an ambassador to the state to challenge its laws.

Throughout the antebellum period some Southerners continually uncovered "evidence" that England was the major source of antislavery and abolitionist agitation, that to the extent New England and the North attacked slavery they did so as the tools of a foreign nation. Anglophobia, fears of the fragility of republican government as it came under attack from abusive power, the defense of slavery, and New Anglophobia, all mixed together into a brew that never failed to stimulate strong Southern emotion. Aside from the continuing agitation over the Negro Seamen controversy and English attempts to suppress the slave trade, new incidents kept England and antislavery continuously before the Southern public, creating a pool of hostility that could easily be redirected at the

North and New England. Consider the Southern reaction to the 1833 English abolition of slavery in the West Indies. By the late 1820s emancipation seemed inevitable, and many in the South carefully analyzed the events to determine how it had come to pass. They wanted to glean lessons from the English experience that would be useful in fending off the threat of American abolition. They concluded that abolition operated by stealth, that the English example proved that the earlier, apparently innocuous, movements against the slave trade or for the African colonization of free blacks inevitably led to ultimate abolition. The lesson that at least some Southerners learned from the West Indies was that attacks on slavery must be met at the frontier—at the point at which they did not seem clearly to threaten abolition. One needed to maintain a careful watch. Ironically, of course, these were the very terms in which traditional republican thought warned about the dangers to liberty. It was also the way gentlemen thought about threats to their honor.

As early as 1827, when the American Colonization Society petitioned Congress for federal aid to transport free blacks to Africa, many planters in the South Carolina low country thought they recognized the action as analogous to the course English abolitionists had once pursued. Robert Turnbull, in his pamphlet on the crisis that threatened American slavery, argued that the English experience demonstrated that abolition operated in a series of steps, that when [William] Wilberforce first approached the Parliament with the idea of ending the slave trade, he was "even *more cautious* than the Colonization society. He took special care not to profess that the abolition of the slave trade was but the *first* step towards an object which he then had most deeply at heart." For Turnbull, the progress of English abolition exposed the real meaning of the apparently harmless Colonization Society's antislavery activity in the United States: it would set the nation down the road to abolition. It was no surprise to many that a few years later the radical abolitionist William Lloyd Garrison should emerge in America. He had been expected. That his arrival coincided with English emancipation only heightened concern.

The close cooperation between American and British abolitionists constantly reconfirmed Southern fears. "[W]hen Garrison was in England," explained one proslavery pamphleteer in 1836, "an arrangement was made with individuals in that country to obtain for their designs English cooperation. It will be seen hereafter," he warned, "that English funds and English influence are at work to disturb and distract this country." Similarly, in the midst of the controversy surrounding the acceptance of abolitionist petitions in Congress, Georgia Senator Alfred Cuthbert simply declared that abolition was un-American; "it originated on the foreign soil of England." In an 1844 letter published in the *Charleston Mercury* and later republished in pamphlet form, Langdon Cheves, old "war hawk" of the War of 1812, also noted the links between English and American abolition: "These Foreign Societies have their agents and orators, with whom they correspond, on the floor of Congress." Cheves even believed that the threat extended to the Whig party. He predicted that if a Whig was elected president "it will be through the aid of these 'Foreign Societies.'". . .

One of the most disturbing evidences of American-English abolitionist cooperation was the 1840 World's Antislavery Convention in London. As Southerners watched in horror, to London flocked much of the leadership of American abolition—William Lloyd Garrison, James G. Birney, William Jay, Wendell Phillips, Lucretia Mott, Lydia Child, and dozens of others. There they fought among themselves on strategy and there they paid homage to the venerable leaders of the successful English abolitionist movement. As they rose in united silent tribute to British abolitionist Thomas Clarkson, expressing a unity they evidenced on few other issues, they helped dispel any lingering Southern doubts of the close connections between English and American abolitionism. James G. Birney, 1840 Liberty party candidate for president of the United States, provided additional evidence, spending the entire period of his campaign and election at the London conference. When the conference published an address that was delivered to the governors of all the slaveholding states under the frank of United States Congressman Seth M. Gates, Southerners gave voice to a flood of abolitionist and Anglophobic criticism. Governor James K. Polk of Tennessee singled out Gates for special condemnation. One wealthy slaveholder in Georgia offered to pay $500 to anyone who would deliver Gates to Savannah. There they knew how to deal with traitors.

Virginia Senator Henry Wise delivered a two-day speech in the Senate in which he voiced all the fears stimulated by the World's Antislavery Convention. He was prompted to speak in response to a resolution that censured John Quincy Adams for introducing abolitionist petitions seeking the dissolution of the Union. Wise labeled the petitions British-inspired. He warned of a British-trained black army in Jamaica, poised to attack Cuba and the United States. He spoke ominously of "English influence abroad . . . in league with the same English influence at home." Wise even told of an interchange of "emissaries" between British and American abolitionists. He believed that Joseph Sturge, a "British monarchist," had come to the United States to destroy the Union. Similarly, Wise argued, James G. Birney's speech at the World's Antislavery Convention offered proof that "American emissaries" had gone to England "to beg for British influence, British prayers, and, if need be, for British gold."

Stirring further Southern Anglophobia were the host of slavery-related issues surrounding the negotiations that resulted in the Webster-Ashburton Treaty of 1842. These issues had long stimulated Southern Anglophobia and would continue to do so even after the treaty had been signed. One set of problems had to do with American coastal vessels containing slaves that, by weather or some other mishap, ended up in the British Bahamas. English policy was to free the slaves, and many in the South saw this policy as an open encouragement to slave revolt. In fact, in October 1841, the American ship *Creole* set sail from Hampton Roads, Virginia, with a few whites and 135 slaves. Several days into the voyage the slaves mutinied and brought the vessel into Nassau where they were given their freedom. The incident seemed to embody all that Southerners had feared. The Virginian John Tyler was president at the time, and his reactions typified the response of many in the South. As Lord Ashburton described it: "The President as a Virginian, has a strong opinion about [the] Creole case, and is not a little disposed to be obstinate on the subject." Tyler, he wrote at another time, "is very sore and testy about the Creole."

Another issue raised by the *Creole* case, but with implications far beyond it, was the problem of extradition. The blacks on the *Creole* had killed some of the white crew, but they could not be tried for their crime because no extradition agreement then existed between England and America. This issue was connected to the continuing problem of fugitive slaves who escaped to Canada. Southerners demanded some provision for their extradition because they had "stolen themselves" or the personal property they brought with them. They had also committed a murder in the act of freeing themselves. England, of course, did not want to enter the business of returning fugitive slaves.

The continuing British attempt to suppress the African slave trade also arose during the Webster-Ashburton negotiations and stirred Southern Anglophobia. England wanted the right to "visit" American ships suspected of carrying slaves. But, as had long been the case, even those who did not support the slave trade could not bring themselves to allow the English to board American vessels. It conjured up the same images that had led to the War of 1812—the images associated with English naval officers boarding American ships to search for deserters and to impress sailors.

Of course, those who favored the slave trade even more readily resorted to Anglophobic arguments. When, for example, Edward B. Bryan attempted to convince Southerners to reopen the trade during the 1850s, he elaborated a full English conspiracy theory. "This alliance [between Britain and Northerners to stop the slave trade]," he contended, "was originally proposed by the British Government, and, as it now stands, there is not an American feature in it." He charged, among other things, that the 1820 American law declaring slave traders pirates had been a British invention and that the antislave trade provisions of the Webster Ashburton Treaty (authorizing English and American squadrons to suppress the trade) had been agreed to because "the British [abolition] societies established branches in New England, and sent preachers to expound their doctrines."

Southern Anglophobia also received periodic support from foreign policy clashes over such objects of American expansion as Texas and Cuba. The Anglophobic Texas hysteria reached severe proportions in the early 1840s. Texas had fought for independence from Mexico and presented itself as a candidate for annexation to the United States. In 1843 President Tyler, already aware that abolitionist forces in America opposed annexation because it meant the extension of slavery, received indications from Duff Green in London that England also had abolition plans. Green reported that Great Britain planned to offer financial aid to an independent Texas in exchange for the abolition of slavery. Green apparently misunderstood British intentions, but given his own Anglophobic fears as well as those of Tyler, one can understand why the idea of an English abolitionist conspiracy proved so attractive. John C. Calhoun and Secretary of State Abel P. Upshur also received news of the plot from Green and they tried to spread the word in Southern newspapers. Southerners responded with pro-annexation meetings and numerous articles warning of the danger to the South if Texas should fall under the influence of English abolition.

The Anglophobic Cuba hysteria reached its peak during the 1850s. The United States, especially expansionists in the slave states, had long hoped to steal Cuba from Spain and extend the American empire into the Caribbean. But the cries of the expansionists became more insistent as England put pressure on both Spain and Cuba to abolish slavery. Cuban planters added their voices to the chorus as they began to lobby for annexation to the United States as a way of avoiding English-inspired abolition. By 1853 the "Africanization" of Cuba scare won wide attention in the South. For many, the horrible image of "Cuba as a free colony but a few leagues distant from our most populous Slave States" was too terrifying to contemplate. These kinds of fears helped win widespread Southern support for John A. Quitman's ill-fated filibustering expedition to conquer Cuba for the South. That Senator Salmon P. Chase of Ohio, a founder of the emerging Republican party in the North, expressed his "sympathy" and "best wishes" to the emancipation movement in Cuba, whether inspired by the English or the French, only reconfirmed old Southern fears of an Anglo-American abolitionist conspiracy. . . .

The movement for Southern literary nationalism also had roots in Anglophobia. In fact, Anglophobia was the central obsession of one of the antebellum South's greatest literary figures, William Gilmore Simms. Like many other South Carolinians, as a child he had been exposed to stories of British revolutionary violence. Simms's grandmother had told him about his great-great-grandfather who fought the English in Charleston and about his great-grandfather who rode with Francis Marion and helped liberate Charleston. Many of Simms's novels were patriotic stories of the Revolution. As editor of one of the most influential Southern publications, the *Southern Quarterly Review*, he gave a great deal of space to articles that aired many of the central themes of Anglophobia, including everything from the World's Antislavery Conference, to the *Creole* affair, to the English plot against Texas slavery. Like Hammond, he even addressed his own major proslavery work to an English abolitionist. Meanwhile, he kept up a steady stream of writing calling for a distinctive Southern literature that would be independent of

England. Later, he would advocate a Southern literature independent of New England as well. Simms's Anglophobia moved smoothly into New Anglophobia. The movement for Southern literary nationalism pursued precisely this path.

Anglophobia was an essential, perhaps the central, ingredient in the movement for Southern nationalism. Consider how it worked. It was by no means a single coherent set of ideas but a series of arguments and images with considerable emotional power. Southern Anglophobia conjured up memories of the American Revolution and the War of 1812- -republican battles for liberty against tyranny. When slavery became a central object of English assault, it was added to the older set of images, becoming just another part of the attack on American liberty. When circumstances placed New England and the North on the side of England during a long series of conflicts over such events as the Negro Seamen acts, the World's Antislavery Convention, the *Creole,* Texas, and Cuba, the South transferred its entire stock of Anglophobic and republican fears and images onto New England and the North. Northerners just seemed to copy everything that England had already done—encourage slave revolts, fail to return fugitive slaves, prevent the extension of slavery, develop an abolitionist movement, exploit labor, and threaten liberty with power. Southern nationalism drew much of its power from the fact that it was a variant of an extant American nationalism. Both nationalisms could trace their roots to a fear of enslavement by the English. Both nationalisms could point to England as the symbol of evil—a symbol that tied together otherwise inconsistent ideas and images. When Southerners were told by the South Carolina secession convention that "the Southern states now stand exactly in the same position towards the Northern States that the Colonies did toward Great Britain," and that "the people of the Southern states are compelled to meet the very despotism their fathers threw off in the Revolution of 1776," the analogy evoked a series of images and ideas rooted in the close connection of republicanism, Anglophobia, and New Anglophobia. An American patriotism had become a Southern patriotism. . . .

*

Disagreement need not lead to war. Any modern nation-state consists of economic, ethnic, religious, and social groups with widely divergent values and interests. Yet these groups often can live together in an uneasy peace, working within a common political structure even as they disagree. South and North lived together in this way for all of the antebellum period. Despite the divergent ideals, despite the divergent labor systems, despite the bitter disputes over the tariff, the territorial expansion of slavery, fugitive slaves, and a host of other issues, South and North remained for a long time in a single political system. Why the system broke down, why the standard methods of dispute resolution ultimately failed, why sectional disagreement ended in secession and civil war, is one of the most profound historical puzzles. The breakdown must be understood as the failure of a political structure. A careful analysis of the political culture of slavery can help us understand that failure.

The success of secession depended on a widely shared Southern view that political leaders and political parties had become corrupt, that the existing political structures could no longer resolve disputes because they had become hopelessly perverted. In fact, what largely differentiated radicals from moderates throughout the various sectional crises was this sense of political corruption. Radicals saw no hope of redress within the existing structures; moderates held on longer to the possibility of redress, but they too eventually became disillusioned. By the eve of the Civil War the vision of a corrupt American politics had triumphed in the South. Let us first examine evidence of this attitude and then seek its origins.

The sense of political corruption reached its peak earliest in the most radical Southern state, South Carolina. The South Carolina vision of corruption is worth describing in some detail because it was later reduplicated in many other states. John C. Calhoun had warned of the danger as early as the 1832 nullification crisis. Drawing on the tradition of seventeenth- and eighteenth-century republican thought, Calhoun repeatedly argued that the nation needed disinterested statesmen who could resist such temptations as executive patronage and the desire for spoils. A great danger to the Republic lay in the nation falling into the hands of corrupt spoilsmen, men who sought money and power in politics. By the late antebellum period many in South Carolina, as they looked at political life in Washington and the North, thought that Calhoun's fear had become reality. Langdon Cheves saw in Washington "men known to the nation by no distinction of talent or public service, the Hales, the Giddings, the Sewards." He feared "the ambition of low-minded politicians who are determined to govern and to crush all power in the Southern states." Lewis M. Ayer in 1855 conceded that the government might have been pure under the hands of the virtuous statesman Washington, but "it was too purely artificial to withstand the selfish passions, wicked prejudices, and lustful appetites for ruthless rule, of the degenerate and fanatical brood who have succeeded to the control of its powers, and who have extracted from 'its page sublime,' a breed of lust, hate, and crime." Isaac Hayne wrote Charles Cotesworth Pinckney, Jr., in 1860, offering his sarcastic analysis of the state of American politics: "Who would live under a Government where a man had to be honest to obtain office, or really great to be thought so? How much more preferable it is to attain distinction by a little dextrous wire-pulling."

Many Carolinians associated the general decline in political virtue with party activity. As one writer in the *Southern Quarterly Review* dramatically phrased it, party "blasts where it is excited, and virtue, withering, shrinks from its presence." H. W. Connor wrote Calhoun from Charleston in 1845 that he hoped that political parties would soon disintegrate. "There is no principle of cohesion amongst them," he informed Calhoun, "except the common love of plunder and so corrupt have the politicians of both parties become that they dare not confide long enough in each other to commit an act of party pillage." Connor fervently hoped for a reorganization of party on the basis of principle, and Calhoun thereby catapulted into the presidency. It was a hope that never became a reality.

By the 1850s, party behavior and the decline of political virtue were closely correlated in the minds of Carolinians. One newspaper from Due West in Abbeville District, for example, in an 1850 editorial complained about "the Dignity Departing" from Congress. The senators had become obsessed with "long details of personalities and party matters" and the House was full of "Buncombe speeches, and party squabbles." W. Allston Pringle told the citizens of Charleston about the evils of party behavior. "Politics," he argued, "whose ends should be the general welfare, have become a game, and a means of livelihood. Party tactics, through which the public voice should be fairly heard, have so disfigured and deformed the government, that public service rather debases than elevates. The Constitution itself which was thought so comprehensive and noble in its aspirations, is regarded as the charter of a private corporation to be used and employed for the promotion of private views." In other words, Pringle believed that party spoilsmen had come to control the government. Their desire for plunder would force them to advocate strengthening government power. "These adventurers," Pringle maintained, "who live upon the abuses which they create, and whose only object is the plunder of the treasury, and a share of the power of the general government, find their ends best attained by every measure which tends to strengthen that government." One year later, Henry L. Pinckney, Jr., reaffirmed these ideas in another oration to Charlestonians. In national politics, he saw only "avarice and ambition." "The pride of party and the greed of gain," he declaimed, "the lust of power and the love of self, that mark the conduct of the North, have driven a faithful and loyal people to the last refuge of despair."

The same message reached Carolinians over and over again in the years just before the Civil War. The Reverend J. C. Coit, in his address to the people of Chesterfield District, analyzed the two motives that competed to guide the behavior of "our civil rulers at Washington." "First; moral: those resulting from their official obligation to the Constitution and liberties of the people. Second; personal: those that spring from their obligations to party, and from their love of money, power and fame." Coit believed that the second motive now dominated. "Under such temptations," he argued, "our federal rulers have proved too frail a depository, for such a trust as the civil government of a people politically free. The Constitution has proved an ineffectual barrier to their encroachments. Fortified by military power and party combinations, the central government has now assumed a position, which, if maintained, will be fatal to the political liberties of the people."

The belief in party as a correlate of corruption clearly affected the Carolinian attitude toward participation in the national party conventions. Just before the 1856 Democratic Convention, for example, the *Unionville Journal* warned Carolinians to remain aloof from party activity. "[L]et other states," admonished an editorial, "if they choose, continue to countenance these self-constituted bodies of politicians, whose object is power, for the sake of plunder, but let her [South Carolina] wash her hands of them." Carolinian experience with party conventions did little to change this belief. One Spartanburg newspaper, after the 1860 Charleston Democratic Convention, reported the impressions of J. P. Reed who watched

Stephen Douglas struggle for the nomination and split the party. "Instead of meeting with statesmen like those of old who had so much distinguished and illustrated our country's name, he found that our political leaders had become corrupt, and like petty spoilsmen were anxious for the loaves and fishes of office."

Even a Carolinian who had cooperated with the national Democratic party, Francis W. Pickens, was troubled by the sense that virtue in national politics seemed in jeopardy. Just before the 1856 election, for example, he wrote privately to Armistead Burt, expressing his deepest fears of political corruption: "If Buchanan is defeated we will be near the beginning of the end and we must solemnly prepare to meet great events. If he is elected and the selfish and designing get control of him and bring into power the camp followers who have pressed as to their plunder of victory, then there will be still great confusion, and his Administration will lead the country into inextricable difficulties." He hoped Buchanan would be a statesman, but he remained uncertain.

Gradually during the antebellum period Carolinians became convinced that only men who had no principles could be elected in the Northern states, and that only unprincipled men could possibly become president. The presidency seemed the great prize of the most skilled plunderer. Claudian B. Northrop, probably with the difficulty of Calhoun becoming president in mind, complained bitterly in 1843 about the scramble for presidential office: "What has become of the dignity of our free empire, when its republican throne, which Washington with modesty reluctantly filled, has been the prize of dishonest bribery and popular delusion; and is no more regarded as the free-will offering of the country's approbation to high public merit, but as the rightful prey of the robber bands which may seize the state." Calhoun's inability even to win the Democratic nomination also greatly disturbed James Hamilton who, in 1844, complained of a Democratic party in a condition "which compels it to pass over the *first* of its Men and to rally on those scarcely above mediocrity." By 1846 Hamilton had become so disillusioned he suggested the White House be inscribed with the label: "*The Temple of Demagogism inscribed to the Genius of Mediocrity dulness Ignorance and Deceit.*". . .

The idea that Northern spoilsmen had gradually come to dominate the political offices of the nation coincided with and was reinforced by a prevailing Southern stereotype of Northern society: the "Yankee" as a man of insatiable greed who measured worth only by wealth. "It is a melancholy fact," one *Southern Quarterly Review* article reasoned, "and a subject of common observation, that *public* spirit is at its lowest ebb among us, whilst the commercial and political are evidently in the ascendant. Our councils no longer, as in former days, are governed by that noble self-sacrificing patriotism, which can recognize nothing but country, and legislate for no interest which embraces anything short of the general welfare." Political corruption, in other words, had risen with the commercial market.

If Carolinians sensed the spread of political corruption in general in the North they believed the antislavery politician was the most corrupt of all. John Townsend, for example, warned in 1850 that it was impossible to compromise with antislavery political leaders. "Fanatics in religion," he wrote of his enemies, "fanatics in politics, the ravening demagogue, hunting after office, and the spoils of party. And when, from the beginning of time, to the present hour, have *such* men been satisfied with concessions." By the time the Republicans came to power in 1860, Carolinians knew precisely what kind of men had finally taken control of the nation. "Well, we have a Republican speaker," Susanna Sparks Keitt [wife of the secessionist congressman, Lawrence M. Keitt] wrote in February. "I expect the old United States Treasury was pulled at today and tonight feels quite exhausted." James Henry Hammond still believed in 1860 that if only the abolitionists, whom he equated with Republicans, could be defeated for the presidency in one or two more elections, "the politicians would give it up because it could not gain them Spoils and Power." The Reverend William O. Prentiss, after the election of Lincoln, told Charlestonians in unequivocal terms precisely what kind of administration had just taken control: "That party [the Republicans] has sold its offices to the highest bidder; its Justices have dispensed justice for reward; its Governors have shared in embezzlements and peculations; its Representatives have been expelled from Congress for bribery." Carolinians simply despised these new politicians. It even offended their honor. "I care nothing for the 'Peculiar Institution,'" R. N. Hemphill wrote W. R. Hemphill just one week before secession in December 1860, "but I can't stand the idea of being domineered by [a pack] of Hypocritical Scoundrels, such as Sumner, Seward, Wilson, Hale, etc., etc."

That Abraham Lincoln himself did not initially seem the most malevolent or most cunning Republican political leader failed to blunt the feeling among Carolinians that statesmen no longer had control of the government, the feeling that spoilsmen were ascendant. The very features which made Lincoln so attractive to many Northerners—his "man of the people" quality and poor upbringing, his earthy sense of humor—made him seem the epitome of the low and vulgar politician Carolinians had been watching with trepidation for years. As Susanna Sparks Keitt wrote with amazement to a Philadelphia friend at the time of Lincoln's inauguration: "Did you think the people of the South, the Lords Proprietors of the land, would let this low fellow rule for them? No. His vulgar facetiousness may suit the race of clock makers and wooden nutmeg venders— even Wall Street brokers may accept him, since they do not protest— but never will he receive the homage of southern gentlemen." The whole Lincoln style of politics offended many Carolinians. Susanna Sparks Keitt could never submit to rule by a man who "exhibits himself at railway depots, bandies jokes with the populace, kisses bold women from promiscuous crowds." If Abraham Lincoln was not the most skillful of the new Republican spoilsmen, in the minds of Carolinians he was at best an unskilled spoilsman and at worst the foolish tool of the most malevolent, far from the kind of statesman needed to control the impending Republican search for plunder. Of course, when war finally broke out, Carolinians quickly realized that Lincoln was no buffoon, that he was as skilled in the unrestrained use of power as any of the most hated Republican leaders. . . .

It was precisely because everyone in South Carolina feared the disease of political corruption that secession could be viewed as an act of purification, an operation that cleanly removed the spreading cancer. W. Alston Pringle told Charlestonians in 1850: "If you wish the government to be venerated and respected, you must purge it of its impurities,—you must rescue it from the thraldom of party— you must restore it to the people, its rightful owners—you must shape its measures to its proper ends." Pringle advised either the transformation of public opinion in the North or secession. W. F. Colcock told the assembled Carolina Southern Rights Associations that they could "be assured that the secession of a single state of this union will bring up for judgment the mightiest questions of a modern age. Statesmen, sir, not venal politicians, not hireling presses, not pensioned libelers, but statesmen will find materials for the exercise of their highest intelligences, their profoundest wisdom."

The imagery of purification dominated the final secession crisis. "We cannot coalesce," explained the Reverend William O. Prentiss to Charlestonians in late 1860, "with men whose society will eventually corrupt our own, and bring down upon us the awful doom which awaits them." Susanna Sparks Keitt in 1861 tried to convey to one of her Northern friends the reasons for South Carolina's secession and conjured a similar image of purification. She recalled a sight they had once seen together in Europe—the "bright and limpid" waters of the Rhone, "fresh from the cold purity of the glacier's bosom" as it mingled with the "turbid Arno." "Frantically," she remembered, "it resisted the muddy impurity of its embraces; for miles and leagues waged the war between Dark and Bright; but finally the struggle ceased. Together in the same current bed they must run; so, mingled waters—the turbid sullying the clear and securing back nought of its purity—together they quietly flowed into the sea." The secession of South Carolina, for Susanna Sparks Keitt, would isolate political pollution, just as the sundering of the two rivers might keep the Rhone forever "fresh from the cold purity of the glacier's bosom.". . .

South Carolinians may have been the earliest and most vocal proponents of the danger of political corruption, but the same disillusionment spread to other Southern states as they edged closer to secession. The states of the lower South seemed most susceptible to the fear. The distrust of parties and political leaders took several different forms in Alabama. Voters became increasingly cynical about their elected representatives, calling them "tricksters" and throwing them out of office in increasing numbers during the late 1850s. The fire-eaters kept up a steady barrage of warnings about the corruptions of parties and politicians. They warned that Southern men who sought federal office became "traitor[s] to the South, bought with the hope of conciliating Northern favor"; they complained of Southern politicians who "as soon as they get in sight of the Presidential mansion and Treasury office are at once transformed into the most national beings in the world"; they spoke of the danger of "the trammels of party," of the "demoralizing influence of party spirit," of "the hot party agitations which has [*sic*] for years past stirred up and floated into Congress some of the very drugs [*sic*] of society, too light and too filthy to comprehend any duty save that of obedience to party leaders."

In Georgia speakers warned citizens of "old and effete political parties," of "basely corrupt" leaders. They explained: "We have but little virtue, heroic virtue or patriotism now amongst our public men." If Lincoln were elected he would use "patronage for the purpose of organizing in the South a band of apologists." The governor guessed: "So soon as the Government shall have passed into Black Republican hands, a portion of our citizens, must, if possible, be bribed into treachery to their own section by the allurements of office." Georgians hoped that secession would "sweep away the past corruptions of the Government."

Perhaps at no other time in American history have so many people expressed disillusionment with political leaders and parties as in the South on the eve of secession. They feared the corruption emanating from the federal government and the North, but they also saw it eating away at the integrity of their own political structures. Secession became the vehicle of purification. . . .

George M. Fredrickson

WHITE SUPREMACY AND THE AMERICAN SECTIONAL CONFLICT

In recent years, historians as well as Americans in general have become aware of the pervasiveness of racial prejudice and discrimination in the history of the United States. George M. Fredrickson has been one of the most penetrating analysts of the nature and role of racial thought and behavior in the nation's past. In this selection from his magisterial comparison of race relations and slavery in the United States and South Africa, he discusses the impact of race on the coming of the Civil War.

From *White Supremacy: A Comparative Study in American and South African History* by George M. Fredrickson. Copyright © 1981 by Oxford University Press, Inc. Reprinted by permission.

After first claiming that racism was a central feature of the sectional conflict, Fredrickson then offers a complex and intriguing explanation of how racism actually shaped the contest that led to war. On the one hand, he acknowledges that the dominant white populations of both sections were racist, and therefore there was, on this score at least, little difference between them. On the other hand, the racial feelings of the South possessed a far greater intensity, he contends, than did their equivalents in the North. Indeed, so powerful and obsessive was southern concern to maintain white supremacy that it was fundamental to the region's social and political existence.

George M. Fredrickson (born 1934), who teaches at Stanford University, is the author of *The Inner Civil War: Northern Intellectuals and the Crisis of the Union* (1965); *The Black Image in the White Mind: The Debate on Afro-American Character and Destiny, 1817-1914* (1971); and *White Supremacy: A Comparative Study in American and South African History* (1981).

In a provocative effort to reinterpret the causes of the American Civil War, the historian Allan Nevins wrote in 1950 that "the main root of the conflict (and there were minor roots) was the problem of slavery *with its complementary problem of race-adjustment.* . . . Had it not been for the difference in race, the slavery issue would have presented no great difficulties." Subsequent scholarship has cast some doubt on this formulation, primarily by plumbing the depths of northern prejudice and discrimination. David Potter, writing in 1968, summed up this work as showing "that the dominant forces in both sections spurned and oppressed the Negro." It was therefore "difficult to understand why the particular form which this oppression took in the South should have caused acute tension, as it did, between the sections." The most compelling recent work bearing on the causes of the sectional struggle has tended to relegate racial attitudes to a subordinate position and has stressed irreconcilable differences in the hegemonic interests and ideologies of the dominant classes of the two sections.

But one does not have to deny importance to these broader configurations to recognize that racial considerations played a significant role in shaping and intensifying the conflict. The North as a whole may have had little use for blacks, and the dominant planter class of the South may have had a greater stake in slavery than simply racial control. But the question persists as to why the white South as a whole, and not just the slaveholding minority, reacted with such intensity to the prospect of any tampering with slavery or limitation of its expansion. It also remains unclear how the North, with all its Negrophobia, could eventually consent to the sudden liberation of four million slaves on American soil, and, shortly thereafter, to their enfranchisement. Although very few white Americans actually endorsed the principle of racial equality on the eve of the Civil War, significant differences of opinion did in fact exist on the question of what racial differences meant for the future of American society.

Our prime source of confusion has been a failure to distinguish between what the psycho-historian Joel Kovel has described as the "dominative" and "aversive" varieties of "racism." "In general," he writes, "the dominative type has been marked by heat and the aversive type by coldness. The former is closely associated with the American South, where, of course, domination of blacks became the cornerstone of society; and the latter with the North, where blacks have so consistently come and found themselves out of place. The dominative racist, when threatened by the black, resorts to direct violence; the aversive racist, in the same situation, turns away and walls himself off." Whatever its validity for other historical periods, this typology can be readily applied to antebellum sectional differences. It was the South that believed it needed blacks as a servile labor force and social "mudsill" (permanent menial class) and developed elaborate rationalizations for keeping them in that position. The North, on the other hand, revealed its basic attitudes in laws that excluded black migrants from entering individual states and in a spate of theorizing, especially in the 1850s, that advocated or prophesied the total elimination of the black population of the United States through expatriation or natural extinction. Some historians have even argued that a principal motive for the northern crusade to prevent the extension of slavery to the federal territories was an aversion to blacks.

But this contrast is misleading, and makes subsequent events incomprehensible, unless another distinction is introduced—namely a crucial difference in the *salience* of the racial attitudes that predominated. "Dominative racism" was a much more significant component of the southern world-view than "aversive racism" was of the northern. Hence it would be an easier matter for Northerners to subordinate their racial sensibilities to other considerations, such as

the imperatives of nationalism or the desire for a consistent application of democratic-egalitarian principles. In the South it was necessary to translate all social and political values into racial terms; for
it was not just slavery, but *black* slavery, that was the keystone of
the social and economic order.

The specific developments leading to the sectional confrontation of 1861 take on an added dimension when viewed in the
perspective of comparative racial attitudes. In the 1830s, a northern
minority, for whom William Lloyd Garrison was the most prominent spokesman, caused a nation-wide furor by calling for the immediate abolition of slavery and eventual incorporation of freed
blacks into American society as full citizens. Spawned by the evan-
gelicalism of the "Second Great Awakening" and its millenarian or
perfectionist offshoots, the abolitionist movement was a logical outcome of the spirit of radical reform that constituted one kind of
response to the unsettling political, social, and economic changes of
the Jacksonian era. As their own relations with blacks sometimes
revealed, the abolitionists were not entirely free of the aversive
prejudice that was widespread in the North. Where they differed
from the majority was in their principled adherence to nonracial
principles in the realm of public policy and social organization. The
most effective sanction for their position was a literal interpretation
of the Declaration of Independence. If "all men are created equal"
and "endowed by their creator with certain inalienable rights," it
was sheer hypocrisy for Americans to hold blacks as slaves and deny
them the essential rights of citizenship. Many abolitionists, perhaps
a majority, were not in fact convinced that blacks as a race were
intellectually equal to whites. But to them this consideration was
basically irrelevant. Like Jefferson, they grounded their belief in
equality on the doctrine of an innate moral sense shared by all
human beings rather than on an identity of rational capabilities.
Furthermore, Christianity taught them that the strong had no right
to oppress the weak; and the economic and political liberalism that
they shared with most other Americans made no provision for
competency tests as a basis for legal equality and participation in a
free labor market. Although they condoned such "natural" inequalities as were based on achievement and cultivation, the abolitionists
stood firmly against artificial barriers to the advancement of any
individual or group. In a real sense, therefore, they represented the

egalitarian conscience of the competitive liberal-democratic society that was emerging in the North.

As is often the reaction of those condemned for not living up to their own principles, a northern majority responded to the abolitionist movement of the 1830s with bitter hostility. Antislavery meetings were broken up by mobs, and individual abolitionists were manhandled or even lynched. State legislatures all over the North passed resolutions condemning this new and militant agitation of the slavery issue. The common complaint against the abolitionists, and the one that was most likely to inspire violence, was that they threatened the supremacy and purity of the white race. Charges that the abolitionists promoted interracial marriage or "amalgamation" set off two of the most savage riots of the tumultuous 1830s—in New York in 1834 and Philadelphia in 1838. The participation of lower-class whites in these disorders was induced to a great extent by the status anxieties generated by a competitive society. For those who had little chance to realize the American dream of upward mobility, it was comforting to think there was a clearly defined outgroup that was even lower in the social hierarchy.

Among the better situated and more thoughtful critics of the abolitionists, another concern was the effect of this new crusade on the preservation of the Union and the success of the republican experiment. Conservative Northerners believed, with considerable justification, that sustained antislavery agitation in their own section would be viewed by the South as a threat to the constitutional "compromise" on slavery and an occasion for "calculating the value of the Union." But there was usually a more profound basis for objecting to the abolitionist program than a purely patriotic devotion to sectional peace and harmony. Since 1817, northern elites had given substantial support to the colonization movement with its unshakable conviction that a combination of white prejudice and black incapacity precluded full citizenship for freed slaves. Hence they endorsed the view that the abolitionist program of "immediate emancipation" would open the doors to the kind of heterogeneity and disorder that was deemed incompatible with the preservation of a stable republican government and a social order dominated by men of property. So long as the blacks remained in the United States in large numbers, they reasoned, it was better that they be firmly enslaved rather than becoming a discontented underclass with just enough freedom to provoke violence and chaos by agitating for their rights.

Despite the widespread northern revulsion to abolitionism in the 1830s and 40s, much of the slaveholding South was thrown into a panic by the very existence of such a movement. Although they clearly exaggerated the extent of northern support for Garrison and his immediate followers, the proslavery polemicists who emerged to do verbal battle with the abolitionists correctly sensed that northern opinion had a potential affinity for antislavery doctrines. Where the abolitionist position seemed most vulnerable was in its prescription of racial egalitarianism as the norm for American society. Partly for strategic reasons, therefore, the earliest defenders of slavery as a "positive good" chose to stress the argument that blacks were a distinct and inferior variety or species of humanity whose innate deficiencies—moral as well as intellectual—made them natural slaves permanently unsuited for freedom or citizenship. It followed that race was a necessary and proper criterion for determining social and legal status in any society that contained a large proportion of such natural "inferiors." This justification of Afro-American servitude as a legitimate application of the quasi-scientific doctrine that there were vast and irremediable differences in the character and capabilities of whites and blacks quickly became the dominant mode of proslavery apologetics in the United States. In his celebrated speech of 1837 defending the South against abolitionist assaults, John C. Calhoun gave central importance to racial distinctions: "where two races of different origin, and distinguished by color, and other physical differences, as well as intellectual, are brought together," he contended, "the relation now existing in the slaveholding states between the two is, instead of an evil, a good— a positive good."

Much of the popularity of the racial defense of slavery stemmed from the fact that its appeal extended far beyond the one-quarter of the southern white population that was actually involved in the ownership of slaves. It is sometimes forgotten that the South turned to a more militant defense of servitude at precisely the time when it was succumbing to Jacksonian pressures to extend the franchise and otherwise increase the democratic rights of the white population. One implication of an appeal to racism by slaveholders was to project an ideal of "*Herrenvolk* equality" by justifying equal citizenship for all whites and a servile status for all blacks on the grounds that there were innate differences in group capacities for self-government. An ideological marriage between egalitarian democracy and biological racism pandered at once to the democratic sensibilities and the racial prejudices of the "plain folk" and was thus well suited to the maintenance of inter-class solidarity between planters and non-slaveholders with the South. It could also create a bond between the southern planter elite and the insecure and often Negrophobic lower-class whites who helped make up the rank-and-file of the Democratic Party in the North. The Alabama "fire-eater" William Yancey summed up the *Herrenvolk* ideology before a northern audience in 1860: "Your fathers and my fathers built this government on two ideas; the first is that the white race is the citizen and the master race, and the white man is the equal of every other white man. The second idea is that the Negro is the inferior race." In such a fashion, the contradiction between the principles of the Declaration of Independence and the practices of slavery and racial subordination—a prime source of the antislavery appeal—could be overcome. Only whites were deemed to be "men" in the sense that they qualified for natural rights. By placing a heavy stress on biological differences whites could conceive of themselves as democratic while also being racially exclusive.

But not all white Southerners were entirely satisfied with such a formulation. There was a tendency among an elite of slaveholding intellectuals to deny the idea of equality more comprehensively. Yet even these unabashed proponents of "aristocracy" as a universally valid basis for social order found an important use for the concept of biological inequality among races. It became a particularly convenient device for sorting out the "mudsill" from the more privileged members of a hierarchical society. If all blacks were naturally "childlike" creatures incapable of taking responsibility for themselves—the standard image of the plantation myth—then it was justifiable to subject them to a form of patriarchal rule inappropriate for adult white males. All white men thereby became potential "aristocrats," and the conservative conception of a rank-ordered society could be preserved without confronting the horrendous task of reducing lower-class but enfranchised members of the dominant race to an inferior civil status. In one fashion or another, therefore, the concept of natural racial inferiority could serve to mitigate the conflict between the paternalistic and pre-modern aspects of the plantation community and the individualistic, formally democratic social and political order prevailing outside its gates. Depending on its context or the audience to which it was addressed, the doctrine that there were innate moral and intellectual differences between whites and blacks could make the latter into perpetual children requiring paternal supervision or into a class of sub-humans who had to be excluded from the community of enfranchised equals prescribed by the liberal-democratic tradition.

If the slavocratic South and its northern sympathizers had remained content with defending slavery where it was already established as a necessary means of disciplining an allegedly inferior race, it is unlikely that such a drastic sectional polarization would have occurred in the 1850s. Abolitionism in its pure form remained unpopular in the North, aversion to blacks continued to be the dominant racial attitude, and it was generally acknowledged that the price of union was a continued respect for the barriers against antislavery action that had been entrenched in the Constitution. But by this time a large number of Northerners had been so antagonized by a southern defense of the principle of slavery that contravened their conception of a democratic society, and so alarmed by what they regarded as the deleterious social and economic consequences of the institution, that they were prepared to resist strenuously any efforts to extend its influence. The abolitionists had failed to arouse much sympathy for blacks as human beings, but their secondary contention that slavery degraded free white labor and retarded capitalistic economic development because it gave slaveholders an unfair advantage in the competition for land, labor, and capital had struck a more responsive chord. Consequently, the issue of the status of slavery in the federal territories, which arose first in connection with the vast areas acquired as a result of the Mexican War and then resurfaced when efforts were made to organize the territories of Kansas and Nebraska in 1854, became the direct source of sectional controversy and conflict.

A northern conviction that Congress had the right and the responsibility to ensure that the territories were "free soil" had first emerged as the platform of a third party in 1848; after the Kansas-Nebraska Act of 1854 opened up the area west of the states of Iowa and Missouri to the possible extension of slavery, this idea became the fundamental tenet of a new sectional party that had already won the support of a majority of northern voters by 1856. The early successes of the Republican Party stemmed in large part from a belief that there was a southern conspiracy to extend slavery, with all its blighting effects on the prospects for a free-labor economy, to frontier areas where it had no constitutional right to go. What was more, slavery had been expressly prohibited in the Kansas-Nebraska region by the Missouri Compromise of 1820. Consequently, the fury of Northerners who supported the new party was aroused by a sense that they were no longer dealing with a minority section that was simply exercising its constitutional rights by defending its "peculiar institution" as a local exception to a national pattern of free labor. They now saw themselves engaged in a struggle with an aggressive "slave power" that was seeking to make its labor system the national norm. Such expansionism, Republicans believed, would directly threaten the capacity of the North—and ultimately the nation as a whole—to realize its potential as a progressive, middle-class democracy based on a free-market economy.

Historians have cast doubt on the proposition that a coordinated and self-conscious "slave-power conspiracy" was actually behind the Kansas-Nebraska Act, but they are generally agreed that the territorial issue, once it was raised, provoked a militant response in the South that drove its leaders to contest every acre of the federal domain, whatever the actual prospects of slavery being permanently established there, and even in some cases to call for annexation of new territory south of the continental United States in the hope of establishing a "Caribbean slave empire." The logic of the "positive-good" defense of slavery clearly justified its expansion, and long-standing fears of northern political dominance dictated efforts to prevent the admission of additional free states to the Union.

Direct concerns about black-white relations and the destiny of the black population in the United States affected this sectional quarrel in ways that may at first glance seem secondary or peripheral. Opponents of the Republicans, in both the North and South, attempted to discredit the new party by charging that it advocated the equality and even the amalgamation of the races. But Republican spokesmen, including Abraham Lincoln, generally responded to such demagogic accusations by professing their own commitment to white supremacy and then blaming slavery and the South for race mixing and the growth and spread of a black population within the United States. Many Republicans, again including Lincoln, advocated colonization or deportation of blacks as the only solution to the race problem. In the meantime, they sometimes condoned or even endorsed the discriminatory laws and exclusion from the suffrage that made blacks non-citizens in most of the northern states.

Despite the Republicans' apparent acquiescence in white supremacy and their repeated disavowal of any attempt to interfere with slavery where it was already established, southern spokesmen and their northern sympathizers continued to invoke the prospect of a collapse of white control, followed by some type of racial cataclysm, as the worst disaster to be anticipated from the Republicans' gaining national power. There is a strong temptation to dismiss such prophecies as either cynical propaganda aimed at a Negrophobic electorate or as the expression of some form of collective paranoia. But there was a strain of realism in the charge that Republicans were covert enemies of the kind of white dominance that the South believed essential to its survival. First of all, it was assumed—with some justification—that the Republican program for containing slavery to its present limits would mean its further demise. Indeed, Republican leaders occasionally admitted that their long-range goal was, in Lincoln's words, to put slavery "on the path to ultimate extinction." The notion that slavery had to expand or die was based partly on the economic imperatives of the institution; it had always required fresh lands to maintain its profitability, and the expectation of further growth of the plantation economy was essential to maintaining the value of the South's enormous investment in human chattel. Any threat to the future of slavery as an institution was *ipso facto* an assault on white supremacy, or so it seemed at the time.

Historians, knowing how the South succeeded in re-establishing black subordination after the Civil War, may be tempted to disassociate racial concerns for the defense of slavery. If the South needed a model for subjugating blacks without owning them, it has been suggested, they needed only to look at the North, with its "black codes," social segregation, and disfranchisement. But this point of view fails to take account of the antebellum perception of the crucial significance of racial demography. The orthodox position on the relationship of slavery and racial control, a view that predominated in the South until it was disproved by the inventiveness of post-war segregationists, was set forth in 1844 by John C. Calhoun when he differentiated between the effects of abolition "where the numbers are few," as in the North, and where blacks were numerous, as in the South. In the former case, the freedmen would rapidly sink to a degraded and "inferior condition." "But . . . where the number is great, and bears a large proportion to the whole population, it would be still worse. It would substitute for the existing relation a deadly strife between the two races, to end in the subjection, expulsion, or extirpation of one or the other. . . ."

The fear that any restriction on the ability of slavery to expand or any weakening of the power or authority of the master class would lead to an inter-racial struggle for survival was close to the heart of southern opposition to Republicanism. As the historian William Barney has pointed out, expansion was viewed not only as an economic necessity but also as "a racial safety valve." To pen up the rapidly growing black population within the existing limits of the South would allegedly fuse a "Malthusian time bomb" and increase the danger of social chaos or even massive slave insurrection. Failure to allow the South to carry its surplus slaves into new territories, Jefferson Davis warned, would "crowd upon our soil an overgrown black population, until there will not be room in the country for whites and blacks to subsist in; and in this way destroy the institution and reduce the whites to the degraded position of the African race.

The lack of Republican sympathy for the white South's racial plight might easily be attributed to a variety of ulterior motives. But, despite the "aversive racism" that Republicans often manifested, their fundamental ideology had no real place for racial domination of a legalized kind, and Southerners were correct in perceiving it as a potential threat to any kind of formalized and rigid racial hierarchy that they might devise. The northern middle-class conception of the good society, as reflected in Republican rhetoric, harbored no justification whatever for the existence of a permanent "mudsill" class; the dominant social and political ideal was "equality of opportunity," or, as Lincoln put it, "equal privileges in the race of life." A competitive society would, of course, result in differences in wealth, power, and social status, but such inequalities would be "natural" and not the "artificial" result of caste distinctions. In the language of modern sociologists, Republicans stood for a social hierarchy based on achievement rather than ascription. This clashed sharply with the southern defense of a social order based, as Barrington Moore has put it, on "hereditary privilege."* To the extent that Northerners repudiated the principle of ascription and defined their own society in opposition to it, they were in effect denying legitimacy to their own practice of legalized discrimination against blacks. Since Republicans had no desire for a subordinated menial class, the only alternatives—at least in theory—were exclusion of blacks and the maintenance of racial homogeneity, or the establishment of a color-blind legal and political system. Clearly the preference in the 1850s was for exclusion or deportation; but when that proved impracticable, and when the North found a need for emancipation and a use for freed blacks during the Civil War, a dominant group was able to sublimate its racial prejudices and make an effort to live up to its egalitarian principles. The final fruit of Republican idealism, and a logical extension of its original principles, was Radical Reconstruction.

The Confederate cause, on the other hand, was not simply the defense of slavery as an institution, but also—and inseparably—a struggle to preserve a social order based squarely on "dominative racism." Slaveholders had many reasons for valuing the peculiar institution; for them it was an obvious source of personal wealth, privilege, and prestige. James L. Roark is probably correct in his assertion that their "commitment to slavery was far more profound than a simple fear of black equality." Nevertheless, the most plausible rationale that they could devise for their practice of enslaving other human beings was that blacks were moral and intellectual inferiors who would lead orderly and productive lives only if under the direct control of white masters. Not only did slaveholders believe this, but the urgent need to ensure the loyalty of the non-slaveholding white majority caused them to emphasize it increasingly as they mobilized the southern states for secession and civil war. As Roark has also pointed out, one of the greatest anxieties of secessionist planters was that class conflict would divide the whites, but they assuaged

---

*Moore's formulation fails to make it clear, however, that the only form of ascription or hereditary privilege that could in fact achieve firm legitimacy in the South was derived from racial criteria.

their fears by appealing to racial solidarity. In his words, "the centripetal force they relied most heavily upon was white supremacy. . . ." Only by stressing the non-slaveholders' social and psychological stake in slavery as a system of racial control could they hope to maintain a united front against a Republican-dominated government that was thought to be bent on the "ultimate extinction" of the institution.

The central role of "dominative racism" as a rationale for secession and a defining feature of southern nationalism was most vividly set forth in Alexander Stephens' famous "cornerstone speech," delivered shortly after his election as Vice President of the Confederacy in 1861. "Many governments have been founded on the principles of subordination and serfdom of certain classes of the same race," he explained; *such were, and are, in violation of the laws of nature.* Our system commits no such violation of nature's laws. With us, all the white race, however high or low, rich or poor, are equal in the eyes of the law. Not so with the Negro. Subordination is his place. He, by nature, or by the curse against Canaan, is fitted for that condition which he occupies in our system." The basis of the new Confederate government was precisely this great truth: "Its foundations are laid, its cornerstone rests upon the great truth that the Negro is not equal to the white man, that slavery—subordination to the superior race—is his natural or normal condition."

An uncompromising commitment to white supremacy was thus a central and unifying component of the separate southern identity that crystallized on the eve of the Civil War. The North was also a prejudiced society in the sense that its white population was generally hostile to blacks and accepted the prevailing belief that they were inferior to whites. But the legalized racial discrimination that existed in the North created an ideological anomaly because it failed to jibe with a growing commitment to middle-class democracy and an open competitive society. Hence it was peripheral or even contradictory to the larger social and political aims of a reformist leadership and could be jettisoned in good conscience or even with self-righteousness. But without its commitment to hierarchical bi-racialism the South was not the South. Only by drawing on the region's deep and salient sources of racial anxiety could the architects of the Confederacy muster the conviction and solidarity necessary for a sustained struggle for independence.

The Secession Crisis

Steven A. Channing

SECESSION IN SOUTH CAROLINA

Steven A. Channing's treatment of South Carolina's secession is note-worthy for its claim that the Carolinians' decision was based not so much on the need to protect slavery as on a deep concern about an imminent loss of control over blacks. That is, fear of racial unrest drove them into secession.

If fear, amounting to hysteria, propelled them, then they undertook secession in an atmosphere of frenzy wherein rational calculation was virtually impossible. By stressing irrationality, Channing suggests that so drastic a move as secession could not occur without some degree of passion and excitement. Indeed, it is inconceivable that a war could break out or a revolt begin in an atmosphere of calm. But that does not necessarily mean that secession itself was an irrational, perhaps paranoid, course of action. It could, as Channing implies, flow logically from the fears already aroused.

Steven A. Channing (born 1940) is the author of *Crisis of Fear: Secession in South Carolina* (1970), from the conclusion of which this selection is taken.

The secession of South Carolina was an affair of passion. The revolution could not have succeeded, and it certainly would not have instilled the astounding degree of unanimity in all classes and all sections that it did, were this not so. The emotional momentum was a function of the intensity of the fear which drove the revolution forward. Divisions, doubts about the wisdom or efficacy of secession were met, or overturned. The ostensible leaders of the movement could not agree on whether they had created this tempest, or had themselves been picked up and carried along by it. Barnwell politician Alfred Aldrich described events in terms which Rhett [Robert Barnwell Rhett was probably the leading secessionist in South Carolina], and many others could appreciate.

Stephen Channing, *Crisis of Fear: Secession in South Carolina,* Copyright © 1970 by Steven A. Channing. Reprinted by permission of Simon & Schuster.

I do not believe the common people understand it, in fact, I know that they do not understand it; but whoever waited for the common people when a great move was to be made. We must make the move & force them to follow. This is the way of all revolutions & all great achievements, & he who waits until the mind of every body is made up will wait forever & never do any thing.

But there were many of Aldrich's associates who strongly disagreed with this description. Poet William Gilmore Simms drew endless pictures of the "landsturm," his romantic image of the essentially popular nature of the movement for secession. Alfred Huger, with his accustomed anxiety warned his friend Joseph Holt that "this revolution is beyond the reach of human power. . . . We have no leaders of any prominence," Huger lamented, "the masses are in the front-rank and cannot be restrained." Such a state of affairs did not frighten everyone. Augustus Baldwin Longstreet, then president of South Carolina College in Columbia, wrote to the editor of the Richmond *Enquirer* on December 6 to refute charges that the secession movement in Carolina had been "gotten up" by the politicians for their own selfish purposes.

Never was there a greater mistake. It is the result of one universal outburst of indignation on the part of the people at Lincoln's election—the unanimous and almost spontaneous resolve, from the mountains to the sea-board, that they never should come under Black Republican rule. . . . You might as well attempt to control a tornado as to attempt to stop them from secession. They drive politicians before them like sheep.

Where was the truth in the kaleidoscope of power? Which way did the lines of action-reaction go, and who ruled whom? Textbook truths usually lie "somewhere in the middle." The answer to this riddle of authority and response probably rested in a like balance. Much has been written to show the deep division of the Southern people, including South Carolinians, on the question of secession. It nearly failed, it is said. More to the point is the fact that it was at last consummated. Against the twin forces of Unionism and fear of secession the revolution carried the day. Analyzing political feeling in the state, all who supported the movement were, of course, prosecessionists, and many of those who opposed immediate action were disunionists as well. Of those who resisted separate secession many may certainly be described as either timid men, men who wanted security, saw it in Southern nationalism, but also feared the unknowable changes that a revolution might bring; men who wanted secession to come, but only as a cooperative venture by a sizable portion of the slave states; or men who believed disunion to be inevitable, if not desirable, but craved some "overt act" of aggression by Lincoln to cite for their consciences and the eye of history. That immediate secession triumphed over these sentiments is the remarkable phenomenon, not the fact that there was still a voice of conservatism in the lower South. Secession has been castigated as a usurpation because a majority allegedly did not support it wholeheartedly; yet these same historians applaud the glories of the American Revolution when all agree that barely one-third favored independence.

The Secession Convention which came together in Columbia on December 17, and in Charleston three days later signed the declaration creating the independent republic of South Carolina, was as representative as it was distinguished. The wealthy, the powerful, the famous were there, as were many unassuming figures from districts across the state. Some had been elected as the traditional leaders in their home districts and parishes. Others perhaps gained the vote of their neighbors at the election on December 6 because of their ardent work for the revolution; one of the representatives from Williamsburg District had gained fame in his association with the Kingstree *Star* during its campaign against abolitionist influences in the region. The people had indeed responded to Lincoln's election with a ferocious roar; but that in part had been planned and hoped for by men such as Aldrich. Still, once those potent fears of secession which so damaged the plans of disunionists elsewhere were mollified or quelled in South Carolina, the movement for secession *was* a popular revolution, Simms's "landsturm." Shortly after the consummation of secession, Isaac Hayne wrote Charles Cotesworth Pinckney, Jr., to tell him the good news. The feeling in favor of the step throughout the state was so strong, Hayne wrote, that no one, not even the old gadflies [Benjamin F.] Perry and [James L.] Orr, had "dared to oppose the onward current." When the signed ordinance of secession was held up in crowded Institute Hall a thunderous shout filled the large chamber, and Hayne, "who put but little faith in the shout of the mob, felt at last that in *this,* the people were in earnest." Affairs had been put into such shape by the leaders as to compel a decision for secession. The people did not hesitate to endorse the compulsion. Plebiscitory democracy triumphed in South Carolina.

*

Secession was the product of logical reasoning within a framework of irrational perception. The party of Abraham Lincoln was inextricably identified with the spirit represented by John Brown, William Lloyd Garrison, and the furtive incendiary conceived to be lurking even then in the midst of the slaves. The election of Lincoln was at once the expression of the will of the Northern people to destroy slavery, and the key to that destruction. The constitutional election of a president seemed to many, North and South, an unjustifiable basis for secession. But it was believed that that election had signalled an acceptance of the antislavery dogmas by a clear majority of Northerners, and their intention to create the means to abolish slavery in America. Lincoln was elected, according to South Carolinians, on the platform of an "irrepressible conflict." This, as James Hammond believed, was "no mere political or ethical conflict, but a social conflict in which there is to be a war of races, to be waged at midnight with the torch, the knife & poison." Submission to the rule of the Republicans would be more than a dishonor. It would be an invitation to self-destruction. Implementing the power of the Presidency, and in time the rest of the Federal machinery, slavery would be legally abolished in time. What would that bring? Baptist minister James Furman thought he knew.

> Then every negro in South Carolina and every other Southern State will be his own master; nay, more than that, will be the equal of every one of you. If you are tamed enough to submit, Abolition preachers will be at hand to consummate the marriage of your daughters to black husbands.

South Carolinians were repeatedly called on to explain the reasons for secession to their uncomprehending Northern friends and relatives. The description these Northerners received of the dominant new party—and of themselves—must have shocked them. "Who are these Black Republicans?" Sue Keitt, wife of the congressman [Lawrence M. Keitt], wrote to a woman in Philadelphia. "A motley throng of Sans culottes and Dames des Halles, Infidels and freelovers, interspersed by Bloomer women, fugitive slaves, and," worst of all, "amalgamationists." The Republican party was the incarnation of all the strange and frightening social and philosophical doctrines which were flourishing in free Northern society, doctrines which were not only alien but potentially disruptive to the allegedly more harmonious and conservative culture of the slave South. It has been suggested that slavery was merely a handle seized upon by extremists in both sections to wage a battle founded in far deeper antagonism. The election of 1860 proclaimed to the South that it must accept a new order of consolidation, industrialization, and democratization. According to this interpretation, secession spelled the rejection of these terms for the preservation of the Union by the old ruling classes.

There is no doubt that those who dominated political life in South Carolina feared the nature of the new social order rising in the North, and feared the party that stood for this order. "The concentration of absolute power in the hands of the North," Lawrence Keitt predicted, "will develop the wildest democracy ever seen on this earth—unless it shall have been matched in Paris in 1789— What of conservatism?—What of order? —What of social security or financial prosperity?" Many Carolinians believed that two separate and distinct civilizations existed in America in 1860, one marked by "the calculating coolness and narrow minded prejudices of the Puritans of New England in conflict with the high and generous impulses of the cavalier of Virginia and the Carolinas." By pecuniary choice and racial compulsion the South had "opted" for slavery and out of that decision had arisen a superstructure of social attitudes and institutions which marked the uniqueness of the slaveholding South.

Moreover, just as Northerners failed to comprehend the Southern view of the world, many Carolinians refused to admit that there was, or could be, any moral or idealistic quality in the antislavery pillar of the Republican party. Hammond affirmed that if the Republicans could have been defeated at the polls in 1860 and 1864, abolitionism would have been abandoned, for "no great party question can retain its vitality in this country that cannot make a President." A number of his fellow citizens declared that they too rejected the "mock humanity" of the Republicans. The issue was one of political power, they said, of controlling the national government, of party spoils. There was an almost pathetic element in this refusal to admit, and inability to see, the sincerity of the moral quality of abolitionism. Nevertheless, particularly in the private correspondence of unassuming soldiers and farmers, one can see frequent references to resistance to the threat of Northern despotism, to the need to protect certain vaguely understood "rights and privileges," often guaranteed by the Constitution. "I care nothing for the 'Peculiar institution'" claimed one former Unionist, "but I can't stand the idea of being domineered over by a set of Hypocritical scoundrels such as Summer, Seward, Wilson, Hale, etc. etc."

Still, the conclusion is inescapable that the multiplicity of fears revolving around the maintenance of race controls for the Negro was not simply the prime concern of the people of South Carolina in their revolution, but was so very vast and frightening that it literally consumed the mass of lesser "causes" of secession which have inspired historians. James Hammond recognized the question of economic exploitation, and the fact that Southerners believed in Northern financial and commercial domination is clear. Nonetheless, the issue went virtually unnoticed in private exchanges throughout the year. Some leaders denounced what they thought was the injustice of the colonial status of the economic South, but this did not touch the hearts of the people, great and low. Attempts to organize such devices as direct steamship trade with Europe, use of homespun cloth, and conventions to promote Southern economic self-sufficiency were, like the more transparent plans for commercial non-intercourse, aimed at wielding the economic power of the region to gain political ends, specifically an end to agitation of the slavery question.

The glorious potential of an independent Southern nation held great emotional appeal for many, but no one was prepared to enter into the perilous business of nation building without some more basic incentive. South Carolina's spokesmen revelled in the contemplation of the political, economic, and social power of the South. They were eager to prove to the North and to the entire world that the South could establish a great nation in her own right. Yet who could fail to see that this was in part a rationalization for the strong desire to escape the moral obloquy heaped upon slaveholders by the North for so many years past; in part an element in the pro-slavery argument, which held a civilization based upon the peculiar institution to be the highest possible culture; and in part a function of the secession persuasion designed to attract and calm adherents to the cause.

As for the "dry prattle" about the constitution, the rights of minorities, and the like, there never was any confusion in the minds of most contemporaries that such arguments were masks for more fundamental emotional issues. [William Henry] Trescot welcomed the speeches of William Seward because they eschewed textual interpretations of the Constitution, and frankly posed the only true and relevant question: "Do the wants of this great Anglo Saxon race, the need of our glorious and progressing free white civilization require the abolition of negro slavery?" Charles Hutson, son of William F. Hutson, a Beaufort rice planter and a signer of the secession ordinance, phrased the matter more directly. Writing from an army camp near Mt. Vernon, Virginia, in September 1861, Hutson commented on a sermon which described the cause of secession as the defense of the noble right of self-government. "It is insulting to the English common sense of the race which governs here," the young soldier retorted, "to tell them they are battling for an abstract right common to all humanity. Every reflecting child will glance at the darkey who waits on him & laugh at the idea of such an abstract right." And when the family of planter John Berkeley Grimball was torn apart by the secession crisis, his son Louis bitterly denounced his sister for charging that South Carolina had willfully destroyed the Union. "What are you writing?" he gasped. "You speak as if we are the aggressors, and would dissolve the union in Blood shed upon a *mere abstract principle,* when the fact is we are oppressed and are contending for all that we hold most dear—our Property—our institutions—our Honor—Aye and our very lives!" To understand what the revolution was all about, he advised his sister to return home from the North, and become a slaveholder herself. So, writing on a broader canvas, Arthur Perroneau Hayne assured President Buchanan that his acquiescence in secession was a noble act of humanity to the white people of the South.

> Slavery with us is no abstraction—but a *great* and *vital fact*. Without it our every comfort would be taken from us. Our wives, our children, made unhappy—education, the light of knowledge—all *all* lost and our *people ruined for ever. Nothing short of separation from the Union can save us.*

The people of 1860 were usually frank in their language and clear in their thinking about the reasons for disunion. After the war, for many reasons men came forward to clothe the traumatic failure of the movement in the misty garments of high constitutional rights and sacred honor. Nevertheless, there were two "abstract rights" which were integral to secession, state sovereignty and property rights. No historian could surpass the discussion of these questions by wartime governor Andrew Gordon Magrath. From the fastness of his imprisonment in Fort Pulaski in 1865 Magrath looked back upon the cause of secession with a detachment which had not yet been colored by the sterilization and obfuscation of the post-war remembrance. There were tangential reasons for the revolution, Magrath allowed, but the central "motive power" was the belief that the ascendancy of the Republican party threatened to disturb their "right of property in slaves." To his credit, Magrath did see the rich variety of implications enmeshed in this property right. For those who did not own a slave, Lincoln's election implied that they might never be able to purchase that essential key to social and economic elevation. In addition, the former jurist understood that the people of the antebellum South conceived slavery to be the basis of stability for their social order, the foundation of their economy, and the source of their moral and cultural superiority. State sovereignty was an issue only because the retreat to the inviolability of state's rights had always been a refuge for those fearful of a challenge to their property. Certainly, the "right of property in slaves" is closer to the heart of the problem than "fear of the antislavery movement," or similar propositions which raise more questions than they answer.

Mid–nineteenth century Americans lived in an age of romanticism. Men had fought for lesser glories than independence and Southern nationalism; and once the terrible momentum was begun, who could say for certain what myths, compulsions, and desires drove men on into revolution and civil war. But somewhere in the intellectual hiatus of the war the clear and concrete understanding of the cause of it all, an understanding shared by those who joined to tear away from the Union, was lost. For the people of South Carolina perpetuation of the Union beyond 1860 meant the steady and irresistible destruction of slavery, which was the first and last principle of life in that society, the only conceivable pattern of essential race control. Perpetuation of the Union, according to Senator Hammond, meant servile insurrection, and ultimately abolition. "We dissolve the Union to prevent it," he told a Northerner in

1861, "and [we] believe, I believe it will do it." Secession was a revolution of passion, and the passion was fear.

Here we have in charge the solution of the greatest problem of the ages. We are here two races—white and black—now both equally American, holding each other in the closest embrace and utterly unable to extricate ourselves from it. A problem so difficult, so complicated, and so momentous never was placed in charge of any portion of Mankind. And on its solution rests our all.

The nation was led into war in 1861 by the secession of the lower South, not by the desire of the Northern people either to end slavery or bring equality to the Negro. Subsequent generations of Americans came to condemn the racist fears and logic which had motivated that secession, yet the experience of our own time painfully suggests that it was easy to censure racism, but more difficult to obliterate it. . . .

Bertram Wyatt-Brown

HONOR AND SECESSION

In his *Southern Honor: Ethics and Behavior in the Old South* (1982), Bertram Wyatt-Brown made an important, and provocative, contribution to historians' understanding about the nature of southern society before the Civil War. He contended that a public ethos prevailed in the South, based on the idea that a person's self-worth was derived from the esteem and respect he was accorded by his peers. By contrast with the custom outside the South, southern men were concerned less with personal achievement and inner convictions of rectitude and integrity than with how society valued them, that is, with their public reputation and status. In this setting a humiliating remark in public might require an immediate response in the form of a challenge to a duel to reestablish manhood and honor.

In the essay that follows, Wyatt-Brown examines the South's resort to secession as a response to the public humiliation and degradation that the North had been inflicting on the region throughout the era of controversy over slavery. The constant denigration of southerners' morality because they ran a slave system came to a head with the election to the presidency of Abraham Lincoln, an avowed opponent of slavery. So obvious an indignity as this had to be repudiated publicly and dramatically. Secession was the form it took. Underlying this emphasis on the centrality of honor in southern life is the assumption that, in quite basic ways, the South was a different society from the rest of the United States, and not just in its practice of slaveholding. But, of course, the persistence of honor was not unrelated to the existence of slavery, with its concomitant master-slave relationship and need for hierarchy and deference.

Bertram Wyatt-Brown (born 1932) teaches at the University of Florida and is the author of *Lewis Tappan and the Evangelical War Against Slavery* (1969); *Southern Honor: Ethics and Behavior in the Old South* (1982); and *Yankee Saints and Southern Sinners* (1985), a collection of his own essays of which this excerpt is a chapter.

The reluctance of those with the most to lose was only one of several indications that more than just slavery was at work in the secessionist dynamic. Slavery was itself inseparable from other aspects of regional life, most especially from the southerners' sense of themselves as a people. That self-perception can be called the principle of honor. In modern times the term has so little meaning that it occupies, says sociologist Peter Berger, "about the same place in contemporary usage as chastity." Nevertheless, though sometimes seen as simply a "romance" to prettify the harsh reality of race control, it was a powerful force in the nineteenth-century South.

Honor may be described in a number of ways, both characterologic and social. It can be considered as general demeanor or gentlemanliness; virtue, that is, trustworthiness and honesty; entitlement; or class rank. Certainly southerners believed that dependability for truth-telling was a prime aspect of honorable character, but it was more than that and also more than a fascination with titles like Colonel and Judge, forms of address that southerners were notoriously prone to crave. Honor will be used here in two separate sociological and ethical senses: the southern mode, which might be called traditional honor, and the mid-nineteenth-century northern one. The latter represented, to use Berger's term, an *"embourgeoisement"* of the concept—diminishing its feudal and communal overtones and adding an institutional, impersonal, and middle-class element.

In regard to traditional honor, the concept involves process more than merely an idealization of conduct. First, honor is a sense of personal worth and it is invested in the whole person. Yet that whole covers more than the individual—it includes the identification of the individual with his blood relations, his community, his state, and whatever other associations the man of honor feels are important for establishing his claim for recognition. The close bonding of honor with an extended self, as it were, contrasts with the kind of honor that would place country before family, professional duty before other matters of importance. Second, honor as a dynamic connecting self and society requires that the individual make a claim for worthiness before the community. And third, it involves the acceptance of that self-evaluation in the public forum, a ratification that enables the claimant to know his place in society and his moral standing. "I am who I say I am" (or, more accurately, "I am who I seem to be"), says the man of traditional honor. We more likely might say, "I am who I am because of what I do." The timocratic community replies, "You are who you say you are." The exchange is completed with the registry of that reply upon the tablet of the individual's personality. He incorporates what is said and thought of him as part of his identity. Although honor can be directly internalized—to act *as if* a public were watching—it has few inner referents. Unlike the man of conscience, the individual dependent on honor must have respect from others as the prime means for respecting himself. Shifting fortunes, personal rivalries, worrisome doubts that one has been properly assessed make the ethical scheme an elusive, tense, and ultimately insecure method of self-acceptance. Western man has always known that traditional honor, being dependent upon public sanction, is a fickle mistress. Outward shows or honors—"place, riches, and favour, / Prizes of accident"—sometimes matter as much as or more than merit, to borrow from Shakespeare, the southerners' most admired playwright.

Ambiguities abound. On the one hand, moderation, prudence, coolness under duress, and self-restraint are admired and even idealized. The southern "Nestors" who urged calm deliberateness before entering on secession hoped to have these qualities approved in the public arena. On the other hand, the man of honor feels that defense of reputation and virility must come before all else. Otherwise, he is open to charges of effeminacy and fear. As Ulysses complains of his warrior colleagues:

> They tax our policy and call it cowardice,
> Count wisdom as no member of the war,
> Forestall prescience, and esteem no act
> But that of hand.

In political terms, honor was not at all confined to those at the top of the social order. It is the nature of the ethic that it must be recognized by those with less status; otherwise, there would be none to render honor to claimants. In the American South, common folk, though not given to gentlemanly manners, duels, and other signs of a superior élan, also believed in honor because they had access to the means for its assertion themselves—the possessing of slaves—and because all whites, nonslaveholders as well, held sway over all blacks. Southerners regardless of social position were united in the brotherhood of white-skinned honor—what George M. Fredrickson has called herrenvolk democracy, though we might refer to it as people's timocracy.

It was upon this basis that John C. Calhoun and others came to admire the Periclean Greeks, devoted as the ancients were to *timē* (honor), democracy, republicanism, and small-community autonomy. In the Greek city-states "the passionate drive to show one's self in measuring up against others," said Hannah Arendt, was the actual basis for politics. To some extent, the same held true in the South. Politics was an arena in which peers—not necessarily the greatest magnates—were rivals for public acclaim and power. As a forum for self-presentation and public service, politics was a simple system to which elaborate bureaucracies, heavy taxes, statutory refinements, and other complexities were alien. Even the notion of party organization, as opposed to community consensus and unanimity on key principles, was suspect, at least among the firebrands for disunionism. In all societies where honor of this kind functions, the great distinction is drawn between the autonomy, freedom, and self-sufficiency of those in the body politic and the dependency, forced submissiveness, and powerlessness of all who are barred from political and social participation—that is, slaves or serfs. For the southern free white, dependency posed the threat of meaninglessness. Slaveholding ennobled, that is, enhanced one's status and independence because ownership provided the instruments for exercising power, not over the slave alone, but over those without that resource. By the same social perception, thralldom degraded and humbled. "The essence of honor," says one writer, "is personal autonomy" or freedom to do what one wishes, and its absence indicates powerlessness.

Under these circumstances, the reasons why the southerner felt so threatened by northern criticism should be clear. The dread of public humiliation, especially in the highly charged political setting, was a burden not to be casually dismissed. In general terms, whenever the public response to claims for respect is indifferent, disbelieving, hostile, or derisive, the claimant for honor feels as blasted, as degraded as if struck in the face or unceremoniously thrown to the ground. He is driven to a sense of shame—the very opposite of honor. The response is twofold: first, a denial that he, a persecuted innocent, seeks more than his due; and second, his outraged "honor" requires immediate vindication, by force of arms if need be. This was especially true for the antebellum southerner because he could hardly escape doubts that his section was perceived by the world as inferior, morally and materially. "Reputation is everything," said James Henry Hammond. "Everything with me depends upon the estimation in which I am held," confessed secessionist thinker Beverley Tucker. Personal reputation for character, valor, and integrity did not end there. Individual self-regard encompassed wider spheres. As a result, the southerner took as personal insult the criticisms leveled at slave society as a whole. . . .

Many examples might be used to illustrate the way in which honor and high-toned language pervaded local politics in the South. But only one will be offered here: a public letter sent to the early fire-eater John A. Quitman of Mississippi in 1851. The occasion was his release from trial over his violation of a federal neutrality act by aiding the ill-fated Cuba filibusterer, Narciso López. General Quitman, a hero of the Mexican War, had resigned the governor's chair after indictment, but now had the opportunity to regain the office sacrificed to save the state from association with his embarrassment. The committee used the formal language of deference in expressing gratitude for General Quitman's "chivalrous and patriotic defense not only of the rights of our common country but the rights of the South against the assaults of its enemies." Words such as *defamed* and *persecuted* referred to his injured innocence. The prosecutor's nolle prosequi was small vindication; only his return to the governorship could accomplish that. Preparatory to the upcoming campaign, the admiring supplicants offered to hold a barbecue in Quitman's honor, a distinctly informal affair compared to the style of the invitation. In reply, Quitman acknowledged that their celebration was "peculiarly gratifying." It demonstrated that they approved his conduct, and therefore he was "honored with their confidence and esteem." (He won nomination but later withdrew.) Although scarcely a major incident, the correspondence over the barbecue pointed toward a sectional distinction the significance of which might easily be dismissed. The late-nineteenth-century southern scholar William Garrott Brown once noted, "It is a superficial historical philosophy which dilates on the economic and institutional differences between the two sections, and ignores smaller divergences as appeared in the manners and speech of individuals."

The formality of language made all interchanges less threatening. Ritual words of praise and acceptance ensured a feeling of trust. Words, thoughts, and gestures that ordinary southerners and their leaders knew so well provided that sense of reliability. It was so necessary in the absence of those institutional safeguards which Stanley Elkins described as mediational devices for social and psychological security. Ritual speech softened the harsh world of personal rivalry, vengeance, threat, and hierarchy. It made the common white feel secure and it strengthened the confidence and persuasiveness of the leader. The discrepancy between language and deed, between barbecues and ragtag parades on the one hand and lofty and punctilious deferences on the other helped to ritualize honor. Often such use of language in the Old South is perceived as meaningless, but it was genuinely functional. By these means the planters and militia officers who organized the occasion, the ordinary citizens who attended it, and the former Mexican War general, John Quitman, running for the governor's seat reconfirmed shared attitudes. The exchange and celebration dedicated them all to the defense of the South against its enemies.

In still larger perspective, the employment of honor in its linguistic and political character helped immeasurably to reinforce the social order. The grandiloquent phrase, the references to manliness, bravery, nobility, and resolute action, for example, were scarcely reserved for politics alone, but political correspondence, public letters, editorials, and speeches all employed a tone that sounded bombastic and overblown to the unaccustomed ear. By and large, it was the rhetoric of gentlemen. Lesser folk often admired it. It sanctified the existing social system to lace speeches with Shakespearean and classical phrases, so long as they were familiar to the listeners. However exaggerated its character, the political vocabulary spoke to the most visceral feelings that southerners possessed.

Given the character of southern politics and its ethical framework, the road to secession does not seem so puzzling. In responding to northern criticism and self-assertiveness, the South's defenders had to emphasize vindication and vengeance. As a result, the purpose of so much southern rhetoric in the prewar period was to impugn the motives and policies of the abolitionists in and out of Congress. Any number of examples might be cited to show how southern anguish at criticism reflected the psychological processes of injured pride. Abolitionists like Garrison thought that their sermons against slavery would force the slaveholder to listen to his conscience, but the effort was futile. Instead, antislavery polemics evoked feelings, not of guilt, but of anger and indignation. As John S. Preston, a South Carolina proslavery advocate, declared, "There is not a Christian man, a slaveholder [in the South], who does not feel in his inmost heart as a Christian" that his fellow churchmen of the North have spilled "the last blood of sympathy [on the point of the] sword of the church. . . . They set the lamb of God between our seed and their seed."

Preston Brooks's assault on Charles Sumner in May, 1856, helps to illustrate the means for southern vindication. What outraged Brooks and his accomplice Lawrence Keitt, the South Carolina congressman, was the Massachusetts senator's tasteless vilification of Senator Andrew Pickens Butler, Brooks's kinsman, during the "Bleeding Kansas" speech. In addition, Sumner had dwelt upon the alleged ineffectuality, even cowardice, of South Carolina troops during the American Revolution. By the rules of honor, Brooks was under no obligation to call for a duel with Sumner because one fought on the field of honor only with one's social and moral peers. By southern standards, Sumner fell considerably below that status. In handling inferiors, a one-on-one horsewhipping was much more appropriate. The fire-eater Keitt explained the matter to the House after the event. By the ancient code, he said, "a churl was never touched with the knightly sword; his person was mulcted with the quarter-staff." This incident points to the sense of degradation that Yankees could feel when faced with southern aggression. "We all or *nearly* all felt," a Bostonian wrote the wounded Sumner, "that we had been personally maltreated & insulted." According to William Gienapp, the attack on Sumner, perhaps more than the troubles in Kansas, aroused northern opinion against the South. Even in conservative circles formerly hostile to the Massachusetts senator's course, concerns for northern self-respect and for free speech were evident.

For both sides, Brooks's violence heightened an awareness of honor's demands. But before such means of vengeance, there had been an escalation of verbal confrontations. The abolitionist rhetoric need not be described; our concentration is upon southern epithet and abuse. Southern spokesmen inflated antislavery denunciations to the level of treachery, betrayal, insurrection, and devilish anarchy. Antislavery attacks stained the reputation by which southern whites judged their place and power in the world. Such, for instance, was the reason why slaveholders insisted on the right to carry their property into the free territories at will. It was not solely a matter of expanding slavery's boundaries, though that was of course important. No less significant, however, was southern whites' resentment against any congressional measure which implied the moral inferiority of their region, labor system, or style of life. Such reflections on southern reputation were thought vile and humiliating. For example, in late 1846, Robert Toombs, senator from Georgia, took exception to the Wilmot Proviso, by which slaveholders would be barred from bringing slaves into lands seized from Mexico. Southern whites, he argued, "would be degraded, and unworthy of the name of American freemen, could they consent to remain, for a day or an hour, in a Union where they must stand on ground of inferiority, and be denied the rights and privileges which were extended to all others." Fear for personal losses from antislavery territorial laws did not matter half as much as the symbolism of such antisouthern measures: its signification of still more dire consequences to come. As Toombs remarked in Congress during the sectional crisis of 1850, the right to enter any territory with slaves involved "political equality, [a status] worth a thousand such Unions as we have, even if they each were a thousand times more valuable than this." This issue was no small matter, in his opinion. He elevated the question of slaveholder's territorial prerogatives to the level of a casus belli, at least to his own satisfaction. "Deprive us of this right," he warned the Senate, and it becomes "your government, not mine. Then I am its enemy, and I will then, if I can, bring my children and my constituents to the altar of liberty, and like Hamilcar, I would swear them eternal hostility to your foul domination."

The world of honor is Manichean—divided between Good and Evil; Right and Wrong; Justice and Injustice; Freedom and Slavery; Purity and Corruption. It was also apocalyptic—with the terms of reference being perfect peace or total war: stability or deference and affection toward the worthy, or servile rebellion, rapine, and slaughter of innocents. This style was scarcely incompatible with Protestant theology. But the primal character of the vision must be recognized, too. Dread of bloody revolt belonged to the world of honor, where few outsiders could be trusted. A telling example came from a speech of William L. Yancey at the Democratic convention in Charleston in which he vindicated the southern cause in these terms: "Ours is the property invaded; ours are the institutions which are at stake; ours is the peace that is to be destroyed; ours is the honor at stake—the honor of children, the honor of families, of the lives, perhaps, of all—all of which rests upon what your course may ultimately make a great heaving volcano of passion and crime." Harboring sentiments like these, southern leaders had no reason to question the use of violence as the best retort to obloquy. Thus, in 1858, Jefferson Davis roused a Democratic rally in New York City against Republican "higher law" politicians such as William H. Seward. The "*traitors* [to the Constitution], *these . . . preachers should be tarred and feathered, and whipped by those they have thus instigated.*"

In societies where honor thrives, death in defense of community and principle is a path to glory and remembrance, whereas servile submission entails disgrace. So it had been in Revolutionary America, at least as South Carolina nullifier Issac Hayne portrayed the struggle for independence. The British imposition of "a three pence a pound tax upon Tea" had been just such a cause for revolution. With obvious reference to the current "tyranny" of unpopular tariff exactions, Hayne argued that the sums involved were not the issue at all. The Parliamentary tea tax would have driven no American into penury. But this and other British measures required patriots to accept meekly the statutory symbols of British imperialism, a surrender of liberty that was dishonorable and therefore unbearable. Nullifiers like Hayne, as well as secessionists later, often posed the splendors of honor against the degeneracy and cowardly temptation of peaceful capitulation. Robert Barnwell Rhett in 1828 assaulted the Unionist faction of South Carolina, stressing the dangers of lost self-confidence: "If you are doubtful of your selves . . . if you love life better than honor,—prefer ease to perilous liberty and glory, awake not! stir not!—Impotent resistance will add vengeance to ruin. Live in smiling peace with your insatiable oppressors, and die with the noble consolation, that your submissive patience will survive triumphant your beggary and despair." Dread of shameful subservience became a more pronounced southern theme after Lincoln's election. For instance, Alcibiade De Blanc of Saint Martin Parish introduced to the Louisiana secession convention a resolution that spoke to the southern fear of lost racial honor. The new president's party would force, he said, the southern people to accept an "equality [of blacks] with a superior race . . . to the irreparable ruin of this mighty Republic, the degradation of the American name, and the corruption of the American blood." . . .

Nearly every major sectional issue from Tallmadge's amendment to the Missouri enabling act to the Free-Soil Wilmot Proviso had brought out expressions from proslavery advocates that connected slaveholding with southern honor and fear of shame. According to William L. Yancey's "Alabama Platform," the Wilmot Proviso was a "discrimination as degrading as it is injurious to the slaveholding states." Words like degraded, shamed, demoralized, and humiliated all referred to the horrors of lost self-esteem. As northern contemporaries believed, southern polemics far exceeded the actual causes. Just how would the Wilmot Proviso affect the ordinary planter in South Carolina or Alabama? Surely his control over his work force was scarcely less secure than before the measure was introduced in Congress. Loss of honor was the great issue, though by no means disconnected from slavery's protection.

So far, this exposition may have helped to explain the ethical language of the two sections, but it does not illuminate how honor played a role in the process of disunionism itself. At once, a vexing problem appears: the failure of all southerners to reach the same conclusion about the crisis. If honor were as pervasive as claimed, one might argue, then why such curious divisions throughout the South? The answer is complex and can only be touched upon here. Honor, like any ethical scheme from Christianity to Confucianism, provides only *general* rules of behavior, from which variety one may readily choose according to personal temperament, experience, or reading of circumstance. (One might as well expect uniformity about the dispensing of worldly goods in Christian doctrine.) Although traditional honor seemed the exclusive preserve of secessionists, the ethic could also be used to defend the status quo rather than revolutionary disunionism.

In ethical and strategic terms, the options were clearly drawn between the need for immediate vindication with a call to arms and the equally "honorable," Ciceronian course of moderation and coolness under provocation. Over the years, southern Unionists had roundly denounced and successfully turned aside the secessionist plea for hot-blooded action. Even at the close of the era, they did not believe that John Brown's raid or Lincoln's election required rebellious measures. Was there not a higher law of honor that demanded of the true-hearted southerner prudence after the results of the 1860 election were known? At the Alabama secession convention, delegate John Potter of Cherokee County, for instance, spoke to the issue. The secessionists tell us that "our honor must be vindicated," he observed. If that be the case, he said, then at least it was one powerful argument for disunion. But there is, Potter continued, "a morbid sense of honor" which often leads to extremes, and it "involves [men] in disgrace while they vainly seek to maintain their false view of true honor."

Potter and many others urged a policy of calculation and patience. The slave states should confer about their grievances and weigh the costs of resistance before plunging into the unknown, they begged. From the time of Cicero to the outbreak of the Civil War, gentlemen had often responded to the passions of the moment by appealing to the Stoic-Christian tradition of honor that repudiated recklessness and intemperate behavior. But the Unionists of the South—by and large, the more securely placed large-scale planters—well knew that their calls for calm deliberation could be impugned as cowardice. For this reason among others, the Constitutional Unionists and those southerners who had voted for Douglas generally proclaimed themselves "conditional" Unionists. That position meant not only a readiness to negotiate or await the verdict of other slave-state allies but also a willingness to accept secession if that policy won overwhelming popular support. It was a part of the honor code itself that community consensus forced dissenters to surrender to popular decision even if the dissenters thought the policy foolish. Otherwise, one ran the risk of communal disloyalty.

Because of the fears for slavery's future that Lincoln's election engendered, the advantages lay with those in the Lower South who insisted that the inaction of continued Unionism would mean disaster and disgrace. The secessionists largely relied upon two tactics, one negative and the other more moderate. The first involved outright intimidation, sometimes violence. Nowhere was community will to repress dissent more evident than in South Carolina upon news of the "Black Republican" victory. Venerable, wealthy, and Unionist, the state supreme court chief justice John Belton O'Neall found that his neighbors no longer shared his sentiments or accepted his leadership. At the Newberry County Courthouse, he urged repudiation of the autumn madness: "Freemen—descendents of the Patriots of '76—it is your duty to prevent such a disastrous [policy as secession]." In reply, the townsfolk pelted him with eggs.

In other states the pressure toward consensus for disunion grew as well. In Atlanta, the *Daily Intelligencer* labeled Unionists "Southern Abolitionists [who ought to be] strung up to the nearest live oak and permitted to dance on nothing." In Alabama, boasted the Hayneville *Chronicle,* "not a half dozen papers" had the temerity to challenge the inexorable will of the outraged populace. The Unionist John Hardy of the *Alabama State Sentinel* in Selma received an offer of $10,000 to shut down his press. When the bribe failed, Yancey and friends pursued him with a libel suit. After two so-called abolitionists were killed by lynch law in Fort Worth, Texas, the local Unionist editor had to sell his paper to secessionists or face a similar fate. An Arkansas mob seized from a steamboat a traveling newspaper distributor from Saint Louis and hanged him for the crime of carrying Horace Greeley's New York *Tribune.* Such activities as these did not at all belie southern claims as liberty-lovers.

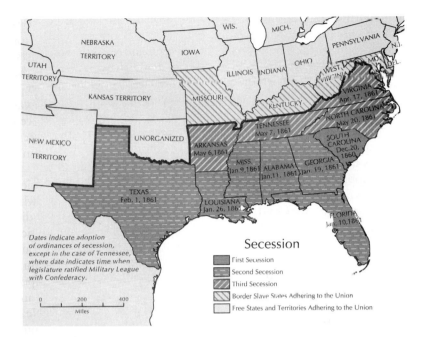

Map of Secession. The southern states did not secede all at once. As this diagram shows, they left in three distinct stages over a five-month period. Thus, the Union broke up piecemeal, and the secession crisis lasted a number of months.

Southerners simply meant something different by the term. As historian Donald Robinson points out, secessionist editors justified such suppressions of a free press "on the ground that the South was fighting for its very life and could ill afford dissension among its people."

    The power of popular coercion also intimidated the Unionist delegates to state secession conventions. At the Alabama meeting, for instance, Yancey darkly impugned the integrity of the Unionist opposition. He called them Tories no less subject to the laws of treason than the Loyalists of the American Revolution had been. At once Robert Jemison of Tuscaloosa leapt to his feet. "Will the gentleman go into those sections of the State and hang all those who are opposed to Secession? Will he hang them by families, by neighborhoods, by counties, by Congressional Districts? Who, sir, will give the bloody order? Is this the spirit of Southern chivalry?" Convinced that the South's material interests and even the safety of slavery lay in preservation of the Union, Jemison appealed to the higher laws of honor by which interpretation popular clamors should not deter the statesman from following the dictates of sound judgment. He put these concerns for public well-being and peaceful prosperity in terms of honor in order to meet secessionist objections that "principle" should overrule all other considerations, regardless of costs in blood, treasure, and risks to slavery itself. In like manner, Mississippi Unionists tried to show that genuine honor required a course quite different from the one secessionists proposed. A "fictitious chivalry," they said, offered only brave words but perversely claimed to be frightened of mannish Boston bluestockings and pious abolitionists. Honor, the Mississippi Unionists explained, demanded that the Gulf states do nothing precipitous: if they seceded at once, they would, in effect, leave their Upper South brethren in the clutches of hostile free-state majorities.

Nonetheless, the submissionists, as they were dubbed, generally received the worst of this line of reasoning. Albert Gallatin Brown of Mississipi gave them the lie in 1860: "If it should cost us the Union, our lives, let them go," he cried. Better that than meekly to "submit to a disgrace so deep and so damning" as abject submission to Black Republican rule. The message that he and others delivered was not casually thrust aside. James L. Alcorn, a Unionist politician and a Delta planter with vast holdings, confided to a friend that the belligerence of the secession majority at the state convention had become almost intolerable. "Should we fail to commit ourselves [to secession], it will be charged that we intend to desert the South. . . . The epithet of coward and submissionist will be everywhere applied to us. We shall be scouted by the masses!" He and his Unionist colleagues signed the secession ordinance under duress, but they naturally had to claim that their action was as honorable and manly as their previous opposition had been. Both positions, they insisted, served the interests of the community and the glory of their state. When a similar tide of secession enthusiasm swept North Carolina after Lincoln's mobilization order, former Whig Jonathan Worth sighed in resignation, "I think the South is committing suicide, but my lot is cast with the South and being unable to manage the ship, I intend to face the breakers manfully and go down with my companions." . . .

The contest over secession was not one that involved matters of conscience or the more legally serious problem of treason. Rather, nearly all politically active southerners assumed the right of secession; the question was the wisdom of the decision. The secessionists, though, had always insisted that advocacy of peace and patience was simply another name for cowardice. Historian John Barnwell points out that the secession extremists proudly accepted their critics' charge of being Hotspurs [the nickname given to Harry Percy, the rival of Prince Hal, later Henry IV, in Shakespeare's play, *Henry IV, Part I*] whose fate served the South as an inspiring example to be followed—possibly into the grave. "Harry Percy failed," the hotheads retorted, not because of his rashness and arrogance but because his kinsmen and allies proved faithless. If southerners were equally untrustworthy, then by the rules of manly honor they deserved defeat and disgrace.

Like the Northumberland rebel [Harry Percy was the son of the Duke of Northumberland], most southern radicals throughout the antebellum years were likely to be men on the threshold of their careers, not well-established and aging property holders. Benjamin Perry, a South Carolina Unionist, noted that the upcountry secessionists in the 1850s were "a set of young enthusiasts inspired with notions of personal honor to be defended and individual glory, fame and military laurels to be acquired." Critics might object to their choler and recklessness, but these truculent southerners had an answer. Even if the South's break for freedom were crushed by northern might, they said, the chance for vindication had to be seized. James Jones, one of the South Carolina ultras, predicted, "If we fail, we have saved our honour *and lost nothing*." The alternative was too demeaning to be considered: the slavery of "*Submission*." The honor that Shakespeare's . . . [Harry] Percy represented could only save injured pride and animate a spirit of defiance. Perhaps it was fitting that the young should stand in the vanguard of secessionism. They were soon to be the first to meet enemy fire in the field. Whether that circumstance was just or not, the words of the victorious Prince Hal were, for many a fallen Confederate, soon and sadly to apply. He addressed Hotspur, slain and lying at his feet: "Thy ignominy sleep with thee in the grave, / But not rememb'red in thy epitaph."

Daniel W. Crofts

THE UNIONIST OFFENSIVE

The drive for secession was resisted in every southern state. In the Upper South—Virginia, Tennessee, and North Carolina—the opponents of secession were so numerous and influential that they succeeded temporarily in stopping the movement in its tracks. They did this either by defeating the call for a secession convention or by voting down an ordinance of secession in the convention itself.

Daniel W. Crofts explains the origins and objectives of these opponents of secession—whom he calls Unionists—and shows how they operated in Virginia, perhaps the pivotal state in the Upper South. In his book *Reluctant Confederates,* from which this excerpt is taken, he emphasizes the strength of this opposition and suggests that had the Lincoln administration encouraged Upper South Unionism, those states might have been kept from ultimately seceding. By raising the possibility that secession could have been restricted to only seven Lower South states, Crofts suggests that the formation of a viable Confederacy, and therefore the outbreak of war, could perhaps have been prevented. Implicit in this proposition is the notion that the war was avoidable, a view not much in evidence among historians in recent years.

Daniel W. Crofts (born 1941) is the author of *Reluctant Confederates: Upper South Unionists in the Secession Crisis* (1989). He teaches at Trenton State College.

Upper South Unionism coalesced during the first two months of 1861. Though confronted by grave obstacles, Unionists possessed one key advantage: popular support for secession had grown since November but had not yet gained a majority in any upper South state. Unionists faced the task of arresting and reversing the growth of secession sentiment in their home states, while also urging Congress to enact Union-saving measures. The two objectives were, of course, interconnected, but each may best be treated separately. This [excerpt] will focus on the first.

The great Unionist achievement, during a winter otherwise marked by frustration and failure, was the mobilizing of popular majorities across the upper South to thwart secession. Why did the upper South refuse to follow the lead of the lower South? That crucial question requires a two-pronged answer, involving both slavery and party. Relatively smaller concentrations of slaves and slaveowners, plus statewide political arenas in which the two major parties competed on close terms, made the upper South less receptive to secessionist appeals. The combination of fewer slaveowners and more formidable political opposition to the secession-leaning Democratic party kept Virginia, North Carolina, and Tennessee in the Union during early 1861.

Plantation regions dominated the seven seceding states in the deep South. It was no coincidence that the first states to leave the Union had the greatest commitment to slavery. Support for secession, both in the upper and lower South, tended to be strongest in high-slaveowning areas and weakest in the low-slaveowning regions of the upcountry. However formidable the slaveowning interest in Virginia, North Carolina, and Tennessee, a larger share of each state's electorate resided in the upcountry than anywhere in the lower South.

Somewhat less well known, but of comparable importance in understanding the relative weakness of secession in the upper South, was a set of partisan arrangements that differed markedly from those in the lower South. Competitive two-party politics in the upper South gave antisecessionists an indispensable base. The Whig party organization and electorate provided the foundation for what would soon be called the Union party in Virginia, North Carolina, and Tennessee.

Whig and Opposition parties throughout the lower South were much weaker and generally weakest in the upcountry. The tendency for lower South Whigs to reside in the "black belts" enervated whatever latent Unionism they possessed. But in the Upper South, Whigs had greater residual strength, which was by no means confined to plantation regions. In North Carolina, notably, a cluster of low-slaveowning counties in the piedmont regularly provided the largest Whig margins in the state. Voters in this Whiggish "Quaker Belt" spearheaded statewide opposition to secession. They gained reinforcements from party loyalists in the mountains and the northeast. Each Tennessee party received comparable support from high- and low-slaveowning regions. But a bloc of strong

Whig counties around Knoxville provided a militantly antisecession nucleus for the broader East Tennessee region, and Whiggish counties in the fertile Cumberland Valley of Middle Tennessee proved especially hospitable to a qualified wait-and-see conditional Unionism. Western Virginia was slightly more Democratic than eastern Virginia, but the unique geographical position of the trans-Allegheny, coupled with its long history of estrangement from the east, made the west almost unanimously pro-Union. Whig strongholds in the Virginia valley and western piedmont also rejected secession, including, for example, Jefferson County, the site of John Brown's assault in October 1859. Even in Southampton County, the Virginia tidewater locale where the slave rebel Nat Turner had rampaged thirty years before, Whigs voted overwhelmingly pro-Union. The inability of secessionists to carry even a bare majority in Southampton well illustrated the linkage between Unionism and Whig party loyalties.

Upper South Unionism thus had both a regional and a party base. A popular outpouring of antisecession sentiment among upcountry nonslaveowners provided the most conspicuous element of Union strength. But Unionism had the potential to become a dominant political force because it extended beyond the upcountry to draw support from the Whig rank and file. The latter included a broad spectrum of southerners, among them more than a few slaveowners from the fertile lowlands. Thomas P. Devereux, one of the wealthiest plantation owners in North Carolina, berated South Carolina for her "folly" and confidently awaited a Union-saving compromise. A conservative orientation was especially pronounced among Union Whigs in eastern Virginia, many of whom deplored the democratic revisions in the 1851 Virginia constitution. They blamed secession on the new breed of "worthless, disgusting politicians" who pandered to popular fears.

Although some embraced Unionism to preserve or rebuild existing social hierarchies, the antisecession insurgency in the upper South had unmistakable egalitarian overtones. Far more than in the lower South, class resentments surfaced in late 1860 and early 1861. One of Edmund Ruffin's correspondents told him in late November that secession sentiment in the Southside Virginia counties of Lunenburg and Nottoway had increased greatly since the election but that "disaffection" among "the poorer class of non slaveholders" had also appeared. Some antisecessionists stated flatly that "in the event of civil war or even servile insurrection, they would not lift a finger in defense of the rights of slaveholders." An observer in Hertford County, North Carolina, a tidewater area just below the Virginia border, was similarly "mortified" to find many nonslaveowning "plain country people" unwilling to fight "to protect rich men's negroes." Nor were nonslaveowning Virginians in the Shenandoah Valley willing "to break up the government for the mere loss of an election." Similar reports emanated from West Tennessee, where "the nonslave holders (or a large majority of them) when approached on the subject declare that they will not fight if war fol[l]ows a dissolution of the union." And in towns and cities across the upper South, "workingmen" organized and demonstrated against secession.

Sensitive to the egalitarian stirrings, some secession sympathizers cautioned against trying to rush the states of the upper South out of the Union prematurely. "You cannot unite the *masses* of any southern State much less those of North Carolina against the Union and in favor [of] slavery *alone*," surmised an astute secessionist. Nonslaveowners would resist any movement that appeared controlled by "the *avarice* and the *selfishness* of *Negro Slavocracy*." But by prudently waiting until the federal government attacked the seceding states, secessionists could "change the issue" to "a question of popular liberty." Once the second consideration was introduced, nothing could hold North Carolina in the Union. A Southern Rights supporter from Virginia reasoned along the same lines. "You can't make the great mass of the people, especially the non slaveholders understand . . . the nice principles on which the secessionists are now attempting to act," he observed. Indeed, he feared that secessionist clamor ran the potential danger "of creating a party with sympathies for the incoming administration, here in our midst." He therefore thought it best "to *prepare* for resistance" without seeming to follow the lead of "disunionists *per se*." He foresaw, too, that "the non slaveholder will fight for his section as soon as the slaveholder if you can convince him that *his* political rights are really threatened."

Such caution was appropriate. Large regions of Virginia, North Carolina, and Tennessee opposed secession with at least as much fervor and with even greater unanimity than it was supported in other areas of those states. Spontaneous Union meetings gathered in upcountry locations at the same time secessionists seized the organizational initiative in many plantation districts. For example, a well-attended public meeting on November 29 in Hawkins County, East Tennessee, resolved that "the doctrine of secession" was "subversive of all just principles of government." The meeting reaffirmed Andrew Jackson's view that secession was "treason." An estimated eight hundred to a thousand people likewise gathered on December 28 in intensely Unionist Randolph County, in the North Carolina piedmont, to condemn secession as "unwise and suicidal" and to deplore the "folly and madness" of extremists North and South.

For the Breckinridge wing of the Democratic party [refers to John C. Breckinridge, the rival Democratic candidate to Stephen Douglas in the 1860 presidential election], which provided the political backbone for the secession movement, the antisecession groundswell in parts of Virginia, North Carolina, and Tennessee posed a deadly threat. Breckinridge had readily carried most Democratic areas of the upcountry. Any significant slippage of Democratic loyalties there, when coupled with the already manifest disaffection from the party of those who voted for Douglas in 1860, seriously endangered the prospects for statewide secession. It likewise threatened the narrow statewide Democratic majorities in all three states.

Several important Democrats led the Unionist exodus from the Breckinridge Democracy. Congressman Sherrard Clemens from Wheeling, the major town in northwestern Virginia's panhandle, condemned South Carolina's "hot and indecent haste." Her action, Clemens charged, "affords no remedy for alleged grievances but would intensify every one of them." Publicly urged to resign by the local Democratic newspaper editor, Clemens refused to back down. He bitterly announced to a Union meeting that if one had to be a disunionist to be an accepted member of his party, he was "no longer a Democrat." Two other Virginia Democratic congressmen, John T. Harris from the Shenandoah Valley and John Millson of the Norfolk region, likewise broke with the party to oppose secession. In North Carolina, editor William W. Holden insisted that voters who had supported Breckinridge had not endorsed secession. He made a blistering attack on Governor John Ellis, a fellow Democrat, who had called for a state convention and a conference of southern states. Holden charged that secession would bring disas-trous consequences—bitter internal strife, chronic warfare, an in-crease in foreign influence, economic stagnation, high taxes, large standing armies, and a "military despotism." The most prominent Breckinridge Democrat to oppose secession was, of course, Senator Andrew Johnson of Tennessee. Insisting that southern rights could best be protected in the Union, he fiercely criticized South Carolina and her allies for trying to coerce Tennessee and the states of the upper South.

A rank-and-file rebellion against disunionist Democratic lead-ership doomed immediate secession in Virginia, North Carolina, and Tennessee. Only by embracing secession with near unanimity could Breckinridge supporters have carried the three states out of the Union because most Bell and Douglas partisans opposed seces-sion and Douglas had siphoned enough normal Democratic votes to allow Bell to carry Virginia and Tennessee. But by early 1861 the Democratic party was more gravely divided than it had been in November 1860.

Nowhere in the upper South, therefore, did secession become statewide majority sentiment during the first months after the pres-idential election. Nor, however, did unconditional Unionism. Many Unionists agreed that the South had grievances against the free states and that redress was in order. Unionists also abhorred the idea of using armed force to challenge secession, and many warned that they would fight on the side of the South if war came. Thus, probably the largest segment of thinking in the upper South during the secession winter favored new constitutional guarantees of sup-posedly endangered southern rights, coupled with a hands-off policy by the federal government toward the seceding states. Conditional Unionists [as this group may appropriately be called] thus reflected . . . a mixture of ultimatumist and anticoercionist ideas.

In Tennessee, for example, only 23.6 percent of voters favored secession in February 1861; 76.4 percent favored either conditional or unconditional Unionism. By using the subsequent June vote to estimate that 35.1 percent of February voters were unconditional Unionists, it may be calculated that 41.3 percent of the February electorate were conditional Unionists. Proportionately fewer uncon-ditional Unionists lived in Virginia and North Carolina, and there was more substantial prosecession sentiment in the two eastern states than in Tennessee. But in all three states, the conditional Unionists stood out as the largest of the three groups.

For Unionists to consolidate their position, they first needed to establish clear demarcations between Unionism and secession. That task was complicated by the conditional nature of much Union sentiment. More Unionists than not could imagine circumstances that would compel them, however reluctantly, to support secession. Some conditional Unionists also flirted with a deliberately ambiguous policy called "reconstruction," which in effect accepted secession as a tactic to achieve reunion.

Virginia Senator R. M. T. Hunter, the chief theoretician of reconstruction, publicized his ideas early in December. He wished to keep the South united, to keep the peace, and to "reconstruct" the Union "upon safe terms." His support for a southern conference made Hunter's proposal attractive to those who had doubts about separate state secession, but his insistence that the South should unite "either within or without the Union" had quasi-secessionist overtones. Because his proposition was put forward at a time when the states of the deep South appeared certain to secede, Hunter in effect advised the upper South to do likewise, at least for tactical reasons. But his alleged motives were to reconstruct the Union— even if the secession of the entire South proved necessary to set that process in motion.

Hunter's formulation temporarily offered his allies in the Democratic party a way to bid for the support of both secessionists and conditional Unionists. A centerpiece of the "reconstruction" scheme, obviously inspired by John C. Calhoun, would have given the slave and free states each a veto power over national policy decisions, along with the right to control the appointment of government officials within each region. Reasoning that the South would be safe in the Union only if the Constitution were amended to encompass the minority veto, Hunter and his followers rejected as inadequate proposed compromises and guarantees regarding the disputed issue of slavery in the territories. "Unless we can have securities of political power," one insisted, "I say this Union ought to be . . . dissolved." Another proposed amending the Constitution to specify that no candidate could be elected president without "a majority of the Southern members of the Electoral College." That requirement would "place the government of the country in the hands of its moderate men" and would offer a strong motive "to ambitious men in all sections, to calm, and not to inflame sectional irritation and prejudice." Concessions of "political power" would be of far more value to the South than any "theoretical acknowledgement of our right of property and our right of equality." These demands for constitutional revision appeared so drastic as to ensure that they could never be enacted. And as it became clear that the lower South considered disunion irrevocable, reconstruction appeared more and more a secessionist subterfuge.

By January Unionists had become contemptuous of the reconstruction ploy. "Let us not deceive ourselves with any such delusion as a reconstruction of the Government, in the event of a separation of the North and the South," warned Congressman William B. Stokes of Tennessee. "Dismemberment will not be followed by a reunion of these States. Disunion means war—civil war." Louisville editor George D. Prentice also erupted angrily at talk of reconstruction. This word "now flowing so glibly from the lips and pens of precipitators here, is that hideous thing D I S U N I O N," Prentice exclaimed. "Let patriots shun it as they would shun the abyss to which it points." John A. Gilmer likewise condemned the idea of reconstruction as "fallacious" and "dangerous," designed by disunionists as a "syren song" to "decoy" and "deceive" the people of the South. "Reconstruction!" he snorted. "You might as well tell me, after you had taken a delicate watch, and put it under the ponderous blows of a forge hammer, that you only did it that you might reconstruct, with perfection, its complex machinery." Virginia Congressman John T. Harris spoke out with similar vehemence: "Reconstruct! Reconstruct! As well try to reconstruct the shattered vase or to tie up Niagara in a handkerchief, and put it in your pocket." As soon as the upper South left the Union, he predicted, secessionists there would adopt the chant used by their counterparts in the cotton states: "We are out forever; we want no guarantees; we will never come back."

By rejecting reconstruction, Unionists in the upper South acquired a more unmistakable identity than their "cooperationist" counterparts in the lower South. Voters in the upper South had no difficulty in differentiating between Unionists and their opponents.

Upper South Unionists firmly opposed secession, either as a tactic or in cooperation with other states.

*

In considering how Unionists challenged secession in their home states, the place to start is Virginia. For reasons that stretched back over two and one-half centuries, Virginia occupied a unique place in both American and southern consciousness. Home of the first permanent English settlement in North America and incubator of the social system that would come to be called southern, Virginia had been the dominant state in the nation during the revolutionary and early national periods. Rapid western expansion had drained population from Virginia and the older states of the Southeast, but she remained the most populous state in the South, with more whites and slaves in 1860 than any other southern state.

Of all the states in the upper South, Virginia had the strongest inclinations toward secession. A web of social, political, and cultural ties linked her to the deep South. Though few Virginians favored disunion per se, many were electrified by the action of the deep South. Unionists watched with dismay as secession momentum intensified in large parts of the piedmont and tidewater. Their alarm increased by late December and early January, when state conventions in the deep South quickly adopted secession ordinances, without submitting their decision to popular referendum. Fearing that "demagogues and extremists" would capitalize on "popular excitement" to call a convention in Virginia and win control of it, Unionists looked for some alternative or at least delay. "We cannot see what any one, who wishes to preserve the Union can accomplish by a convention," one noted. But public sentiment in favor of a convention increased through December, making Unionists doubtful that they could block it altogether.

The secession issue overshadowed everything else by the time the legislature met in special session in early January. "We shall have two distinctly marked and very zealous parties here," observed former U.S. senator and former ambassador to France William Cabell Rives, "one for secession before the 4th of March," the other hoping the Union could be saved. "The secession party is already strong, and has been rapidly gaining ground up to the present time," he noted, "but I cannot but hope, as soon as a definite plan for pursuing

"A Consoling Thought" cartoon, April 1861. This cartoon is a critical depiction of President Lincoln's stance during the secession crisis. Because his policy appeared to lack firmness and urgency, Virginia's secession seemed only a matter of time. (*Chicago Historical Society*)

redress in a constitutional method shall be brought forward in opposition to secession, the progress of the latter will be checked."

The unprecedented public excitement in Richmond that greeted the assembling legislature made it appear, at first, that Rives had underestimated secessionist strength. "Times are wild and revolutionary here beyond description," one Virginia legislator reported. Governor John Letcher's message combined a vigorous condemnation of northern encroachment on southern rights with a cautionary warning against calling a convention or acting hastily, but many legislators were swept up in the secession enthusiasm. The Richmond correspondent of the *Wheeling Intellegencer,* the most important unconditional Union newspaper in the state, reported that "nothing is heard but resistance to the General Government, and sympathy with the cause of South Carolina." His editor feared that "nine tenths" of the members of the legislature had "gone crazy." Alexander H. H. Stuart, a state senator and former secretary of the navy, wrote on January 8 that "madness rules the hour. You can hardly imagine the extent of the insanity. I have scarcely a ray of hope left." He reported that several prominent Virginia congressmen had come to Richmond from Washington "to poison the minds of the legislature." Stuart, doubtful that anything could be done "to stay the storm," feared that war might soon erupt.

The strength of Virginia secessionists proved illusory. They wanted the legislature to empower a state convention to secede from the Union, following the example set in the deep South. But a coalition of moderates balked. The legislature did agree to call a convention, but under ground rules that hedged against immediate secession. Only the timing of the convention suited secessionists: an election would be held on February 4, with the delegates then selected to meet on February 13. By apportioning delegates on the "white basis," as in its lower house, the legislature assured that regions west of the Blue Ridge, where secession was weak, would hold a majority. A proposal to give voters the chance to approve or disapprove the holding of a convention failed by a narrow vote. But the legislature did allow voters to decide on February 4 whether any change in the relationship between Virginia and the federal government proposed by the convention should be subject to popular referendum. Thus, at the same time voters chose delegates, they would also vote for or against reference.

At the same time the legislature acted on the convention bill, it invited all other states to appoint delegates to a special meeting in Washington, D.C. The Virginia-sponsored gathering, scheduled for February 4 and soon dubbed the "Peace Conference," raised hopes for a Union-saving compromise. The legislature also dispatched representatives to meet with President Buchanan and the authorities of the seceding states to urge against any hostilities and to invite the latter to attend the Peace Conference. The plan for the Peace Conference, credited to Union Democrat James Barbour, Union Whig George W. Summers, and perhaps others, provided antisecessionists with an excellent basis to argue that peaceful restoration of the Union remained possible. The Unionists who devised the idea of a Peace Conference thus laid a clever and effective trap for secessionists, who found themselves in the awkward position of asserting that the state's peacemaking efforts were futile. The Peace Conference stratagem would pay Virginia Unionists rich dividends on election day in early February.

The action of the legislature pleased Unionists and alarmed secessionists. The editor of the *Wheeling Intelligencer* applauded the legislature's "returning sense of moderation." Giving voters the right to decide whether they wanted a popular referendum on any convention action removed "the deadly feature that was most to be feared." By contrast, the editor of the *Richmond Enquirer* condemned the "stupid" reference amendment, bitterly regretting that the legislature had "emasculated" the convention bill.

The legislature scheduled the election of convention delegates for the same day the Peace Conference would meet in Washington. The contest received national attention as the first clear indication of how the upper South would respond to the secession crisis. Though undertaken in haste and handicapped by midwinter weather and bad roads, the Virginia campaign was intense and spirited. Union ranks included almost all supporters of Douglas in 1860, almost all Whigs who lived west of the Blue Ridge, a large majority of Whigs from the piedmont and tidewater, plus a substantial increment of "moderate Breckinridge men," especially those from the West, who were retrospectively dismayed to find "so many Disunionists" among their former political allies. Unionists worked hard to put old party animosities on the shelf. In counties entitled to more than one representative, Union nominations often went to a Whig and a Douglas Democrat. Opponents of secession began to refer to their coalition as a "party." As the February election approached, they felt encouraged about the prospects of "the Conservative and anti-precipitation Union party."

Union efforts in Virginia were enhanced by authoritative reassurances from Washington about the prospects for a satisfactory settlement of the sectional crisis. Stephen A. Douglas wrote a public letter stating that "there is hope of preserving peace and the Union. All depends on the action of Virginia and the Border states. If they remain in the Union and aid in a fair and just settlement, the Union may be preserved.—But if they secede under the fatal delusion of a reconstruction, I fear that all is lost. Save Virginia, and we will save the Union." Kentucky Senator John J. Crittenden and the four Union congressmen from Virginia—Alexander Boteler, John T. Harris, John S. Millson, and Sherrard Clemens—assessed the situation similarly. Conditional Unionist leader James Barbour urged voters to be guided by the opinions of Douglas and Crittenden, who were "above all men in America . . . devoting their energies to secure a pacific adjustment to the pending controversy."

Unionist success in seizing the middle ground threw Virginia secessionists on the defensive. The case for secession hinged on the assumption that the North would never accept an adequate plan for sectional reconciliation, so that Virginia had to side with the South. But the calling of the Peace Conference and the reassurances from Douglas and Crittenden made many Virginians hopeful. The Southern Rights Democrats who dominated Virginia's congressional delegation—Senators R. M. T. Hunter and James M. Mason, plus eight of the state's twelve representatives—tried desperately to regain the advantage. They issued a statement endorsing Southern Rights convention candidates, declaring that Congress would not enact a suitable compromise, and strongly implying that the Union could be reconstructed only if Virginia seceded quickly.

But the argument that the state's secession could effect a reconstruction of the Union had become untenable by late January. Virginia's spokesman to the seceded states, Judge John Robertson, was told repeatedly that they did not intend to come back. Nor would they attend the Peace Conference. The *Richmond Whig* pronounced the idea of seceding so as to reconstruct an "utter absurdity" and a "ridiculous idea." The reference issue also hindered the secession cause. Unionists supported reference on the obvious democratic grounds of wanting citizens to approve any change in the relationship between Virginia and the federal government. Secessionists argued lamely that the convention might need to act quickly, making it inexpedient to wait for a popular referendum. Only in eastern Virginia did the antireference argument receive much of a hearing. In many counties in northwestern Virginia, all candidates for the convention favored reference.

By the end of January, perceptive secessionists recognized the likelihood of "a defeat in Virginia and all the rest of the border States." An observer from Georgia reported that several economic issues had aided Unionists. The "manufacturing interest of Virginia" suspected that a southern Confederacy would destroy tariff barriers and "establish free trade." Worries that "navigation of the Mississippi will be obstructed and that the slave trade will be reopened" had also weakened the secession cause in the upper South. Unless organizers of the southern Confederacy proceeded "with the greatest caution," they ran the danger of having "the border slave States strongly bound with our foes against us and making common cause with them to conquer."

The election surpassed Unionist hopes. Fewer than one-third of the 152 delegates elected favored secession. The provision to refer the action of the convention to a popular referendum also carried by an emphatic majority, 103,236 to 46,386. Voters east of the Blue Ridge divided almost evenly on reference, 32,294 to 32,009. But western voters overwhelmingly favored it, 70,942 to 14,377. . . . Voters in most counties west of the Blue Ridge favored reference by a notably larger margin than the combined Bell, Douglas, and Lincoln vote in 1860. . . . [In over fifty western counties] significant numbers of Breckinridge supporters must have voted pro-Union. Nowhere in the northwestern trans-Allegheny could secessionists achieve even the feeble 31 percent antireference vote they averaged statewide. Except for a handful of ardently Democratic counties in the Valley and the southwest, secession attracted solid support only in traditionalist bastions in the piedmont and tidewater, characterized by large slaveholdings or Democratic loyalties (and usually both). Virginia, unlike the states of the deep South, decided against hasty action and chose instead to use its influence to mediate the sectional crisis. "Lord, how dumfounded are the secessionists here!" crowed one Virginia Unionist. "But a few days ago they were high up stairs and clamoring from the house tops. But 'such a getting down stairs, I never did see.'"

Several observers recognized that the Virginia election had "annihilated all existing party organizations" and set in motion a fundamental rearrangement of political forces in the state. The Southern Rights Democrats who dominated the state congressional delegation suffered an obvious popular rebuke after committing their prestige to the secession cause. The *Richmond Whig* applauded the independence of the "masses," who had "ignored old party divisions" and "emancipated themselves from the thraldom of party leaders." As a consequence, the *Whig* predicted the rise of "new organizations" based on "the great question of the day." Conservatives of all earlier political persuasions would unite to form "a new Union party," and the "destructives" would coalesce in a competing minority party: "'UNION' or 'DISUNION' is the issue; and 'UNIONISTS' or 'DISUNIONISTS' must be the party organizations and designations."

A massive mailing of speeches and documents contributed to the Union victory in Virginia. The effort was coordinated by Joseph C. G. Kennedy, head of the U.S. Census Bureau. Kennedy asked census takers to send him information about secession sentiment in their localities and then arranged to have Union documents sent to areas where they would be useful. He kept a reported twenty clerks at work to address the mailings and lined up southern Unionist congressmen to frank the documents for free delivery. Virginia received first priority, but Tennessee and North Carolina became the principal destinations in February. Robert Hatton reported to his wife that he was "worn out" from "franking and directing documents, speeches, etc., to Tennessee, hoping to influence our election for members of the convention." He dispatched "about fifteen hundred speeches a day" for several weeks. John A. Gilmer, probably the wealthiest of the congressmen involved, later reported that he paid to have speeches reprinted and to hire clerks. Others also paid substantial amounts out of pocket for reprints. "Night after night," from the close of office hours until midnight, the mailing operation continued.

Fragments of his surviving correspondence show that Kennedy, a Pennsylvanian with Whiggish antecedents, worked closely both with upper South Unionists and with conciliatory Republican leaders such as William H. Seward and Charles Francis Adams. Kennedy reassured southern census takers that Lincoln would "satisfy all reasonable men, North and South," and "inaugurate an era of peace and good will." By rejecting secession, the border slave states would be "certain to secure all Southern rights and guarantees." To preserve the interest of southern census takers in the Union cause, Kennedy informed them that they would be paid "at the earliest moment funds are provided by the Treasury. If things settle peaceably, there will be no delay; if revolution comes, God only knows what will follow." The responses Kennedy received from his Virginia census takers filled him with "apprehension." But two days after the Virginia election, a relieved Kennedy jubilantly encouraged southern Unionist congressmen to continue franking documents.

More volunteers would "make the work lighter as our hearts are by the result in Virginia."

Howls of protest about the mailing operation soon came from secessionists and Southern Rights supporters, who arraigned "this creature Kennedy" for developing "a system of espionage to pry into the feelings of the people" and for "turning out every man in the Census Bureau who entertains the right of secession." Southern Rights devotees in Virginia complained about the promulgation of "incendiary documents"; those in North Carolina wailed that "Gilmer and company," working with "the Census Bureau and the Black Republicans," were "flooding the state with submission and coercion speeches." Allegations that recipients of a mass mailing of Union documents to eastern Virginia included some free blacks provoked an uproar in the Virginia convention. Secession newspapers made similar accusations during the North Carolina campaign. The complaints were doubtless true. Free blacks and whites were listed together on the same census sheets. Tired clerks could easily, if inadvertently, have dispatched Union documents to free blacks. Secessionists did more than complain. Southern Rights postmasters regularly tampered with the mails, and a secession delegate to the Virginia convention boasted that Union documents in one town had been "collected and publicly burned."

Secessionist obstruction testified to the impact of the mailings, prompting Unionists to follow up on their Virginia victory by blanketing North Carolina and Tennessee. A local political leader told North Carolina Congressman Zebulon B. Vance that "the people seem to want information and want to hear from you." Vance promised to send "thousands of Union documents" into his district, so that "*every man* shall have one." He also urged his friends to help circulate the material. Congressman Gilmer likewise did all he could to place documents "in the hands of each voter" in North Carolina. . . . Tennessee and North Carolina soon followed Virginia's lead in rejecting immediate secession and adding insult to secessionist injury by refusing to countenance state conventions. . . .

David M. Potter

WHY THE REPUBLICANS REJECTED BOTH COMPROMISE AND SECESSION

Historians have discussed a number of scenarios in their attempts to determine the policy of the new Republican administration when it was faced with the actuality of southern secession in early 1861. They range from the assertion that Lincoln provoked a confrontation at Fort Sumter to the claim that he wanted to play for time and do nothing but was drawn into action by the exigencies of the situation in Charleston harbor. Whatever policy the incoming Lincoln administration pursued would have a decisive effect on whether war could be avoided or, if not, on how it would break out. Therefore, it is important to know exactly what Lincoln and the Republicans intended, as well as the extent to which they achieved these aims. Did Lincoln foresee war and accept it as unavoidable? Or did Lincoln work to avert it and then stumble into it—yet another instance of James G. Randall's "blundering generation" of political leaders?

In this selection, David M. Potter distills the argument of his *Lincoln and His Party in the Secession Crisis* (1942). He concluded that Lincoln's policy was conciliatory in intent and rested on the assumption that, in the absence of further provocation, the opponents of secession—who probably constituted a majority in the South—would stall, and soon reverse, the movement for withdrawal. Thus, rejecting compromise, secession, *and* war as the alternatives, Lincoln opted for a fourth approach. This policy was intended, Potter thought, to avoid war but in fact failed to achieve that end. Based on an incorrect assumption, it alas failed to avert war.

David M. Potter (1910–1971) taught at Yale and Stanford universities. A major historian of the South and the Civil War, he wrote, among other books, *Lincoln and His Party in the Secession Crisis* (1942), a collection of essays, *The South and the Sectional Conflict* (1968), and *The Impending Crisis, 1848–1861* (1976), which won him a Pulitzer Prize in history posthumously.

Historians have a habit of explaining the important decisions of the past in terms of principles. On this basis, it is easy to say that

David M. Potter, "Why the Republicans Rejected Both Compromise and Secession," in *The Crisis of the Union, 1860–61*, edited by George Harmon Knoles. Copyright © 1965 by Louisiana State University Press.

the Republicans rejected compromise because they were committed to the principle of antislavery and that they rejected secession because they were committed to the principle of union. But in the realities of the historical past, principles frequently come into conflict with other principles, and those who make decisions have to choose which principle shall take precedence. When principles thus conflict, as they frequently do, it is meaningless to show merely that a person or a group favors a given principle: the operative question is what priority they give to it. For instance, before the secession crisis arose, there were many Northerners who believed in both the principle of antislavery and the principle of union, but who differed in the priority which they would give to one or the other: William Lloyd Garrison gave the priority to antislavery and proclaimed that there should be "no union with slaveholders." Abraham Lincoln gave, or seemed to give, the priority to union and during the war wrote the famous letter to Horace Greeley in which he said: "My paramount object is to save the Union and it is not either to save or to destroy slavery. What I do about slavery and the colored race, I do because I believe it helps to save the Union, and what I forbear, I forbear because I do not believe it would help to save the Union." Lincoln was always precise to almost a unique degree in his statements, and it is interesting to note that he did not say that it was not his object to destroy slavery; what he said was that it was not his paramount object—he did not give it the highest priority.

To state this point in another way, if we made an analysis of the moderate Republicans and of the abolitionists solely in terms of their principles, we would hardly be able to distinguish between them, for both were committed to the principle of antislavery and to the principle of union. It was the diversity in the priorities which they gave to these two principles that made them distinctive from each other.

A recognition of the priorities, therefore, may in many cases serve a historian better than a recognition of principles. But while it is important to recognize which principle is, as Lincoln expressed it, paramount, it is no less important to take account of the fact that men do not like to sacrifice one principle for the sake of another and do not even like to recognize that a given situation may require a painful choice between principles. Thus, most Northern antislavery men wanted to solve the slavery question within the framework of union, rather than to reject the Union because it condoned slavery; correspondingly, most Northern Unionists wanted to save the Union while taking steps against slavery, rather than by closing their eyes to the slavery question.

In short, this means—and one could state it almost as an axiom—that men have a tendency to believe that their principles can be reconciled with one another, and that this belief is so strong that it inhibits their recognition of realistic alternatives in cases where the alternatives would involve a choice between cherished principles. This attitude has been clearly defined in the homely phrase that we all like to have our cake and eat it too.

Perhaps all this preliminary consideration of theory seems excessively abstract and you will feel that I ought to get on to the Republicans, the crisis, and the rejection of compromise and secession; but before I do, let me take one more step with my theory. If the participants in a historical situation tend to see the alternatives in that situation as less clear, less sharply focused than they really are, historians probably tend to see the alternatives as more clear, more evident, more sharply focused than they really were. We see the alternatives as clear because we have what we foolishly believe to be the advantage of hindsight—which is really a disadvantage in understanding how a situation seemed to the participants. We know, in short, that the Republicans did reject both compromise and secession (I will return to the details of this rejection later) and that the four-year conflict known as the Civil War eventuated. We therefore tend to think not only that conflict of some kind was the alternative to the acceptance of compromise or the acquiescence in secession, but actually that this particular war—with all its costs, its sacrifices, and its consequences—was the alternative. When men choose a course of action which had a given result, historians will tend to attribute to them not only the choice of the course, but even the choice of the result. Yet one needs only to state this tendency clearly in order to demonstrate the fallacy in it. Whatever choice anyone exercised in 1860–61, no one chose the American Civil War, because it lay behind the veil of the future; it did not exist as a choice.

Hindsight not only enables historians to define the alternatives in the deceptively clear terms of later events; it also gives them a deceptively clear criterion for evaluating the alternatives, which is in terms of later results. That is, we now know that the war did result in the preservation of the Union and in the abolition of chattel slavery. Accordingly, it is easy, with hindsight, to attribute to the participants not only a decision to accept the alternative of a war whose magnitude they could not know, but also to credit them with choosing results which they could not foresee. The war, as it developed, certainly might have ended in the quicker defeat of the Southern movement, in which case emancipation would apparently not have resulted; or it might have ended in the independence of the Southern Confederacy, in which case the Monday morning quarterbacks of the historical profession would have been in the position of saying that the rash choice of a violent and coercive course had destroyed the possibility of a harmonious, voluntary restoration of the Union—a restoration of the kind which William H. Seward was trying to bring about.

I suppose all this is only equivalent to saying that the supreme task of the historian, and the one of most superlative difficulty, is to see the past through the imperfect eyes of those who lived it and not with his own omniscient twenty twenty vision. I am not suggesting that any of us can really do this, but only that it is what we must attempt.

What do we mean, specifically, by saying that the Republican party rejected compromise? Certain facts are reasonably familiar in this connection, and may be briefly recalled. In December, 1860, at the time when a number of secession conventions had been called in the Southern states but before any ordinances of secession had been adopted, various political leaders brought forward proposals to give assurances to the Southerners. The most prominent of these was the plan by Senator John J. Crittenden of Kentucky to place an amendment in the Constitution which would restore and extend the former Missouri Compromise line of 36° 30', prohibiting slavery in Federal territory north of the line and sanctioning it south of the line. In a Senate committee, this proposal was defeated with five Republicans voting against it and none in favor of it, while the non-Republicans favored it six to two. On January 16, after four states had adopted ordinances of secession, an effort was made to get the Crittenden measure out of committee and on to the floor of the Senate. This effort was defeated by 25 votes against to 23 in favor. This was done on a strict party vote, all 25 of the votes to defeat being cast by Republicans. None of those in favor were Republicans. On March 2, after the secession of the lower South was complete, the Crittenden proposal was permitted to come to a vote. In the Senate, it was defeated 19 to 20. All 20 of the negative votes were Republican, not one of the affirmative votes was so. In the House, it was defeated 80 to 113. Not one of the 80 was a Republican, but 110 of the 113 were Republicans.

Another significant measure of the secession winter was a proposal to amend the Constitution to guarantee the institution of slavery in the states. This proposed amendment—ironically designated by the same number as the one which later freed the slaves— was actually adopted by Congress, in the House by a vote of 128 to 65, but with 44 Republicans in favor and 62 opposed; in the Senate by a vote of 24 to 12, but with 8 Republicans in favor and 12 opposed.

While opposing these measures, certain Republicans, including Charles Francis Adams, brought forward a bill to admit New Mexico to statehood without restrictions on slavery, and they regarded this as a compromise proposal. But this measure was tabled in the House, 115 to 71, with Republicans casting 76 votes to table and 26 to keep the bill alive. Thus, it can be said, without qualification, that between December and March, no piece of compromise legislation was ever supported by a majority of Republican votes, either in the Senate or the House, either in committee or on the floor. This, of course, does not mean either that they ought to have supported the measures in question, or that such measures would have satisfied the Southern states. It is my own belief that the balance between the secessionist and the non-secessionist forces was fairly close in all of the seceding states except South Carolina, and that the support of Congress for a compromise would have been enough to tip the balance. But the Crittenden measure would possibly have opened the way for Southern filibustering activities to enlarge the territorial area south of 36° 30′—at least this was apparently what Lincoln feared—and the "thirteenth" amendment would have saddled the country with slavery more or less permanently. When we say, then, that the Republicans rejected compromise, we should take care to mean no more than we say. They did, by their votes, cause the defeat of measures which would otherwise have been adopted by Congress, which were intended and generally regarded as compromise measures. In this sense, they rejected compromise.

When we say the Republican party rejected secession, the case is so clear that it hardly needs a recital of proof. It is true that at one stage of the crisis, many Republicans did talk about letting the slave states go. Horace Greeley wrote his famous, ambiguous, oft-quoted, and much misunderstood editorial saying that "if the cotton states shall become satisfied that they can do better out of the Union than in it, we insist on letting them go in peace." Later, when the situation at Fort Sumter had reached its highest tension, a number of Republicans, including Salmon P. Chase, Simon Cameron, Gideon Welles, and Caleb Smith, all in the cabinet, advised Lincoln to evacuate the fort rather than precipitate hostilities; but this hardly means that they would not have made the issue of union in some other way. Lincoln himself definitively rejected secession in his inaugural address when he declared: "No state upon its own mere motion, can lawfully get out of the Union. . . . I . . . consider that in view of the Constitution and the laws, the Union is unbroken; and to the extent of my ability I shall take care, as the Constitution itself expressly enjoins upon me, that the laws of the Union be faithfully executed in all the States." After the fall of Fort Sumter, he translated this affirmation into action by calling for 75,000 volunteers, and by preparing to use large-scale military measures to hold the South in the Union. The fact that no major figure in the North, either Republican or Democrat, ever proposed to acquiesce in the rending of the Union and that no proposal to do so was ever seriously advocated or voted upon in Congress, is evidence enough that the Republicans rejected secession even more decisively than they rejected compromise. They scarcely even felt the need to consider the question or to make an organized presentation of their reasons. It is true that some of them said that they would rather have disunion than compromise, but this was a way of saying how much they objected to compromise, and not how little they objected to separation. It was almost exactly equivalent to the expression, "Death rather than dishonor," which has never been understood to mean an acceptance of death, but rather an adamant rejection of dishonor.

Here, then, in briefest outline is the record of the Republican rejection of compromise and of secession. What we are concerned with, however, is not the mere fact of the rejection, but rather with its meaning. Why did the Republicans do this? What was their motivation? What did they think would follow from their decision? What did they believe the alternatives to be? Specifically, did this mean that the choice as they saw it was clear-cut, and that they conceived of themselves as opting in favor of war in a situation where they had a choice between secession and war? As I come to this question, I must revert to my comments earlier in this paper by pointing out again the tendency of historians to see the alternatives with preternatural clarity and the fallacy involved in attributing to the participants a capacity to define the alternatives in the same crystalline terms.

Peace or war? Compromise or conflict? Separation or coercion? These alternatives have such a plausible neatness, such a readiness in fitting the historian's pigeon holes, that it is vastly tempting to believe that they define the choices which people were actually making and not just the choices that we think they ought to have been making. We all know, today, that economists once fell into fallacies by postulating an economic man who behaved economically in the way economists thought he ought to behave. But even though we do know this, we are not as wary as we should be of the concept of what might be called an historical man who behaved historically in the way historians thought he ought to have behaved. It is very well for us, a hundred years later, to analyze the record and to say there were three alternatives, as distinct as the three sides of a triangle, namely compromise, voluntary separation, or war. Indeed this analysis may be correct. The error is not in our seeing it this way, but in our supposing that since we do see it in this way, the participants must have seen it in this way also.

Nothing can be more difficult—indeed impossible—than to reconstruct how a complex situation appeared to a varied lot of people, not one of whom saw or felt things in exactly the same way as any other one, a full century ago. But in the effort to approximate these realities as far as we can, it might be useful to begin by asking to what extent the choices of compromise, separation, or war had emerged as the possible alternatives in the minds of the citizens as they faced the crisis. Did they see the Crittenden proposals as embodying a possibility for compromise, and did a vote against these proposals mean an acceptance of the alternatives of war or separation? Did a policy which rejected both compromise and war indicate an acceptance of the alternative of voluntary separation? Did a decision to send food to Sumter and to keep the flag flying mean an acceptance of war? By hindsight, all of these indications appear plausible, and yet on close scrutiny, it may appear that not one of them is tenable in an unqualified way.

Did a vote against the Crittenden proposals indicate a rejection of the possibility of compromise? If Republicans voted against the Crittenden proposals, did this mean that they saw themselves as rejecting the principle of compromise and that they saw the possibilities thereby narrowed to a choice between voluntary separation or fierce, coercive war? If they repelled the idea of voluntary separation, did this imply that they were prepared to face a choice between political compromise or military coercion as the only means of saving the Union? If they urged the administration to send food to the besieged men in Sumter and to keep the flag flying there, did this mean that they had actually accepted the irrepressibility of the irrepressible conflict, and that they regarded peaceable alternatives as exhausted?

Although it makes the task of our analysis considerably more complex to say so, still it behooves us to face the music of confusion and to admit that not one of these acts was necessarily seen by the participants as narrowing the alternatives in the way which our after-the-fact analysis might indicate. To see the force of this reality, it is necessary to look at each of these contingencies in turn.

First, there is the case of those Republicans, including virtually all the Republican members in the Senate or the House, who refused to support the Crittenden proposals. To be sure, these men were accused of sacrificing the Union or of a callous indifference to the hazard of war; and to be sure, there were apparently some men like Zachariah Chandler who actually wanted war. (It was Chandler, you will recall, who said, "Without a little blood-letting, the Union will not be worth a rush.") But there were many who had grown to entertain sincere doubts as to whether the adoption of the Crittenden proposals, or the grant of any other concessions to the South, would actually bring permanent security to the Union. The danger to the Union lay, as they saw it, in the fact that powerful groups in many Southern states believed that any state had an unlimited right to withdraw from the Union and thus disrupt it. Southerners had fallen into the habit of asserting this right whenever they were much dissatisfied and declaring they would exercise it if their demands were not met. They had made such declarations between 1846 and 1850, when the Free-Soilers proposed to exclude slavery from the Mexican Cession. They had done so again in 1850 when they wanted a more stringent fugitive slave law. The threat of secession had been heard once more in 1856 when it appeared that the

Republicans might elect a Free-Soiler to the presidency. On each occasion, concessions had been made: the Compromise of 1850 made it legally possible to take slaves to New Mexico; the Compromise also gave the slave owners a fugitive act that was too drastic for their own good; in 1856, timid Union-loving Whigs rallied to Buchanan and thus helped to avert the crisis that Frémont's election might have brought. Each such concession, of course, confirmed the Southern fire-eaters in their habit of demanding further concessions, and it strengthened their position with their constituents in the South by enabling them to come home at periodic intervals with new tribute that they had extorted from the Yankees. From the standpoint of a sincere Unionist, there was something self-defeating about getting the Union temporarily past a crisis by making concessions which strengthened the disunionist faction and perpetuated the tendency toward periodic crises. This was a point on which Republicans sometimes expressed themselves very emphatically. For instance, Schuyler Colfax, in 1859, wrote to his mother about conditions in Congress: "We are still just where we started six months ago," he said, "except that our Southern friends have dissolved the Union forty or fifty times since then." In the same vein, Carl Schurz ridiculed the threat of secession, while campaigning for Lincoln in 1860: "There had been two overt attempts at secession already," Schurz was reported as saying, "one the secession of the Southern students from the medical school at Philadelphia . . . the second upon the election of Speaker Pennington, when the South seceded from Congress, went out, took a drink, and then came back. The third attempt would be," he prophesied, "when Old Abe would be elected. They would then again secede and this time would take two drinks, but would come back again." Schurz's analysis may have been good wit, but of course it was disastrously bad prophesy, and it had the fatal effect of preparing men systematically to misunderstand the signs of danger when these signs appeared. The first signs would be merely the first drink; confirmatory signs would be the second drink. James Buchanan recognized, as early as 1856, that men were beginning to underestimate the danger to the Union simply because it was chronic and they were too familiar with it: "We have so often cried wolf," he said, "that now, when the wolf is at the door it is difficult to make the people believe it." Abraham Lincoln provided a distinguished proof of Buchanan's point in August, 1860, when he wrote: "The people of the South have too much of good sense and good temper to attempt the ruin of the government rather than see it administered as it was administered by the men who made it. At least, so I hope and believe." As usual, Lincoln's statement was a gem of lucidity, even when it was unconsciously so. He hoped and believed. The wish was father to the thought.

The rejection of compromise, then, did not mean an acceptance of separation or war. On the contrary, to men who regarded the threat of secession as a form of political blackmail rather than a genuine indication of danger to the Union, it seemed that danger of disunion could be eliminated only by eliminating the disunionists, and this could never be accomplished by paying them off at regular intervals. The best hope of a peaceful union lay in a development of the strength of Southern Unionists, who would never gain the ascendancy so long as the secessionists could always get what they demanded. Viewed in this light, compromise might be detrimental to the cause of the union; and rejection of compromise might be the best way to avoid the dangers of separation or of having to fight the disunionists.

If the rejection of compromise did not mean the acceptance of either separation or war, did the rejection of separation mean an acceptance of a choice between compromise and coercion as the remaining alternatives? This was the choice which history has seemed to indicate as the real option open to the country. But, though the unfolding of events may subsequently have demonstrated that these were the basic alternatives, one of the dominating facts about the Republicans in the winter of 1860–61 is that they rejected the idea of voluntary disunion and also rejected the idea of compromise, without any feeling that this narrowing of the spectrum would lead them to war. At this juncture, what may be called the illusion of the Southern Unionists played a vital part. Both Lincoln and Seward and many another Republicans were convinced that secessionism was a superficial phenomenon. They believed that it did not represent the most fundamental impulses of the South, and that although the Southern Unionists had been silenced by the clamor of the secessionists a deep vein of Unionist feeling still survived in the South and could be rallied, once the Southern people realized that Lincoln was not an Illinois version of William Lloyd

Garrison and that the secessionists had been misleading them. Lincoln and Seward became increasingly receptive to this view during the month before Lincoln's inauguration. Between December 20 and March 4, seven Southern states had held conventions, and each of these conventions had adopted an ordinance of secession. But on February 4, the secessionists were defeated in the election for the Virginia convention. Within four weeks thereafter, they were again defeated in Tennessee, where the people refused even to call a convention; in Arkansas, where the secessionist candidates for a state convention were defeated; in Missouri, where the people elected a convention so strongly anti-secessionist that it voted 89 to 1 against disunion; and in North Carolina, where anti-secessionist majorities were elected and it was voted that the convention should not meet.

It clearly looked as though the tide of secession had already turned. Certainly, at the time when Lincoln came to the presidency, the movement for a united South had failed. There were, altogether, fifteen slave states. Seven of these, from South Carolina, along the south Atlantic and Gulf coast to Texas, had seceded; but eight others, including Delaware, Kentucky, and Maryland, as well as the five that I have already named, were still in the Union and clearly intended to remain there. In these circumstances, the New York *Tribune* could speak of the Confederacy as a "heptarchy," and Seward could rejoice, as Henry Adams reported, that "this was only a temporary fever and now it has reached the climax and favorably passed it." The Southern Unionists were already asserting themselves, and faith in them was justified. Thus, on his way east from Springfield, Lincoln stated in a speech at Steubenville, Ohio, that "the devotion to the Constitution is equally great on both sides of the [Ohio] River." From this it seemed to follow that, as he also said on his trip, "there is no crisis but an artificial one. . . . Let it alone and it will go down of itself." Meanwhile, Seward had been saying, ever since December, that the Gulf states would try to secede, but that unless they received the backing of the border states, they would find their petty little combination untenable and would have to come back to the Union. Again we owe to Henry Adams the report that Seward said, "We shall keep the border states, and in three months or thereabouts, if we hold off, the Unionists and the disunionists will have their hands on each others throats in the cotton states."

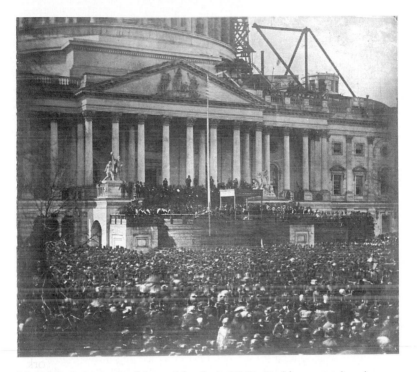

Lincoln's inaugural address, March 4, 1861. Besides conveying the portentousness and solemnity of the occasion, this daguerrotype is also symbolic. The unfinished new capitol building that looms over the event below can be seen as a representation of the Union that was also incomplete and was actually breaking up as Lincoln spoke. (*Chicago Historical Society*)

Today, our hindsight makes it difficult for us to understand this reliance upon Southern Unionism, since most of the unionism which existed was destroyed by the four years of war; and it was never what Seward and Lincoln believed it to be in any case. But it seemed quite real when five slave states in rapid succession decided against secession. Thus, in terms of our alternatives of compromise, separation, or war, it is interesting to see that an editorial in the New York *Tribune* on March 27, 1861, specifically examined the alternatives and specifically said that there were only three; but the three which it named were not the three we tend to perceive today. The fact that this editorial, rather closely resembling one in the New York *Times,* was probably inspired by the administration, gives it additional interest.

The *Tribune* began by saying that there were but three possible ways in which to meet the secession movement. One was "by prompt, resolute, unflinching resistance"—what I have been calling the alternative of war; the second was "by complete acquiescence in . . . secession"—that is, separation. But instead of naming compromise as the third alternative, the *Tribune* numbered as three "a Fabian policy, which concedes nothing, yet employs no force in support of resisted Federal authority, hoping to wear out the insurgent spirit and in due time re-establish the authority of the union in the revolted or seceded states by virtue of the returning sanity and loyalty of their own people." As the editorial continued, it explained the reasoning which lay behind the advocacy of this policy.

> To war on the Seceders is to give to their yet vapory institutions the strong cement of blood—is to baptize their nationality in the mingled life-blood of friends and foes. But let them severely alone—allow them to wear out the military ardor of their adherents in fruitless drilling and marches, and to exhaust the patience of their fellow-citizens by the amount and frequency of their pecuniary exactions—and the fabric of their power will melt away like fog in the beams of a morning sun. Only give them rope, and they will speedily fulfill their destiny—the People, even of South Carolina, rejecting their sway as intolerable, and returning to the mild and paternal guardian-ship of the Union.
>
> In behalf of this policy, it is urged that the Secessionists are a minority even in the seceded States; that they have grasped power by usurpation and retain it by terrorism; that they never dare submit the question of Union or Disunion fairly and squarely to the people, and always shun a popular vote when they can. In view of these facts, the Unionists of the South urge that the Government shall carry forebearance to the utmost, in the hope that the Nullifiers will soon be overwhelmed by the public sentiment of their own section, and driven with ignominy from power.

It seems reasonably clear that this editorial defined quite accurately the plan of action which Lincoln had announced in his inaugural. In that address, although affirming in general terms a claim of federal authority which, as the *Tribune* expressed it, conceded nothing, he made it quite clear that he would, as the *Tribune* also said, "employ no force" in the immediate situation. He specifically said he would not use force to deliver the mails—they would only be delivered unless repelled. He specifically said that federal marshals and judges would not be sent into areas where these functions had been vacated. "While the strict legal right may exist in the government to enforce the exercise of these offices, the attempt to do so would be so irritating that I deem it better to forego for the time the use of such offices." Without officials for enforcement, Lincoln's statement that he would uphold the law became purely a declaration of principle, with no operative or functional meaning. Finally, after having first written into his inaugural a statement that "all the power at my disposal will be used to reclaim the public property and places which have fallen," he struck this passage from the address as it was ultimately delivered. It was at about this time that Senator William P. Fessenden of Maine wrote that "Mr. Lincoln believed that gentleness and a conciliatory policy would prevent secession"—as if secession had not already occurred.

Finally, there is a question of whether even the decision to send supplies to Fort Sumter involved a clear acceptance of the alternative of war as well as a rejection of the alternatives of separation or compromise. Professor Stampp and Richard Current [each had written a book on Lincoln in the secession crisis] have both argued with considerable persuasiveness that Lincoln must have known that the Sumter expedition would bring war, since his informants from Charleston had warned him that such an expedition would be met with military force; and they have shown too that anyone with as much realism as Lincoln had in his makeup must have recognized that the chances for peace were slipping away. Yet I think their argument is more a reasoning from logic—that Lincoln must have seen the situation as we see it—and not an argument based primarily on expressions by Lincoln himself, showing that he had abandoned his belief in Southern Unionism and accepted the alternative of war. Indeed, insofar as we have expressions from him, he continued to believe in the strength of Southern Unionism. Even when he sent his war message to Congress on July 4, he said: "It may well be questioned whether there is today a majority of the legally qualified voters of any state, except perhaps South Carolina, in favor of disunion. There is much reason to believe that the Union men are in the majority in many, if not in every one of the so-called seceded states."

The crisis at Fort Sumter has possibly had almost too sharp a focus placed upon it by historians, and I do not want to dissect that question all over again in this paper. I will state briefly that, in my opinion, Lincoln pursued the most peaceful course that he believed was possible for him to pursue without openly abandoning the principle of union. That is, he assured the Confederates that food only would be sent into Fort Sumter, and nothing else would be done to strengthen the Union position unless the delivery of the food was resisted. While this may be construed, and has been construed, as a threat to make war if the food were not allowed, it can equally well be regarded as a promise that no reinforcement would be undertaken if the delivery of the food was permitted. Lincoln's critics, who accuse him of a covert policy to begin in an advantageous way a war which he now recognized to be inevitable, have never said what more peaceable course he could have followed that would have been consistent with his purpose to save the Union. Thus, they are in the anomalous position of saying that a man who followed the most peaceable course possible was still, somehow, a maker of war.

But as I suggested a moment ago, this focus upon Fort Sumter can perhaps be intensified too much. Even if Lincoln anticipated that there would be shooting at Sumter (and he must have known that there was a strong likelihood of it), what would this tell us about the choice of alternatives leading to the American Civil War? We may again revert to the somewhat arbitrary practice of answering this question in terms of the alternatives as they appear to us now. If the situation is viewed in this way, one would say we have three options neatly laid in a row: separation, compromise, war. If a man rejects any two of them, he is choosing the third; and since Lincoln and the Republicans rejected separation or compromise, this means that they exercised a choice for war. As a statement of the way in which the historical process narrows the field of possible action, this may be realistic; but for illumination of the behavior of men it seems to me very misleading. It assumes two things: first that choices are positive rather than negative; second that a choice of a course which leads to a particular result is in fact a choice of that result. Neither of these assumptions seems valid. What often happens is not that a given course is chosen because it is acceptable, but that given alternatives are rejected because they are regarded as totally unacceptable;

thus one course remains which becomes the course followed, not because it was chosen, but because it was what was left.

When Lincoln ordered the Sumter expedition to sail, it was not because he wanted to do so; it was because he hated even worse the contingency of permitting the Sumter garrison to be starved into surrender. As he himself said, he had been committed to "the exhaustion of peaceful measures, before a resort to any stronger ones." But by mid-April at Sumter, the peaceful measures had all been exhausted; and the course that Lincoln followed was taken not because it was what he had chosen, but because it was what was left. That course resulted, as we now say, in the bombardment of Sumter, and the bombardment of Sumter was followed by four years of fighting which we call the Civil War. But even though the sending of the expedition led to events which in turn led on to war, it does not follow that the choice to send the expedition involved an acceptance of the alternative of war.

If deeds and consequences could be thus equated, our view of human nature would have to be more pessimistic than it is; and at the same time, our view of the future of humanity might perhaps be somewhat more optimistic. For it would imply that men have deliberately caused the succession of wars that have blotted the record of human history—certainly a harsh verdict to pronounce on humanity—and it would also imply that they have a certain measure of choice as to what forces of destruction they will release in the world—a proposition which would be comforting in the age of nuclear fission. But when we examine the situations of the past, how seldom does it appear that men defined the alternatives logically, chose the preferable alternative, and moved forward to the result that was intended? How often, on the other hand, do we find that they grope among the alternatives, avoiding whatever action is most positively or most immediately distasteful, and thus eliminate the alternatives until only one is left—at which point, as Lincoln said, it is necessary to have recourse to it since the other possibilities are exhausted or eliminated. In this sense, when the Republicans rejected both compromise and secession, thus narrowing the range of possibilities to include only the contingency of war, it was perhaps not because they really preferred the Civil War, with all its costs, to separation or to compromise, but because they could see the consequences of voting for compromise or the consequences of accepting separation more readily than they could see the consequences of following the rather indecisive course that ended in the bombardment of Fort Sumter. They did not know that it would end by leaving them with a war on their hands, any more than they knew it would cost the life of one soldier, either Rebel or Yank, for every six slaves who were freed and for every ten white Southerners who were held in the Union. When they rejected compromise, because they could not bear to make concessions to the fire-eaters, and rejected separation, because they could not bear to see the Union broken up, this does not mean that they accepted war or that they were able to bear the cost which this war would make them pay. It may really mean that they chose a course whose consequences they could not see in preference to courses whose consequences were easier to appraise.

Historians try to be rational beings and tend to write about history as if it were a rational process. Accordingly, they number the alternatives, and talk about choices and decisions, and equate decisions with what the decisions led to. But if we examine the record of modern wars, it would seem that the way people get into a war is seldom by choosing it; usually it is by choosing a course that leads to it—which is a different thing altogether. Although war seems terribly decisive, perhaps it requires less positive decision to get into wars than it does to avert them. For one can get into a war without in any way foreseeing it or imagining it, which is easy. But to avert war successfully, it has to be foreseen or imagined, which is quite difficult. If this is true, it means that the Republicans may have rejected separation and compromise not because they accepted the alternative, but precisely because they could not really visualize the alternative. When they took the steps that led them into a war, they did so not because they had decisively chosen the road to Appomattox or even the road to Manassas, in preference to the other paths; instead they did so precisely because they could not grasp the fearfully decisive consequences of the rather indecisive line of action which they followed in the months preceding their fateful rendezvous.

Kenneth M. Stampp

THE REPUBLICANS' POLICY: A REPLY TO DAVID M. POTTER

At first reading, Kenneth M. Stampp's response may seem to diverge on only minor points from David M. Potter's position. In fact, it makes several different, and significant, assertions. First, Stampp argues that Lincoln operated on the premise that war was quite likely; that is, he did not set out to avert war. Stampp then explains that the new president's policy was to take a firm, yet not provocative, stand rather than to conciliate the South. And finally, he claims that the strategy succeeded because it forced the Confederates to make the overtly belligerent move that initiated hostilities. While quite different in these respects from Potter's analysis, Stampp's explanation still rejects the possibilities at both extremes—either that Lincoln provoked war by forcing the Confederates into a showdown at Fort Sumter or that his policy rested on the idea of "masterly inactivity," as William H. Seward, his secretary of state, recommended. The interpretations of both Stampp and Potter, although different from each other, lie within the confines of these two extreme positions.

Kenneth M. Stampp's book on the secession crisis is *And the War Came: The North and the Secession Crisis* (1950), where he had set out more fully the approach that differed with Potter's. As noted earlier, he has written a number of important books on the Civil War era.

I assume that we are concerned not only with Lincoln and the Republican members of Congress but also with Republican governors, Republican members of the state legislatures, and rank-and-file Republican voters as well. For the vast majority of these Republicans also rejected compromise and secession.

As I see it, Professor Potter's argument runs something like this: (1) Men do not like to think that the principles they cherish may conflict with each other. This prevents them from seeing realistic alternatives when the alternatives force them to choose between their principles. (2) The alternatives are never as clear to the participants in a crisis as they are to historians with their hindsight. The

Kenneth M. Stampp, "Comment on 'Why the Republicans Rejected Both Compromise and Secession,'" in *The Crisis of the Union, 1860–61*, edited by George Harmon Knoles. Copyright © 1965 by Louisiana State University Press.

power of hindsight makes it difficult for historians to see a historical situation as the participants saw it. (3) With our hindsight we know that the Republicans rejected compromise and secession and that the result was the Civil War. Therefore, we tend to think the Civil War that actually occurred was the clear alternative to accepting compromise or secession. (4) Hindsight also enables us to judge alternatives in terms of results that participants could never have anticipated. Thus the rejection of compromise and secession led to a four-year war, to the preservation of the Union, and to the abolition of slavery; but no one in the winter of 1860–61 could have known that these would be the results.

Up to this point there is nothing in Professor Potter's argument with which I would disagree, except the conclusion he draws from it as stated here. The "supreme task of the historian," he says, "is to see the past through the imperfect eyes of those who lived it." In my opinion, this is one valid way to see the past; but having accomplished it, the historian's task is but half done. The other way to see the past is with all the wisdom and perspective that experience and hindsight can give us. It was hindsight that enabled Professor Potter to describe Carl Schurz's remarks about the approaching crisis as "disastrously bad prophesy" and to show how Schurz helped to prepare men to "misunderstand the signs of danger." It was hindsight once more that enabled him to discern the element of tragedy in human existence as he did so brilliantly in the last pages of his paper—how men throughout history, without willing it, maneuver themselves into situations that culminate in disaster. We must use hindsight as Professor Potter uses it: not to judge and condemn the men of the past, but to understand *why* their best-laid plans so often went astray.

But for the problem at hand—that is, determining why Republicans rejected compromise and secession—Professor Potter believes that we must see the situation as the participants saw it. He objects, therefore, to describing the alternatives as compromise, peaceful secession, or war, because we can see that these were the alternatives only with hindsight. When the Republicans rejected compromise and peaceful secession, he says, they were not necessarily choosing war. I think Professor Potter is correct in this, but I do not think this is the most fruitful way to consider the alternatives. There is another way that brings the alternatives as the Republicans of 1860–61 saw them much closer to the alternatives as we, with our hindsight, see them now. The alternatives were these: (1) compromise, (2) acquiescence in secession, or (3) *the use of whatever force might be necessary to collect federal revenues and to recover or maintain possession of federal property.* These were the alternatives as most Republicans understood them then, and they were the real alternatives as we know from our hindsight.

But from the perspective of 1861, the consequence of using force against the South to collect the revenues and hold federal property was not *necessarily* war. A few Republicans thought it would be; others feared it might be; but many others hoped it would not be. The use of force might have resulted only in a few minor skirmishes, followed by the quick submission of the Southern rebels. The crisis might have been over in a few weeks. Better still, a sufficient demonstration of federal power might have resulted in the immediate collapse of the Confederacy without so much as a skirmish. Thus Republicans could, as most of them actually did, reject compromise and peaceful secession and choose coercion (they called it "the enforcement of the laws") without favoring war or believing that their choice would lead to war. I do not think that even Zachariah Chandler wanted war. After all, he asked only for "a little blood-letting." I believe that when the alternatives are understood in this way, we have a partial answer to the question of why the Republicans rejected compromise and peaceful secession. Thus, even if Republicans believed that Southerners were serious about secession, they could reject compromise and peaceful secession without feeling that war was the only remaining alternative. A mere show of force might have been enough. This generalization is in agreement with the position Professor Potter takes in the concluding pages of his paper, but not with the position he takes in the middle part.

In the middle part, Professor Potter would say that I have begged the question, for I have presupposed not only that Southerners were serious about breaking up the Union but also that Republicans *knew* they were serious and considered alternatives accordingly. This is a presupposition that Professor Potter will not accept, and this is crucial to his explanation of why the Republicans rejected compromise and peaceful secession.

Many Republicans, he thinks, had come to the conclusion that Southerners had got into a bad habit of threatening to secede whenever they failed to get what they wanted. Therefore, according to Professor Potter, Republicans considered the threat of secession to be a form of political blackmail. To compromise with men such as these would only strengthen the disunion movement and make matters worse. More than that, Professor Potter believes that many Republicans thought secessionism lacked basic strength and that most Southerners were actually Unionists at heart. Given time and encouragement, Southern Unionists would suppress the secessionists and regain control; and the Union would be restored without either compromise or war. Thus the alternatives were not compromise, peaceful secession, or force (as I have suggested that Republicans understood them); rather, the alternatives were compromise, peaceful secession, or a "Fabian policy which concedes nothing, yet employs no force" but depends instead on voluntary reunion "through the returning sanity" of the Southern people. Therefore, Professor Potter suggests that Republicans rejected compromise and peaceful secession because they believed the alternative was not war but a reliance on Southern Unionism. Whether he believes that this was the position of *most* Republicans is not clear. Professor Potter says *many*, and among them he includes Lincoln and Seward.

Assuming this generalization to be true for many Republicans, it is still necessary to explain why those who did *not* rely on Southern Unionism (however many there were) rejected compromise and peaceful secession; and I have suggested that it was because they saw the "enforcement of the laws" as an alternative that would not necessarily lead to war. But at this point I would like to consider the alternative of voluntary reunion which Professor Potter believes many Republicans favored. I think the best way to consider it is to take a look at the Northern Democrats and to note what *they* were saying during the crisis. Most Democrats, like the Republicans, rejected peaceful secession; but, unlike the Republicans, they strongly favored compromise, and almost none of them showed any faith in voluntary reunion. Indeed, they repeatedly warned that the inevitable alternative to compromise was *war*—a long and sanguinary war, from which the country would not recover for decades.

Thus we seem to have many Republicans rejecting compromise and saying hopefully and mistakenly that Southern Unionists would soon suppress the secessionists and restore the Union; and we seem to have the Democrats begging for compromise and making what in retrospect proved to be the most realistic predictions about the consequences of rejecting compromise. Are we to conclude from this that the Democrats were a more perspicacious lot than the Republicans? I think not. Rather, it is much more likely that neither the Republicans nor the Democrats were quite sure what the ultimate consequences of rejecting compromise would be. (This, I believe, is nearly the position that Professor Potter takes in the concluding pages of his paper—a position that he does not entirely reconcile with the one he takes in the middle section.)

Why did the Democrats predict war? I would suggest that their desire to achieve a compromise tempted them to paint the most horrible picture of the consequences of *not* compromising. In short, they were trying to frighten people into accepting a compromise. As for the Republicans, their opposition to compromise tempted them to paint a more cheerful picture of the consequences of not compromising. Voluntary reunion was not so much an alternative as a political strategem used by some Republicans who, as a matter of fact, either did not know what the consequences of rejecting compromise would be or preferred the alternative of enforcing the laws.

This is not to say that there were no Republicans who really believed a Unionist reaction would take place in the South. I think there were some, especially in the early weeks of the crisis before South Carolina seceded and seized Fort Moultrie. After that, the evidence indicates that the number of Republicans who believed in this easy solution dwindled rapidly. To put it another way, a growing number of Republicans—I think the great majority of them by January—began to suspect that the federal government might have to take positive action, that is, enforce the laws, in order to suppress the secessionists. Seward, we know, continued to have faith in voluntary reunion almost to the outbreak of war. But not Lincoln. He seems to have believed in this remedy in November and early December, but there is considerable evidence that he had begun to change his mind when South Carolina seceded.

The evidence is available in Lincoln's collected works. On December 21, he wrote to Francis P. Blair, Sr., that if the forts were surrendered before the inauguration they would have to be retaken afterward. On the same day he wrote to Elihu B. Washburne asking him to tell General Scott "to be as well prepared as he can to either *hold* or *retake* the forts, as the case may require, at, and after the inauguration." On December 22, Lincoln wrote to Major David Hunter: "If the forts fall, my judgment is that they are to be re-taken." On the same day he wrote to Peter Sylvester: "If Mr. B[uchanan] surrenders the forts, I think they must be retaken."

The most revealing of these letters was one, dated December 29, to James Watson Webb, editor of the New York *Courier and Enquirer.* Webb had written to ask Lincoln's views on how to deal with secession, to which Lincoln replied: "I think we should hold the forts, or retake them, as the case may be, and collect the revenue. *We* shall have to forego the use of the federal courts, and *they* that of the mails, for a while. We can not fight them into holding courts, or receiving mails. This is an outline of my view; and perhaps suggests sufficiently the whole of it." There is here not a hint of voluntary reunion as a way of dealing with the crisis; and I am inclined to agree with Professor Potter that "Lincoln was always precise to a unique degree in his statements."

Actually, Lincoln, in his letter to Webb, outlined precisely the policy he described in more detail in his inaugural address. This was the policy he believed in from late December until March 4; and I think it is the policy he followed when he became President. He would permit the federal courts to suspend operation if necessary, and Southerners could go without mail service if they wanted to. Moreover, there would be no invasion, no use of force, except (and this is a big exception) what may be necessary to "hold, occupy, and possess the property and places belonging to the government, and to collect the duties and imposts." This being the case, I do not interpret Lincoln's statement that he would uphold the laws as "purely a declaration of principle, with no operative or functional meaning" as Professor Potter does. I believe that Lincoln was as precise in his statements here as Professor Potter has found him to be elsewhere.

I see no evidence that Lincoln became increasingly receptive to the idea of voluntary reunion during the month of February. Professor Potter describes what was happening in Virginia, North Carolina, Tennessee, Arkansas, and Missouri, where secession was defeated. But he ignores what was happening in Montgomery, Al-abama, where the Confederate States of America took form that very month; the fact that not one of the seceded states sent repre-sentatives to the peace conference that was then meeting in Washington; and the fact that the Texas convention, on February 1, approved secession by a vote of 166 to 7. To me, Lincoln's remarks on the way to Washington in February, as well as his inaugural address, indicate that he had come to the disagreeable conclusion that as President he might very well have to use force against the secessionists. Hence he was doing his best to prepare the people for it and to assure them that the responsibility for violence would lay with the South: "In *your* hands, my dissatisfied fellow countrymen, and not in *mine*, is the momentous issue of civil war."

Why, then, did the Republicans reject compromise and peaceful secession? A few, no doubt, because they believed that Southern Unionists would be able to suppress the secessionists by themselves; a few because they could both anticipate and accept the alternative of civil war; most because they were willing to take their chances with the alternative of enforcing the laws.

And why should so many Republicans have preferred the risks of enforcing the laws to compromise or peaceful secession? For a variety of reasons: some because they believed it was a dangerous precedent to compromise with men who were committing treason; some because they thought it was morally wrong to make further concessions to the Slave Power; some because their national pride was deeply offended by the Southern effort to dismember the federal Union; some because they believed that the failure of the American experiment in self-government would dishearten liberal political forces in the whole western world; and some, no doubt, because they were afraid that compromise would destroy the Republican party, as it had destroyed the Whig party.

Lincoln, in his second inaugural address, explained precisely the ultimate consequence of the Republican rejection of both compromise and peaceful secession: "Both parties deprecated war, but one of them would *make* war rather than let the nation survive, and the other would *accept* war rather than let it perish, and the war came."

Phillip S. Paludan

THE AMERICAN CIVIL WAR AS A CRISIS IN LAW AND ORDER

The question at the heart of Phillip S. Paludan's essay is, Why did the North resist southern secession by force rather than just let the South go? For an answer, Paludan looks beyond the policymakers in Washington who were the protagonists in the explanations offered by Potter and Stampp and most other historians. As a result, he discovers the existence of attitudes and priorities in northern society that made it impossible to ignore the South's action.

The animating spirit behind the drive to counter the South was the concern, Paludan concludes, that secession was an act of lawlessness that, if left unchecked, could result in an undermining of obedience to authority and of deference to institutions in the North itself. In arguing this point, Paludan takes direct issue with David Herbert Donald, while he also adopts a different position from Arthur Bestor on the contribution of the legal and constitutional framework to the sectional conflict and the coming of war.

Phillip S. Paludan (born 1938) teaches at the University of Kansas and is the author of *A Covenant with Death: The Constitution, Law, and Equality in the Civil War Era* (1975); *Victims: A True Story of the Civil War* (1981); and *"A People's Contest": The Union and Civil War, 1861–1865* (1988).

Despite thousands of volumes written about the Civil War we still know almost nothing about one of the central questions that that struggle poses: why did men rush to fight for their endangered country? Indeed why did they believe that secession endangered it? We know with some precision why the South seceded. The answer is obvious at first glance and remains clear upon deeper investigation—the South seceded because it saw in the election of Lincoln a threat to the survival of slavery, the foundation for the Southern way of life. Tradition, psychology, and economics all spoke clearly the same message—without slavery we cannot survive. And so secession came.

Phillip S. Paludan, "The American Civil War Considered as a Crisis in Law and Order," *American Historical Review* (October 1972), vol. 77, No. 4, pp. 1013, 1017–22, 1024–34. Used by permission of the author.

But a description of the decision for secession is not a description of why the war came. Although the South prepared for war there would be none unless the North contested the Southern action. Lincoln's assertion that "both parties deprecated war; but one of them would make war rather than let the nation survive; and the other would accept war rather than let it perish," is imprecise and thus misleading. The decision to make war for the Union was made not in Richmond or Montgomery but in Washington, and Boston and New York, and Indianapolis, and Columbus, and Springfield. This decision was made by Lincoln and by thousands of men who throughout the secession winter and especially after Sumter rushed to the colors. To understand why the war came we must look not at secession but at the Northern response to it. . . .

If we are to understand the reason that the North went to war for the Union we need to . . . direct our attention toward the local experience, toward the environments in which the majority of Northerners lived. To focus locally is to ask the question about why men fought for the Union in a different and I hope more useful and precise way. The question changes form the general "Why fight for the Union?" to "What was there in the daily experience of most Northerners that made them sensitive and responsive to those images the Union evoked?"

As the North reacted to the secession crisis one theme was repeated constantly, and it suggests a crucial fact about Northern society. Again and again newspaper editors and political leaders discussed the degree to which secession was likely to produce disorder, anarchy, and a general disrespect for democratic government. The future president Andrew Johnson pictured for his congressional colleagues "this Union divided into thirty-three petty governments, with a little prince in one, a little potentate in another, a little aristocracy in a third, a little democracy in a fourth and a republic somewhere else . . . with quarreling and warring amongst the little petty powers which would result in anarchy." Congressman Zachariah Chandler announced that if secession were tolerated "I shall arrange for emigration to some country where they have a government. I would rather join the Comanches; I will never live under a government that has not the power to enforce its laws." The conservative Philadelphia *North American* called secession "Lawlessness on a Gigantic Scale" and remarked, "The world must regard with

Departure of the New York State Militia, April 19, 1861. This engraving—the original was in color—depicts the glamor and festiveness of the scene at Broadway and Courtland Street in New York City, as the state volunteers, with their new uniforms and equipment, went off to war. (*Gift of the Mr. & Mrs. Karolik Collection. Museum of Fine Arts, Boston.*)

profound astonishment the spectacle of national lawlessness which the southern States of this Union now exhibit. . . . Resistance to law, . . . contempt for order . . . defiant rebellion against the entire structure which we call the United States government." The Boston *Traveller* argued that had the founders of the country provided for peaceable secession they "would have organized anarchy." Allow Southern states to secede, the Douglas-supporting Burlington *Weekly Sentinel* said, and "the Union with all its glory . . . high hopes . . . power, with all its interest has gone and stands in history as another monument of the inability of man to govern himself under the forms of constitutional law." . . .

*

Northern determination to uphold government and order against the threat of anarchy was not simply rhetoric. Both speakers and listeners responded to such sentiments naturally, for in talking about the need for order and stable government they were discussing the topic about which the vast majority of Northerners were experts in practice if not in theory. In raising the issue of law and order the speakers struck Northerners quite literally where they lived. No issue, with the possible exception of acquiring wealth, had attracted so much energy and debate in the prewar years. From the Mayflower Compact and the organization of colonial governments, through the writing of the Articles of Confederation, the creation of the Constitution, the ratification of thirty-two state constitutions from 1776 to 1860 in the states that did not secede (fifteen in the last fifteen years before secession), the debates and elections over constitutions that failed, the countless creations of county, town, and city governments, these Americans had been engaged in government-making. Add to this the millions of words expended debating constitutional questions in the prewar era, the numerous court cases that attracted national attention, the almost constant elections in the country with their concomitant discussions of governmental issues, and it is possible to describe the prewar years as a time of continual concern with questions of government, order, and law. . . .

The avalanche of oratory debating questions of law, government, and the Constitution had special meaning for Northerners. It was not merely theorizing about ideals but was a practical debate about the way they lived. Government in the pre–Civil War North was not "them"; it was "us." The national government was days if not weeks away, and its constitutional powers were strictly limited. It regulated interstate commerce, ran the post office, dealt with Indians, conducted such foreign policy as there was, and paid and administered an army and navy that totaled around 28,000 men as of 1860. In 1861 there were about 36,500 paid civilian employees of the national government, and approximately 30,000 of these were local postmasters. The national government did not tax the public at large. It had no powers in matters of health, education, welfare, morals, sanitation, safety, or local transportation. In short, practically every activity that affected the lives of Americans was the province of either state or local government—and more often than not it was local. An observer in 1850 described the structure of government:

> The President has one postmaster in every village: but the inhabitants of that village choose their own selectmen, their own assessors of taxes, their own school-committee, their own overseers of the poor, their own surveyors of highways, and the incumbents of half a dozen other little offices corresponding to those which, in bureaucratic governments, are filled by appointment of the sovereign. In all these posts, which are really important public trusts, the villagers are trained to the management of affairs, and acquire a comprehensiveness of view, a practical administrative talent, and a knowledge of business. . . . This training is very general; for owing to our republican liking for rotation in office, the incumbents of these humble posts are changed every year or two.

Nowhere was this description more true than in the states of the Middle West. Indeed the recent frontier experiences of that region guaranteed a widespread personal involvement in questions of government, law, and order. In the two generations before the Civil War, wilderness and Indian territory had been transformed into states: Ohio, 1803; Indiana, 1816; Illinois, 1818; Michigan, 1837; Iowa, 1846; Wisconsin, 1848; Minnesota, 1858. Such state-making had been preceded by community-making on a vast scale. The early years of settlement in these states lend some support to the popular image of a wild, uncivilized frontier. The predominant pattern, however, was that of a successful struggle for community order, a struggle without much opposition once the permanent settlers arrived. These pioneers carried in their baggage the experience with and devotion to the government institutions of the East. Indeed many of those who came to the West were conservative members of Eastern communities who wanted to re-establish the sort of order they believed was being undermined by liberal domination of their homelands. Their commitment to stability and order can be seen in the fact that they founded churches and schools in the first days of community building. Henry Ward Beecher noted in the 1850s that the frontier settlers "drive schools along with them as settlers drive flocks. They have herds of churches, academies, lyceums; and their religious and educational institutions go lowing along the western plains as Jacob's herds lowed along the Syrian hills."

The institutions the settlers of the Midwest founded were copies of those they had known in the East. The New England model was widely emulated, and it ensured the formation of stable communities, as whole communities often moved together, locating their towns on land that was already plotted and organized into townships. Such activity minimized mad scrambles for land. In some cases settlers found that the apparatus of county and town government preceded them into a region, and they were bound by law and inclination to adopt that organization. . . .

The frontier regions, some of them settled only fifty years before, some in the process of settlement in 1860, demanded the most widespread involvement. From earliest cabin raisings, to the creation and maintenance of towns, to the sustaining of large cities, people took part actively. Men without prior experience were drafted as officials or rushed to file for office as eagerly as they filed their land claims. For example, in Hamilton County, Ohio, an election was called for delegates to the constitutional convention of 1802. Of the ninety-four candidates who filed for ten positions, twenty-six received between 121 and 1,635 votes. "Everybody," one Indiana pioneer wrote, "expected at some time to be a candidate for something; or that his uncle would be; or his cousin, or his cousin's wife's cousin's friend would be; so that everybody and everybody's relation's friend, were forever electioneering." Such involvement in politics continued unabated into the decades before the war. As Henry Clyde Hubbart writes of the older Middle West, "The people of the free West in the forties and fifties were a political people. This was true in all senses of the term politics whether the word be held to mean political ideas and philosophy; or social attitudes . . . or in a narrower sense political party programs or activities; or in a still narrower sense, the designs and manipulations of politicians and petty factions." Large numbers of Americans, then, took a personal and active part in creating the institutions of government that made civilized life possible in the West. Commenting on what they see as the crucial element in the frontier experience, Stanley Elkins and Eric McKitrick conclude, "Here was a society in which the setting up of institutions was a common experience."

Concern for the government and politics was not confined to the frontier areas of the West. Indicators of involvement in such questions appear in the East as well. In the first place, the founding of towns and the consequent opportunities and demands for participation were not limited to the West. Five of the twenty-seven towns that in 1851 made up Oneida County in New York had been founded between 1827 and 1846. Between 1823 and 1836 there were four towns established in that state's Herkimer County. Erie County, New York, saw the founding of new towns in 1851, 1852, 1853, and 1857. Bucks County, Pennsylvania, just outside Philadelphia, had newly created towns up to 1838, and Venango County in Pennsylvania organized townships in 1845 and 1850 and would continue to do so up to 1876. Towns that had been long established would often rededicate themselves to maintaining the communities they had and to carrying out the ideals of their founding. Again and again, then, Americans in the nonseceding states involved themselves in government-making, considered the problems of self-rule, and thereby made government their own responsibility.

Involvement in the governing and political process was not limited to forming governments. Rotation in office apparently was frequent. Herkimer County in twenty-six years re-elected a member of Congress only three times; of twelve state senators, only one man repeated in thirteen years. The town of Caroline in New York saw twenty-six men in the office of town supervisor in a forty-nine-year period. The longest tenure was four years, and only two men held the job that long. The town of Queensbury, New York, had fifty-nine different justices of the peace from 1795 to 1873 and 143 different constables from 1766 to 1873. Town records contain thirteen pages listing seventy men each as highway commissioners from 1766 to 1873, most of them single termers. Similarly great rotation in office occurred in the offices of town and ward supervisor in Buffalo from 1854 and in Venango County, Pennsylvania. A sample of New England towns suggests similar facts of rotation. Worcester, Massachusetts, between 1848 and 1859 had seven different mayors and forty-nine different aldermen out of seventy-two possible positions. Ward supervisor positions show the same pattern. Taking only two wards we see twenty-two different supervisors for thirty-six possible jobs in Ward One and twenty-six different supervisors out of thirty-six possibilities in Ward Four. Roxbury, Massachusetts, rotated officeholders with similar frequency.

One did not have to be an officeholder to maintain an intense interest in public affairs. Visitors noted how passionately Americans were involved in politics, the turbulence and intensity of elections, and the apparent bitterness of party strife. Their observations are borne out by statistics. For the years 1848 to 1872 Walter Dean Burnham estimates the mean turnout for presidential elections to be an impressive 75.1 per cent. (By way of comparison, the national turnout in the 1968 election was 61.6 per cent.) In off-year elections an estimated 65.2 per cent of those eligible voted. (The 1970 off-year elections for the House brought 44.9 per cent of the eligible voters to the polls.) When the South is removed from the sample the figures are more impressive still. Between 1868 and 1880 the mean turnout in presidential elections was 82.6 per cent in the North. In Michigan between 1854 and 1872 the mean turnout in presidential years was 84.8 per cent, in off-years 78.1 per cent. For Ohio from 1857 to 1879 these figures read 89.0 per cent and 78.4 per cent. In New York from 1834 to 1858 the mean turnout in presidential years was 84.8 per cent and in off-year elections 81.5 per cent. Further evidence of involvement is seen in the fact that there was a very small amount of roll-off in the voting process. (Roll-off is the tendency to vote only for major offices and to ignore lesser ones.) Between 1857 and 1879 in Ohio the mean roll-off was 0.6 per cent. New York from 1834 to 1858 witnessed a 1.6 per cent roll-off. From 1854 to 1872 Michigan's mean roll-off was 0.9 per cent. Additional testimony to the intensity of political concern is seen in two notable statistics. First, there was very little split-ticket voting. Political preferences tended to be strong and tenacious. Certainly mid-nineteenth-century voters hoped that the best man would win, but they tended to think that the best men were devoted to Democratic, Whig, or Republican principles. Second, there was very little party switching, with the understandable exception of the election of 1840. When either of the major parties won large majorities, these came not as the result of changes in political allegiances but because of abstentions by the voters of one party. Either one voted for his party or he did not vote; it was a rare man who viewed politics so dispassionately that he could stomach voting for the opposition party.

In the prewar period, then, Americans made their own governments, enforced their own laws, staffed their own institutions, and gave intense attention to questions of government, politics, and law. There existed compelling personal reasons to be devoted to the preservation of law and order.

*

There was violence in prewar American society—a great deal of it. Indians, abolitionists, immigrants, Negroes, Mormons, Masons, as well as the WASP majority all received their share. But violence is not necessarily the opposite of law and order. Modern riots and disruptions have provoked and energized a "law-and-order" movement, but that should suggest that violence may be the instrument of stability as well as disorder. In fact, when we look carefully at the violence of the pre–Civil War years, as well as our own, we discover how much of it, though not all, resulted from efforts to preserve, not to destroy, the existing order. Abolitionists were attacked by "gentlemen of property and standing" for threatening the existing economic and racial status quo. Indians were seen as savage threats to the expansion of a prosperous and comparatively well-organized society. Immigrants threatened to inject foreign ideas and practices into a political system that demanded consensus. Mormons outraged the morals of their neighbors and seemed to endanger the prevailing ideology by their exclusiveness. Masons were charged with an anarchistic atheism that would destroy the Christian sinews of society. And Negroes who forgot their assigned place knew that their punishment would not be restrained by charity.

Much of this violence was part of the persistent vigilante tradition in American society. Although hardly the sort of law and order that civil libertarians admire, vigilantism is "as American as cherry pie" and springs from the same sentiment that is the focus of this essay—the belief that individual Americans are responsible for the preservation of stability, that the law is an expression of popular sentiment, and that the people have the duty to maintain it even if procedural due process is not respected. Vigilantism is, as Richard M. Brown argues, socially conservative—an attempt to secure and maintain a society that respects property, stability, and order. To the degree that he feels personally responsible for maintaining order, therefore, every American is potentially a vigilante.

Michel Chevalier saw this in 1833 and thought that it was admirable. Local saloonkeepers, he observed, were often the "police commissioner," and the tavern regulars "would in case of necessity be ready to act the part of constables." In a society that lacked a powerful state, he concluded, "This is real self-government; these are the obligations and responsibilities that every citizen takes upon himself when he disarms authority."

Recognition of the strength and pervasiveness of such law-and-order sentiment and of the personal involvement of Americans in the creation and sustenance of government suggests weaknesses in the predominant historiography describing prewar society. David Donald, Stanley Elkins, and Rowland Berthoff have emphasized the unstructured and hence disordered nature of pre-1860 America. Burgeoning popular rule and expanding self-esteem weakened faith in old institutions, Donald argues, and social mobility further weakened society's sinews. Elkins emphasizes the breakdown of key institutions in explaining why Northern intellectuals attacked slavery with such unrestrained intensity. Quoting Henry James, as does Donald, Elkins describes American society: "No State, in the European sense of the word, and indeed barely a specific national name. No sovereign, no court, no personal loyalty, no aristocracy, no church, no clergy, no army, no diplomatic service, no country gentlemen, no palaces . . . no cathedrals . . . no great universities nor public schools . . . no literature . . . no political society." Americans are "an unsettled people," Berthoff insists, adding to the strictures of Donald, Elkins, and James a family structure weakened by growing industrialism, the explosive fears of immigrant impurities, and the extraordinary mobility of this people. . . .

Doubtless, Berthoff and Donald . . . do describe essential characteristics of antebellum America. Industrialization did threaten the family and weaken established economic patterns. The lust for wealth encouraged roaring boom towns and boomtown mentalities: a callousness about anything but the acquisition of wealth. Certainly many feared that immigrants threatened the stability of American society, and there was a unifying force in seeming to defend democracy against an insidious invasion of "popery." Surely America would have been more unified had the national government consistently compelled, by its energy, the admiration of its people. Mobility did uproot Americans and not only transformed communities left behind but influenced the form of those that were created. And there is a strong element of truth in Berthoff's suggestion that the Union garnered devotion because it was an "overarching abstraction" that compensated for the breakdown of families, churches, and old elites. But there is more, I believe, to the fight for Union, and more to prewar society than this.

What is omitted in all these discussions is the factor that must be included in any description of the structure of society and the meaning of nationhood: the daily experience of the people with government. The weakness of current historical literature on the subject is its failure to consider common experience as an important element of social unity, its failure to discuss the ubiquitous personal familiarity of Americans with the institutions of law and order.

But evidence abounds to suggest the importance of this experience—primarily in the record of daily activities but also in the observations of visitors and of the nation's literary figures as well. Despite the protean nature of prewar society visitors noted again and again the ease with which Americans preserved and developed the tools of self-rule. They were struck especially by the facility with which the American people created the communities and associations they needed. "These people associate as easily as they breathe," Fredrika Bremer noted. The need for American settlers to work together, encouraged by the absence of government energy, produced a capacity for self-generated unity that overcame the natural centrifugal tendencies of equality, Tocqueville observed. After over twenty years in this country, the German-American political thinker Francis Lieber was still struck by "the thousandfold evidences of an all pervading associative spirit in all moral and practical spheres."

What they were describing of course was the fact of democratic government—the constantly demonstrated ability of the people to make government and use it for their purposes. On the national level, as representatives from Maine tried to solve the issue of Southern slavery and senators from Alabama sought to establish a government for Kansas territory, in short, as national legislators wrestled with moral issues fomenting in places unfamiliar to them, democratic government was demonstrating its limitations. But in the range of life most people lived, self-government was creating abilities and commitments that would ensure that democratic government would endure in the United States whatever its national infirmities.

Men were developing a sense that government was them and that they were responsible for order. . . .

But what is striking is the fact that throughout the disunion crisis of 1860–61 men spoke not merely of a national economy or of the ties of sentiment that bound them to their birthplace but constantly and passionately of the destruction of self-government should secession succeed. They were thus seriously concerned with the preservation of the institutions of government that they were a part of, and they linked their experience with that government to the survival of the Union. Local personal experience was somehow bound to the preservation of national institutions. How?

First of all, they knew that the Union was a federal union, that local government performed administrative functions that Washington could not, and should not, supply. Local government was an inextricable part of the nation's governing process. Functions of local and national government were divided, and debates raged over state versus national rights and powers. Yet the division of power and responsibility existed not for its own sake but because men believed that a national government could not function, nor could it remain the government of a free people, if it took to itself the governing of a vast continent. Men wanted to preserve local government so that the nation could function and continue to be free.

Second, and perhaps of greatest importance in establishing the connection between local self-government and the survival of the Union, was this fact: not only was local government an administrative necessity; it was the fundamental characteristic of this nation. The country had been founded with the ideal of self-rule in mind, had fought a revolution to secure it, and had created a constitution that respected it. Americans endorsed and validated this national ideal every time they established institutions of self-government.

Americans were not attached to a place; constant migration demonstrated that. They were not devoted to the land; the image of the land as real estate, the continuing land speculation attested to that. What made them Americans was that they ruled themselves wherever they went. The Scotsman Alexander McKay saw this with notable insight. What distinguished this people, he observed, was "the feeling which they cherish towards their institutions." Europeans loved the land that they and their ancestors had occupied for centuries. But "the American exhibits little or none of the local attachments which distinguish the European. His feelings are more centered upon his institutions than his mere country. . . . His affections have more to do with the social and political system with which he is connected than with the soil he inhabits." Europeans tended to be miserable when separated for long periods from their birthplace, but "give the American his institutions and he cares but little where you place him." McKay admitted that in places like New England there was strong local feeling but what was "astonishing" was "how readily even there an American makes up his mind to try his fortunes elsewhere, particularly if he contemplates removal to another part of the Union, no matter how remote . . . providing the flag of his country waves over it, and republican institutions accompany him on his wanderings." Local institutions of democratic self-government were thus a nationalizing force, and devotion to them was the imperative bond of union.

Of course not every Northern soldier would go to war against the South with the words "law and order" on his lips. Many would enlist in the excitement of the moment. Many would seek the cheap glory of a short war and sign up for ninety days to march under the banner "the Union forever." A response of simple outrage at being attacked was natural enough and was probably widespread. Many believed that the time had come when war might purge the nation of many of its corrupting impurities—the willingness to value material wealth over nobility of character, the inclination to serve personal selfishness rather than the good of society. Republicans naturally were unwilling to destroy their party and repudiate the principles on which they had been elected by yielding to Southern threats and then rebel gunfire. The vast majority accepted the assertion of Richard Henry Dana that the North should not "buy the right to carry on the government, by any concession to slavery." For these reasons and others men went to war.

Yet admitting these expressions of anti-Southern sentiment does not weaken the argument so far advanced for the importance of the idea of law and order in generating a willingness to fight. The source of much of this sentiment was a widespread fear that the institutions of self-government that maintained ordered liberty were threatened by slavery and the South. To describe the incidents of the 1850s that spawned or encouraged anti-Southern feelings is practically to catalog apparent threats by slavery on such Northern institutions.

The outrage against the Fugitive Slave Law was provoked in part by the Northern belief that this law defied local custom and traditions of self-government. The Kansas crisis was often described as proof that local government might be despoiled by slavery and its supporters. When Presidents Pierce and Buchanan supported the proslavery government in Kansas, despite the Free-Soil majority in the territory, their action was taken by many as a sign that the corrupting hand of slavery had captured the nation's executive office. When the Supreme Court produced the Dred Scott decision opponents saw evidence that courts were not immune from the same corruption. When Charles Sumner was attacked in Congress the event was described as more than the beating of one fire-eater by another; it was declared to be one more Southern attack on the principle of free speech in a free government and hence on Congress itself. The impact of these events would lead many of the North's conservative legal thinkers, men devoted to the preservation of existing legal and governmental institutions, to take anti-Southern positions even though they deplored the extremism of abolitionism. A potent source of anti-Southern sentiment was thus a widespread fear that slavery and its proponents endangered the institutions of self-government of the nation. Such a threat, of course, would shake Northerners profoundly, for it involved institutions that were an inextricable part of their experience as citizens of a democracy.

Examining the strengths of democracy on the eve of secession one perceptive author hit the mark: More than any other government, wrote Henry Flanders, democracy identified the citizen with his government and thus instilled a powerful patriotism. The citizen in such a state was "an indirect but influential agent in the administration of its affairs, watches with eager interest its course and whenever difficulty or danger impends, with something more than a sense of duty or spirit of loyalty, acts boldly and greatly in its service." Such people were deeply devoted to the law, he continued, for "in doing homage to law, they do homage to themselves, the creators and preservers of law." Three years later, with the war raging, Andrew Preston Peabody was equally struck by the way in which self-government created patriotic citizens. Men who made the laws themselves felt personally responsible for them and their survival. Peabody's language was ornate, but the meaning for the war was precise: "He in whom resides an aliquot portion of the sovereignty" he wrote, "will bear his kingly estate in mind on the numerous occasions in daily life on which he might else forget even his manhood."

Urging the energetic prosecution of the war James Russell Lowell had observed that "our Constitution claims our allegiance because it is law and order." Northerners did not forget their responsibility for that law and order. Foreign observers might have doubted that the nation with the least powerful national government in the world, a nation apparently so centrifugal, could and would find soldiers for a struggle to maintain unity, but those who knew the nation were not surprised. Exulting in the proof of strength that was indubitable by 1864 an obscure writer in the *Atlantic Monthly* remarked, "The bubble of Republicanism, which was to display such alacrity at bursting, is not the childish thing it was once deemed. . . . We have proved that we are a nation equal to the task of self-discipline and self-control." The daily experience of Americans with self-government, with fashioning and maintaining law and order, had done its work well.

SUGGESTIONS FOR ADDITIONAL READING

The literature on the coming of the Civil War is massive. Nevertheless, there are some valuable discussions of the trends and issues in the historiography that offer insight and perspective. Although rather outdated now, Thomas J. Pressly's *Americans Interpret Their Civil War* (1954) is perhaps the most thorough treatment of the historical writing on the subject before 1950. Other useful surveys can be found in Howard K. Beale, "What Historians Have Said About the Causes of the Civil War," in *Theory and Practice in Historical Study: A Report of the Committee on Historiography of the Social Science Research Council* (1946); Arthur M. Schlesinger, Jr., "The Causes of the Civil War: A Note on Historical Sentimentalism," *Partisan Review* (October 1949); Pieter Geyl, "The American Civil War and the Problem of Inevitability," in Geyl, *Debates with Historians* (1958); and David M. Potter, "The Literature on the Background of the Civil War," in Potter, *The South and the Sectional Conflict* (1968). More recently, Eric Foner, "The Causes of the Civil War: Recent Interpretations and New Directions," in Foner, *Politics and Ideology in the Age of the Civil War* (1980) and several pieces in Kenneth M. Stampp, *The Imperiled Union: Essays on the Background of the Civil War* (1980) have provided assessments of current trends in the historiography.

The first published accounts of the coming of the Civil War were written by participants in the sectional crisis. Besides those of Henry Wilson and Alexander H. Stephens, book-length treatments were produced by Edward A. Pollard, *The Lost Cause* (1866); Robert L. Dabney, *A Defence of Virginia* (1867); Jefferson Davis, *The Rise and Fall of the Confederate Government,* 2 vols. (1881); Horace Greeley, *The American Conflict,* 2 vols. (1864–1866); John A. Logan, *The Great Conspiracy: Its Origin and History* (1886); and a memoir of his own presidential term by James Buchanan, entitled *The Administration on the Eve of the Rebellion: A History of Four Years Before the War* (1866). Although not a public figure, George Washington Williams was a contemporary who, in 1883, published his *History of the Negro Race in America from 1619 to 1880.*

At the turn of the century, the emerging historical profession generated several multivolume histories of the United States that made significant contributions to an understanding of how the war arose. Among them were James Ford Rhodes, *History of the United States from the Compromise of 1850 to the Restoration of Home Rule at the South,* 7 vols. (1893–1906); Edward Channing, *A History of the United States,* 6 vols. (1905–1925), esp. vol. 6; and James Schouler, *History of the United States of America Under the Constitution,* 7 vols. (1880–1913). More interpretative and succinct were the studies written by Frederick Jackson Turner in his *The Frontier in American History* (1920) and *The Significance of Sections in American History* (1932) and by the future president, Woodrow Wilson in his *Division and Reunion, 1829–1889* (1893).

During the first decades of the twentieth century, there emerged several versions of what became known as the "irrepressible conflict" interpretation of the coming of the Civil War. The most important were Charles A. and Mary R. Beard, *The Rise of American Civilization,* 2 vols. (1929), esp. chaps. 17 and 18; Arthur C. Cole, *The Irrepressible Conflict, 1850–1865* (1934); Ulrich B. Phillips, *The Course of the South to Secession* (1939); and Frank L. Owsley, "The Fundamental Cause of the Civil War: Egocentric Sectionalism," *Journal of Southern History* (February 1941) as well as the essay included in this anthology. See also Vernon L. Parrington, *Main Currents in American Thought,* 3 vols. (1927–1930), esp. vol. 2, and Louis M. Hacker, *The Triumph of American Capitalism* (1940), esp. part 3, for other Beardian approaches.

The revisionist response arose in the interwar years, and the main works in this "repressible conflict" school were James G. Randall's "Blundering Generation" article (*Mississippi Valley Historical Review,* June 1940) and his "The Civil War Restudied," *Journal of Southern Hitory* (November 1940) and *Lincoln the Liberal Statesman* (1947); Avery O. Craven, *The Repressible Conflict, 1830–1861* (1939), *The Coming of the Civil War* (1942), and a collection of his essays, *An Historian and the Civil War* (1964); and Charles W. Ramsdell, "The Natural Limits of Slavery Expansion," *Mississippi Valley Historical Review* (October 1929) and "The Changing Interpretations of the Civil War," *Journal of Southern History* (February 1937). Also in the "revisionist" mold were Gilbert H. Barnes, *The Antislavery Impulse, 1830–1844* (1933); George F. Milton, *The Eve of Conflict: Stephen A. Douglas and the Needless War* (1934); and Roy F. Nichols, *The Disruption of American Democracy* (1948).

Since the 1950s an enormous number of books have appeared on various aspects of the era before the Civil War, ranging from general surveys to detailed monographs. Among the former, the most significant have been Allan Nevins's massive study, *Ordeal of the Union*, 2 vols. (1947) and David M. Potter's *The Impending Crisis, 1848–1861* (1976), probably the best one-volume treatment of the onset of the war. Useful contributions were also made by James M. McPherson, *Battle Cry of Freedom: The Civil War Era* (1988), specifically chaps. 1–10; James G. Randall and David H. Donald, *The Civil War and Reconstruction* (2d ed., 1969), chaps. 1–9; William R. Brock, *Conflict and Transformation: The United States, 1844–1877* (1973); David Herbert Donald, *Liberty and Union* (1978); Roger Ransom, *Conflict and Compromise: The Political Economy of Slavery, Emancipation, and the American Civil War* (1989); Richard H. Sewell, *A House Divided: Sectionalism and Civil War, 1848–1865* (1988); and Bruce Levine, *Half Slave and Half Free: The Roots of the Civil War* (1992). Since most of these books are surveys covering more than just the coming of the war, only the first section of each volume is likely to be relevant.

Because the more specialized studies are so numerous, the listing that follows is necessarily selective. The list is broken down into categories:

Economic and Social Developments During the Antebellum Era. On economic change, see George Rogers Taylor, *The Transportation Revolution, 1815–1860* (1951); Paul W. Gates, *The Farmer's Age: Agriculture, 1815–1860* (1962); Douglass C. North, *The Economic Growth of the United States, 1790–1860* (1961); Thomas C. Cochran, *Frontiers of Change: Early Industrialism in America* (1981); Merritt R. Smith, *Harpers Ferry Armory and the New Technology: The Challenge of Change* (1977); and Robert V. Bruce, *The Launching of Modern American Science, 1846–1876* (1987). Social change can be traced through Carl N. Degler, *At Odds: Women and the Family in America from the Revolution to the Present* (1980); Mary P. Ryan, *Cradle of the Middle Class: The Family in Oneida County, New York, 1790–1865* (1981); Ellen Carol DuBois, *Feminism and Suffrage: The Emergence of an Independent Women's Movement in America, 1848–1869* (1978); Jonathan Prude, *The Coming of Industrial Order: Town and Factory Life in Rural Massachusetts, 1810–1860* (1983); Sean Wilentz, *Chants Democratic:*

New York City and the Rise of the American Working Class, 1788–1850 (1984); Alan Dawley, *Class and Community: The Industrial Revolution in Lynn* (1976); Carl F. Kaestle, *Pillars of the Republic: Common Schooling and American Society, 1780–1860* (1983); Morton J. Horwitz, *The Transformation of American Law, 1780–1860* (1977); Richard D. Brown, *Knowledge Is Power: The Diffusion of Information in Early America, 1700–1865* (1989); John D. Unruh, *The Plains Across: The Overland Emigrants and the Trans-Mississippi West, 1840–1860* (1979); and Lee Soltow, *Men and Wealth in the United States, 1850–1870* (1975). Broadly conceived studies of developments before the Civil War are Richard D. Brown, *Modernization: The Transformation of American Life, 1600–1865* (1976) and Robert H. Wiebe, *The Opening of American Society: From the Adoption of the Constitution to the Eve of Disunion* (1984).

Biographies of Principal Figures. Abraham Lincoln, the preeminent political leader of the Civil War era, has been studied extensively, namely in Benjamin P. Thomas, *Abraham Lincoln: A Biography* (1952); Stephen B. Oates, *With Malice Toward None* (1977); and perhaps best of all, though not a study of his life, Richard N. Current, *The Lincoln Nobody Knows* (1958). Other important biographical studies include David Donald, *Charles Sumner and the Coming of the Civil War* (1960); Glyndon Van Deusen, *William Henry Seward* (1967); Robert W. Johannsen, *Stephen A. Douglas* (1973); and Robert V. Remini, *Henry Clay: Statesman for the Union* (1991). Among the major biographies of southerners are Drew Gilpin Faust, *James Henry Hammond and the Old South: A Design for Mastery* (1982); Robert E. May, *John A. Quitman: Old South Crusader* (1985); Thomas E. Schott, *Alexander H. Stephens of Georgia* (1988); Craig M. Simpson, *A Good Southerner: The Life of Henry A. Wise of Virginia* (1985); and John Niven, *John C. Calhoun and the Price of Union: A Biography* (1988).

Abolitionism and Antislavery. Martin Duberman, ed., *The Antislavery Vanguard: New Essays on the Abolitionists* (1965), reopened the case for the abolitionists. Many books followed, among which the most significant are Aileen Kraditor, *Means and Ends in American Abolitionism: Garrison and His Critics on Strategy and Tactics, 1834–1850* (1969); Lewis Perry, *Radical Abolitionism: Anarchy and the Government of God in Antislavery Thought* (1973); Merton Dillon, *The Abolitionists: The Growth of a Dissenting Minority* (1973);

Ronald G. Walters, *The Antislavery Appeal: American Abolitionism After 1830* (1976); James B. Stewart, *Holy Warriors: The Abolitionists and American Slavery* (1976); Lewis Perry and Michael Fellman, eds., *Antislavery Reconsidered: New Perspectives on the Abolitionists* (1979); Lewis S. Gerteis, *Morality and Utility in American Antislavery Reform* (1987); and David Brion Davis, *The Problem of Slavery in Western Culture* (1966) and *The Problem of Slavery in the Age of the American Revolution, 1770–1823* (1975). African-American abolitionists are treated in Benjamin Quarles, *Black Abolitionists* (1969); Jane H. and William H. Pease, *They Who Would Be Free: Blacks' Search for Freedom, 1830–1861* (1974); and R. J. M. Blackett, *Building an Antislavery Wall: Black Americans in the Atlantic Abolitionist Movement, 1830–1860* (1983). Biographies of leading abolitionists are John L. Thomas, *The Liberator: William Lloyd Garrison* (1963); James B. Stewart, *Wendell Phillips: Liberty's Hero* (1986); Nathan I. Huggins, *Slave and Citizen: The Life of Frederick Douglass* (1980); and William S. McFeely, *Frederick Douglass* (1991). Other aspects of the crusade against slavery can be discovered in Leon Litwack, *North of Slavery: The Negro in the Free States, 1790–1860* (1961); Leonard L. Richards, *'Gentlemen of Property and Standing': Anti-Abolition Mobs in Jacksonian America* (1970); Blanche G. Hersh, *The Slavery of Sex: Feminist Abolitionists in America* (1979); Richard H. Sewell, *Ballots for Freedom: Antislavery Politics in the United States, 1837–1860* (1976); Ronald G. Walters, *American Reformers, 1815–1860* (1978); David J. Rothman, *The Discovery of the Asylum: Social Order and Disorder in the New Republic* (1971); and Michael Fellman, *The Unbounded Frame: Freedom and Community in Nineteenth Century Utopianism* (1973).

The System of Slavery in the South. Investigation of the South's "peculiar institution" has been both extensive and penetrating during the past thirty years or so. After Kenneth M. Stampp's *The Peculiar Institution: Slavery in the Ante-Bellum South* (1956) and Stanley M. Elkins's *Slavery: A Study in American Institutional and Intellectual Life* (1959), there appeared John W. Blassingame, *The Slave Community: Plantation Life in the Antebellum South* (1972); Herbert G. Gutman, *The Black Family in Slavery and Freedom, 1750–1925* (1976); Lawrence W. Levine, *Black Culture and Black Consciousness: Afro-American Folk Thought from Slavery to Freedom* (1977), esp. chaps. 1 and 2; Albert G. Raboteau, *Slave Religion:*

The *'Invisible Institution' in the Antebellum South* (1978); Deborah G. White, *Ar'n't I a Woman: Female Slaves in the Plantation South* (1985); Charles Joyner, *Down by the Riverside: A South Carolina Slave Community* (1984); Ira Berlin, *Slaves Without Masters: The Free Negro in the Antebellum South* (1974); and Peter Kolchin, *Unfree Labor: American Slavery and Russian Serfdom* (1987). Very important are four books by Eugene D. Genovese: *The Political Economy of Slavery* (1965); *The World the Slaveholders Made* (1969); *Roll, Jordan, Roll: The World the Slaves Made* (1974); and *From Rebellion to Revolution: Afro-American Slave Revolts in the Making of the Modern World* (1979). In *Reckoning with Slavery*, ed. Paul David, the statistics of the institution of slavery are reexamined in the light of Robert W. Fogel and Stanley L. Engerman's controversial *Time on the Cross: The Economics of American Negro Slavery* (1974), while Peter Kolchin's "Reevaluating the Slave Community: A Comparative Perspective," *Journal of American History* (September 1983) and Peter J. Parish, *Slavery: History and Historians* (1989) assess the contributions of the recent scholarship.

Politics and Society in the Old South. Disputatious interpretations of the South's slave society can be found in Eugene D. Genovese, *The Political Economy of Slavery* (1965) and *The World the Slaveholders Made* (1969); Bertram Wyatt-Brown, *Southern Honor: Ethics and Behavior in the Old South* (1982); J. Mills Thornton III, *Politics and Power in a Slave Society: Alabama, 1800–1860* (1978); James Oakes, *The Ruling Race: A History of American Slaveholders* (1982); Kenneth S. Greenberg, *Masters and Statesmen: The Political Culture of American Slavery* (1985); and Carl N. Degler, *The Other South: Southern Dissenters in the Nineteenth Century* (1974). Other books on the prewar South are John McCardell, *The Idea of a Southern Nation: Southern Nationalists and Southern Nationalism, 1830–1860* (1979); George M. Fredrickson, *The Black Image in the White Mind: The Debate on Afro-American Character and Destiny, 1817–1914* (1971), chaps. 2 and 3; Gavin Wright, *The Political Economy of the Cotton South* (1978); William J. Cooper, Jr., *The South and the Politics of Slavery, 1828–1856* (1978); Don E. Fehrenbacher, *The South in Three Sectional Crises* (1980); Bruce Collins, *White Society in the Antebellum South* (1985); Elizabeth Fox-Genovese, *Within the Plantation Household: Black and White Women of the Old South* (1988); Steven Hahn, *The Roots of Southern Populism:*

Yeoman Farmers and the Transformation of the Georgia Upcountry, 1850–1890 (1983); and William W. Freehling, *The Road to Disunion, Volume I: Secessionists at Bay, 1776–1854* (1990).

The Politics of the Sectional Crisis. The Mexican War and its aftermath brought the sectional dispute to a head. This episode is treated in Paul W. Schroeder, *Mr. Polk's War: American Opposition and Dissent, 1846–1848* (1973); Robert W. Johannsen, *To the Halls of Montezuma: The War with Mexico in the American Imagination* (1985); Frederick Merk, *Manifest Destiny and Mission in American History* (1963); Chaplain W. Morrison, *Democratic Politics and Sectionalism: The Wilmot Proviso Controversy* (1967); and Holman Hamilton, *Prologue to Conflict: The Crisis and Compromise of 1850* (1964). The crisis decade of the 1850s is examined in Eric Foner, *Free Soil, Free Labor, Free Men: The Ideology of the Republican Party Before the Civil War* (1970) and Michael F. Holt, *The Political Crisis of the 1850s* (1978), the two differing interpretations that provide the framework for analyzing the political road to war. Also valuable are William E. Gienapp, *The Origins of the Republican Party, 1852–1856* (1987); Don E. Fehrenbacher, *Prelude to Greatness: Lincoln in the 1850s* (1962); James A. Rawley, *Race and Politics: "Bleeding Kansas" and the Coming of the Civil War* (1969); Joel H. Silbey, *The Partisan Imperative: The Dynamics of American Politics Before the Civil War* (1985); Barbara J. Fields, *Slavery and Freedom on the Middle Ground: Maryland in the Nineteenth Century* (1985), Don E. Fehrenbacher, *Slavery, Law and Politics* (1981) on the Dred Scott case; Stanley W. Campbell, *The Slave Catchers: Enforcement of the Fugitive Slave Law, 1850–1860* (1970); Robert E. May, *The Southern Dream of a Caribbean Empire, 1854–1862* (1973); Kenneth M. Stampp, *America in 1857: A Nation on the Brink* (1990); James L. Huston, *The Panic of 1857 and the Coming of the Civil War* (1987); Dale Baum, *The Civil War Party System: The Case of Massachusetts, 1848–1876* (1984); and Mark W. Summers, *The Plundering Generation: Corruption and the Crisis of the Union, 1849–1861* (1988). On nativism, see Jean H. Baker, *Ambivalent Americans: The Know-Nothing Party in Maryland* (1977); Michael F. Holt, "The Politics of Impatience: The Origins of Know Nothingism," *Journal of American History* (September 1973); and Ray Allen Billington, *The Protestant Crusade, 1800–1860* (1938), a much earlier but still useful work. See also Richard Franklin Bensel, *Yankee Leviathan: The Origins of*

Central State Authority in America, 1859–1877 (1990), on state power and secession.

The Secession Crisis. For the view from Washington, see David M. Potter, *Lincoln and His Party in the Secession Crisis* (1942); Kenneth M. Stampp, *And the War Came: The North and the Secession Crisis, 1860–1861* (1950); Richard N. Current, *Lincoln and the First Shot* (1963); and a provocative, older article from a revisionist, Charles W. Ramsdell, "Lincoln and Fort Sumter," *Journal of Southern History* (September 1937). Studies of the southern states during the crisis are Ralph Wooster, *The Secession Conventions of the South* (1962); Steven A. Channing, *A Crisis of Fear: Secession in South Carolina* (1970); William L. Barney, *The Secessionist Impulse: Alabama and Mississippi in 1860* (1974); Michael P. Johnson, *Toward a Patriarchal Republic: The Secession of Georgia* (1977); Walter L. Buenger, *Secession and Union in Texas* (1984); J. Mills Thornton, *Politics and Power in a Slave Society,* chap. 6; and Daniel W. Crofts, *Reluctant Confederates: Upper South Unionists in the Secession Crisis* (1989). A very useful collection of public lectures on aspects of the secession crisis is George H. Knoles, ed., *The Crisis of the Union, 1860–1861* (1965).

Several other essay collections contain valuable pieces on the coming of the Civil War, namely David Donald, *Lincoln Reconsidered: Essays on the Civil War Era* (1961); David M. Potter, *The South and the Sectional Conflict* (1968), esp. "The Civil War in the History of the Modern World: A Comparative View" and "The Historian's Use of Nationalism and Vice Versa"; C. Vann Woodward, *American Counterpoint: Slavery and Racism in the North-South Dialogue* (1971); Eric Foner, *Politics and Ideology in the Age of the Civil War* (1980); and Bertram Wyatt-Brown, *Yankee Saints and Southern Sinners* (1985).